MANAGING
BUSINESS RISK

MANAGING BUSINESS RISK

a practical guide to protecting your business

fourth edition

consultant editor: jonathan reuvid

Recommended by the
Institute of Risk
Management

KOGAN
PAGE

London and Philadelphia

Publisher's note

Every possible effort has been made to ensure that the information contained in this book is accurate at the time of going to press, and the publishers and authors cannot accept responsibility for any errors or omissions, however caused. No responsibility for loss or damage occasioned to any person acting, or refraining from action, as a result of the material in this publication can be accepted by the editor, the publisher or any of the authors.

First published in Great Britain and the United States in 2003 by Kogan Page Limited
Second edition 2005
Third edition 2006
This edition 2007

120 Pentonville Road
London N1 9JN
United Kingdom
www.kogan-page.co.uk

525 South 4th Street, #241
Philadelphia PA 19147
USA

© Kogan Page and Contributors, 2003, 2005, 2006, 2007

ISBN-10   0 7494 4949 7
ISBN-13   978 0 7494 4949 0

The views expressed in this book are those of the authors, and are not necessarily the same as those of the Institute of Risk Management.

British Library Cataloguing-in-Publication Data

A CIP record for this book is available from the British Library.

Library of Congress Cataloging-in-Publication Data

Managing business risk : a practical guide to protecting your business / Jonathan Reuvid, [consulting editor]. – 4th ed.
     p. cm.
   Recommended by Institute of Risk Management.
   ISBN-13: 978-0-7494-4949-0
   ISBN-10: 0-7494-4949-7
1. Risk management. I. Institute of Risk Management. II. Reuvid, Jonathan.
   HD61.M26 2007
   658.15'5–dc22
                                                2007001960

Typeset by JS Typesetting Ltd, Porthcawl, Mid Glamorgan
Printed and bound in Great Britain by Cambridge University Press

DO YOU KNOW THE SECRETS OF

GOOD RISK MANAGEMENT?

Being able to identify and manage risk is increasingly recognised as a key leadership skill.

The Institute of Risk Management can equip you with the knowledge, tools and techniques fundamental to managing your organisation's risks.

Courses for individuals

- professional qualification (MIRM)
- introductory qualification (CIRM)
- two-day training for directors
- a range of distance-learning modules

Enterprise-wide training

- enterprise-wide risk management training (MoRU)
- adaptable to your organisation's needs
- choice of delivery – use your own in-house trainers, or IRM course providers

For information on risk management qualifications, training, events, jobs, and membership, contact:

Rebecca Brueton
info@theirm.org
+44 (0) 20 7709 9808
www.theirm.org

On-line training

New!

- Suitable for SMEs
- Practical on-line risk management training (PRORIM)

irm

The Institute of Risk Management
Delivering high quality risk management education

Protect yourself against FX risk

Exposure to exchange rate volatility is an unavoidable aspect of international trade and without an effective strategy to manage this risk it can have a detrimental affect on your bottom line.

At Currencies Direct we understand that no two businesses are the same and as a result our currency specialists will work with you to develop a solution tailored to your specific requirements, helping your business to mitigate risk and maximise profit.

Forward Contracts

Forward contracts help your business to manage future risk by allowing you to lock in a rate today for the delivery of funds in the future. Whether you're buying or selling currency locking in a rate helps to protect your business against changes in the market, thus protecting your profits from erosion.

Currencies Direct can book contracts from as little as three days anywhere up to two years, with the option of closed or open settlement dates – allowing the flexibility needed to meet the demands of international business. In addition we only require a small deposit so setting up a contract has minimal impact on your cash flow.

key benefits
- **Lock in exchange rates today for delivery up to two years ahead.**
- **Forecast budgets, profit margins and price lists without currency fluctuations affecting your bottom line.**
- **Low contract minimums and minimal deposit requirements.**

Limit Orders

Businesses involved in international trade can often find themselves in a situation where valuable time is spent monitoring the currency markets in order to secure favourable rates. At Currencies Direct we recognise this and offer all our clients a limit order service free of charge.

Limit orders enable you to set a target rate at which you want to buy or sell your currency. Our specialists will help you to determine a rate that is appropriate for existing market conditions and will then monitor the market for you. As soon as the target rate is reached the order is executed.

key benefits
- **The market is monitored on your behalf and your order automatically executed if your target rate is reached.**
- **No obligation to make a purchase if your target rate is not reached.**

Information provided by Currencies Direct.

www.currenciesdirect.com   Tel: **0845 389 0910**   Email: c**orporate@currenciesdirect.com**

Enterprise Risk Management «

Companies need to become more effective at evaluating and managing the uncertainties they face as they strive to create sustainable value for their stakeholders.

Enterprise Risk Management (ERM) is the corporate-wide application of risk management to improve the performance of an organisation's business. It transforms risk management into a proactive, continuous, value-based, activity.

ERM encourages opportunity-seeking behaviour, helping managers develop confidence in their understanding and management of the risks they are taking on. It is a source of competitive advantage, and can have a positive effect on reputation and brand.

Siemens Insight Consulting has a series of ERM services that encompass assessment, evaluation, measurement, policy review and risk education.

These services can benefit companies that want to establish ERM as a core corporate competence as they:

- Engage in multiple projects

- Respond to market changes

- Invest in capital projects

- Engage in large contracts

- Comply with regulatory obligations

- Manage multiple subsidiaries or contracts with outsourcing arrangements.

The benefits of Insight's service:

- Reduce governance risk

- Improve ability to respond to a changing business environment

- Improve opportunity management

- Reduce unacceptable performance

- Improve risk mitigation

- Increase risk awareness and improved reporting

- Increase operating savings

- Reduce capital costs.

Siemens Insight Consulting subscribes to the CESG Listed Advisor Scheme (CLAS) and CHECK services. We are certified against BS 7799, a preferred supplier of services to the UK Government and an accredited Catalist supplier.

If you'd like to discuss how Siemens Insight Consulting could help you manage risk in your organisation, phone 01932 241000 or email us at insight@insight.co.uk

Project Risk Management «

Poorly managed projects can leave organisations exposed to erosion of profits, loss of customers, reputational damage, late entry to markets, exposure to contract penalties, liquidated damages or litigation.

Project risk management is a systematic, methodical approach to identifying, assessing and responding to identified threats and opportunities to secure project objectives.

Siemens Insight Consulting provides a comprehensive project risk management service, based on both broad experience and best practice methods.

Our experience spans the telecommunications, water, rail, media, heritage, pharmaceutical, transportation, property, health, IT and education sectors.

The benefits of Insight's services include:

• Informed decision making

• Evaluation of options based on their risk profile

• Identification of the threats and opportunities

• Definition of realistic contingencies

• Generation of confidence limits of achieving the primary objectives

• Making the risk ownership of contracts explicit

• Guiding decisions on risk share

• Identification of concrete responses to identified threats.

www.siemens.co.uk/insight

Insight Consulting

SIEMENS

Chiltern.

Managing risk +
enhancing control =
good governance

There is increasing pressure on executive and non-executive directors to demonstrate that their business has sound systems of risk management and internal control.

Chiltern's specialist Risk and Control team provides independent support and advice to help businesses assess their business risks and controls with a focus on improving business performance.

We help our clients to answer the questions:

◆ **Corporate governance**
   How good is our governance framework?

◆ **Risk management**
   Do we understand our risk profile?

◆ **Internal control**
   How effective are our internal controls?

◆ **Internal audit**
   What internal audit capabilities do we need?

For more information on how Chiltern can help your business please contact:

Louis Cooper
T 020 7153 2290   E cooperl@chilternplc.com

Chiltern plc   T +44 (0)20 7339 9000
3 Sheldon Square   F +44 (0)20 7339 9010
London   E enquiries@chilternplc.com
W2 6PS   www.chilternplc.com

SUCCESS *m*

the power of financial management in business

CIMA professionals take the lead in management accounting.

CIMA is the financial qualification most aligned to today's business needs*.

CIMA Professionals drive some of the world's most successful organisations.

CIMA professionals work as an integral part of multi-skilled management teams and carry out a range of activities:

- the generation and creation of value through effective strategic decision making and deployment of resource
- formulating business strategy to create wealth and shareholder value
- plan long, medium and short run operations
- determine capital structure and fund that structure
- measure and report financial and non financial performance
- implement corporate governance procedures, risk management and internal controls.

*Based on Bath School of Management syllabi research – 2006

For further information about CIMA, the Chartered Institute of Management Accountants visit **www.cimaglobal.com**

HASTAM

HASTAM's mission is to improve the management of health, safety and environmental risks within organisations. To achieve this, HASTAM works in partnership with their clients to provide the highest quality bespoke services and products – just the support an organisation needs, just when they need it.

Much of HASTAM's work involves the provision of health, safety and environmental consultancy and training. Having been established since 1984, HASTAM can provide a wealth of expertise, ensuring they deliver innovative solutions which are practical and cost effective. Many of HASTAM's services are based around OHSAS 18001, the subject of a chapter in this book, by two HASTAM Directors, Tony Boyle and Mike Thomas. Whilst HASTAM services follow 18001, they are not restricted to organisations seeking accreditation – the principles represent HASTAM's view of best practice, as described in their chapter.

HASTAM's services include a gap analysis to identify how close an organisation is to complying with 18001, and the preparation of a description of an OH&SMS, written procedures and a legal register. HASTAM can then provide ongoing support and internal audit.

Training which they provide is wide ranging and tailored to the specific needs of clients. Examples include courses on the principles of health and safety management for directors, managers and supervisors. These courses are often supplemented with detailed courses on topics such as risk assessment or incident investigation, addressing the client's procedures. They are normally run in-house, allowing for practical sessions where appropriate. The courses can be certificated through organisations such as IOSH or NEBOSH or by HASTAM themselves.

HASTAM's most recent innovation is a behavioural safety programme (SAM) which expands a client's overall management system by building in a novel approach to behaviour modification. Incorporating, as appropriate, consultancy, training, and ongoing support, HASTAM's package enables a step change to new levels of performance.

In addition to training and consultancy services, HASTAM produces off-the-shelf products designed to simplify health, safety and environmental management, including the widely used audit and monitoring system, CHASE.

To see how HASTAM can help you,
visit their website at **www.hastam.co.uk** *or e-mail* **mike@hastam.co.uk**

scrutiny:

Photo Sirotti

Businesses today need to withstand close investigation - from authorities, shareholders, special interest groups and the media.

At DNV, we assist our clients in reaching new standards and expectations for sustainable business conduct. Combining technology, operations, management and risk competencies, we help our clients safely and responsibly improve their business performance, in an ever changing and demanding world.

Enterprise Risk Management • Safety and Environmental Risk Management • Operations Excellence • Verification • Technology Qualification • IT Risk Management • Training

a new reality
a different approach
:DNV

www.dnv.com

MANAGING RISK

Contents

YOU GET THE BUSINESS UP WE'LL KEEP IT RUNNING.

AND RUNNING...

AND RUNNING...

With HP Business Continuity & Recovery Services you'll be ready for any eventuality, making business interruption a thing of the past. And if the worst happens (perish the thought) we'll have you working again in no time. Our multi-vendor team of specialists has the expertise to support other equipment too, not just HP. Whatever happens, your business will keep running, and running, and running...

Visit hp.com/go/businesscontinuity
or call 0870 443 6919

the easy, low cost, Business Continuity solution

Sometimes things let you down

If your office is not available to your employees, it's unlikely that your business is available to your customers. The same is true of your information systems or perhaps, even just one business critical application. That's why we have business continuity centres all around the UK, which provide alternative offices and IT services to ensure that your business can continue to operate, even when something goes seriously wrong. It means that customers can still call you. You can still call your customers. You can receive and process orders and your reputation remains intact. What's more, once your customers learn what happened they will see how well you've coped with a difficult situation and how you've protected their interests, and your reputation and customer loyalty will improve. But we've saved the best news 'til last - these business continuity services are inexpensive and very straightforward to implement.

DISASTER
COVER
Direct

To find out more, call us on 08701 22 02 40 or visit www.disaster-cover.co.uk

Part 4: Risks for Financial and Corporate Managers

RISK

AND HOW IT CAN SPUR

SHAREHOLDER
VALUE

The typical shareholder isn't overly fond of risk, yet strategic risk is essential for improving returns. That's where Enterprise Risk Management comes in. Named a leader in the field by Forrester,* Protiviti can partner effectively with your organisation to identify and assess your risks. Address those risks most critical to your success. Evaluate your progress. And advance on to your next priorities. All the

while, you'll be building an infrastructure that delivers a constant, clear view of your risks so you can limit or capitalise on them. It's a model for continuous improvement, and it's precisely how we've helped many Fortune 1000 companies grow their value—something the typical shareholder is quite fond of, indeed.

For a complimentary copy of our 144-page Guide to Enterprise Risk Management, please visit protiviti.com/shareholdervalue.

protiviti®
Independent Risk Consulting

Know Risk. Know Reward.™

Foreword

Managing business risk is everyone's business

Today, risk management is firmly on the agenda of every organization. Whether the context is business or public life, the general public, media, employees and investors all hold senior management and boards accountable for risk management, or at least for perceived risk control failures.

Risk management today is still a relatively young discipline. As Peter Bernstein describes so well in his history of the discipline, *Against the Gods*, our ability to understand, let alone control, risk was historically constrained by a combination of religious beliefs and an underdeveloped application of mathematics.

More recently commentators have started to talk of so-called 'enterprise risk management' (ERM), meaning the application of risk management techniques to all aspects of any enterprise and, particularly, to the creation of rewards as well as the control of hazards. In truth, enterprise risk management is just risk management. However, the term is invaluable in differentiating the discipline from many of its components, ones without which ERM would not exist today.

Thus, for instance, health and safety, insurance, corporate governance, business continuity, and market and credit risk management are all important management tools in their own right. However, true ERM also considers other causes of risk and methods of their control: hence the emerging importance of areas such as people risk, intellectual property, information risk and that wonderful catch-all term 'operational risk management'.

In order to make sense of this alphabet soup, a number of standards are now in circulation, particularly AS/NZS 4360, the IRM/Airmic/Alarm Risk Management Standard, and COSO from the United States. Each of these is best thought of as a 'tool' rather than a standard *per se*. Thus AS/NZS 4360 provides a comprehensive 'how to do' guide for the practitioner, the multilingual IRM standard is a simple plain-language guide for the average business manager, and COSO approaches the subject with a strong audit/regulatory slant. As this book goes to press, an International ISO

Standard is under development, and in the UK a British Standard awaits publication – yet more tools.

In some ways, this focus on tools can miss the point. As with any tools, it's the way they are used that matters most. Senior management and boards are fundamentally custodians of an organization's stakeholder value. As custodians, they must care and nurture that which is entrusted to them and pass it on to their successors in an improved state. Taking risk is a fundamental component of this or, as Erica Jong said, 'If you don't risk anything, you risk even more.'

Risk management should thus be a very major board focus. This focus has three most critical components:

- First, *choice*: Every business decision involves an evaluation of choices. The choices organizations take must assume an analysis of the relative risks involved in each possible outcome. Decisions must take due accord of maximizing reward (upside risk) and minimizing hazard (downside risk).
- Second, *sustainability*: Sustainable businesses are ultimately more successful than 'firework businesses' that fizz brightly and then explode with a loud bang. The proper evaluation of longer-term options is a key outcome from any strategic planning process. Acting on those options accordingly as external influences change is, if anything, even more important. Also of critical importance is the recognition that not everything can be controlled: corporate resilience (or continuity) planning must consider the impact of not just local failure (for instance, a major fire or storm) but also global catastrophes (terrorism, pandemics, etc).
- Third, *people*: Probably most important of all, an organization's culture, including the tone set by the board and CEO, is the most critical element of successful and intelligent risk management. At one end of the spectrum, the high-profile risk management failures of the 1990s dotcom boom and the corporate greed scandals of the early 21st century show what happens with an unfettered approach to the assumption of risk regardless of reward. At the other end, recent examples from public life where simple, innocent everyday activities like playing conkers or holding bonfires are banned in the name of risk management show what can happen in a 'running scared' culture.

    Risk management tone and culture are therefore critical and in turn determine other vital risk management influences such as remuneration policy ('what gets paid gets done') and how communication is structured in an organization (one-way – 'top down'; or two-way – with all key stakeholders involved).

So, what will the future hold? Certainly, managing risk is undoubtedly everyone's business: the trend towards the greater integration in management of risk will continue. Embracing that challenge, risk managers will need to evolve and develop a wider range of knowledge and skills than may hitherto have been the case. These skills aren't just technical in nature: successful risk practitioners will be those who have the influencing and negotiation skills to ensure that the balanced or enterprise risk message is heard and acted upon at the top table.

Moreover, the ability to spot trends and identify significant future risk trends will become increasingly vital, not just in risk management *per se*, but in business management as a whole. Those who can master that will certainly prove their value both to their own organizations and to the profession as a whole.

Steve Fowler
Chief Executive Officer
Institute of Risk Management

Contributors' notes

ACE European Group has established branch offices in 17 countries across Europe, Freedom of Services permission to provide insurance services to clients in 27 EEA countries and affiliates in Egypt, Bahrain, Pakistan and Russia. ACE Europe Group comprises the operations of ACE Europe, ACE Global Markets and ACE Tempest Re (Europe). ACE Europe provides a range of tailored Property and Casualty, Accident and Health and Personal Lines solutions for a diverse range of clients. The ACE Group of Companies is a global leader in insurance and reinsurance serving a diverse group of clients. Headed by ACE Limited (NYSE: ACE), a component of the Standard & Poor's 500 stock index, the ACE Group conducts its business on a worldwide basis with operating subsidiaries in more than 50 countries.

Odd Andersen is a director in DNV. He is an economist and MBA from IMD in Lausanne, Switzerland. Odd has worked with clients in the finance, ICT and public sectors. He has also worked on implementation of risk management systems. This includes raising awareness of the 'new risk reality', the challenge for corporations and the public sector to manage new types of risk (eg environmental, brand/reputation, ICT, corporate governance) and to take a wider and longer-term view on risks.

Richard Archer is a consultant with DNV who carries out management consultancy assignments. He specializes in applying the principles of business risk and uncertainty management to simplify complex business problems. Assignment topics are commonly for decision support, management system assessment and gap analysis, project risk management and enterprise risk management. Richard is the primary author of *EFQM Framework for Risk Management* and is a lead instructor on the DNV enterprise risk management two-day course. He has two economics degrees and a diploma in applied management from Warwick Business School.

Eric Bloem is Group Insurance Manager in the Group Finance division of Heineken International.

Tony Boyle, BSc, MSc, PhD, CPsychol, AFBPsS, CFIOSH, MIRM has extensive consultancy experience in various countries. He has developed audit systems and

OH&S management systems based on OHSAS 18001 for a number of organizations. Tony has published over 50 articles, papers and book chapters including *Health and Safety: Risk management*, a textbook published by IOSH covering the risk management and human factors material required for the NEBOSH Diploma in Occupational Safety and Health.

David Breden is Managing Director, HSBC Insurance Brokers and the architect of OpRisk Modeller, a secenario-based commercial risk mapping tool developed by HSBC to meet the needs of the Basel II AMA quantification requirements. He has been involved in operational risk management since 1995 and is a Fellow of the Institute of Operational Risk.

Stephen Capon is the Manager of Country and Credit Risk Management, Political Risks and Credit, ACE Global Markets (ACE's specialist international business, underwriting through ACE European Group and ACE's Lloyd's Syndicate 2488).

John Cassey joined Protiviti's Integrity Risk practice in October 2006, helping to develop forensic accounting and fraud investigation services. He brought with him over 25 years' experience in detecting and investigating fraud, tracing and recovering assets and stolen funds, and advising businesses on how to reduce the threat of fraud. John spent nearly 18 years in HM Revenue and Customs (formerly HM Customs and Excise), where he was a senior officer in the Investigation Division, before working in the commercial sector, where he has held senior positions in major corporations. He has extensive experience throughout the world in interviewing suspects and witnesses, often in a hostile environment.

Centre for Decision Analysis and Risk Management at Middlesex University is both a research centre within the School of Health and Social Sciences and an umbrella organization bringing together university groups with an interest in risk, risk assessment and risk management. The university offers the postgraduate certificate, postgraduate diploma and MSc in risk management.

Centre for Effective Dispute Resolution (CEDR) is the thought leader for dispute resolution in Europe and the internationally acclaimed trainer in mediation and conflict management skills. An independent non-profit organization supported by multinational business and leading professional bodies, CEDR has the mission to encourage and develop mediation and other cost-effective dispute resolution and prevention techniques in commercial and public sector disputes.

Centre for Technology Management sits within the Institute for Manufacturing at Cambridge University's Engineering Department, and its main research areas are strategic technology management, innovation and design management and technology enterprise. The recently completed Business Appraisal of Technology research project was sponsored by the Engineering and Physical Research Council under the Innovative Manufacturing Research initiative. The project involved academics from the Institute for Manufacturing and significant industrial collaboration.

Robert Chapman has supplied risk management services to over 40 companies. He holds a PhD in risk management, has provided services in Ireland, Denmark, Holland, France and Dubai, as well as the UK, and has published two books on the subject of risk management as well as numerous journal articles and papers.

Chartered Institute of Management Accountants (CIMA) is the only international chartered accountancy body with a sole focus on business. It is the fastest-growing UK-based accountancy body, in terms of members in both the UK and worldwide, and is the voice of over 158,000 members and students in 161 countries.

Chartered Institute of Purchasing and Supply (CIPS) is the leading international body representing purchasing and supply management professionals. It is the worldwide centre of excellence on purchasing and supply management issues. CIPS has approximately 42,000 members in 134 different countries, including senior business people, high-ranking civil servants and leading academics. The activities of purchasing and supply chain professionals can have a major impact on the profitability and efficiency of all types of organization.

Chiltern plc is the UK's leading independent tax adviser. The firm also provides a range of non-audit corporate services in areas such as corporate governance, risk management and internal control. Chiltern is recommended as a leading adviser by International Tax Review's *World Tax 2007* – for the third year in succession. The firm supports its clients' global activities through the exclusive UK membership of Taxand, the first global alliance of independent and specialist tax firms, and through Moores Rowland International, a worldwide association of independent accountancy, tax and business practices.

Commercial Security International Limited (CSi) is a London-based company providing discreet and professional investigation and corporate security solutions for companies, institutions, governments and private individuals.

Companycare Communications has a 20-year track record of success acting on a global basis as a PR and marketing communications consultancy for a range of national and international clients within the technology, media and telecoms sectors. The consultancy also has a thriving corporate business and recently launched a consumer division, Escapade. Current clients include Siemens, 3M, the GSM Association and Bic.

Louis Cooper is Head of Risk and Control Services at Chiltern plc. He is a corporate governance, business risk and internal control specialist with experience in design, coordination and delivery of business risk advisory services. Roles include acting as 'subject matter expert' on the requirements of the UK Combined Code, Turnbull Guidance and US Sarbanes–Oxley section 404 reporting. Louis advises both national and international clients on a range of business assurance issues including corporate governance frameworks, risk management systems, internal control procedures and internal audit activities.

Andrew Cromby is a partner and Head of Dispute Resolution at KSB Law LLP. A commercial litigator specializing in corporate disputes, he acts for businesses including companies and partnerships and deals with high-value, complex litigation including domestic and international arbitrations, mediations and other forms of alternative dispute resolution. Andrew adopts a robust and pragmatic approach to dispute resolution and focuses on achieving his clients' commercial objectives whilst minimizing the disruption inherent in any formal dispute.

James (Jim) W DeLoach, Jr is a managing director with Protiviti and responsible for the company's governance services and enterprise risk management market offerings. For more than 30 years he has provided advice and counsel on auditing and risk management to clients across different industries. He also works closely with competency and industry leaders to focus the company's efforts in delivering independent risk consulting services to the marketplace. Jim has delivered numerous presentations on risk management and governance matters to companies and groups in 26 countries. He is also a prolific and widely published author of books and articles covering various aspects of business risk assessment and management, including *The Bulletin*, Protiviti's newsletter on corporate governance and risk management issues, and Protiviti's Sarbanes–Oxley resource guides.

Marie-Gemma Dequae is the President of the Federation of European Risk Management Associations (FERMA) and corporate risk manager worldwide for the global transformation and materials group Bekaert. She has a PhD in applied economics.

DNV is a leading international provider of services for managing risk, with more than 6,500 employees in 300 offices in 100 countries. As an independent foundation with the objective of safeguarding life, property and the environment, DNV assists customers in managing risk by providing three main categories of service: classification, certification and consultancy. Services are offered primarily to high-risk, capital-intensive industries where they can make a significant contribution to the management of risk, thereby aiding decision-making processes, reducing costs and improving operational availability.

Deborah Evans is Business Manager, Corporate Reporting and Assurance for LRQA, responsible for global verification services including corporate sustainability reports and greenhouse gas emissions for the UK and EU Emission Trading Schemes and Kyoto Protocol mechanisms of CDM and JI. She holds a degree in environmental science and a postgraduate diploma in environmental impact assessment.

Guy Facey is head of KSB Law's international practice. He advises on a broad range of corporate projects, involving corporate finance, mergers and acquisitions, flotations and international corporate structure. Transactions with China are a significant part of his practice. He has considerable experience in the aviation sector and transacts in Italian, French and, to a lesser extent, Mandarin Chinese.

Clare Farrukh, CEng, MIChemE is carrying out research concerned with the development of practical tools for industry, including a fast-start roadmapping technique and the coordination of a recent project on technology valuation. She has a degree in chemical engineering, an MSc in organizational behaviour and spent six years as a process engineer.

Federation of European Risk Management Associations (FERMA) represents over 5,000 individual members in risk management associations in 13 European countries.

Andrew Fields is a Senior Manager in KPMG's Risk and Sustainability Services practice. Andrew has over 15 years' experience advising large multinational clients on risk management and has worked with more than 30 large FTSE, public sector and international organizations advising on the design, build and operation of risk management systems.

Allan Gerrish is the Lead Business Continuity Consultant at ICM Computer Group. An MBCI, Allan held various management positions in the financial services industry before joining ICM in 2004 to develop their business continuity consultancy offering in line with financial services standards and to develop and promote ICM's established risk control culture.

Anne Goodenough is currently undertaking PhD research at the University of Gloucestershire where she is also a part-time member of the teaching staff and guest lecturer in the Department of Natural and Social Sciences.

Allison Grant is a partner and head of KSB Law's Employment department. She advises on all employment and industrial relations law issues, including health and safety. Her focus is on helping employers maintain good employment practice. Allison has considerable experience covering unfair dismissal, redundancy, disciplinary issues, equal pay, TUPE, breach of contract and discrimination law.

Leigh Griffiths is a Business Continuity Manager at Hewlett-Packard.

HASTAM specializes in the application of formal management systems to OH&S. Established in 1984, HASTAM works in partnership with its clients to provide a range of bespoke training and consultancy services to complement in-house resources. The CHASE software system has been developed for use in monitoring and auditing performance.

Heineken International has wide international presence through a global network of distributors and breweries. Heineken owns and manages one of the world's leading portfolios of beer brands and is one of the world's leading brewers in terms of sales volume and profitability. Its principal international brands are Heineken and Amstel, but the group brews and sells more than 170 international premium, regional, local and speciality beers, including Cruzcampo, Tiger, Zywiec, Bira Moretti, Ochota, Murphy's and Star.

Hewlett-Packard is a technology solutions provider to consumers, businesses and institutions globally. The company's offerings span IT infrastructure, global services, business and home computing, and imaging and printing.

Robert (Bob) B Hirth is the Managing Director of Internal Audit Services for Protiviti and a member of the firm's Operating Committee. Bob has more than 25 years of professional services experience working with a broad range of global, public and local private organizations in a variety of industries, helping them address their most significant business risks and issues. His experience includes business and operational consulting as well as internal audit and business risk management. He has attended and presented at hundreds of audit committee and senior management meetings. Bob has served numerous organizations on high-pressure, priority and sensitive business risk issues both nationally and overseas in more than 10 countries. He has also been involved in assisting emerging, large and fast-growth public companies to establish their internal audit functions and has provided full outsourcing, co-sourcing and other advisory and business risk management services to more than 50 organizations.

Ian Hodgskinson is responsible, as Business Stream Director, for the services that LRQA provides to clients. He is a member of the executive team of the Lloyd's Register Group. With a metallurgy degree and metals industry background, Ian became a member of the small team that started LRQA in 1985. He has played a major role in the development and application of LRQA's own management systems that have enabled the company to become a major global organization.

Sean Holohan joined Protiviti in October 2004 as Director of Integrity Risk Services with responsibility for fraud risk management and for further development of the fraud prevention and investigation service lines. On the technology side, Sean has created an experienced computer forensics team at Protiviti, capable of assisting clients to capture digital evidence simultaneously over multiple locations. Sean previously worked for two Big Four accountancy firms and spent five years as a senior inspector for the Law Society investigating dishonest solicitors in England and Wales.

HSBC Insurance Brokers is one of the largest international insurance broking, risk management and employee benefits organizations in the world. It is the only major insurance broker that forms part of a global banking group. As a member of the HSBC Group, HSBC Insurance Brokers shares an international network with offices in countries and territories in Europe, the Asia-Pacific Region, the Americas, the Middle East and Africa.

Dr Francis Hunt has research interests in technology valuation, support solutions engineering and open source software development, and lectures on the engineering IA mathematical methods course. He has a degree in mathematics and a PhD in artificial neural networks from the Ecole des Mines de Paris, and worked at Pi Research as a software engineer.

ICM Computer Group delivers optimum business availability in a way that is tailored to its customers' needs though a unique combination of managed availability and business continuity services. With a product and services portfolio that is unrivalled in the UK, no other company can do more to ensure clients' operational availability.

KPMG LLP is a UK limited liability partnership operating from 22 offices across the UK with over 9,000 partners and staff. The firm recorded a turnover of £1.28 billion in the year ended September 2005. KPMG is a global network of professional firms providing audit, tax and advisory services. It operates in 144 countries with more than 104,000 professionals working in member firms around the world. The independent firms of the KPMG network are affiliated with KPMG International, a Swiss cooperative. KPMG International provides no client services.

Gillian Lees is one of CIMA's technical specialists with a focus on corporate and enterprise governance, including risk management and the use of the CIMA Strategic Scorecard™.

Elisabeth Lewis Jones has a wealth of crisis experience, from a fatal plane crash to the high-profile BSE/CJD scare. She has worked in-house at Birmingham Airport, was the MD of one of the Midlands' largest PR consultancies and in 2004 co-founded Liquid Public Relations. Elisabeth is a director of the Chartered Institute of Public Relations (CIPR) and has been elected its President for 2008.

Liquid Public Relations was founded by Elisabeth Lewis Jones and Menna Rees-Steer in 2004 with the philosophy of providing a full service consultancy offering only senior, qualified practitioners to work on client activity. Operating a system more akin to a chamber of barristers, this senior team provides a strategic approach with hands-on delivery across the private, public and not-for-profit sectors.

Lloyd's Register Quality Assurance Ltd (LRQA) is a member of Lloyd's Register Group and is one of the world's foremost management system assessment, training and verification organizations delivering business assurance to organizations globally. LRQA's approach focuses on the effectiveness of an organization's systems in delivering its business outcomes. Through business assurance, LRQA assesses the capability to manage broader business risks, while providing its clients and other stakeholders with the assurance given by independent verification and certification.

Mike Madgin joined DNV in March 2006. A chartered accountant, he worked previously for a leading professional services firm for over 25 years, where he gained extensive experience of providing information risk management services and developing new services. He has worked in the UK, Africa, Europe, the Far East, the Middle East and North America.

Graham Massie is a director of the Centre for Effective Dispute Resolution (CEDR) and a practising accredited mediator. He is a qualified chartered accountant and has spent 10 years with KPMG in Chicago and London. He has been a company director in the United States and has established his own business consultancy practice, with extensive experience of multinational corporate consultancy.

Neil Miller is a director at Commercial Security International Limited (CSi), a company specializing in fraud and intellectual property investigations.

Dr Rick Mitchell was until recently Group Technology Director of Domino Printing Sciences plc, following 23 years with Philips. He is now a visiting fellow at the Institute for Manufacturing at the University of Cambridge and a visiting professor at Cranfield School of Management and has research interests in R&D project selection.

Dr James Moultrie, CEng, MIMechE is a University Lecturer in innovation and design management. He has extensive experience in engineering and product management in the precision instruments sector. James holds an MBA and MA in industrial design; his PhD focused on assessing and improving design capabilities in small firms.

Norland Managed Services Limited is the UK's leading and fastest-growing independent engineering services provider. Established in 1984, its mission to 'be the market leader through exceptional service and exceptional people'. Norland chooses to work with customers who accept no compromise in quality standards. The business has grown to an annualized turnover of £120 million on the foundation of high customer retention rates, with over 1200 employees at Norland offices in London, Birmingham, Bristol, West London, Manchester, Newbury, Slough and Scotland.

Christopher Parr is a partner in the KSB Corporate department. He has 20 years experience as in-house counsel and of commercial transactions across the oil exploration, industrial gases, chemicals, pharmaceuticals, engineering, steel and construction industries. Christopher advises on corporate projects including mergers and acquisitions, joint ventures, specialized commercial agreements, agency and distribution agreements, international corporate structures and general company/commercial activities.

Dr Robert (Rob) Phaal joined the Centre for Technology Management at the University of Cambridge in 1997, where he conducts research in the area of strategic technology management with a particular interest in technology roadmapping. Rob has a mechanical engineering background with industrial experience in technical consulting, contract research and software development.

Tim Pickard is Area Vice-President, International Marketing at RSA, The Security Division of EMC.

Protiviti is a leading provider of independent risk consulting and internal audit services. The firm provides consulting and advisory services to help clients identify, assess, measure and manage financial, operational and technology-related risks encountered in their industries, and assists in the implementation of the processes and controls to enable their continued monitoring. Protiviti also offers a full spectrum of internal audit services to assist management and directors with their internal audit functions, including full outsourcing, co-sourcing, technology and tool implementation, and quality assessment and readiness reviews.

Caroline Raymond is the founder of Stress in Perspective, a consultancy that has helped numerous organizations develop appropriate stress management strategies. She assisted the Health and Safety Executive with their recent initiatives to reduce work-related stress and has written extensively on the subject. She currently designs and runs the Institute of Occupational Safety and Health's professional development courses on work-related stress.

Carmen M Rossiter is a managing director with Protiviti and leads the company's Toronto practice. She is a risk and control specialist, assisting leading organizations in addressing governance, risk management, control and internal audit issues and in developing enterprise solutions. She specializes in the financial services industry with a focus on banks, insurance companies and pension funds, but has a broad base of experience across all industry sectors. Starting in the audit practice of PricewaterhouseCoopers, she had an industry career that included controllership experience with Crown Life Insurance and strategic and financial planning experience with the Canadian Imperial Bank of Commerce. Returning to public practice in 1995, Carmen was a partner in the risk management practice of PricewaterhouseCoopers until joining Protiviti to launch the Toronto practice in 2004.

RSA is the security division of EMC. It is the expert in formation-centric security, enabling the protection of information throughout its life cycle. RSA enables customers cost-effectively to secure critical information assets and online identities wherever they live and at every step of the way, and manage security information and events to ease the burden of compliance.

Karl Russek has more than 13 years' experience in the insurance industry and environmental liability arena. Prior to joining ACE, he served as Assistant Vice-President, Risk Management for XL Environmental. He also held increasingly senior leadership positions in ECS Claims Administrators Inc before being appointed vice-president and management consultant in 1999. Prior to that position, he was employed in a variety of positions within the environmental engineering and regulatory community. Karl holds a BSc degree in secondary education from the University of Scranton and an MS degree in environmental quality science from the University of Alaska School of Engineering.

Penny Sanders is an associate in the Corporate practice at KSB Law specializing in the law relating to the regulation and compliance of the financial services industry. Penny is a member of the Securities and Investments Institute and advises on all matters relating to compliance with the Financial Services and Markets Act 2000, the FSA Rules and Guidance and the implications of recent European directives on financial services businesses.

Paul Saville-King is a divisional managing director of the Critical Services Division for Norland Managed Services Limited. Paul has a robust background in all aspects of building services, electrical engineering, fire and security and building management systems. He is pioneering the reduction of risk in engineering services through a unique critical engineering and risk management (CERM) business model in collaboration with key account clients, technical experts and consultants from the industry. Paul has qualifications in engineering, business and finance, holds an MBA with distinction from Ashridge and is a full member of the Institute of Incorporated Engineers (IIE), a fellow of the Chartered Management Institute and a member of the BIFM.

Siemens Insight Consulting is the specialist security, compliance, continuity and identity management division of Siemens Enterprise Communications Limited. From the development of policy, strategy and awareness through to the delivery of complete solutions comprising identity management, smart cards, testing, training and managed security, Insight Consulting helps organizations to identify and manage risk in their IT operations.

Thomas Stamm is Chief Casualty Underwriter for Europe at XL Insurance. He has over 20 years' experience in casualty underwriting for large multinational companies across a wide variety of industry sectors and products. He is currently responsible for casualty underwriting in XL Insurance's Continental Europe and Asia region. Thomas is a fellow of the Swiss Insurance Institute and has a bachelor's degree in business administration.

Alan Stanbra has over 25 years of management experience specializing in management systems. He holds an MSc in TQM and business excellence and is both an EFQM assessor and IRCA registered principal auditor, carrying out hundreds of assignments in the UK and globally. Alan was also an examiner for the Institute of Quality Assurance for several years.

Dr Frank Stenner took global responsibility for corporate finance, financial marketing, pension fund management and risk management within the BMW Group as Group Treasurer until September 2006. Previously, as CEO of BMW Bank GmbH he was for many years in charge of BMW Financial Services in Germany and held the position of a regional director for BMW Financial Services Asia/Pacific. He earned his academic degrees of Diplom-Kaufmann and Dr.rer.pol at the University of Hamburg.

Dr Elmar Steurer began his professional career after his PhD at the University of Karlsruhe at the R&D division of Daimler-Benz AG. His research responsibility for the coordination of the financial risk management activities served as a basis to establish the country and counterparty risk controlling function within the treasury of DaimlerChrysler AG. In 2002 he moved to BMW Group to take over responsibility for the issuance of public bonds. Since 2006 he has worked on the project risk management of the treasury with the scope to apply financial risk management methods to the industrial business.

Caroline Summerfield is a partner at KSB Law and has extensive experience dealing with all aspects of commercial property law, particularly in investment property acquisitions and disposals, landlord and tenant matters, property lending transactions and development work. Her clients include house builders. Caroline has developed particular expertise in advising property owners on their obligations under the disability discrimination legislation, having acted for many retailers and their landlords.

Kevin Taylor is a director of Companycare Communications, a PR and marketing communications consultancy. Kevin specializes in the IT sector where his clients have included BT, Kodak, Siemens and the GSM Association. He has also been an official spokesman for BT and London Transport and a radio news reporter. A fellow of the Chartered Institute of Public Relations, Kevin is a member of the Institute's Executive and its honorary treasurer.

Mike Thomas, BSc, CFIOSH, MIoD is Managing Director of HASTAM. He has 30 years' experience of health and safety consultancy and training in the UK and overseas and has a key involvement in HASTAM's CHASE monitoring systems. Mike has recently developed a behavioural safety package with clients. He has given a number of papers on OH&SMS implementation and monitoring performance.

Dr Anne-Marie Warris is Global Product Manager Climate Change for LRQA Centre based in the UK. She is the UK expert to the International Organization for Standardization TC207 (ISO14000) committees, specifically those on greenhouse gas, the joint CASCO/ISO committee of accreditation requirements for greenhouse gas and ISO14001 and the European accreditation committee on greenhouse gas. She is vice-chair of the Emission Trading Group Limited, which acts as a forum for emission trading issues in the UK, chairing its working group on verification, monitoring and reporting. Anne-Marie holds an MBA from London Business School, a PhD in combustion from Imperial College and a Master in Chemical Engineering from Chalmers University in Sweden.

Alena Watchorn heads up the Corporate Finance Insurance Division of HSBC Insurance Brokers, the specialist division dedicated to providing specialist insurance products for corporate transactions including warranty insurance. Alena has spent over 10 years in advising and broking warranty insurance and has led the development of the product including the design of the first buyers' side warranty insurance policy and placement of the largest warranty insurance programme. She has been involved in advising on over 1,000 transactions ranging from small UK private deals to the sale of billion-pound multinational companies. Her team also specializes in environmental insurance, tax opinion insurance, prospectus insurance and other transactional-based insurance products. Alena is a graduate in management science, associate of the Insurance Institute and fellow of the Institute of Risk Management.

John Watt is a senior lecturer in risk management and is Co-ordinator, Centre for Decision Analysis and Risk Management, School of Health and Social Sciences, Middlesex University. He is an environmental scientist by training and has research interests in risk management and environmental pollution effects on health and on cultural heritage. John is programme leader for the postgraduate degrees in risk management and undertakes training and consultancy work in a number of risk areas.

Emma Watkins is the Pensions Specialist at ACE European Group, responsible for developing pension trustee liability insurance. Since joining the company in 2004, Emma has further developed ACE's product to respond to recent legislation and continues to work on increasing awareness of the product in the general insurance and pensions marketplaces. Before joining ACE, Emma managed a multi-disciplined operational area within Hazell Carr Pensions Consulting covering actuarial, documentation and administration disciplines and formed part of their new business presentation team. She assisted in the strategic partnership between Hazell Carr and Prudential, where she originally managed defined benefit administration and pension technical areas. Emma is a member of the NAPF and is part PMI qualified.

Paul Williams is a UK chartered accountant (FCA) and a chartered information technology professional (CITP). He served as International President of the Information Systems Audit and Control Association and its sister body, the IT Governance Institute, from 1999 to 2001.

XL Insurance companies help leading industrial and commercial businesses manage their risks by providing comprehensive, cost-effective and integrated solutions. We offer a broad portfolio of high-quality insurance products and related services including property, casualty, professional and specialist coverage. We are committed to five key values: ethics, teamwork, excellence, development and respect. XL Insurance is the global brand used by XL Capital Ltd's property and casualty insurance companies and specialty underwriting divisions throughout the world.

CREATE A BRIGHTER FUTURE.
MAKE PROGRESS.

KSB Law

...usually when they are least expected. Often when they could have been avoided.

At KSB Law we offer proactive advice on how to avoid damage to your business, including advice on:

- Age discrimination
- Workplace stress
- Disability risk assessment of your premises
- Buying or selling a business
- Regulatory risk
- Warranty claims
- Managing business risk within contracts
- Corporate governance
- Risk Management in China

All of these topics are the focus of chapters within this book and have the potential to damage your company. We aim to help you identify risks before they happen.

To discuss legal risk management contact:
Andrew Cromby
+44 (0)20 7822 7597 acromby@ksblaw.co.uk
or the individual authors on
+44 (0)20 7822 7500

KSB Law LLP
Elan House • 5-11 Fetter Lane • London • EC4A 1QD
60 Victoria Street • St Albans • Herts • AL1 3XH

www.ksblaw.co.uk

Introduction

As Steve Fowler points out in his Foreword, risk management is on the agenda of every company's board of directors and the introduction, execution and monitoring of its disciplines involve all levels of management. The growing pervasiveness of risk management techniques in all kinds of business is mirrored in the scope of this fourth edition of *Managing Business Risk*. The contents range from the formulation of strategies and good practice in their implementation to specific risks in operational, financial and corporate management, from risks in innovation and expansion to aspects of environmental risk and to the areas of employment and human relations and IT management and usage, where risk management techniques are more commonly employed.

Managing Business Risk is used by the UK's Institute of Risk Management (IRM) as recommended reading in its professional qualification programmes and we welcome in this edition a thought-provoking chapter from the Federation of European Risk Management Associations (FERMA) on the evolution of risk management across the countries of the European Union. Other chapters in Part 1 of the book address the areas of strategic risk and corporate governance. For the first time we include a chapter on strategic risk management written specifically for the directors and managers of small businesses.

Part 2 focuses on good practice in implementing risk management strategies, with contributions from leading international consultants in risk management and from two major multinationals, BMW Group and Heineken International, that have introduced risk management strategies into their businesses with excellent results. In Part 3, which covers risk issues in operational management, there are echoes of the previous edition in the seven specific topics addressed but all the chapters are new contributions from experienced risk management practitioners.

Six key areas of risk that are primarily the concern of senior financial and corporate office management are highlighted in Part 4, and Part 5 features the particular risks that arise in many businesses as a result of innovation and expansion.

The next two parts, 6 and 7, deal with the more familiar territory of employment, human relations and IT management and usage and are essential reading for all managers with responsibility in those areas.

Finally, in Part 8, three aspects of managing environmental risk are explored, including an overview of international developments, the related business impacts of climate change, and occupational health and safety.

As usual, I take this opportunity of expressing my appreciation to all those who have written for this edition; I am sure that readers will find many chapters of relevance and interest to them. My particular thanks go to those contributors who have sponsored the book and provided multiple contributions, in particular ACE European Group, DNV, HSBC Insurance Brokers, KSB Law LLP and Protiviti.

The pace of change in risk management techniques and their application remains brisk and will surely lead us into new areas for the next edition of *Managing Business Risk*. We look forward to the challenge.

Jonathan Reuvid

1

Risk Management Strategy and Corporate Governance

Evolution in risk management

Marie-Gemma Dequae, Federation of European Risk Management Associations (FERMA)

Every organization takes risk in order to meet its business objectives. Without risk, there would be no reward. At the same time, those risks must be managed in a disciplined and systematic way. Not only does risk management protect the organization from loss, but also appropriate risk management techniques allow the organization to take those risks necessary to meet its business objectives.

The International Federation of Risk and Insurance Management Associations (IFRIMA), the international umbrella organization for risk management associations throughout the world, says that risk management is a central part of any organization's strategic management.[1] It is the process whereby organizations methodically address the risks relating to their activities, with the goal of achieving sustained benefits across the portfolio of activities. This is often called enterprise risk management (ERM) and its objective is to add maximum value to these activities.

The foundation of an ERM programme is a disciplined, consistent process throughout the organization and should include:

1. *Risk identification and assessment.* This step includes identification of the significant risks that face the organization and includes development of risk registers and risk mapping, along with both quantitative and qualitative analysis of the exposures.

2. *Risk mitigation strategies.* The development of risk mitigation strategies is key to the management of risk issues, and action plans need to be included in the overall business plans of the organization to ensure successful implementation.
3. *Residual risk transfer.* Once all risk mitigation strategies have been evaluated and implemented as appropriate, the residual risk has to be effectively managed through a combination of insurance, hedging and other alternative techniques to ensure the best possible coverage at the lowest possible transfer cost.
4. *Risk reporting.* The organization needs the ability to report on risks internally, specifically to senior management and the board of directors.
5. *Monitoring.* This part of the process is designed to ensure adherence to and effectiveness and relevance of policies and procedures relating to risk management.

The value added by risk management relates directly to the mission of the organization, its long-term viability and its business imperatives. In order to achieve this value, risk management can and should be applied by taking an integrated approach:

■ taking into consideration all types of risks;
■ adopting a consistent approach and methodology for each type of risk;
■ ensuring that policies and strategies are developed with a positive and professional risk/opportunity approach.

This can and should be achieved by developing policies and activities in three significant areas:

1. *Contribution to the overall business objectives of the organization.* All organizations must take risk in order to be successful. Risk management, appropriately applied, will allow the organization to take those risks that are necessary to its overall value and to leverage opportunities from the ability to take and manage risks.
2. *Establishment of a consistent, transparent framework for corporate governance.* Good corporate governance requires that effective risk management programmes be established by boards of directors and implemented by management. These programmes must be comprehensive and transparent, promoting risk consciousness throughout the organization and allowing for comprehensive reporting externally to shareholders and regulators.
3. *Protection for the company from adverse variances and catastrophes.* Protection from adverse variances and catastrophes requires consideration of both internal and external risk factors. In addition, achieving appropriate protection requires a combined focus on risk mitigation and risk transfer through insurance, hedging or other financial instruments. The practice of hazard and insurable risk management has matured significantly over the years and has protected organizations from catastrophic risk exposures to their properties and personnel and for their liabilities.

Implementation of a risk management programme will differ from one organization to another. Nevertheless, it is important that the implementation plans include the manner in which risk management will be embedded into the culture of the organization. This should include the definition of roles, training and integration into the reward system. Without operationalizing risk management into the organization's culture, the programme will become just words on paper.

The skill set for risk management will vary considerably depending upon the industry. It can include expertise in investments, finance, actuarial science, law, engineering, risk transfer, business processes, internal audit, etc, or combinations thereof. Risk management is a collaborative process requiring commitment and consensus within an organization. The culture and business purpose of the organization will drive the type of process and risk mitigation strategies to ensure successful implementation.

Finally, in order to integrate risk management properly into the strategic management of the organization, the risk manager must be positioned at a high enough level in the organizational structure to ensure the success of the programme.

Standards

The development of enterprise risk management has taken place in tandem with that of corporate governance regulations, many of which require organizations to confirm that they have identified and assessed their risks and that internal controls are in place to manage those risks. In Europe, the UK has taken the lead, followed by Germany and France, and other countries have now put corporate governance in their legislation.

In addition, industry and risk specific standards, guidelines and frameworks have been developed by many professional and self-regulatory organizations, such as the Committee of Sponsoring Organizations (COSO) on behalf of the audit profession, the Basel Committee on Banking Supervision for banking institutions and the Global Association of Risk Professionals (GARP) on behalf of financial risk managers.

When it comes to enterprise risk management, IFRIMA encourages the development of best practices and guidelines for risk management. It believes that a detailed international risk management standard would not be practical because there is no one risk management standard. Instead, IFRIMA considers a generic best practice/guideline document as beneficial for the development of risk management throughout commerce and countries. IFRIMA members in Australia, Europe and Canada have developed and adopted risk management standards.

In Europe, the Federation of European Risk Management Associations (FERMA) has adopted the Risk Management Standard first published in the UK in 2002. It is now available in 15 languages, including all major European languages, as well as Chinese, Japanese and Arabic. Anyone interested can download it free from the website at www.ferma-asso.org.

The Standard sets out a standardized and enterprise-wide process. It gives guidelines on how to start the process, what steps to take, how to organize it in a company or group of companies, etc. Risk reporting and communication are very important – to keep the internal side of the reporting transparent between the business units and the individual managers. The Risk Management Standard also gives advice on how to organize and establish the roles of the different people involved in risk management, and the risk management process.

The Standard is a very useful tool. It also refers to the International Organization for Standardization (ISO) standards, because a lot of confusion can come out of terms that have a different meaning in one country as against another. It is important to get the right terms for everyone.

The results of a survey of 460 European risk managers carried out on behalf of FERMA were published in October 2006 and showed that senior management is now the driving force behind risk management in many European companies. Nearly 80 per cent of the risk managers said their board/supervisory committee (44 per cent) or CEO (34 per cent) directly sponsors risk management. Other responses strengthened the picture of top-level involvement in risk management and of a profession that has grown in scope and confidence.

The vast majority of risk managers surveyed said they report to the board (24 per cent) or CEO (27 per cent). A further 46 per cent report to the CFO. The risk management professional deals with the board or supervisory committee at least once a year in two-thirds (63 per cent) of the companies.

The results of the survey demonstrate the seriousness with which senior management now regards risk management. We believe that corporate governance regimes have emphasized the role that risk management can play in the success of a business, which makes it a matter for the boardroom. With the spread of corporate governance legislation, for instance in Spain, Italy and Slovenia, we expect this trend to continue.

European directives

Next after adapting risk management to the internal side of the organizations, it is important to have a look at the outside world and the legal environment. In Europe, European Union directives and their evolution have a significant impact on enterprise risk. Among the directives that will affect the risk environment are:

■ *Insurance intermediaries directive.* The Insurance Mediation Directive is intended to create a single market in insurance via a 'passport' for EU retail insurance intermediaries. It is under review in Germany, where there are some problems in implementing the directive due to the high number of intermediaries.
■ *Environmental directive.* FERMA is participating in the negotiations on financial responsibility for environmental damage in order to make the measures acceptable for industry.
■ *Solvency 2.* This new capital adequacy regime for insurance companies, including internal controls, better risk management and corporate governance issues, has to be implemented in July 2007.
■ *Reinsurance directive.* Its goal is to bring the reinsurance industry under a standard-ized prudential regime such as exists for the life and non-life insurance sectors.

■ *Audit directive.* The eighth version of this directive, likely to go into effect in mid-2008, requires group-level audit committees with clearly defined responsibilities, including oversight of the company's internal audit, internal control and risk management systems.

■ *Flood directive.* The aim is to help member states prevent and limit floods and flood damage by identifying the river basins and coastal areas at risk and then creating flood risk management plans. The first assessments should be completed in 2012.

■ *Motor insurance directive.* This is a fifth version in the series aimed at creating the free movement of vehicles through the EU.

■ *Company law directives.* The fourth and seventh directives are to be amended, with corporate governance rules that would confirm collective responsibility of board members for financial statements and key non-financial information.

The latest changes and developments in risk management in Europe

Going back in time, risk management has developed a lot, starting with businesses optimizing their insurance buying process. In the past, separate subsidiaries or units bought separate policies. The early risk managers in the 1980s and early 1990s tended to buy global insurance coverage. From this development, we saw that, in order to keep insurance coverage complete and consistent, you have to work on the risk management process, and you have to be aware of all the risks in all the different parts of your group.

A major trend in business today is the creation of very large international groups through mergers and acquisitions. As a result, businesses have become more complex and operate in different sectors and different territories.

It is important for risk management to be involved from the first steps to have global solutions to risk issues. When you are making an acquisition, you need all the information on risks in the target company, not only operational and accidental risks, but also human resources risks, like employers' liability and pension promises. Information about all types of environmental risks, product liability issues and litigation is also crucial. At the moment of acquisition, the risk manager begins the important job of looking at the risk management procedures and practices of both companies and integrating them and their insurance programmes, together with organizing a lot of training of people. Post-completion, the main objective is to integrate everything in the risk management processes, procedures and contracts as soon as possible

The kinds of risks have also evolved and there are now more risks where the insurance market is not offering solutions, for example reputation risks, terrorism, etc. Therefore, enterprise risk management has become very important as we now need to look at risks from a total global perspective.

The most recent developments in FERMA

One of the major aspects of FERMA has always been education, and in October 2006 we launched an e-learning course. 'Prorim' is aimed at businesses that do not have a professional risk manager and it was supported in its development by the European Commission's Leonardo da Vinci programme for vocational training. Prorim consists of six modules accessed by the internet, and it is distributed in Germany, Italy, France and the UK in their respective languages.

Risk managers are expanding their understanding of the risk issues related to climate change, and in October 2007 FERMA will hold its biennial forum with the theme of risk management in motion: global responsibility and sustainability. We expect 1,000 attendees.

The European risk benchmarking survey carried out for us by Ernst & Young in Paris and AXA Corporate Solutions mentioned above received a very good response rate of about 20 per cent. FERMA is really becoming a body with some common objectives. In the last three years, we have seen growing interest in risk management from Eastern Europe and have welcomed the Russian and Bulgarian risk management associations into membership. Poland, too, is likely soon to join.

The European Commission is worried about the free market competition and the management of services within financial institutions and business insurance. Thus, it is carrying out a survey with insurers and brokers, and FERMA was the appointed representative body for commercial insurance buyers for the European Commission.

Your dialogue with the insurance industry

We have a lot of dialogue. If you look at evolution in the insurance industry, people are getting more risk management minded. From the insurers' perspective, risk management means that they have to be very careful about what risks to assume. If you look at the insurance contract of 20 years ago, the excluded risks then would be one page long. In contracts today, there are many more exclusions. Insurers are very reluctant to take on risks that cannot be calculated actuarially. However, from a risk management perspective, we need coverage of risks where we can't really estimate what is going to happen, even after having worked on the full process of risk management.

Just in terms of natural phenomena, storms are getting more frequent and severe, and the impact of events is getting more international, for example flood activity, storms, tsunamis, earthquakes, etc. That means it becomes much more difficult for us to manage these risks, so we need more risk transfer and risk financing. We, therefore, have to work with the insurers to look at acceptable solutions for both sides.

Another aspect of communication and working together with insurers is the globalization of activities, and I'm referring to the Asian situation. Every country has its own insurance legislation, eg Chinese risks have to be insured in China, and there is some new regulation on reinsurance. Development of insurance regulation is very important for us. We need insurance that is present in all the countries where we, as industrial and commercial companies, have a presence, and this is improving.

The whole process of negotiating with the insurers can be much improved. There is still a lot of work to be done with contract certainty, by which we mean the timely agreement of contract terms and delivery of documentation.

Following concern about lack of transparency over brokers' remuneration, FERMA proposed a simple charter to major brokers in 2005, but it now seems they are unlikely to sign. It is possible some countries will introduce regulation. In Belgium, we were able to have a position paper between the association of the big brokers and the national risk managers association. The French risk management association also made an agreement with brokers in their country, which soon after became the subject of regulation. The whole problem is that you can get transparency on the business interest contracts but not on personal lines. We hope our discussions have at least improved the situation.

In the United States, the Risk and Insurance Management Society (RIMS) has improved its quality improvement process (QIP) with integrity and transparency. FERMA is participating in the activities developed by RIMS in these areas. It is interesting to see the differences between different countries. We have to be partners in risks. As risk managers, we want to transfer the risk to the insurer, and the insurer needs to know what we are doing, so there must be an open discussion and transparency between the partners.

Note

1. IFRIMA White Paper, *Enterprise Risk Management*, 2004.

Strategic risk and good governance

Gillian Lees, Chartered Institute of Management Accountants (CIMA)

Introduction

It is no exaggeration to say that an organization must understand its strategic risks if it is to succeed in the long term. Evidence has shown that, when risks materialize, it is the strategic risks that account for the greatest impact on shareholder value compared to financial and operational risks. What we are talking about here is the risks that prevent the organization from achieving its strategy, for example a failure to integrate an acquisition successfully, misaligned products or intense competitive pressures. It is also important to consider the upside of risk – it is equally possible to fail by not taking advantage of strategic possibilities.

However, a McKinsey survey of 1,000 directors worldwide in 2005 showed that, while 75 per cent wanted to spend time on strategy and risk as opposed to accounting and compliance issues, only 11 per cent claimed to have a complete understanding of current risks and 8 per cent had an understanding of long-term risks. A more recent survey has revealed some progress in board understanding of risk, but the fact remains that more could and should be done to improve this, particularly within the context of an ever-accelerating pace of change. A key priority for boards is to ensure that they do not spend too much time on compliance issues at the expense of strategy.

Getting the balance right

The framework of enterprise governance has been developed in order to emphasize the importance for boards of balancing conformance with performance. It was developed as part of a project undertaken by the International Federation of Accountants (IFAC) and CIMA following the major corporate scandals in the early years of the 21st century, including Enron, WorldCom and Parmalat. The aim of the project was to explore what went wrong in companies and what has to be done to ensure that things go right. A series of 27 case studies was undertaken, covering:

- 10 countries, including the UK, United States, France, Australia and Italy;
- 10 industry sectors, including telecommunications, retail, insurance and banking;
- both corporate governance and strategic policies and practices;
- successes, such as Tesco, and failures, such as Enron and WorldCom.

There is little doubt that such scandals have brought corporate governance issues to the forefront of debate. Many countries have reviewed their corporate governance arrangements, including the UK with its revised Combined Code. The United States has gone even further by enacting the stringent Sarbanes–Oxley Act, which includes a requirement under section 404 for companies to state that their internal financial controls are effective.

However, the IFAC/CIMA project concluded that, while corporate governance failure was a factor in some cases, there were many other examples of companies running into difficulties as a consequence of their strategic choices and/or their failure to implement strategy effectively. Good corporate governance was a necessary, but not sufficient, foundation for success. In other words, bad governance could ruin a company, but could not, on its own, ensure its success. In a similar vein, Dutch research looked at Europe's largest business failures over the past 25 years and concluded that nearly two-thirds failed for legitimate reasons – what the researchers term the risks of entrepreneurship – rather than because of fraudulent or unethical behaviour (Bollen *et al*, 2005).

Enterprise governance focuses on both conformance and performance aspects of business and is illustrated in Figure 1.2.1.

The core message of enterprise governance is that organizations must balance conformance requirements with the need to deliver long-term strategic success through performance.

In terms of risk management, the framework clearly illustrates the importance of paying sufficient attention to the need to create wealth or value and to exploit valuable opportunities. With such recent attention on corporate governance and control, it is not surprising that some commentators have argued that the pendulum has swung too far in that direction and that the importance of entrepreneurial leadership needs to be re-emphasized. Risk management is not just about loss prevention, but also about the seizing of opportunities. This is the so-called upside of risk management where the emphasis is on realizing the rewards associated with particular risks. Viewed in this way, effective risk management may enable the organization to take more risks in order to improve overall returns and shareholder value.

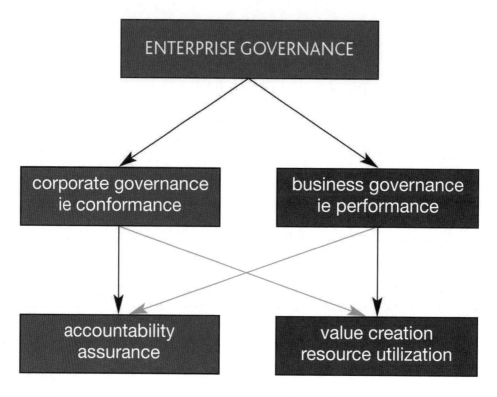

Figure 1.2.1   The enterprise governance framework

The role of the board in practice

A strategically minded board that engages effectively with management has the potential therefore to make a considerable impact on the organization's long-term success. However, there are some very good reasons as to why boards struggle in practice to make effective contributions to their organization's strategic development:

- *Lack of time and crowded agendas.* An obvious reason in recent years has been the substantial demands of compliance issues, for example the Sarbanes–Oxley Act for companies listed in the United States and the transition to international accounting standards in Europe. Fortunately, there are signs that the pendulum is swinging back into balance with boards beginning to refocus their attention on strategy.
- *Greater complexity of business combined with information overload.* This can make it difficult for non-executive directors, with a part-time involvement, to really understand the organization in depth and to engage in constructive debate with management. Information that is poorly organized or presented in different formats at each meeting also makes a director's life challenging. There is often simply too much information for the board to digest properly.

■ *Lack of robust processes and oversight mechanisms at board level for dealing with strategy.* This is in contrast to other issues for which the board is responsible and for which there are dedicated committees, such as the audit, remuneration and nomination committees. These enable boards to exercise effective oversight of these areas.

Clearly, boards need some tools and techniques to help them to understand and manage their strategy, including strategic risks. The CIMA Strategic Scorecard™ aims to address this need, and we will now look at this in more detail.

The objectives of the CIMA Strategic Scorecard™

The CIMA Strategic Scorecard™ ('the scorecard') is a pragmatic and flexible tool that is designed to help boards to fulfil their responsibilities to contribute to and oversee strategy effectively. It should be noted that it remains the role of the management to develop and propose the strategy, while the board's focus is to challenge the strategy constructively, endorse it and monitor its implementation. The objectives of the scorecard are:

■ to assist the board, in particular the non-executive directors, in the oversight of an organization's strategic process;
■ to provide an integrated and dynamic framework for dealing with strategy at board level that focuses on the major strategic issues facing the organization and ensures that strategy is discussed at board level on a regular basis;
■ to provide strategic information in a consistent and summarized format to help directors to obtain sufficient grasp of the material so that they can offer constructive, informed input;
■ to assist the board in dealing with strategic choice, transformational change and the attendant risks;
■ to provide assurance to the board in relation to the organization's strategic position and progress;
■ to assist the board to identify key points at which it needs to take decisions.

Although the scorecard is aimed primarily at board-level use, we have found that it offers considerable benefits to the organization's management:

■ Introducing the discipline of having to prepare and update the scorecard helps management to keep its focus on the major strategic issues.
■ It facilitates discussion within the management team and thus helps the team to refine its proposals prior to exposure to the board.
■ It can help to identify gaps in knowledge and analysis and can improve the quality of information presented to the board.

■ Because the scorecard improves the quality of the board's contribution, this can lead to a more constructive relationship with management with consequent benefits for governance and performance.

The four dimensions of the scorecard

The scorecard has four dimensions as set out in Figure 1.2.2.
    Each dimension is summarized below:

■ *Strategic position.* This dimension focuses on information that is required to assess the organization's current and likely future position. It covers externally focused information such as economic, political and regulatory developments and market share as well as internal issues such as competences and resources. The board discussion focuses on reviewing the information and considering its implications.
■ *Strategic options.* The focus of the scorecard now shifts towards decision making. Strategic options can be defined as those options that have the greatest potential for creating or destroying stakeholder value. Typically, there are no more than four to five under consideration at any one time.
■ *Strategic implementation.* At this point, the emphasis of the scorecard is to identify milestones for the board and monitor implementation of the agreed strategy. Decisions on appropriate action may be required if things are not proceeding as planned.
■ *Strategic risks.* This dimension underpins the others by focusing specifically on the major strategic risks that pose the greatest threat to the achievement of the organization's strategy or, conversely, present the greatest opportunities. Other issues that need to be considered here are the determination of the organization's risk appetite and implementation of effective risk management policies and processes. This dimension is covered in more detail below.

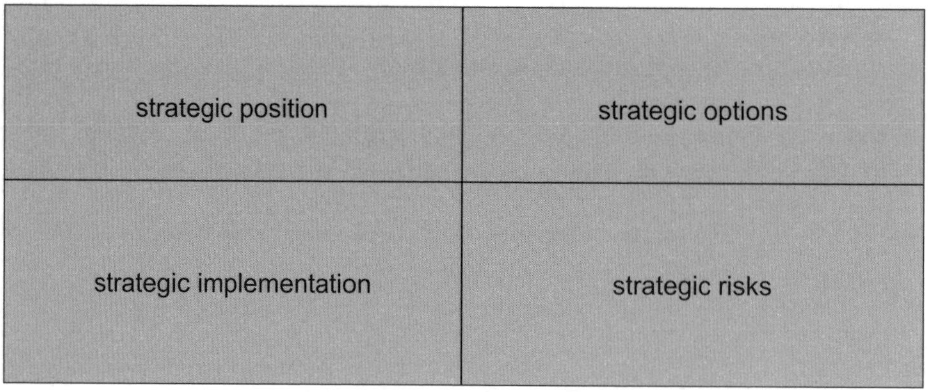

strategic position	strategic options
strategic implementation	strategic risks

Figure 1.2.2   The CIMA Strategic Scorecard™

The scorecard in practice

When presented to the board, the scorecard is set out in the form of tables with relevant headings for each dimension. These can be modified to suit the individual organization. These headings basically prompt management to provide an adequate description of the activity being undertaken, including when the last information was put to the board and when new information will be presented in future. The board needs to agree with management which high-level issues and activities are to be included. The board can then pose challenging questions in relation to all these items. Depending on the answers provided, the board can decide whether it is satisfied, whether action needs to be taken and/or whether it needs to explore a specific issue in more depth – perhaps by referring to more detailed supporting analysis.

This supporting analysis will have been used by management to undertake the detailed strategic planning and management; so, in effect, each dimension is supported by a variety of tools and techniques. Organizations can use the ones that are most relevant for their circumstances.

In addition to the four tables for each of the four dimensions of the scorecard, an additional item is a simple summary list of all the issues covered in each dimension on one page. This may sound very basic, but it provides a clear and useful snapshot of all the major issues and challenges facing the organization – very useful to incoming non-executive directors who need to understand the business very quickly. A sample summary table is shown in Figure 1.2.3.

Strategic position	Strategic options
This section lists the key areas of importance for the organization. No more than 10 issues and listed in order of importance, eg: – regulatory developments; – technological developments; – competitors; – competences.	This section lists the major strategic options and should contain no more than five: – merger in related business; – outsourcing major process; – major divestment and refocus of business.
Strategic implementation	**Strategic risk**
This section lists major strategic projects that are in progress. They should be different from items listed under 'Strategic options': – development of major new delivery channel; – major relocation; – expansion into Eastern Europe.	This section lists the key strategic risk issues, in terms of appetite, process and actual risks: – risk appetite; – process issues; – strategic risks; eg reputation. – employee retention;

Figure 1.2.3   The CIMA Strategic Scorecard™ summary table

The scorecard is typically presented to the board on a quarterly or half-yearly basis.

The strategic risk dimension in detail

The CIMA Strategic Scorecard™ provides a useful framework both for integrating strategic risk into the overall context of strategy and, in turn, for ensuring that strategy is dealt with effectively at board level.

There are three key components to strategic risk management:

■ *Risk appetite:* as its name suggests, this covers the organization's desire, capacity and capability to assume risk. Every organization has a risk appetite regardless of whether it is aware of it or not and it provides an overall direction for the organization's strategy. It is important therefore that the board and management undertake the key task of determining and articulating the risk appetite of the organization.
■ *Strategic risks and opportunities facing the organization:* the nature and extent of these, the likelihood of their occurrence and/or potential for exploitation, ability to manage risks and so on. To a large extent, these need to be considered in respect of each of the other three dimensions, but the strategic risk dimension provides a useful check and balance to ensure that this is actually happening.
■ *Process issues:* how risks are actually managed within the organization, training issues, risk identification and prioritization, stress testing, risk monitoring processes, whether any risks are currently materializing and so on.

The strategic risk dimension could be regarded as encompassing or driving the other three dimensions, for example a major motor company has considered repositioning the strategic risk dimension so that it is the first to be considered in the sequence. An alternative approach, suggested by a large media company, is to view the strategic risks dimension as the 'strategy for risk' and add what it has termed the 'risk wrapper' to the entire scorecard with suggested interventions for each of the dimensions of the scorecard. This makes for a powerful and integrated strategic risk management tool.

However the board chooses to view it, what really matters is that it spends adequate time and attention on all three components of strategic risk and that risk management is fully embedded in the overall strategy.

Current developments

CIMA is currently undertaking further work on developing the scorecard so that it can evolve into a robust and practical tool. As a first step, it undertook a trial itself, and some of the outcomes show the potential benefits of the scorecard in preventing the over-management of risk. The key points arising from the trial are that the scorecard has:

■ helped management to identify gaps in knowledge and analysis and helped to maintain focus;

- provided an invaluable structure to help identify and prioritize options, monitor progress and ensure that risks are identified;
- helped the governing Council and management to focus on the issues that really matter, both internal and external;
- shown how difficult it can be to maintain a high-level view – the temptation is always to get caught up in the detail;
- forced directors and Council members to 'lift their eyes above the horizon' and to avoid the comfort zone of detail. In this way, it has proved to be valuable in encouraging effective strategic thinking.

A trial is now well advanced in a major housing association, and initial indications are that the scorecard has enabled the board to discuss strategic issues and strategic options and to give a clear direction to their strategy in a very interactive way. Further trials are planned in organizations in both the private and the public sector.

Conclusion

Successful organizations are those that are able to identify the right strategy and then harness all their effort into ensuring that everything that they do supports that strategy. This applies to risk management, which must be fully integrated into the organization's key strategic objectives with a full understanding of the major strategic risks. By supporting high-level strategic thinking and embedding strategic risk firmly into the scorecard framework, the CIMA Strategic Scorecard™ should make a valuable contribution to effective risk management.

References and further reading

Bollen, L H H *et al* (2005) *Classification and Analysis of Major European Business Failures*, Maastricht Accounting, Audit and Information Management Research Center, www.fdewb.unimaas.nl/aim

CIMA (2005) *The CIMA Strategic Scorecard*, CIMA discussion paper, free download from www.cimaglobal.com/cimastrategicscorecard

IFAC/CIMA (2004) *Enterprise Governance: Getting the balance right*, free download from www.cimaglobal.com/enterprisegovernance

Corporate governance

Guy Facey, KSB Law LLP

Background

Various corporate scandals in the UK in the 1980s and 1990s (Maxwell, BCCI, Polly Peck) acted as a wake-up call and led to the Cadbury Code of Best Practice (known as the Cadbury Report), which was published in 1992. Various other reports followed on from this, not only in the UK but internationally, and the UK is seen as one of the leading countries for corporate governance standards.

Defining 'corporate governance'

Corporate governance means 'the system by which companies are directed and controlled' (Cadbury Report 1992). It mainly deals with relationships between constituent parts of a company: the directors, the board and the shareholders. However, it is more commonly used in the wider sense of 'good governance' or the body of rules that regulate the transparency, accountability and proper dealings in the conduct of an organization's business. From the company's point of view it is probably best seen as a system of risk controls or checks and balances.

In the last few years, principally as a result of corporate scandals but also resulting from shareholder pressure generally, there has been a wave of new regulation in the UK and the United States. Much of the regulation takes the form of requiring companies to provide better information to shareholders and to the public in what is known as the 'comply or explain' corporate governance culture. Much of the focus has also been on non-executive directors, who do not have full-time service contracts with the company

Table 1.3.1   Reports and reviews of corporate governance in the UK

1992	Publication of the Cadbury Report to address concerns over financial irregularities.
1995	Publication of the Greenbury Report to address issues of internal control.
1998	Publication of the Hampel Report to address issues of compliance with the Cadbury and Greenbury reports, which led to the publication of the Combined Code of Corporate Governance 1998.
1998	DTI initiates three-year in-depth review of company law.
1999	Publication of Turnbull Guidance, *Internal Control: Guidance for directors on the Combined Code.*
2002	Publication of the White Paper on *Modernising Company Law* following the three-year review.
2003	Publication of the Smith Report on guidance on audit committees and the Higgs Report on the role and effectiveness of non-executive directors, which led to changes in the Combined Code of Corporate Governance 1998.
2003	Financial Services Authority (FSA) review of the UK Listing Rules, placing emphasis on corporate governance.
2004	Review of the impact of Turnbull Guidance.
2005	Publication of *Internal Control: Revised guidance for directors on the Combined Code.*
2005	Publication of the company law reform White Paper.
2005	FRC initiated a review of the Combined Code.
2006	FRC consultation with shareholders on the Combined Code.

but provide their skill and experience and often sit on several boards. The aim of the rules is to protect shareholders' rights, enhance disclosure and transparency, facilitate the effective functioning of the board and provide an efficient legal and regulatory framework, which is essential for companies and for the economy as a whole.

The history of corporate governance in the UK

In response to a number of high-profile corporate scandals, a series of reports and reviews have been published, all of which have had an influence on corporate governance in the UK. A selection of these is shown in Table 1.3.1.

The UK corporate governance law is also significantly influenced by EU law. In May 2003, the European Commission issued the *European Action Plan on Company Law and Corporate Governance*, which proposed a total of 24 measures to be implemented by all member states. As a response the DTI published the *UK Approach to EU Company Law and Corporate Governance* in 2005.

Where the law on corporate governance is found

The basic source of corporate governance law in the UK is the Companies Act and case law, which apply in various degrees to all companies, whether public or private, quoted or unquoted. The main source of corporate governance for listed UK companies is the Combined Code of Corporate Governance and the Listing Rules. Therefore, if your company is not listed, the Companies Act and common law rules will apply to you. If you are thinking of listing, be it on Ofex/Plus, AIM or the Full List of the London Stock Exchange, then you should be aware of the Code and the Listing Rules.

Company law

The Companies Act 1985 is the main statute regulating companies. It contains extensive provisions on the conduct of directors, including conflicts of interest, loans from the company, misleading the auditors and dealings in the company's shares. Many of the offences carry a fine or a prison term. In many cases the Companies Act relaxes the standard of duty imposed on directors of private companies (as opposed to public companies) or allows the shareholders of the company to waive the requirements of the Act.

Directors are also bound by the company's memorandum and articles of association. The articles of association are the internal rules governing the conduct of a company's affairs. They also deal with the relationship between the managing director, the chairman and the board and the shareholders. The duty of directors is to act within the powers granted to them by the company's memorandum and articles of association. They also have common law duties (as discussed below).

Currently, directors' common law and fiduciary duties to the company are not set out in the Companies Act (but see 'The Companies Bill' below). They are embodied in a vast body of case law dating back to the 19th century and beyond. These common law rules impose considerable responsibilities on directors and should not be underrated. The case law continues to be refined by modern decisions, for example in cases of white-collar crime and civil cases of disputes between shareholders. Broadly speaking, the common law duties comprise duties to exercise skill and care; to act in good faith in the best interests of the company; not to fetter discretion; to avoid conflicting interests and conflicting duties; and not to make a secret profit.

Some of these rules are incorporated into Acts. For example, the basic statement of the duty of skill and care at common law is effectively summarized in section 214(1) of the Insolvency Act 1986:

> for the [above] purposes, the facts which a director of a company ought to know or ascertain, the conclusions which he ought to reach and the steps which he ought to take are those which would be known or ascertained, or reached or taken, reasonably diligent persons having both:

- [*the so-called objective test*] the general knowledge, skill and experience that may reasonably be expected of a person carrying out the same functions as are carried out by that director in relation to that company; and
- [*the so-called subjective test*] the general knowledge, skill and experience that the director has.

To take an example, where a company is proposing to make a material investment in something that depends heavily on technology, it might be thought that a non-executive director sitting on the board could rely on the subjective test and claim that, not being a technology expert, he or she does not have the technical knowledge to make a judgement on the risk of the investment. The director would however be wrong if he or she did not demonstrate a reasonable level of knowledge, skill and experience under the more general, objective test. In those circumstances the director might be expected to insist on a report from a technology expert to the board in order to be shown to have discharged the duty of care.

Commentators have observed that the non-executive directors of Equitable Life will have to overcome this hurdle. The case brought by Equitable Life against its former directors for breach of the duty of skill and care and of fiduciary duty is seen as the first full examination of non-executive directors' duties by an English court. This case is still ongoing and the implications are yet to be revealed as the court proceedings move forward. In the context of the duty of skill and care, it is interesting to note that in interim proceedings (brought by the non-executive directors to relieve them of liability – under section 727 of the Companies Act 1985 – on the basis that they had acted 'honestly and reasonably') the judge, who rejected the application, commented that:

> I do not think this statement [ie that directors are entitled to trust the full-time executives for information] does represent the modern law at least if (as the applicants were inclined to submit) it means unquestioning reliance upon others to do their job. It is well known that the role of non-executive directors in corporate governance has been the subject of some debate in recent years. For present purposes… it… suffices to say that the extent to which a non-executive director may reasonably rely on the executive directors and other professionals to perform their duties is one in which the law can fairly be said to be developing and is plainly 'fact sensitive'. It is plainly arguable, I think, that a company may reasonably at least look to non-executive directors for independence of judgment and supervision of the executive management.

The Combined Code

The main source of rules on corporate governance for listed companies is the Combined Code on Corporate Governance. It was originally published by the Financial Reporting Council (FRC) in 1998. Subsequent to the Higgs Report on non-executive directors and the Smith Report on audit committees, a new version of the Combined Code was published in July 2003. The 2003 Code amounts to a significant revision of the 1998 Code. In 2005, the FRC initiated a review on the implementation of the Combined

Code and a small number of changes were made in an updated version of the Code published in June 2006.

The Combined Code does not have the effect of law but follows the UK model of governance represented by transparency and reporting and allowing institutional investors and others to apply pressure, the 'comply or explain' regime. This is reinforced by the Listing Rules, which require listed UK companies to provide a statement on how the company has applied the principles of the Code in a manner that would enable shareholders to evaluate how they have been applied. If not, they have to specify which provisions have not been complied with, for what period and the reasons for non-compliance.

The full text of the Code can be seen on the FSA website. It contains 17 main principles of good governance, most of which have in addition supporting principles and more detailed code provisions that amplify the principles. The supporting principles are drafted in general terms to allow companies flexibility in interpreting and implementing them.

The 17 main principles set out standards of good practice in relation to issues such as board composition and development, remuneration, accountability and audit, relations with shareholders and institutional investors:

■ *The chairman:* should ensure that shareholders' views are communicated to the board, and should facilitate the effective contribution of non-executive directors and ensure constructive relations between executive and non-executive directors. The role of chairman and chief executive should not be exercised by the same individual.

■ *The chief executive:* should not go on to become chairman of the same company. In exceptional cases, where the board decides that he or she should do so, it should consult with major shareholders and explain its reasons.

■ *Appointments to the board:* a formal and transparent procedure should be used for the appointment of executive directors. There should be a nomination committee for board appointments. In addition, the terms and conditions of non-executive directors should be made available for inspection.

■ *The audit committee:* in the revised Combined Code the role of the audit committee has been strengthened. Examples of its roles are: to monitor the integrity of the company's financial statements; to review the company's internal financial controls; to make recommendations to the board on the appointment/removal of the external auditors; and to monitor the independence of the external auditors.

■ *Shareholder consultation:* in its annual report the board is required to state what steps it has taken to consult with major shareholders.

The June 2006 Combined Code made the following main changes to the 2003 Code:

■ It amended the existing restriction on the company chairman serving on the remuneration committee to enable him or her to do so where considered independent on appointment as chairman (although it is recommended that he or she should not also chair the committee).

■ It provided a 'vote withheld' option on proxy appointment forms to enable share-holders to indicate if they have reservations on a resolution but do not wish to vote against it. A 'vote withheld' is not a vote in law and is not counted in the calculation of the proportion of the votes for and against the resolution.
■ It recommended that companies publish on their website the details of proxies lodged at a general meeting where votes are taken on a show of hands.

Associated guidance

The Turnbull Guidance, published by the Institute of Chartered Accountants in England and Wales in 1999, provides guidance to companies on how to apply the section of the Combined Code dealing with internal controls (section C.2). It emphasizes that management of risk is the responsibility of the board of directors. In some cases risk management is delegated to the audit committee. In some companies, where risk management is particularly high-profile or where the company is of a larger dimension, the board may appoint a risk management committee.

In 2004 the Financial Reporting Council initiated a review to evaluate the impact of the guidance. The findings of the review are positive that the principles-based approach of previous guidance had been very successful. Consequently only minor changes were made in the Revised Guidance published in October 2005. The section of the guidance relating to the Code provision on internal audit has been removed and incorporated into the Smith guidance on audit committees. Boards are now required to confirm in the annual report that necessary action has been or is being taken to remedy any significant failings or weaknesses identified from their review of the effectiveness of the internal control system, and to include in the annual report such information as considered necessary to assist shareholders' understanding of the main features of the company's risk management processes and system of internal control.

The Smith Report and the Higgs Report, containing best practice guidance relating to non-executive directors and audit committees respectively, have no formal status and companies are not required to follow them when applying the Combined Code.

The Listing Rules, Disclosure Rules and Prospective Rules

The new Listing Rules, Disclosure Rules and Prospective Rules came into effect on 1 July 2005, ending a modernization and simplification process begun by the FSA on 30 July 2002 in order to implement EU directives under the Financial Services Action Plan.

The new Listing Rules removed the Combined Code from its annexe. However, continuing obligations such as the class tests and related regimes have been retained in the Listing Rules. Minor amendments are made to the Model Code covering dealings by those with managerial responsibilities and employee insiders. Chapter 7 of the Listing Rules contains high-level principles that are enforceable like other rules.

Issuers are to interpret the Listing Rules in line with the spirit and purpose of the Listing Principles. Pursuant to these principles, a listed company must take reasonable steps to enable its directors to understand their responsibilities and obligations as directors.

The new Disclosure Rules contain rules and guidance on listed companies' obligations to disclose and control inside information and notify transactions by 'persons discharging managerial responsibilities'. Under the new rules, the requirements to notify directors' transactions required under the previous Listing Rules are replaced and extended to cover persons discharging managerial responsibilities and their connected persons.

The new Prospectus Rules are not fundamentally different from the rules existing before 1 July 2005.

Guidelines from shareholder groups

The Institutional Shareholders' Committee (ISC) published a statement of principles in October 2002, which is aimed at encouraging institutional shareholders and investment managers to play a more active role in companies they invest in. They are expected:

- to publish their policies in relation to active engagements with companies they invest in;
- to monitor the companies' performance and maintain a dialogue with them;
- to intervene where necessary;
- to evaluate the impact of their policies and report back to their clients.

The ISC comprises four large institutional investor groups: the Association of British Insurers (ABI), the National Association of Pension Funds (NAPF), the Association of Investment Trust Companies and the Investment Management Association.

The ABI has also published a number of guidelines, including comment on the need to focus on managing long- and short-term risks and issues relating to social responsibility. The NAPF is to launch a web-based service for UK investors to give them access to analysis in thousands of companies worldwide.

Shareholder pressure is a key feature of the corporate governance climate in the UK. An active participant in this is the ABI. For example, they have criticized as being a 'Pandora's box' proposals by a Dutch chemicals and life science company to pay enhanced dividends to long-term shareholders; at GlaxoSmithKline, shareholders first voted down plans to pay chief executive Jean-Pierre Gamier £22 million should he be dismissed for poor performance and then put pressure on the board to publish a revised pay policy.

On 30 September 2005 the ISC published an updated version of its statement of principles on the responsibilities of institutional shareholders and agents. However, the changes made since the last version in 2002 are minor.

Board responsibility

The main responsibility for corporate governance falls upon the board of directors. Many of the websites referred to at the end of the chapter contain useful guidance. The board can also use its auditors and lawyers (whether the in-house legal department or an external firm) to assist in writing corporate governance policies, and the company secretary should report to the board on monitoring compliance with corporate governance procedures.

It should be noted that the Combined Code includes an obligation on the board to review the company's systems of internal controls, and the board should report to shareholders confirming that they have done so. (The review should cover all material controls, including financial, operational and compliance controls and risk management systems.)

The UK and United States compared – the international dimension

In the United States, the Sarbanes–Oxley Act was passed – together with changes to the rules of the National Association of Securities Dealers and the New York Stock Exchange – as a result of the Enron and WorldCom scandals. The Act does not take a principles-based approach. Rather, it raises the level of criminal penalties. It is probably true to say that the Sarbanes–Oxley Act was the US government's first significant regulatory effort on corporate governance. The UK approach of improving best practice guidelines contrasts with the United States' more regulatory approach.

Other differences between the United States and the UK are that in the United States it is common to concentrate power in the hands of one autonomous decision maker. In the UK the emphasis on separating the role of the CEO and the chairman is a hallmark of UK corporate governance, and the Higgs Report showed that over 90 per cent of listed companies split these two roles.

A further example is the UK annual report compared with the US proxy statement. In the US the proxy statement is intended to give shareholders a basis on which they can vote at an annual shareholders' meeting. In the UK the annual report is less obviously directed at voting, particularly voting on the composition of the board. This only arises where the board proposes directors for re-election (because they have served their three-year term or have been appointed to the board since the last annual general meeting) or proposes new directors for election. In this case the annual report includes biographical details of directors and details of directors' remuneration.

There is no international corporate governance model although the World Bank and the OECD have begun some initiatives. The European Commission has stated that it does not intend to produce a European corporate governance code, although it considers that the EU should adopt a common approach for some of the essential rules. This was set out in a 2003 consultation paper called 'Modernising company law and enhancing corporate governance in the EU', which focused on the following key areas: an annual corporate governance statement, strengthening shareholders' rights, the composition of the board of directors, directors' remuneration, institutional investors and board structures. The paper also proposed the formation of a European corporate governance forum, which should meet once or twice a year to coordinate national corporate governance codes. Some commentators have expressed doubt as to whether such a body would really add value to the development of corporate governance.

Current developments – where corporate governance law is going

As a result of the political and business climate in the wake of corporate scandals involving misfeasance, we can expect to see more and more regulation coming from the government, the City (mainly the FSA) and the EU. In the light of this, boards of directors should make efforts to ensure that their corporate governance procedures stay up to date.

The Companies (Audit, Investigations and Community Enterprise) Act 2004

This Act came into force on 6 April 2005. It was a direct response to corporate collapses such as Enron and is part of the government's strategy to restore and maintain investor confidence in companies and financial markets. *Inter alia*, the Act amends the overall framework for the regulation of statutory auditors, strengthens the rights of company auditors and increases company investigators' powers and makes provision for the establishment of a new corporate vehicle. In particular, the Act contains measures to reform directors' and auditors' liability. These include allowing companies to indemnify directors in respect of proceedings brought by third parties and pay directors' defence costs as they are incurred, even if the action is brought by the company itself. Directors would still be liable to pay any damages awarded to the company and to repay their defence costs to the company if their defence were unsuccessful.

The Companies Bill[1]

After a long consultation period, the Companies Bill was introduced to the House of Lords in November 2005. On 19 October 2006 the report stage of the Companies Bill was completed, and the bill had its third reading in the House of Commons. The bill received Royal Assent, and most of its provisions are expected to come into effect in October 2007. Formerly known as the Company Law Reform Bill, this bill covers a wide range of company law issues. The bill proposed a number of significant changes. These include codification of directors' duties; measures to allow shareholders to agree to limit auditors' liability; new criminal offences and protection for directors and auditors; and new opportunities for companies to use electronic methods of communication. The codification of directors' duties will introduce a statutory statement of duties, which will replace many existing common law rules.

Such provisions will apply to all the directors of a company, even if they are shadow directors or former directors of the company. Changes in relation to directors' duties include a statutory requirement for directors to have regard to a list of factors in exercising their duty of good faith and to allow independent directors to authorize a director's conflict of interest.

The Corporate Manslaughter and Corporate Homicide Bill

After high-profile rail crashes there have been calls for a new corporate manslaughter offence. Bill 220 2005–2006, the Corporate Manslaughter and Corporate Homicide Bill, was formally introduced in the Commons on 20 July 2006. The bill makes provision for a new offence of corporate manslaughter in England, Wales and Northern Ireland and of corporate homicide in Scotland. The bill contains 24 clauses and two schedules. It is expected that the bill will ensure that companies are liable for any deaths resulting from a general breach of the duty of care by the firm. The new manslaughter offence would apply to corporations, including public bodies, and introduce unlimited fines if it were found that a death followed a serious failing by senior managers in the organization of the corporation.

Corporate governance: QCA guidelines for AIM companies

The Combined Code does not apply to companies quoted on AIM. To fill this gap, the Quoted Companies Alliance published a set of corporate governance guidelines for AIM companies on 13 July 2005. They include a code of best practice for AIM companies, comprising some simple principles, intended as a minimum standard, and recommendations for reporting corporate governance matters. Some of the rules contained go even further than the Code. For example, the role of chairman and chief executive should not be held by the same individual. If they are, there should be a clear explanation of the board procedures that provide protection against the risks of concentration of power. A company should have at least two independent non-executive directors (one of whom may be the chairman). A list of factors potentially prejudicing a director's independence is included in the appendices to the guidelines. Internal controls should be reviewed at least annually.

Operating and financial review/business review

In November 2005 the government took the decision to repeal the mandatory requirement on quoted companies to prepare an operating and financial review (OFR). The repeal came into force on 12 January 2006 and removed the requirement for operating and financial reviews for financial years beginning on or after 1 April 2005. Companies will only be required to produce a business review instead.

Note

1. The Companies Bill is now in law.

References and useful websites

- Full text of the Listing Rules including the Combined Code: www.fsa.gov.uk/ukla/2_listinginfo.html
- Government White Paper, *Modernising Company Law*, July 2002: www.dti.gov.uk/companiesbill/index.htm
- Full text of the Companies Bill (the Companies Reform Bill): http://www.publications.parliament.uk/pa/ld200506/ldbills/034/2006034.htm
- DTI consultative document *Company Law – Flexibility and Accessibility*: www.dti.gov.uk/cld/pdfs/powerscondoc_final.pdf
- Higgs Report, *Review of the Role and Effectiveness of Non-Executive Directors*, Derek Higgs, January 2003: www.dti.gov.uk/cld/non_exec_review
- Smith Report, *Audit Committees: Combined Code guidance*, Sir Robert Smith, January 2003: www.frc.org.uk/images/uploaded/documents/acreport.pdf
- Financial Reporting Council: www.frc.org.uk
- Turnbull Report, *Internal Control: Guidance for directors on the Combined Code*, ICAEW, September 1999: www.icaew.co.uk
- Association of British Insurers (relevant guidelines are included in the Investment Affairs section): www.abi.org.uk
- Institutional Shareholders' Committee statement of principles on the responsibilities of institutional shareholders and agents: www.abi.org.uk/display/file/38/statement_of_principles.pdf
- National Association of Pensions Funds: www.napf.co.uk
- QCA guidelines: http://qcanet.co.uk/guidance_booklets.asp

Strategic risk management for small businesses

John Watt, Middlesex University

Introduction

Approaches to the management of risk vary according to the context within which they are made. We all manage risk throughout the day and, as individuals, have enormous freedom with respect to the way that we do this. This chapter looks at ways that small businesses can take a strategic look at their entire operation and the risks they face in attempting to achieve their objectives, which equates in this case to what the business community often terms 'enterprise risk management'. In publicly owned corporations or large organizations, risk managers must operate in accordance with a formal and transparent framework of policy and process. The details of that framework will vary according to the nature of the business but there are normally common elements that would be expected to be present in a well-governed organization. These might include the following elements of enterprise risk management:

- A risk strategy for the organization is established.
- There is an infrastructure and process for risk governance.

Risk Management in London

The increasing requirement for high level responsibility and accountability for undertaking strategic level risk management is driving a demand for professionals equipped to identify and prioritise risks emanating from a number of different sources. Discipline-specific research within the different specialisations in an organisation needs to be combined into a coherent strategy o protect its mission and objectives. Middlesex University offers postgraduate programmes (MSc/PGDip/PGCert Risk Management, full-time or part-time) that enable a new generation of risk managers to enhance their knowledge of the philosophical and technical issues which permeate risk management decision making. Research at the DARM centre takes a multi-disciplinary approach which encompasses the natural scientific, socio-economic, psychological, legal, philosophical, ethical, and communication dimensions of risk management.

There are a considerable number of approaches to the complex subject of risk in use, and, as risk issues become increasingly interdependent, it is more and more necessary to understand similarities and differences between them and to attempt to facilitate effective collaboration. Our programmes seek to determine and understand the common features of decision making, to examine critically the diverse models and methodologies employed for the technical assessment of risk and to reflect the evolution of the subject area from a largely technical, science based, risk assessment focus to an integrated approach to decision making that involves stakeholders in a transparent dialogue that reflects their concerns alongside the technical evaluation. They represent a combination of expertise from different sectors into an inter- and multi-disciplinary framework.

This programme will appeal to people who are being asked take on a wider risk portfolio (or younger people who aspire to this role) and to decision makers in all areas contributing to strategic risk management. Option modules are available in a wide range of subject areas depending on experience, including:

- Management
- Finance
- Health and Safety
- Environment
- Social Policy
- Clinical Risk

For an informal discussion, contact John Watt: **j.watt@mdx.ac.uk**
For further details on all the programmes and on the work of the Centre please see
www.mdx.ac.uk/risk

DARM
The Middlesex University Centre for Decision Analysis and Risk Management

■ Individual risks are proactively identified.
■ These risks are assessed.
■ A risk appetite is set.
■ Risks are prioritized and managed.
■ The process is reported, monitored and kept up to date.

Small businesses fall between the requirements of individuals and those of large public companies. They have a lot of the flexibility of individuals, since their risk management is often the owner's assessment of the threats and opportunities that confront the company.

There are many ways to define small businesses but a number of generalizations can be made:

■ independent ownership and operation;
■ close control by owners/managers;
■ owners/managers do most of the decision making;
■ owners/managers 'own' most of the risk (since they contribute most if not all of the operating capital, or have borrowed it themselves);
■ a small number of employees[1] (many businesses employ no more than one person);
■ low employee turnover.

This is an important sector and one that the risk management profession needs to take seriously. According to the latest available statistics[2] there were an estimated 4.3 million business enterprises in the UK at the start of 2004. Almost all of these enterprises (99.3 per cent) were small (0 to 49 employees). Only 26,000 (0.6 per cent) were medium-sized (50 to 249 employees) and 6,000 (0.1 per cent) were large (250 or more employees). Small and medium-sized enterprises (SMEs) together accounted for more than half of the employment (58.5 per cent) and turnover (51.3 per cent) in the UK. Small enterprises alone (0 to 49 employees) accounted for 46.8 per cent of employment and 37.0 per cent of turnover.

Some 72.8 per cent of all enterprises (3.1 million) were enterprises with no employees – sole proprietorships and partnerships comprising only the self-employed owner-manager(s), and companies comprising only an employee director. They had an estimated combined turnover of £190 billion.

The challenge for the risk management profession is to provide a level of support that utilizes the close personal involvement described, while adding rigour and objectivity to the perhaps frequently instinctive or intuitive measurement undertaken in small businesses. The small business is made very vulnerable by the reliance on the strengths of a small number of individuals and the consequent pressure on their time and resources. In addition to the characteristics set out above, most of these companies will have some or all of the following characteristics:

■ lack of specialist staff;
■ multifunctional management;

- lack of control over the business environment;
- limited market share.

On the other hand, if the advantages of strategic risk management can be clearly identified, the process of undertaking it should be relatively straightforward given the close linking of the owners, managers and operators of the business.

Just as for large organizations, the tasks of effective enterprise risk management are to establish clear strategic objectives for the enterprise, to understand the risks threatening the realization of those objectives and to put in place a policy and process for the management and oversight of those risks throughout the business. Given the will, it is much easier for the executive management of a small business to be routinely and actively involved in the application of risk management policy and the operation of process than it often is for larger organizations. It should be easier to embed risk management policy throughout the organization, especially if it is directly projected as a performance-enhancing activity for the business.

Drivers of risk management for small businesses

Put simply, the main advantage to having a strategic risk management process for small businesses is that it allows the owners to stand back from what they are doing and evaluate their position. One difficulty that they face is that most risk assessment is tied up with a specific discipline or speciality. They themselves are likely to be familiar with a few of them but may not be sufficiently aware of others. They may recognize the 'obvious', or most apparent, risk that they are facing. For example, the owners of a lumber yard will immediately recognize the risk to staff and customer safety from using saws and other industrial equipment. They may not as easily recognize the threat to the business resulting from the opening of a new DIY superstore in a nearby town. They need to know how to compare such different risks and to identify strategies to cope. In some situations they will need to plan to limit the likelihood of something happening but at other times they will be planning strategies to maximize their prospects for recovery.

There are a number of things that may drive risk management. These include legislation and insurance, internal drivers and business practice.

Legislation and insurance

This is often the issue that dominates for small (and not-so-small) organizations. There are many legislative and regulatory requirements relating to risk management, and these include:

- occupational health and safety legislation;[3]
- fair trading legislation;
- contractual obligations;
- insurance requirements;
- financial reporting requirements;

- environmental legislation;
- business-specific requirements, eg food hygiene regulations for a restaurant.

One common problem that may be encountered in the absence of a strategic risk management policy is that the management of these externally driven requirements can come to dominate a business, thus themselves becoming a threat to its proper functioning. Are there therefore any advantages that may be identified that actually improve the internal working or market position of the company?

Internal drivers

A number are frequently identified, such as:

- increased competitive advantage;
- enhanced quality of product or service;
- increased efficiency, productivity and effective use of resources;
- improvements in health and safety;
- reduced litigation potential;
- improved communication with staff;
- improved management practices;
- improved relationships with clients, employees, suppliers and contractors;
- enhanced business planning and achievement of objectives and goals;
- reduced budget overspends;
- reduced compliance costs;
- faster recovery when things go wrong.

Business practice

There are many good business practice reasons why a business owner should apply risk management, and these include:

- protection of reputation and development of the brand;
- increased transparency in financial management;
- enhanced staff confidence and therefore better retention of key individuals;
- enhanced client confidence;
- protection of assets and the longer-term viability of the business;
- demonstration of accountability especially in the context of tendering for business to organizations with formal risk governance requirements from subcontractors.

Risk management for small businesses

Establishing a risk strategy for the organization

The process of 'top-down' management of the risks faced by a company has been variously labelled and defined – business risk management, holistic risk management, strategic risk management or enterprise risk management. The underlying sense of all of these terms is that somebody looks at what the business is trying to do (its objectives), what opportunities it has and the things that threaten its ability to grasp those opportunities. Therefore, it includes the process of planning, organizing, leading and controlling the activities of the business to optimize the potential impacts of risk on earnings, assets and capital. Risk is thus associated with opportunity (sometimes called upside risk) and threat (or downside risk). The latter often dominates the risk agenda and contributes to a rather negative reaction of many small businesses to the process. An approach that recognizes that taking (upside) risk is the very process that drives innovation and the pursuit of new markets while offering techniques to keep the potential exposure proportionate is more likely to find favour with entrepreneurs than a pro forma, ritualistic compilation of all of the obstacles. It is important to stress that the process optimizes the risk and does not seek to stifle innovation or creativity.

The starting point then is obvious. The owners of the business need first to establish their objectives. What is it that they are trying to do? Initially this will be a statement of the mission and vision of the company – a definition of the business. This develops into a number of operational aims and targets expressed over a number of time periods. For example:

■ One year aims:
  – improve operational performance;
  – develop new products;
  – achieve leadership in the UK market.
■ Targets:
  – to increase sales to £YYY;
  – to increase profits to £XXX;
  – to achieve 15 per cent sales revenue from product A.

The risk management strategy then goes on to establish a structure and process for managing the risks that threaten achievement of these aims and targets. This is known as establishing a risk governance framework – it simply means setting out the ways that hazards and the risks they pose are to be identified, assessed, prioritized and managed. It also establishes the way the process is reported, monitored and kept up to date.

Identification of individual risks

As stated earlier, people starting and running small businesses have identified what they see as a potential opportunity in an area in which they feel confident to operate but there are likely to be many other areas or categories of risk that threaten their success. A structured approach to risk identification might identify risk categories, specific areas or topics to be considered one by one. This stimulates creative consideration and increases the opportunity to identify a broader range of risks, while enabling a better focus within specific categories.

Brainstorming within the company (perhaps in events facilitated by risk management consultants) can assist a business in risk identification and assists the business owner to select the best techniques for risk identification and analysis. Risk assessment tends to be discipline-specific and so technical input may be needed – for example from the bank for financial advice or from a solicitor for legal advice as well as the technical risk assessment for the actual operation of the business.

This process leads to a list of hazards and the risks associated with them sorted for ease of operation into a number of categories. In small businesses the process can and should be straightforward – simple answers to some obvious questions such as 'What might happen?', 'How might it happen?' and 'Why should it happen?' The identification should build on experience and also try to look forward to anticipate risks that might occur that have not yet been experienced.

Risk assessment

Risk assessment has two components – the likelihood of something happening and the severity of the outcome if it were to happen. These are often portrayed by use of a risk matrix. Such a matrix might be divided into a 3×3 grid, one axis depicting the likelihood of occurrence and the other depicting the potential impact. If risks appear in the top right corner of the matrix, they might be considered to be 'critical'. Risks in the lower left corner might be considered to be 'very low'. As discussed earlier, assessment of risk is undertaken by different specialist professions utilizing a range of specific techniques. Consideration of health and safety risks might see a 'critical' outcome as death, with a 'very low' outcome being one that could result in 'injury or illness not resulting in a lost work day'. A project risk management might use categories such as:

■ 'C (Critical): If the risk event occurs, the programme will fail. Minimum acceptable requirements will not be met.'
■ 'N (Negligible): If the risk event occurs, it will have no effect on the programme. All requirements will be met.'

Setting a risk appetite

Risk appetite is a way of expressing the level of risk to which an organization is prepared to be exposed before it decides action is necessary. By setting a risk appetite the business is able to allocate the appropriate amount of resource. This is important but not always easy to see. Owners of small businesses will know that their resources are limited and that anything they decide to spend on mitigating a given risk will not be available to spend elsewhere. But how much should be retained?

Setting an appetite level for each risk has the following advantages:

■ It forces the company to measure clearly and compare its risks and think about the potential losses and gains.

- It helps it to see if resources are wasted on risks (ie money is being spent in areas that offer a low level of threat compared to the threshold of company exposure).
- Equally, it helps the business to recognize that attention should be focused on risks (threats) above the defined level.
- Objectives should be set in line with risk appetite, which helps in setting the right objectives.
- It helps to prioritize the allocation of limited time and resources.

If a risk falls outside the risk appetite threshold, risk management treatments and business controls are required to bring the exposure level back within the accepted range. Risk appetite may in certain circumstances be specified by law – for example for health and safety.

Prioritizing and managing risks

The risk assessment process data need to be analysed against the company's risk appetite to develop a number of consolidated risk categories and strategic risk priorities. These are set out in relation to the calculated risk categories, which ensures a focus on those risks that have emerged as critical or high risks to the existence or liquidity of the business. These consolidated risks are likely to be made up of a number of component parts, each of which will have had its risk assessed. In simple terms this means that the business owner takes a measured, objective look at the business, perhaps using external advisers (consultants, bankers, lawyers or accountants, for example). Professional risk managers may be a useful addition to these advisers, providing assistance in achieving the right level of emphasis on risk. The structured approach means that the business owner is able to see outside his or her own areas of immediate expertise and to avoid being trapped into an undue focus on minor risks driven by external pressures such as litigation or insurance.

Establishing an integrated risk management strategy also includes setting out ways of reporting and monitoring the process and keeping it up to date.

The limitations of risk management, as in any management process, should be clearly recognized by the business owner and management team. These limitations include the following:

- Risk assessment will not make decisions for the business. It can help the owner to make decisions but these decisions will be limited by the depth of the research and analysis of risk and the experience and risk management skill of the individual(s) involved in the risk assessment.
- Risk management will not guarantee freedom from all risk. It is never the intention of risk management to eliminate risk, but rather to prioritize the *appropriate* application of scarce resources and time.
- Risk management will not guarantee that adverse events won't happen. Risk management does however offer significant warning of likely problems and a focus on methods to protect reputation and business continuity.

■ Risk assessments will attempt to identify all significant risks but they are limited by the resources available, including information availability, staff capability, time and budget.

Conclusion – why a small business should develop a strategic risk management strategy

Doing this offers significant advantages to the small business:

■ It ensures that the business focuses on its own mission and objectives and does not get diverted by external influences.
■ It ensures that it is compliant with regulation and best practice.
■ It may offer significant legal protection if something does go wrong.
■ It may also lead to substantial savings in insurance costs.

In general risk management helps a company to avoid surprises and prioritize actions and allows it to avoid over-managing trivial risks. It is important that risk assessments should be fit for purpose (comprehensive enough without being excessive) and that the management strategies are tailored to the needs, resources and opportunities of the individual business. There is clearly a huge opportunity for the risk management profession given the number of small businesses and their importance to the economy.

Notes

1. In the UK, a small company is defined by the Companies Act 1985 as one that has a turnover of not more than £5.6 million, a balance sheet total of not more than £2.8 million and not more than 50 employees.
2. Small and medium-sized enterprise (SME) statistics UK 2004, published on 25 August 2005 by the Small Business Service (SBS), an executive agency of the Department of Trade and Industry.
3. This legislation, for example, does have different implications for businesses of different sizes, with very small businesses (fewer than five employees) not being required to have a written risk assessment.

Resources

A simple guide to risk management for small businesses with a number of clearly described examples and case studies is available at www.smallbiz.nsw.gov.au.

Please feel free to contact either the Middlesex University Centre for Decision Analysis and Risk Management (www.mdx.ac.uk/risk) or the Middlesex University Centre for Environmental and Safety Management for Business (www.mdx.ac.uk/www/cesmb).

Risk management: failing to address the current risk agenda

Andrew Fields, KPMG LLP

Risk management has received a jolt in the past 12 months but unfortunately the risk management capability of many organizations is not reacting quickly enough to the emerging risk agenda. Risk managers face being relegated to obscurity unless they can lead their businesses in responding to these new risk challenges. Now is the time that businesses actually need their risk managers the most. This chapter explores the main emerging themes in risk management and argues that risk managers, in the main, are remaining focused on the operation of internal risk identification processes and are missing opportunities to evolve risk management.

The fallout from Sarbanes–Oxley (SOX) has left many senior executives questioning the value they get from the significant investment being made in risk, internal control and assurance activities in their businesses. The enhanced requirements for risk disclosure in narrative reporting are laying bare to external scrutiny hitherto internal risk management processes. Furthermore, the predominance of the sustainability agenda has meant that the 'external' risk environment is rapidly challenging the 'internal' risk environment as a core focus for risk management attention.

Complacency is no longer an option

But a practical start is

The complexity of today's business environment and the increasing pace of change has left some business leaders feeling uncertain about their most pressing risks and exposures. In addition, investors, credit rating agencies and customers are increasingly looking for assurance that the enterprise is able to communicate, manage and mitigate its risks effectively.

This has put risk management firmly on the business radar but the response has been mixed. Compliance remains the dominant driver for many, leading to a concentration on internal control and financial risk, whilst the change process and emerging risks are often overlooked.

The quality of your risk management is only as good as its weakest point. KPMG's Enterprise Risk Management team can help you to re-engineer your risk management strategy and bring a balance to your overall investment to enhance, as well as protect, your company's performance.

For further information please contact:
Richard Sharman
+44 (0)20 7311 8228
richard.sharman2@kpmg.co.uk

www.kpmg.co.uk

AUDIT ▪ TAX ▪ ADVISORY

KPMG

Risk managers are often frustrated at the continuous challenge they face in proving that they add real value rather than just cost and bureaucracy to their businesses. Moreover, in believing that they do add value, risk managers themselves are eager to operate at more senior levels within their organizations. These new issues are real challenges for business and, as risk is the consistent theme in these issues, there is a clear opportunity for risk managers to grasp this agenda, help their businesses to save money and help senior executives to understand and manage emerging aspects of the 'external' business environment. However, in order to do this, risk managers must raise their game and, in meeting this challenge, grasp the new opportunities presented to them. These opportunities are considered below.

Time for a deSOX

For risk managers, SOX has been a mixed blessing. It undoubtedly raised the profile of risk, internal control and assurance as important management disciplines; yet it also distracted senior management attention and resources away from risk management, whilst leaving business managers 'compliance fatigued' and with a distorted perception of exactly what risk management contributes to organizations. Yet the shadow cast by SOX need not be without its silver lining. As companies meet the challenge of section 404 compliance, senior management is now questioning how it can get the best return on the significant and disparate investments it continues to make in risk, internal control and assurance. As leading organizations move to integrate these activities more closely, the risk manager is emerging as a key player in the ability of business to create this new integrated environment. Not only do risk managers have a unique perspective across the whole enterprise, but also they are the custodians of the risk and internal control data that are the key to closer integration of the different risk management, internal control and assurance activities.

Opportunity 1: SOX-Lite

There is no doubt that the first year of SOX implementation was painful. A recent survey of accelerated filers showed that 60 per cent of companies with revenues of US$20 billion or above invested more than 100,000 work hours in complying with Section 404.[1] That is the equivalent of employing a team of 70 people full time for a year. However, a certain level of sanity has since prevailed with both auditors and US regulators accepting that a risk-based approach can save time and, more importantly, is just as robust.

After at least two years of SOX documenting, testing and reporting, few areas of any business can claim ignorance of the concept of risk, internal control and assurance. Whilst some grumbling remains about the time-consuming, overly prescriptive and detailed regime required by SOX, many companies are beginning to take a more positive view. Indeed, non-SEC-registered businesses have begun to apply the disciplines of SOX without the regulatory imperative as they recognize the extent to which risk management and internal control disciplines actually help to deliver a better-managed business. Senior management, however, is struggling to see how better management discipline can be achieved at a broader level without replicating the effort involved with SOX. Risk management is the SOX-Lite it is looking for.

Having, albeit reluctantly, accepted that 'taking risk knowingly' is something they should be doing, managers are looking for an easier tool to address these wider business-critical risks. 'Just don't make me go through another SOX', they say. This is where the opportunity lies for the risk manager. The risk manager is in the ideal position to offer management a SOX-Lite – a relatively simple management tool (risk profiling) that will provide assurance on the state of risk and control in key risk areas, but that will consume a fraction of the time required by SOX. A robust risk profiling exercise can provide management with immediate consensus on risk priorities and action required, whilst providing a focus for targeted internal control evaluation and focused assurance activity if required.

Opportunity 2: A little bit of SOX never hurt anyone

Many business managers have begun to seek assurance for what they see as far more important business risks, including product innovation, talent retention and dealing with competitive pressures. Indeed, many are questioning why so much time had to be spent on financial reporting risk – a risk that for most companies sits somewhere in the middle of their risk profile, at the potential expense of under-investing in the management of more significant risks.

SOX has provided disciplines that can be adapted to strengthen the risk management process. For many organizations, a weakness in the current approach to risk management is that risk assessment relies on control self-assessment, particularly for key risks. Executives are therefore often nervous about accepting risk information as robust or accurate and hence the ability of risk information significantly to influence decision making is limited. Assertions that controls are 'effective' or 'strong' are made on the basis of management opinion provided with relatively little evidence. It is here that the documentation and testing regimes of SOX can be simplified to provide a 'hybrid' that sits between the full-blown Section 404 analysis and the unsubstantiated management assertion. This would give management greater assurance for its areas of responsibility, whilst giving the risk manager a more robust set of data.

Airing the dirty linen in public

A recent KPMG survey analysed the extent to which narrative reporting will influence analysts' investment recommendations.[2] A key component in narrative reporting is risk disclosure. Of the analysts surveyed, 44 per cent stated that they anticipate changing their rating of a company on the basis of additional insight gained through disclosure in narrative operating and financial review (OFR) – or business review-style reporting.[3]

This suggests that analysts are learning how to use narrative information better rather than the more traditional focus on financial projections and are therefore keen to see more of this style of reporting. Although the OFR legislation was ultimately scrapped, its successor – in the shape of the UK business review – will ensure that this style of reporting is here to stay.

The KPMG research shows that analysts now see the value of narrative reporting and fully intend to make use of the information it provides them with when determining a company's rating. Analysts' support for narrative reporting will surely only increase over time as, firstly, the quality of information improves and, secondly, the need to provide such information becomes mandated by law. The dilemma that companies face is whether they can afford either not to supply narrative reporting information (at least until it becomes mandatory) or to supply information that does not quite match the analysts' expectations.

As it has been established beyond reasonable doubt that analysts are interested in narrative reporting, the next step is to ask exactly what sort of issues they expect companies to be reporting on. With the threat that ratings could be altered as a direct result of narrative reporting, getting this disclosure 'wrong' would represent a significant gamble on the part of business.

In meeting the requirements of the business review, companies will be specifically required to disclose the main trends and factors likely to affect their future development, performance and position and to describe the principal risks and uncertainties facing them. When given a list of typical risk areas (operational, technology, projects, finance, legal and strategic/market risks), it becomes clear that analysts would appreciate more information on just about all of them.

Table 1.5.1 illustrates the responses from analysts when asked in the different areas how useful, if at all, narrative reporting of risk and uncertainties would be in analysing the business strategies and future prospects of the companies they followed.[4]

Table 1.5.1   Usefulness of narrative reporting of risks and uncertainties

	Very useful %	Fairly useful %	Not very useful %	Not at all useful %	Don't know %
1. Operations (eg the possibility of a terrorism incident)	40	48	12	0	0
2. Technology (eg the possibility of an IT system failure)	36	48	16	0	0
3. Projects (eg the possibility of a major project failure)	56	40	4	0	0
4. Finance (eg the failure of a counterparty)	28	56	16	0	0
5. Legal (eg a possible failure to meet regulatory requirements)	28	52	16	4	0
6. Strategic/market (eg a possible loss of reputation or market share)	16	44	36	4	0

A notable exception however is the strategic/market risks, where 36 per cent of analysts claimed that they would find narrative reporting on this area not very useful. This figure is out of kilter with their responses on other risk topics. The potential reason for this is that analysts already feel up to speed with the risks in this area and further narrative disclosure would give little additional insight. This contrasts with analysts' views on disclosure on project risks, where clearly more information is desired. Arguably, the reason for this is that the risks in this area are traditionally less transparent to the analyst, but can be significant in contributing to or destroying value.

As businesses get used to disclosing non-financial information in narrative reporting, a clearer picture of what 'good' looks like will emerge. The crux of the matter is that, as narrative reporting indeed becomes more established, analysts will increasingly want more detail on the business risks that face a company and how they are being managed.

Opportunity 3: Fit for purpose

This new emphasis on risk-specifics opens a company's hitherto internal risks to more scrutiny and will also force a higher level of transparency on the effectiveness of risk management processes.

The approach to risk management, in many organizations, is now dated. Rather than becoming embedded, risk management has often just become tired. The majority of risk management processes were devised during the immediate post-Turnbull period and have not subsequently been significantly revised. Unlike many business processes, the risk management process has tended to remain static rather than to develop and improve.

However, the requirements for risk management have now moved on. Risk disclosure is now regulated and as such directors' liabilities have increased, expectations from analysts have been heightened and requirements for disclosure in 'new' areas (ie projects) are prevalent. The opportunity for risk managers is to use these changes to revisit, revitalize and re-energize their risk management approach in order to ensure that it remains fit for purpose and continues to provide the right information, in the right format, to the right people, at the right point in time.

'The end is nigh'

Over recent years, identifying and proactively managing the issues on the corporate responsibility (CR) agenda have become an increasing challenge for business.

From energy usage and carbon emissions to ethical supply chains, to fair trade, equality and diversity in the workforce and investment in the local community, it appears that the CR agenda encompasses a diverse range of ever increasing issues. The speed with which these issues can mature to present companies with significant stakeholder or regulatory pressure to change practices and behaviours has added another dimension of uncertainty into the business environment.

Table 1.5.2 illustrates how the maturity of CR issues evolves over time from latent levels of maturity (ie CR issues with limited stakeholder awareness) to institutionalized ones (ie CR issues with significant stakeholder awareness).

Table 1.5.2 The maturity of CR issues over time

| Maturity of issues | Evidence | Signals | | |
		Stakeholder modes of engagement	Boundaries, expectation and regulation of issues	Boundaries of corporate responsibility
Latent	Exploratory research, perceptions but little or no evidence	– Opinion leader interest – Activist interest	– No regulation – Limited stakeholder expectations	Undefined boundaries with limited societal debate
Emerging	Detailed research but no conclusions	– NGO lobbying – Media attention – Political awareness	– Growing stakeholder expectations – Civil society regulation	Boundaries being debated by society
Established	Strong consensual evidence emerging	– Multi-sector or multi-stakeholder partnerships (eg GRI, UN Global Compact) – Business associations (eg Responsible Care)	– Coherent stakeholder expectations – Corporate self-regulation – Co- or multilateral regulation	Boundaries emerging
Institutionalized	Evidence accepted	– Political actions – Judicial actions	– Strong stakeholder expectations – State of intergovernmental expectations	Well defined boundaries

The public debate on nutrition, for instance, has matured rapidly and has had a significant impact on business performance across a range of sectors. In the UK, the 2005 Channel Four series *Jamie's School Dinners* propelled the issue of nutrition to the fore, both inside and outside the school environment. The significant media coverage of this issue consolidated stakeholder expectations for food standards and shifted the perceived boundaries of responsibility across the entire value chain with significant implications for businesses. For instance, food manufacturers and retailers have come under increasing scrutiny regarding the quality of food and appropriate labelling. Additionally, media and advertising companies have been criticized for marketing 'junk food' to children. In January 2006, parents and advocacy groups filed a lawsuit in the United States against Viacom and Kellogg's in relation to the marketing of junk food to young children.

Given the sheer unpredictability of the CR agenda, it is difficult for businesses to identify the next CR issue that is going to emerge and hence adequately prepare. Whilst many organizations now do have resources devoted to managing and communicating CR, it must be the role of the risk manager to ensure that CR horizon-scanning is better linked to the overall risk profile in order to ensure that the business has an accurate view of both 'internal' and 'external' risks.

Opportunity 4: Meet the neighbours

As the risk manager's primary focus is on understanding risk to the effective operation of business processes, their understanding of the external CR environment is often somewhat muted. The ability proactively to identify CR issues, both risks and opportunities, is critical to managing responsible business performance. Latent and emerging risks, as described in Table 1.5.2, can be detected through effective engagement with a range of external stakeholders and be used to inform risk strategy.

Risk managers should now seek to work with their colleagues in the CR department to engage better with external stakeholders in order to identify their perspectives on risk. Risk managers should then mesh these 'external' perspectives with the traditional 'internal' risk profile in order to develop an accurate risk profile. Once the CR issues have been identified, the risk manager should develop appropriate management frameworks to assess the business implications of the CR issues, understand boundaries of control and influence, assist the company in developing appropriate mitigation strategies and then work to communicate performance to relevant internal and external stakeholders.

A new start, not a conclusion

The business agenda continues to evolve and keep risk management near the top of executive priorities. Risk managers need to be braver in seeking to show leadership in the risk agenda. Leadership means stepping outside the areas of traditional focus and proactively addressing the areas above. Indeed, there will never be a point in time when businesses have done enough to manage risk and as such risk management will always have a future. Risk managers, however, need to show the way.

Notes

1. 'Life after SOX', *Strategic Risk Magazine*, September 2006.

2. KPMG (2006) *Oil and Gas: What does good business reporting look like?*, November, KPMG, London.
3. ibid.
4. ibid.

2

Good Practice in Implementing Risk Management Strategies

Enterprise risk management and business performance optimization

James W DeLoach, Jr, Protiviti, USA

Today, organizations face an increasingly uncertain future. In order to remain competitive, they must strike a delicate balance between pursuing the opportunities with the highest return and maintaining exposure to risk at an acceptable level.

To stay afloat in this dynamic operating environment, where the need for both strategy setting and risk assessments never ends, organizations can improve business performance with an enterprise risk management (ERM) strategy that is closely integrated with strategy setting; ERM provides organizations with the tools to make better choices in protecting and enhancing enterprise value.

Yet, for an integrated risk management/strategy-setting approach to be effective, risk responses should support the organization's value creation objectives by managing and monitoring the performance variability inherent in its future operations, protecting accumulated enterprise value from unacceptable losses, and leveraging existing core competencies to pursue market opportunities.

Against this backdrop, this chapter outlines the steps an organization may take to create an integrated, enterprise-wide approach that aligns ERM with improving business performance.

Identifying value drivers

When managing enterprise value, organizations must develop an understanding of the sources and drivers of value using the business objectives and strategy as a context. This understanding provides the context for managing risk. As senior managers focus their attention on the enterprise's long-term prospects for generating superior returns, they must:

1. evaluate the key underlying variables in the business plan that are exposed to performance variability and that require specific risk responses;
2. understand the loss exposures or drivers inherent in the enterprise's business model that require specific risk responses; and
3. identify incongruities inherent in the business model where management has, either knowingly or unknowingly, accepted risks that should be avoided, given the entity's risk appetite.

ERM's focus on the critical risk management tasks – identify events, assess risk, formulate risk response, implement control activities, inform/communicate and monitor – provides a flexible framework for addressing these three strategically important issues. Failure to manage the enterprise's exposures to potential future events that can destroy value will reduce even the best-laid plans for creating value to waste.

To identify value drivers (or key underlying variables) effectively, a context is useful. For example, shareholder value is a generally accepted measure of value and is, therefore, an example of a useful context for defining enterprise value. Economic value added (EVA) is an example of such a measure. Other examples providing a context for defining value drivers inherent in the business model include business objectives and strategies, key performance goals and key success factors linked to value creation. Value drivers can be linked to the variables that influence the achievement of the business plan, eg they may be defined in terms of the key underlying variables that cause revenues and expenses to go up and down.

Once the key value drivers are defined, key performance indicators (KPIs) are developed. These KPIs translate concept into action in the business plan, as they are the metrics by which performance against the plan is evaluated and ultimately rewarded. KPIs are converted into reports and are used to monitor performance over time. Managing and monitoring the business will surface opportunities to improve processes, products and services to enhance enterprise value.

The EVA framework: applications for increasing enterprise value

There are several issues to consider when applying ERM to improve business performance. To illustrate, EVA is a useful framework for measuring corporate performance that takes into account a capital charge reflecting the total cost of capital deployed in the business. This framework is used to establish accountability of managers for creating value. The basic formula for calculating EVA is as follows:

EVA = NOPAT − WACoC
where NOPAT is net operating profit after tax and WACoC is weighted-average cost of capital.

There are at least four ways to increase enterprise value under the EVA framework:

- *Create new opportunities:* the enterprise invests in new business activities, which promise attractive returns that are expected to exceed the WACoC.
- *Improve performance:* the enterprise improves performance and increases returns of existing business activities by improving policies, processes, competencies, reporting, technology and/or knowledge in ways that achieve this desired result.
- *Harvest existing value:* the enterprise withdraws from existing business activities generating inadequate returns, ie these activities have generated (or are expected to generate) returns that do not exceed the WACoC.
- *Adjust and align the cost of capital:* the enterprise takes specific steps to reduce the WACoC and/or ensure risks taken are consistent with the enterprise's risk appetite.

ERM and EVA: opportunities for improving business performance

By applying an ERM perspective, we can identify several opportunities for enhancing risk management processes to improve business performance using the application of EVA, as described above, as a context.

Create new opportunities

NOPAT only reflects expected losses that are reasonably estimable. Unless specifically adjusted for risk, an overall WACoC ignores the relative risks inherent in individual business units and activities. To address these inherent risks, management should insist that the methodology used to calculate EVA considers the risk equivalency of alternative activities. Under ERM, a process must be in place to identify the primary risks inherent in individual business units and activities.

Every successful business takes risk in the pursuit of value-added opportunities. For example, when management decides to enter new markets, introduce new products, acquire another entity or exploit other market opportunities, inherent in these decisions are choices to assume additional risk. When risk management is integrated with strategy setting, these choices are transparent because directors and executive management have full knowledge of the consequences of taking risk. That knowledge is a result of the organization's efforts to understand, monitor and track risk during the strategy-setting process.

ERM sets a process in place to identify the priority risks inherent in management's planned actions and price the acquisitions, transactions and deals resulting from those actions to compensate the enterprise appropriately for the risks it is assuming. Failure to make this assessment may result in management committing to undertake activities in which there are significant undesirable risks that exceed the organization's risk appetite, ie unacceptable performance variability, loss exposure and/or business model incongruities. The objective is to understand fully the good things that can happen, the bad things that can happen and the various scenarios in between.

In addition, following the consummation of acquisitions, transactions and deals, a process is in place to monitor the risks and mitigate them if they are subsequently determined to be different from those originally contemplated by the strategy. Effectively integrated with strategy setting, risk management should invigorate opportunity-seeking behaviour by helping managers develop the confidence that they truly understand the risks and have the capabilities at hand within the organization to manage those risks. As a result of these measures, management and the board fully understand the downside of such risks and the severity of their impact. They also know what to monitor over time.

Given the future's unpredictability, management should determine that the enterprise has allocated sufficient capital to provide a cushion for unexpected or unknown extreme losses incurred by individual activities. Herein lies a logical connection between ERM and value creation. If there were no risks, there would be no need for equity capital. Thus, equity capital is the price of exposure to uncertainty. If there were no exposure to uncertainty (ie the future was certain), every organization would be able to fund their activities with AAA-rated bonds.

However, because this scenario does not exist in the real world, equity capital is needed to cover unexpected risks. Anything that can be covered by traditional insurance or with insurance-like structures becomes more certain if the insuring counterparty has an outstanding credit rating and there is an absence of legal loopholes clouding the settlement process. In such conditions, the need for equity capital may be reduced. This discussion leads to the key link between ERM and value creation. Because the board and CEO must ultimately assume responsibility for allocating capital effectively, a risk assessment can be useful in differentiating risk profiles by unit, activity or project.

Improve performance

A robust, comprehensive risk assessment of a given business unit or activity may identify priority risks that expose future revenue streams and cash flows to unacceptable performance variability or loss exposure. Once a consistent risk assessment framework is implemented enterprise-wide, comparison and aggregation across the operating and support units become possible. Capital allocation becomes more meaningful and investment choices become clearer. A more robust risk assessment process reduces the chance of overlooking key risks and incurring unacceptable opportunity costs due to risk-averse behaviour. Risk responses can then be evaluated to reduce the priority risks to an acceptable level. In making such assessments, the identification of potential events or scenarios may provide useful insights as to the soft spots in the enterprise's or unit's business strategy, as well as opportunities to improve performance.

Harvest existing value

Decisions to exit a market or geographic area, or to sell, liquidate or spin off a product group or business must be evaluated carefully. Managers need to understand the 'relative riskiness' of different units, geographies, products or markets. If performance is measured without considering the risks assumed by managers in generating returns for the enterprise through their respective activities, an exit decision could result in withdrawal from a business that is generating superior risk-adjusted returns, even though its gross returns, unadjusted for risk, may appear lacklustre relative to other activities. The analysis supporting this assessment could be as simple as a risk map prepared for each business unit or as sophisticated as deploying a risk-adjusted performance measurement. Furthermore, during strategy setting, management must assess the consequences of taking action to mitigate one risk, as that action could create another risk. An effective risk assessment will facilitate an evaluation of alternatives.

Adjust and align the cost of capital

Under EVA, this step is difficult to take in a way that results in a substantive change that really makes a difference. One reason is that the WACoC is more relevant to the enterprise's specific units and activities than it is for the enterprise as a whole, if those units and activities have unique risk profiles. Companies may get around this issue by assigning different units with a specific WACoC relevant to their specific activities, based upon benchmarks from a market-based surrogate, such as a specific public company or a group of companies with the equivalent activities and risks. If a business unit engages in high-risk activities, its cost of capital should be higher than that of lower-risk businesses, and if its activities are low-risk the enterprise's cost of capital invested in the unit should be correspondingly lower. Market valuations at the corporate level often do not provide sufficient transparency as to the risks undertaken by different units and activities.

During the strategy-setting process, companies that are serious about risk management strive to configure their risk taking with their core competencies, or what they do best, avoiding unduly constraining risk-averse behaviour. The business model of every successful organization exploits to the maximum extent possible the areas in which the company excels relative to its competitors. In leveraging these advantages, however, management needs assurance that the company is not gambling its future. An ERM infrastructure provides the discipline, focus and control by which management 1) capitalizes on competitive strengths while protecting enterprise value and 2) ensures the company only takes those risks it is best equipped to handle within the parameters of its risk appetite, while minimizing exposure to those areas considered 'off-strategy' because of the lack of competence to manage.

Conclusion

In summary, the linkage of ERM to improved enterprise performance is achieved in different ways. By evaluating the effects on business performance of changes to a firm's risk profile from implementing alternative risk responses, management is able to focus on improving the expected return for the enterprise as a whole or alternatively holding the expected return constant and altering the organization's risk characteristics.

Management alters an entity's risk characteristics by reducing:

1. the enterprise's net exposure;
2. the variability of the enterprise's expected returns caused by specific sources of uncertainty (such as exposure to fluctuating currency rates);
3. the likelihood of financial distress in the event of realized changes in key variables (such as changes in interest rates for a highly leveraged company); or
4. other uncertainties in the attainment of expected returns.

In effect, improving business performance arises from integrating risk management with strategy setting.

Such integration means two things. First, it means the risk profile of strategic decisions is evaluated early in the strategy-setting process, leading to a more robust business strategy. Second, it means that policies, procedures, measures and monitoring are established and continuously improved to provide assurance to management and the board that the company is on target with achieving its expected return, while controlling its accepted exposure to risk. These two aspects of an integrated process lead to a stronger focus on improving business performance. The bottom line is that the organization only 'learns once' and shares knowledge and experiences so that risk management capabilities are continuously improved and exposure to unacceptable risks and strategic error is reduced.

A scorecard born and embraced

Eric Bloem, Heineken International

Introduction

Over the last few decades the need to inform external parties has been growing, and corporate governance has increased the demand for consistent information as well. The old-fashioned survey reports produced by brokers and/or insurers were, on a one-to-one basis (one site, one insurance programme), to a certain extent useful. However, they did not deliver fast and efficient information, owing, for example, to:

- The time consumed on location and the time spent on writing reports, leading to high cost and thus a low number of surveys. This resulted in a situation in which only the major sites got attention, whereas we believe that the time and energy spent could be spent more efficiently for all parties involved.
- The method of reporting, which made it difficult to use the report and findings for internal use, something we consider essential in order to get colleagues on board and to invest time and respond in the desired fashion. For example, we think it is worthwhile to report a sprinkler if it does not comply to certain standards. So, in this case the site manager and insurance manager should be made aware of the sprinkler problem and the fact that, so long as it is not repaired or installed according to standard, it will be kept out of the equation.

■ The description of the insured, which is another irritation in the old-fashioned report. The company under study knows best what it does and why with respect to the product or process. This is truly interesting for an insurer, but why the same story in every report? Just refer to a standard description of the client activities, processes, etc and keep it simple. It is better to use the public domain to download the information and focus on the essence of the task.
■ The lack of uniformity in reporting formats, which resulted in a lack of benchmark material for internal use and consequently made it difficult to sell the survey as providing added value. Moreover, it complicated a switch to other insurers. The lack of comparability was also a killer in the advice area. Different surveyors delivered different opinions that were sometimes contradictory.
■ Overkill. Attempts were made to catch 100 per cent of the information possible related to risk management issues, whereas 80 per cent of the information was never utilized.

To conclude: the old-fashioned surveys did not fulfil our objective and we wondered how they ever fulfilled the 'technical' objective of insurers. In any case, they did not help us to initiate the risk management process, as they were perceived as an annual burden, like filling in a tax form, because of the time, cost and energy involved. However, although we learned a lot from a number of good people, unfortunately we all felt more or less like captives.

Why collect information in a scorecard form?

As mentioned in the introduction, the need for information is growing and this applies to both internal and external parties. We also observed that a number of parties involved executed different surveys, investigations, etc for different objectives. The latter, although true, does not equate to a need for different kinds of information. To put it simply: the fact that the final reports, conclusions, etc serve different objectives is no reason to gather the information in a number of different, but almost similar exercises. Commonly used information could be gathered in one sweep, allowing for more time on real priorities. So the starting point for our scorecard was:

■ What is the common information used by different parties?
■ How can we make that information accessible for the parties?
■ How can we prevent double work and cost and so create more time for specific objectives?
■ How can we guarantee the quality of the information?

To conclude: we were looking for lower cost, more information and better utilization of resources and cost, and that needs to be emphasized, for all parties involved. Actually, we also had to find a modus to break with old customs and thus focus on the objective and, to a lesser extent, with old-fashioned procedures. So it all boils down to: 'do less, get more and break with traditions'.

The first scorecard

When we started with a global property programme (in the early1990s) we tried to change the system in order to get the maximum return for combined efforts. Therefore, with more than 80 production operations spread over the world, we had our reservations about collecting and maintaining underwriting information in a sensible manner. Moreover, we believed that the information should be made available in a format that would fit different internal and external purposes.

Although we did not use the name 'scorecard' at that time, we actually tried to construct one. However, we failed. The failure was due to different factors like: complexity, lack of accessibility of the data (except to the IT manager) and no complete buy-in from the major internal and external players. Although it was a lost battle, all people involved agreed that this was something we should have, but that it should be available at low cost, easily accessible, consistent and of an unprejudiced high quality. The idea was good but ahead of its time.

Consequently, we continued with the old-fashioned system of surveys, reporting, etc. Over time, we made some modifications but we continued to believe that, with the same energy and resources, more could have been achieved. Obviously, form rather than content was the dominating factor, something we were not able to change.

Over time, the growing need for information and emphasis on corporate governance issues revived interest in the abandoned system. The awareness that software and hardware had made a quantum leap was the final trigger to take up the old idea. With the lessons learned we started all over again.

Framework to create the environment to get it done

Lack of support was an important reason for the earlier failure. So we first needed to create the environment in order to create a platform for the other important players. In our situation, from an insurance perspective, that is the group safety health department (SHE), the broker and some major reinsurers. Together, we arrived at the following framework. Actually, getting insurers on board was the most difficult part, but that was solved after we explained the objectives and showed the draft framework:

- *Simplicity.* In the initial stage, surveys will always have to be done by an expert. However, in a maintenance stage or in *ad hoc* situations even a non-'survey' expert must be able to handle the system and come back with good-quality information. So, questions almost as simple as multiple choice should be the objective.
- *High quality.* No questions should arise about the quality of the information gathered.
- *Focus.* Complexity would be a killer and, consequently, we needed to keep focused on the essential information and the final objective: the art of 'doing less and getting more'.

- *Justification and acceptance by external parties.* Quality is a subject in its own right but procedures must be embedded in order to guarantee that checks and controls are in place for justification purposes. This is of equal importance for internal and external parties. With respect to the internal value it should be observed that the final objective is that the 'score' will form an integrated part in the premium allocation model and bonus scheme of the local management. With respect to the external target groups or stakeholders we have to realize that the information is used for underwriting information or to scrutinize the premium allocation model. So it had better be good.
- *Buy-in by local (SHE and insurance) managers.* This appears to be a given but the fact was that, although all these people were involved in risk management, they were often not aware of each other's existence and, even if aware, they did not always realize the supplementary nature of their tasks.
- *Communication/software.* All information gathered needed to be available for all parties involved and it was necessary that the software used should not form a hurdle for exchange.
- *Tailor-made reporting for different purposes and management layers.* Serving different purposes also implies reporting to different management layers: something very important for keeping all stakeholders aligned.
- *Cost efficiency.* The system must be able to generate a saving in such a manner that the parties involved would be able to reallocate resources in a more efficient manner.

How did we achieve this?

Simplicity

On this issue, we ended up with the idea that we would have to focus on reporting situations and not on reporting scores.

In this respect, we were able to use the company databases and, more specifically, the SHE database – an extremely rich database filled with information and standards that can be used for all kinds of situations. Together with insurers and brokers we evaluated and fine-tuned the standards related to risk management issues and filled a few gaps.

As the database is embedded in many systems this was a step forward, even without a scorecard. The next step was to determine how many different situations or levels of safety we would have to review. For this purpose, we used the old SHE and insurance reports and in general we were able to boil it down to three well-defined 'common standard' levels. These levels are the benchmark and all the surveyors have to do is to determine whether the situation fits a certain standard. If not, the score will be zero.

Figure 2.2.1 gives an example of such a question.

Thus, the questionnaire describes the potential situation with the scores to be expected and indicates at the same time what one should do in order to achieve a higher score. This simplicity could only be realized because we were able to build on an

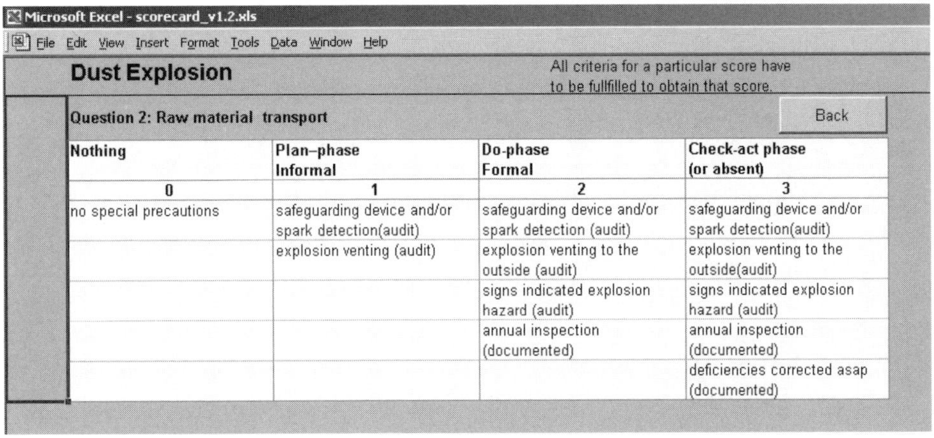

Nothing	Plan–phase Informal	Do-phase Formal	Check-act phase (or absent)
0	1	2	3
no special precautions	safeguarding device and/or spark detection(audit)	safeguarding device and/or spark detection (audit)	safeguarding device and/or spark detection(audit)
	explosion venting (audit)	explosion venting to the outside (audit)	explosion venting to the outside(audit)
		signs indicated explosion hazard (audit)	signs indicated explosion hazard (audit)
		annual inspection (documented)	annual inspection (documented)
			deficiencies corrected asap (documented)

Figure 2.2.1 Scoring criteria on raw material transport in dust areas

existing system and had a good insight into the actual situation. Logical consequences, such as quality and brand name, have always been strong drivers for what we call today 'risk management'.

Consequently, even for a new surveyor it will be easy to understand how the situation can be improved, as it is just a matter of updating the local situation according to the description of the desired level. As reference is made to company standards even brand-new surveyors cannot obscure the discussion by pushing their own 'personal' solutions. Changing standards was, is and will continue to be an issue for group SHE.

Various tests were carried out and the final test was to survey a few newly acquired assets in order to see whether the group standards could be maintained to assess the risk. To a large extent it worked but we also learned a few things such as, for example, discovering an unforeseen situation in the milling department, which is a well-known major potential hazard area for dust explosions and thus worth serious attention. To our way of thinking, a mill must be in a building instead of standing outside. However, owing to the 'never rain' environmental circumstances the mill was situated outside, as there was simply no reason for a building. Desert wind and birds helped to create a dustless environment and, consequently, it was not surprising that the equipment and situation did not meet any of our standard situations and hence that the score became nil. However, measured in a realistic manner, the dust risk was acceptable. This represents a typical situation in which the parties involved (insurers, broker, group SHE and insurance manager) will have to agree about the score. This kind of exception will not lead to any change in the system or questionnaire, as it would lead the way into an old trap: complexity.

High quality

Here we applied a very important lesson: work the existing system and do not try to 'reinvent the wheel'. High quality and consistency were achieved, as we used the previously mentioned internal databases as a backbone and engaged external parties to scrutinize the applicable issues. In fact, this was fine-tuning and formalized standing procedure. In other words, the procedure was already partly in place and embedded.

Focus

Given the complexity of the subject, focus could only be achieved if we were able to define the essentials and generally focus on common factors. In our system this resulted in our focus on fire and explosion risk, while risks like earthquakes, floods and hurricanes were ignored in the scorecard because they are inherent to a location and, fortunately, not too common in our portfolio. Consequently, they do not need to be evaluated in a regular survey. The gathering of this site-specific information through a first visit and updating the background information was sufficient.

Justification and acceptance by external parties

This is an essential element that we achieved in two steps:

- *Internal process.* The local insurance manager (often the financial manager) and the local SHE manager have to sign off the survey. This is a matter of check and balance as our SHE managers are very experienced in surveys and, moreover, are used to external justification. So by their nature they will be prudent. For the insurance/financial manager it is trickier as he or she fully realizes the risk of bad underwriting information, as it implies either that we did not adapt coverage (limits, conditions) or that insurers denied a claim because certain information had been withheld. So in case of doubt, there will be a tendency to report prudently.
- *External process.* In addition to the annual scorecard, the broker and insurer will carry out random surveys. This is partly done to check the results and to give more attention to the set of priorities. The procedure is simple: the observation of the broker and insurer prevails without discussion and the scorecard will be adapted accordingly.

Test

First tests showed that the local SHE managers (mainly in charge of the survey) were very accurate; in 95 per cent of cases the score differed by less than 10 per cent from our estimates (based on old surveys and earlier visits). The 'unexpected' scores were followed up by a survey and without too many problems we were able to explain what went wrong or learned a few things about the questionnaire, answers, etc. So the review of the test helped us to improve quality and show the need for extra information. Only in a few situations did we have to amend the score downwards.

Buy-in by local (SHE and insurance) managers

In essence, there is a major overlap between the subjects that SHE and insurance managers deal with, although from a different perspective. We had to work hard to make it clear that it was not a turf fight but a matter of teaming up in the risk management arena. Once that had been accomplished, the response was very enthusiastic and actually delivered some useful feedback in the design stage.

Something that also helped to get the local managers on board was explaining that, by taking the initiative, we aim to keep control over the process in a positive manner. There were a few reasons for this reaction:

■ There would no longer be contradictory advice.
■ Advice would be standardized according to approved company standards.
■ Scores can and will be benchmarked with other sites.
■ Priorities are indicated in red.
■ The goals or standards will not shift every year.
■ Until group SHE or insurance managers refer to specific situations local management is free to set priorities.

The last points are interesting as this will enable them to work on improving the score (which is what we expect), keeping investment plans, etc in mind, and thus blend it into normal run-of-the-mill activity. Moreover, by working with already approved standards, investments will be challenged to a lesser extent, not only for the required quality but also by pointing out the potential effect by referring to the score.

Communication/software

Owing to the focus and the restrictions, we were able to keep communication/software relatively easy; consequently, the data are in Excel and in this standard medium it is easy to exchange the data.

Reporting customized for different purposes and management layers

We solved this potential problem by testing different formats in the draft period and we have standardized formats that will be generated automatically. For example, a radar screen is used to show at a high level how a site or all the sites of one region score compared to the total of another peer group. In Figure 2.2.2 a typical radar screenshot is displayed, reporting and comparing the scores of the local safety manager and the external surveyor.

Alternatively, a screenshot simply showing the total score is shown in Figure 2.2.3. This score is the average of a number of questions per subject and the shades indicate the status and/or urgency to do something. At SHE level and that of the insurance manager the total breakdown per subject is available, including the remarks and references made (see Figure 2.2.4).

It is also possible to generate a comparison per region and per subject, as in Figure 2.2.5. These were just a few examples of standard reporting.

During the testing stage we discovered that the local managers were intrigued by the score as they started to think aloud about how to improve the scores. Actually, we hoped to achieve a complete buy-in.

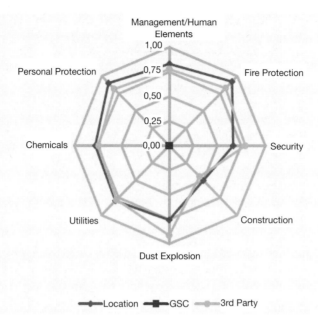

Figure 2.2.2 Radar screenshot of one of the facilities

	Location	GSC	3rd Party
Management / Human Elements	0,50		0,47
Fire Protection	0,58		0,41
Security	1,00		0,79
Construction	0,50		0,44
Dust Explosion	0,33		0,28
Utilities	0,44		0,46
Chemicals	0,50		0,51
Personal Protection	0,62		0,54
Results	0,51		0,46
Frontpage			
Print			
Clear all scores			
Save and close			

Figure 2.2.3 Screenshot of total score per category for one facility by location and third party

Overall results	0,51	0,46
Management / Human Elements	**0,50**	**0,47**
[Go] 1 Calamity plan	0,03	0,03
2 "No-smoking" policy	0,03	0,05
3 Hot work permit procedure	0,03	0,03
4 Internal safety inspections	0,00	0,00
5 Risk assessment procedure	0,02	0,04
6 Cardboard storage	0,07	0,04
7 Empty/idle pallet storage	0,11	0,07
8 Empty/Idle pallet stacking	0,07	0,07
9 Empty crate storage	0,11	0,11
10 Traffic safety	0,00	0,00
11 Forklift truck safety	0,04	0,04
Fire Protection	**0,58**	**0,41**
[Go] 1 Municipal fire brigade	0,06	0,03
2 Site fire squad	0,06	0,07
3 Hand fire extinguishers	0,10	0,12
4 Hose reels	0,14	NA
5 Smoke/ fire detection and alarm in buildings	0,17	0,13
6 Fire detection and extinguishing in control rooms, (production)	0,06	0,07
7 Automatic sprinkler, (see also fire water supply)	0,00	0,00
8 Fire water supply (fire water pump and external supply)	0,00	0,00
9 Major hydraulic systems	NA	NA
Security	**1,00**	**0,79**
[Go] 1 Fencing	0,38	0,38
2 Entry to site	0,63	0,42
Construction	**0,50**	**0,44**
[Go] 1 Main structure	0,11	0,11
2 Insulation materials, (buildings, fermentation tanks)	0,22	0,33
3 Fire separations	0,17	0,00

Note: the scores shown in Figures 2.2.2, 2.2.3 and 2.2.4 imply: 1 = very good and 0 = very bad.

Figure 2.2.4   Screenshot of overall results per topic for one facility by location and third party

Cost efficiency

Cost efficiency is a very important issue for all involved. Using Excel is low-cost; however, the major saving lies in surveys currently being carried out with absolute efficiency. Checking is easy, with the most recent scorecard available, and takes a few hours for an average site, whereas the reports can be made available on the spot. In the past, a survey took at least two days, and included time for reporting. So the scorecard has proved to be a major time saver and has resulted in additional surveys that really add value to the common risk perception. Moreover, we now get a survey done once a year on every production location and there is time left to select the sites to which we need to give extra attention, for example because of divestments or investments.

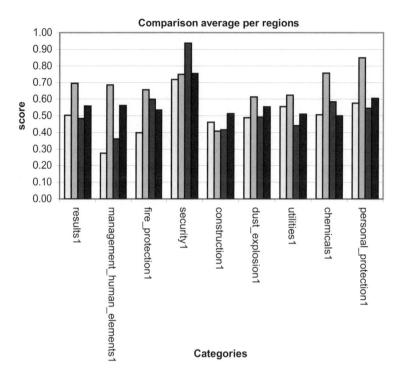

Figure 2.2.5   Comparison of details per region

Conclusion

We managed to get it done and we achieved total acceptance. Moreover, the SHE department took the format as an example for another SHE survey and the insurance department will be involved in fine-tuning the items related to liability risk. So the scorecard was accepted and embraced, given the fact that the format is utilized for other purposes. Our mission was completed although we have some plans for further optimization. One of the objectives is to get it working on a palmtop and introduce online benchmarking at local level.

Acknowledgements

Although this chapter is written from the risk/insurance manager perspective it must be emphasized that setting up and maintaining a successful scorecard is not something one does on its own. Immense support from other internal and external risk management colleagues was needed and will continue to be required for the future. For example, the alignment with the SHE (safety health environment departments) disciplines was essential in the design stage and will continue to be important. The know-how and experience gathered in risk management was simply overwhelming and happened to be firmly embedded in all kinds of procedures on several levels within the organization. To a certain extent we wanted to make this know-how and experience available to external audiences; it just needed to be labelled 'risk management'. The result: hidden but not forgotten, and simply embedded in the structure to serve and protect quality and brand name, in other words a structure that was in place already long before we used fashionable terms like 'risk management'.

Equally impressive was the support from external parties who helped us to translate our know-how about the company into a viable model to measure and report risk. Mention must be made of a few of the people who made a difference at several moments in time: Ole Zeeman and Rene Dirven, both from Aon, Steef Elshout (formerly of Aon) and Harry Limberger from Allianz. Their input was vital to the birth of the model and its content.

Integrated risk management at an international automobile manufacturer

Frank Stenner and Elmar Steurer, BMW Group

Risk and risk management

As a global manufacturer of premium cars, the BMW Group is exposed to a multitude of different risks in each of its divisions. In addition to fluctuations of currencies, interest rates and raw material prices, the growing complexities and shortening of innovation cycles in the development, production and sales processes, as well as the increasing competitive pressure in global markets, result in a higher volatility of financial results.

Therefore, a risk management process has to be installed to make risks across all types of risk and across all business units comparable and to aggregate these to describe comprehensively the overall risk situation of the company. This chapter highlights some milestones of the risk management activities achieved by BMW Group.

It is logical to describe risk from management decisions as probability distributions of their possible outcomes (Karten, 1972: 152). Such probability distributions contain all facts and pieces of information relevant to a decision. A decision under risk is therefore defined as a rational choice between different probability distributions. To characterize probability distributions, a number of operational measures have been developed by decision theory, such as expected value, standard deviation and value at risk.

It is common to use the term 'risk' to describe negative deviations from a planned outcome. The term 'chance' is then reserved to specify the positive deviations. However, in this context, the only difference between both terms is the starting point of the numerical scale. Chance is the opposite side of the risk coin (Karten, 1972: 163).

A company's risk management quantifies risks and chances based on their cash flow impacts. When aggregated across all company activities, the interdependencies between different driving factors are also considered and accumulated in so-called correlation matrices. Risk management provides support to decision makers by:

■ specifying the complete chance/risk profiles;
■ identifying offsets of chances/risks and avoiding their duplications;
■ supporting decisions on capital expenditures and allocations of risk capital.

Further, risk management strengthens the awareness of management to limit negative deviations from agreed targets and to exploit profit potentials to their maximum. To underline this entrepreneurial aspect of risk management for the company culture, the term 'chance/risk management' (CRM) is used in this chapter.

Integration of risk in the company

To identify, evaluate and document risks, a comprehensive CRM system is applied within the BMW Group:

■ Chances and risks of management actions are assessed, and activities to meet agreed targets and to limit downside risks are rolled out in the company's long-term planning, annual budgeting and sub-annual forecasting.
■ Projects to develop new automobiles are decided upon in a transparent analysis of driving forces for risks and chances.
■ Rapid and extensive group-wide reporting to decision makers on the degree of target achievement, a management requirement.
■ A group-wide network of risk managers regularly assesses all essential kinds of risk.

Many risk management systems concentrate on loss potentials, the negative outcomes of decisions. Consequently, actions to avoid risk are of high priority. Entrepreneurial decision makers take a different view; they want to take advantage of profit opportunities by actively controlling acceptable risks. The minimum requirement for an integrated

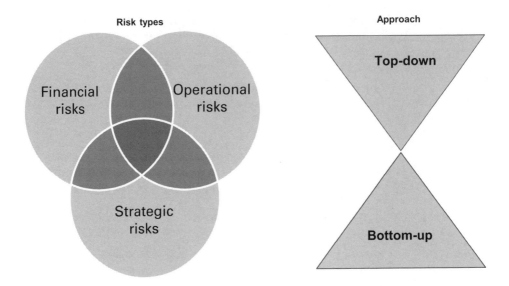

Figure 2.3.1 Integrated risk management

CRM is therefore to strike a balance between the tolerated appetite for risk and the exploitation of profit opportunities to enhance the shareholder value of the company.

The various categories of risk in the business need to be integrated according to their organizational origin, as illustrated in Figure 2.3.1. Relative to their specific business area, risks that are coordinated at a central level from a top-down perspective have to be merged with risks that are controlled at a decentralized level from a bottom-up perspective. In general, financial risks are managed at a central level in manufacturing industry. This includes common guidelines for treasury activities in all business units and the employment of derivative instruments for the activities in the financial market as well as the use of offset opportunities by global sourcing of supplies and plant equipment.

The handling of operational risks can be centralized or decentralized. Regarding their impact on the company's cash flow, however, they are very seldom quantified and aggregated in a way consistent with a company-wide CRM approach. At the BMW Group important operational risks are appraised by the CRM function.

Strategic risks, by their nature, can only be evaluated and managed at a central level. The CRM function, the controlling function and the strategy function need to align their respective activities to achieve maximum impact on the shareholder value of the company. A systematic and professional management of all types of risks is essential for the company to compete successfully in its industry and that is exactly the task of an integrated chance/risk management process. This includes, but is not limited to, strict adherence to risk-handling guidelines. More important is the optimization of a comprehensive chance/risk profile spanning all aspects of the business. In such a way integrated CRM contributes its share to grow the value of the company. To pursue this claim three distinct dimensions of an integrated CRM can be concluded: common understanding, types of risk and methodology, as demonstrated in Figure 2.3.2.

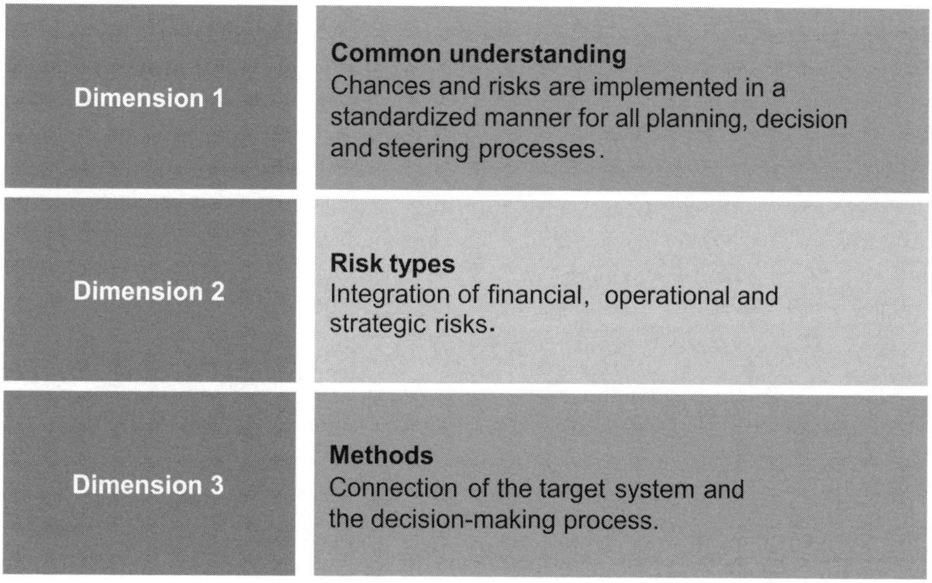

Dimension 1	**Common understanding** Chances and risks are implemented in a standardized manner for all planning, decision and steering processes.
Dimension 2	**Risk types** Integration of financial, operational and strategic risks.
Dimension 3	**Methods** Connection of the target system and the decision-making process.

Figure 2.3.2   Dimensions of integrated risk management

The objective of an integrated CRM, therefore, is to execute a comprehensive and reliable aggregation of chances and risks across distinct types of risk, several company divisions and business fields. For example, typically the entry strategy for a new sales market is designed by the sales division. This approach is then tested and reviewed by the controlling and strategy functions with regard to its profitability and its alignment with the established overall strategy. Additional insight should be gained by asking CRM to look into the ramifications of the suggested sales strategy on other driving forces within the company, such as financial services.

Implementation of an integrated CRM

The CRM function is often closely associated with the treasury function of a company since quantification of chances and risks and the application of an appropriate toolkit of risk-mitigating instruments is an accepted standard for managing risks in financial markets. To highlight the relevance of the transfer of CRM methods from treasury to other business activities, the proven risk management methods applied in treasury are briefly introduced. Subsequently, the process to evaluate chances and risks for projects within the BMW Group is outlined.

Although this approach is relevant for all decisions on capital expenditures and strategies, it is critical for a company-wide acceptance of the CRM methodology that its benefits are convincingly demonstrated with relevant vehicle projects extending from the initial idea to the finished product: successes or failures of new vehicle projects impact very strongly on the future of the company.

Integrated management of financial risks

Price fluctuations in the global foreign exchange, money and capital as well as commodity markets reflect not only on the financial result of the automotive business but also on the result of the financial services business. Management of the liquidity reserve and of pension assets as well as asset/liability management in financial services exposes the company's interest result to the risk of interest rate movements. Credit risks of customers and suppliers in addition to the residual value risk created by the leasing activities in financial services complete the company's portfolio of financial risk exposures. According to the definition of risk as a random event, the impact of these financial risks on the company's cash flows is quantified as probability distributions. The wealth of available statistical data on price changes in the financial markets and the large size of customer portfolios make it possible to assign objective probabilities to the spectrum of possible outcomes. Following that a transfer of risk through forward and option agreements with third parties in the financial markets could become necessary. On the other hand, further opportunities to generate additional profit by expanding the risk position should also be considered.

Approximately 50 per cent of the total turnover of the BMW Group is realized outside the euro zone. To manage the volatilities of financial outcomes an integrated CRM looks first for offsets at an operational level that compensate each other's movements in part or in total. For example, the fluctuations of the revenue cash flows in domestic currency (euro) as a result of sales in a foreign currency (US dollar) can be offset by the expense cash flows for material purchases and/or for production of products in the same foreign currency (US dollar).

Consequently, an international car manufacturer can substantially reduce its total foreign exchange exposure by matching its global production and supplier network with the currency portfolio of its sales revenues. The existing relationship between financial risks and operational activities of the business clearly demands a joint, ie integrated, evaluation of functionally distinct areas of responsibility.

By managing risks jointly, ie by aggregating individual probability distributions rather than adding up their individual risk parameters, the aggregated situation offers a reduced risk exposure, provided that the correlation between the individual risks is not completely positive, ie a correlation coefficient of less than 1. An analysis of the financial risks at the BMW Group clearly supports this approach of risk integration; the aggregated cash flow at risk for all financial risks mentioned in this context was substantially lower than the added cash flow at risk values. This procedure also reduces the number of risk transfer activities and thus reflects positively on the involved transaction costs.

Integrated risk management of vehicle projects

In principle the methods of CRM that are successfully applied for financial risks are also suitable for strategic and operational risks, provided that probability distributions of cash flow outcomes can be established. The CRM at BMW Group has transferred these methods to the management of vehicle projects.

All such projects have to contribute a predefined minimum return to the company's overall enterprise value. This minimum contribution is determined over the full life cycle of the vehicle including all cash inflows and outflows initiated using a dynamic net present value calculation. In this context the role of CRM is selectively to support the decision-making process and to identify as early as possible the need for actions. Drivers for chances and risks are challenged by analysing the probability distributions of the net present values based on the relevant cash flows. Vehicle projects with identical return projections often show very distinct volatilities of their respective outcomes. To identify and to prioritize possible factors of chances and risks, a standard evaluation procedure has been created that is based on three fields of chances and risks: vehicle characteristics, processes and market environment, exhibited in Figure 2.3.3.

This segmentation of possible chance and risk factors essentially reflects the organizational responsibility of the operational functions involved. The sales division is in charge of anticipating the driving factors for volatilities from the market environment. The production division is accountable for any fluctuations in the outcomes from the manufacturing process. Market demands and production know-how in turn define the specifications expected from the proposed end product. The risks resulting from planning and designing such a car are borne by the development division.

It is necessary to create a chance/risk profile at the very beginning of the development process as changes can still be effected with a limited negative impact on the project's total return. As the development of the vehicle reaches its final stages any changes in its specifications will become more costly and this cost impact will certainly limit the extent to which changes remain economically feasible. The CRM

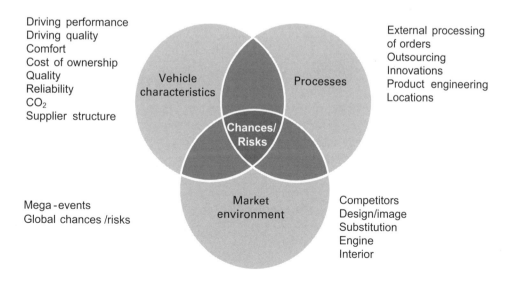

Driving performance
Driving quality
Comfort
Cost of ownership
Quality
Reliability
CO_2
Supplier structure

External processing
of orders
Outsourcing
Innovations
Product engineering
Locations

Vehicle characteristics

Processes

Chances/
Risks

Mega-events
Global chances /risks

Market
environment

Competitors
Design/image
Substitution
Engine
Interior

Figure 2.3.3 Chance and risk factors driving vehicle projects

approach adds value by offering a decision-making tool to balance chances and risks in a structured way at any chosen point in time and to avoid costly misjudgements. It offers a comprehensive view to ensure cost-efficient manufacturing and a fit with corporate strategy.

The chance/risk profile is established in four steps, illustrated in Figure 2.3.4: identification, evaluation, quantification and aggregation. First, the company's appetite for risk is statistically measured as a level of confidence of a project's cash flow, ie the probability of a given outcome is within a predefined or planned interval. Then the most important risk factors are identified and scenarios for positive and negative deviations from the planned result are established for the risk factors, and their respective likelihoods of occurrence are evaluated. Next, the monetary impacts of these scenarios are quantified as deviations from the planned cash flow level. Aggregating all risk and chance drivers by using a correlation matrix will give an overall probability distribution of cash flows. This results in a corresponding expected value and standard deviation, as well as the aggregated cash flow at risk (CFaR) and the aggregated cash flow at chance (CFaC). These risk measures reflect distinct views of the possible deviations of the project's cash flows from the planned outcome. Comparing the expected value with the planned outcome is an indication of how ambitiously the project plan is rolled out.

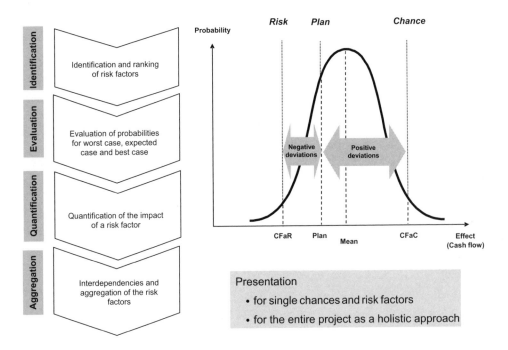

Figure 2.3.4   Approach to assessing chances and risks of vehicle projects

In order to quantify, for example, market expectations, two distinct sources are compared and contrasted. The first is the market experience of the management; the second is statistics and evaluations by industry and consumer associations. Therefore, the data input into establishing the chance/risk profile will always be a mix of objective, factual data and subjective assessments.

Certain projects require the wealth of knowledge of managers amassed over the years rather than statistical coverage. However, statistics and modelling serve to verify the individual expectations. The usefulness of these findings can be enhanced further by drawing in representatives from controlling, group planning/strategy and the CRM functions because they ensure that compromises between risk evaluations put forward by individuals and the overall business requirements are reached. Rather than targeting one single outcome this evaluation process allows the submission of ranges of outcomes for the stream of planned cash flows.

Developing new automobiles inevitably incurs risk. Therefore, applying a chance and risk analysis is not meant to rule out completely all risks but to point out benefits from changing established procedures, eg:

■ early recognition of crucial driving factors;
■ maintaining a balance between chances and risks;
■ stopping costly passing on of decision making in the hierarchy;
■ initiating focused actions early to limit risk exposure;
■ opening up options for new projects.

When applied across the entire portfolio of vehicle projects CRM helps to optimize the risk/return contribution of individual projects by considering also how they mutually impact on each other and what, for example, they contribute to the value of the common brand of the business. This portfolio approach follows very much the lines that a portfolio manager would take when allocating available capital to investments in capital market securities.

Aggregation of chances and risks for the allocation of risk capital

In an ideal world the quantification of all financial, operational and strategic risks as random variables and their aggregation in their respective business segments can – of course – be carried out across the entire enterprise; the total chance/risk position is measured by the aggregation of all risks including the interdependencies between them. This overall probability distribution marks the cash flow at risk in comparison to the mean as an estimation of the worst outcome, not being exceeded with a given probability in a defined planning period. Thus the amount of risk capital is calculated by the difference between the planned result and the worst outcome. Also, benchmarking specific, individual risks against this comprehensive exposure shows their true, relative importance for the success or failure of the business. The methodological challenges involved, that is to run interviews and to do evaluations and complex calculations, as well as the need to determine the risk level that is acceptable, underline the importance of a competent in-house CRM function. The risk appetite of the entire company can only be decided by its top management.

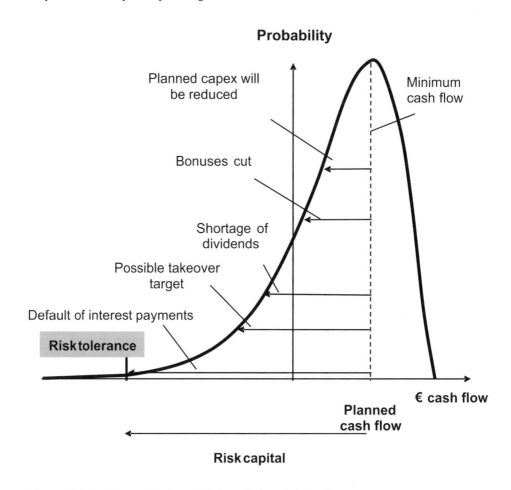

Figure 2.3.5   Determination of risk capital and risk tolerance

The readiness to accept risk will be influenced by the type of industry in which the company is doing business, the intensity of competition there, the company's capital structure and, last but not least, the personal risk attitude of each individual manager. The size of the expressed risk appetite explains the extent to which the organization is able and willing to absorb shortfalls of cash up to an implied probability level in order to protect the company against the failure of serving outstanding debt jeopardizing its existence. On a less critical level, the protection against the failure to go ahead with planned capital expenditures or paying dividends, pensions or bonuses also depends on the risk tolerance shown as defined in Figure 2.3.5. To quantify the risk appetite it is convenient to use the statistical term of 'interval of confidence'. Based on a level of

95 per cent, frequently applied in the manufacturing industry, it is possible to define cash flow at risk limits that control individual types of risk. The remaining 'open' risk of 5 per cent will not be covered by the available risk capital and consequently, in this example, management is prepared to run out of capital with exactly that probability. Depending on the risk capital available and on the risk tolerance defined, a transfer of risk to third parties will be initiated, such as entering into forward contracts, or negotiating risk transfer agreements with business partners. On the other hand, the overall risk position may also be expanded to exploit opportunities for additional returns, such as insourcing attractive business activities.

This process outlines the ranges of possible fluctuations for target achievements critical to the company's performance. The relevant factor that, in the end, determines the acceptable risk tolerance is the amount of equity available. This is the money that may be put at risk.

For a given business strategy, balancing risk appetite against available equity determines the extent to which risk transfers are necessary or the amount of equity that may be returned to shareholders because it is 'not needed'. Last but not least, it also initiates a demand for 'fresh' equity to be raised from the shareholders if justified by the risk/reward balance of its portfolio of projects and business activities in general. Therefore, the limited availability of equity/risk capital is the prime concern of a chance/risk management at an aggregated portfolio level.

Conclusion

The purpose of an integrated risk management approach is to make risks in the business comparable across all types of risk and all business units and to exploit profit potentials without exceeding the company's accepted appetite for risk. This is achieved by properly analysing individual risks and aggregating them to a comprehensive description of the company's risk position. The benefits of systematic chance and risk management for entrepreneurial decisions have been highlighted: the chance and risk profiles of decisions, projects, strategies or the total business can be made more transparent, and the implementation of early warning signals helps to initiate effective countermeasures in time, so avoiding experiencing sudden and emerging activities. It effectively prevents a major crisis from happening. The establishment of such chance and risk profiles for decisions in the treasury business and for vehicle projects can only be viewed as a first step. In a next step, the insights from these CRM processes have to be rolled out across the entire company and the methods of analysis, quantification and risk mitigation have to be applied universally for all important business decisions throughout the company.

Once it is appreciated what the methodological difficulties are that CRM faces when chances/risks are quantified and aggregated and risk capital is allocated throughout the business, some basic requirements should become an integral part of any company's culture: planning based on ranges of outcomes rather than on a single outcome; applying a common definition of risk and of risk correlations; and establishing tools to balance chances and risks.

References and further reading

Gleißner, W (2003) Balanced Scorecard und Risikomanagement als Bausteine eines integrierten Managementsystems, in *Erfolgsfaktor Risiko-Management*, ed Frank Romeike and Robert Finke, Wiesbaden

Jokisch, J (1987) *Betriebwirtschaftliche Währungsrisikopolitik und internationales Finanzmanagement*, Stuttgart

Karten, W (1972) *Die Unsicherheit des Risikobegriffes, in Praxis und Theorie der Versicherungsbetriebslehre, Festgabe für H.L. Müller-Lutz zum 60. Geburtstag*, ed Paul Braess, Dieter Farny and Reimer Schmidt, Karlsruhe, pp 147–69

Merbecks, A *et al* (2004) *Intelligentes Risikomanagement*, Frankfurt and Vienna

Pechtl, A (2003) Ein Rückblick: Risikomanagement von der Antike bis heute, in *Erfolgsfaktor Risiko-Management*, ed Frank Romeike and Robert Finke, Wiesbaden

Pfennig, M (2000) Shareholder Value durch unternehmensweites Risikomanagement, in *Handbuch Risikomanagement*, ed Lutz Johanning and Bernd Rudolph, vol 2, Bad Soden, pp 1296–332

Romeike, F (2003) Bewertung und Aggregation von Risiken, in *Erfolgsfaktor Risiko-Management*, ed Frank Romeike and Robert Finke, Wiesbaden

Contract risk

Robert Chapman, Siemens Insight Consulting

Introduction

The most important lesson of the last few years is that board members can no longer claim to be ignorant of business risk. The board is not immune. When the absence of adequate risk management leads to something going wrong, as it invariably does, the board will be held accountable. Positions will be vulnerable and shareholders will want to hold individuals to account in the aftermath of adverse events. It is a given.

In addition, if the event is sufficiently high-profile, the media are likely to ensure that the news reaches a wide audience. There is no hiding place. The board needs to focus on those areas of risk that can have the greatest impact.

An area of risk management that receives insufficient attention is contract risk. In this chapter, contract risks from a buyer and a supplier perspective are examined, together with examples of good and poor risk management. Good risk management can capitalize on opportunities and secure business objectives. Poor risk management has led to the loss of executive jobs, reduction in share value, damage to reputation and loss of projected earnings.

Board accountability

There is now a proliferation of standards, guides and books contributing to a wealth of knowledge on the subject of risk management. In addition, various forces have converged to push risk management into the consciousness of management and boards. However, effective risk management is not ubiquitous and would still appear to be elusive to some organizations.

The application of robust, effective risk management, even within some FTSE 100 companies, is still weak. While all large companies carry out risk management to some degree, a key challenge for boards all around the world is to develop a new rigour in their processes. There still needs to be a transformation in the application of risk management from conformance to performance. The message has not got through that the mismanagement of risk can carry an enormous price and that effective risk management can improve the balance sheet.

In particular, organizations that are most effective and efficient in managing risks both to existing assets and to future growth will, in the long run, outperform those that are less so. More importantly, a business that cannot manage risks effectively will simply disappear.

The solution is for board members to learn of the potential for adverse events, be sufficiently aware of the sources of risk within the area of business they are operating in, and take pre-emptive action. Steps must be taken to ensure that the objectivity and perspective sought by adding non-executive directors to the board, to support decision making, is not undermined by their lack of understanding of risk management, its tools or its techniques. Board members need to enhance their understanding of risk management and in particular the risks associated with any form of business change.

Identifying the board's appetite for risk management

One of the common questions to be asked when setting up a risk process is to establish the organization's risk appetite. But this can be premature.

The more pertinent question is 'What is the board's appetite for risk management?' To some, talking about risk management is about as exciting as planning a trip to the dentist. When the subject is raised during the 'lift speech', eyes can glaze over and interest is lost. But risk management couldn't be less like root canal treatment. Carried out appropriately it can be energizing and very rewarding. Risk management can be one of the more exciting aspects of business – growth – through looking at new opportunities and how they may be developed.

Identifying responsibility

While it is not the board's responsibility to manage the business, it *is* responsible for overseeing management and holding it accountable. Hence, the duty of the board is not to undertake risk management on a day-to-day basis, but to make sure that frameworks are in place that support the implementation of risk management throughout the organization.

The board should ensure that the information it receives about risk is accurate and reliable. Directors should maintain a healthy scepticism and require information from a cross-section of reliable sources, from the CFO, CEO and senior management to internal and external auditors. Board members should be prepared to ask tough questions and they should make themselves able to understand the answers. In particular, they should be fully conversant with the risk ownership profile of contracts and how risk management dictates behaviours.

Risk management applications

Regardless of the size of an organization, risk management should be applied to at least the following activities, as banks, investors, shareholders and partners will increasingly expect to see evidence of a detailed risk assessment when reviewing business proposals of any substance:

■ entering into a contract;
■ developing strategic development plans (long-range planning);
■ preparing business plans;
■ seeking additional finance;
■ preparing for and implementing organizational change;
■ choosing between options;
■ commissioning new premises or acquiring existing premises to refurbish;
■ carrying out a project;
■ submitting a bid for a major new commission;
■ delivering a major commission;
■ entering into a joint venture;
■ looking to penetrate new markets;
■ installing a new IT system;
■ developing business resilience;
■ acquiring a new company;
■ expanding overseas;
■ evaluating opportunities.

Contracts

Reflecting on the bullet point list above, the one area of risk that all businesses face at some stage is entering into a new contract.

A series of questions need to be asked if an organization is considering entering into a contract. Clearly, the questions will differ, depending on whether the organization is delivering or procuring a service or product.

The three main functions of contracts are to define:

■ *responsibilities* (work to be performed by the contractor and client if appropriate);
■ *risk ownership* (how the risks inherent in the activity will be allocated between the contracting parties);
■ *the client's objectives* (implanting motives in the contractor that match those of the client).

There is a common perception that the best way to manage risk is to transfer it and that such an action results in its removal. Transfer of risk to the wrong party can actually enlarge a risk. Client organizations, when deciding upon the allocation of risks, need to recognize that they will pay for those risks that are the responsibility of the contractor, as well as their own, for contractors will usually include contingencies within their tenders as a means of guaranteeing their return in the event that risks allocated to them materialize.

In addition, clients must recognize that the more risk that is transferred to the contractor, the higher the tender price will be (unless it is a very depressed market) or the more likely it is that tenderers will withdraw.

Hence, when considering the allocation of risk to another party, thought should be given to the following factors:

■ the ability of the party to manage the risk;
■ the ability of the party to bear the risk if it materializes;
■ the effect that risk allocation will have upon the motivation and behaviour of the recipient;
■ the cost of the risk transfer;
■ how risk transfer will affect all of the activity objectives.

The allocation of risks between the parties to a contract should be identified by the client prior to the tender process. The client should include within the tender documents a risk register, which describes the identified risks and the proposed allocation of ownership. The tenderers should be asked to price the risks, identify their proposed response categories and mitigation actions, and confirm the allocation of the risks between the contract parties within their tender. The review of the risk registers within the tender returns will form a significant component of the tender evaluation process. How this is approached will depend on the form of the procurement route adopted.

Clients must recognize that different forms of procurement have very different risk ownership profiles. The main reason why the Scottish Parliament building project failed to meet its objectives (as cited in both the Auditor-General's report and the subsequent Holyrood report) was the choice of the procurement route. The selection of construction management was cited as the single factor to which most of the misfortunes that had befallen the project could be attributed. Surprise was expressed during the Holyrood enquiry about the selection of construction management when it was evident that the Scottish Office (while working to publicly declared fixed budgets and being highly 'risk averse') had chosen a procurement route that offered no fixed budget and had a high degree of attendant risk for the client. In his report Lord Fraser stated: 'it verges on the embarrassing to conclude, as I do, that virtually none of the key questions about construction management were asked. Similarly none of the disadvantages of construction management appear to have been identified.'[1]

Delivering a service or product

When considering risk management of delivery, several questions should be answered, but these questions need to be specific, relevant and engaging:

- How much could we lose if we cannot satisfy the terms of the contract once signed?
- Are we absolutely sure what we are required to deliver if we accept these contract terms?
- What are the critical resources to the delivery of this contract and, if after commencing the contract they were lost or no longer available, how would we recover and how long would it take?
- What would be the damage to our relationship with our client, our reputation and our standing in the market if we do not deliver this contract on time?
- What is our experience of delivering this type of product/service?
- Do we have adequate business continuity plans in place to cope with disruption to our premises?
- Are the production/delivery costs fully understood?
- What changes in the marketplace that are currently expected could impact on the contract?
- If critical members of staff to the contract, for whatever reason, became unavailable, how would the organization respond?
- How would our share value be affected by adverse media in the event the contract resulted in litigation?
- Are there any critical project dependencies?
- Are there any aspects of the service or product that involve novel technology?

Case study: Airbus (delivering a product)

Airbus, the European plane maker, is an organization that has clearly failed to manage its production risks on its A380 'superjumbo' (the world's largest-ever aircraft) and deliver against its contracts with airline carriers.

The A380 has cost Airbus 12 billion euros ($14 billion; £8 billion) to develop, and will be the world's largest airliner, seating more than 500 passengers across twin decks.[2] It is designed to fly between the main international hubs.

In September 2006 it was reported that the first of the 159 ordered at that stage would be handed over to Singapore Airlines, 12 months behind schedule. Airbus has admitted that it will deliver only nine in 2007, instead of the promised 25, up to nine fewer in 2008 and five fewer in 2009. The A380 production problems caused a publicly stated 26 per cent slump in the share price of the majority owner, EADS, when it became public knowledge in June 2006. As a result of these delays, several executives have lost their positions.

In June 2006 it was announced that Airbus chief Gustav Humbert had resigned over the A380 delays. He said at the time: 'the recently announced delay on the A380 production and delivery programme has been a major disappointment for our customers, our shareholders and our employees. As president and chief executive of Airbus, I must take responsibility for this setback and feel the right course of action is to offer my resignation to our shareholders.'[3]

In September 2006 Charles Champion, the executive in charge of the flagship A380 programme, was dismissed, it was reported, because of deliveries being put back by a year resulting in a 2 billion euro (£1.35 billion) reduction in earnings over the next three years.[4] According to Airbus staff, Champion paid the price for failing to inform the Airbus board promptly of the A380's mounting technical difficulties, and for allowing severe production bottlenecks to continue unchecked for months, rather than fix them immediately.

Chief executive Geoff Dixon of Qantas (one of the contracted carriers) has said that Qantas would be seeking compensation from Airbus, under the terms of its contract.[5] Further compensation claims from other airline carriers are likely to follow.

So, in addition to the loss of earnings, Airbus will face further losses through compensation payments to airlines. John Leahy, chief operating officer for customers, declared that it is standard practice to compensate contracted parties[6] and said that 'payments will be made for each day of delay in delivery'.

Airbus at the time was 80 per cent owned by the European aerospace and defence group EADS, and 20 per cent by the UK's BAE Systems. However, BAE Systems has decided to sell its stake in Airbus. Mike Turner, chief executive of BAE Systems, said he had 'no regrets' about the sudden decision to sell off its 20 per cent stake in Airbus for £1.9 billion and insisted that major shareholders were right behind him.[7] This was significantly lower than the anticipated sale figure of £3 billion mooted in April 2006.[8] BAE Systems also predicted that the European plane maker would announce further delays to the delivery of A380 superjumbos and was likely to unveil a hefty cash call in the future.

Procuring a service or product

When considering risks associated with procurement, several questions should be answered, and again these questions need to be specific, relevant and engaging. The following list, while not exhaustive, contains the key issues to be addressed:

■ Has the contracting party appropriate experience?
■ Is the contracting party financially stable?
■ Has the organization sufficient resources?
■ What contractual commitments does the contracting party already have?
■ Is the contracting party currently in litigation with other clients?
■ What is the delivery track record of the organization?
■ How robust are their processes?
■ What are their management capabilities?

- Which of the organization's key representatives will be assigned to the contract?
- Is the organization able to deliver in the required time frame?
- How will relationships be developed to engage the contracting party in delivery?
- How will risk management be addressed?

Case study: Terminal Five (procurement of services)

The British Airports Authority (BAA),[9] when embarking on the Terminal Five (T5)[10] project at Heathrow Airport, gave considerable thought to the contracts they would engage in and the management of risk.

The research they conducted into major construction projects prior to the commencement of T5 highlighted two key areas that seemed to undermine progress: cultural confusion and the reluctance to acknowledge risk.[11] From a slide included in a presentation by Tony Douglas (managing director of T5) (see Figure 2.4.1) it is clear from the lessons learned that process, organization and behaviours, together with leadership, should be a key focus. A key component of all of these aspects of management was the mitigation of risk.

Lessons Learned

- Research from £1bn+ projects
- Process, organisation, behaviours
  - Actively expose & manage risks
  - Actively promote & motivate success (opportunity)
  - Actively address behaviours & all key relationships
- Leadership
  - Change & uncertainty is the norm
  - Risk is the square of the size e.g. 100× risks
  - A different outcome means doing something different
- No solution is a "dead-cert"

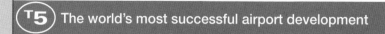

T5 The world's most successful airport development

Figure 2.4.1 Lessons learned

As a consequence of this research, BAA recognized that the risk associated with such a huge infrastructure programme, coupled with the sheer complexity and scale of the work involved, would require a fresh approach to the way the project should be managed if it was to be built on time and within budget.

Risk management was seen as a key driver for programme success. As a consequence it took a unique contractual approach and prepared the T5 Agreement, a bespoke commercial partnering agreement between BAA and contractors and suppliers.[12]

The T5 Agreement is the legally binding contract between BAA and its key suppliers. It is a contract based on relations and behaviours. BAA described it as ground-breaking and considers it is unique in the construction industry. Through the agreement, BAA accepts that it carries all of the risk for the construction project. With this burden removed from contractors and suppliers, BAA believed it would encourage contractors to solve anticipated problems, integrate as teams and focus on proactively managing risk rather than avoiding litigation.

The programme is currently reported to be on budget and programme.

BAA bears out Apgar's[13] argument that those that succeed with new opportunities can better cope with risks and develop 'risk intelligence' as a competitive advantage.

Conclusion

There is a need for businesses to move away from compliance to performance in the way risk management is applied to businesses.

Boards need to become more informed about how risk management can improve bottom-line performance.

One of the largest activities of business that either contribute to or erode performance is contracts. For any business, equal attention needs to be paid to contracts that are entered into both to supply and to receive services.

The degree of risk transfer between a client and a contractor will dictate the behaviour of the contractor, and risk transfer can prove to be a false economy. Risks within a contract need to be made explicit prior to the contract being signed so that each party is fully aware of the risks that it will own and the impact they will have, should they materialize.

Notes

1. The Holyrood enquiry, A report by the Rt Hon Lord Fraser of Carmyllie, QC, 15 September 2004, ISBN 1-4061-0013-7, © Scottish Parliamentary Corporate Body.
2. BBC (2005) 'Airbus confirms super-jumbo delay', 1 June.
3. BBC (2006) 'EADS and Airbus bosses both quit', 2 July.
4. David Gow (2006) 'Airbus sacks third chief over A380 debacle', *Guardian*, 5 September.

5. BBC (2005) 'Airbus confirms super-jumbo delay', 1 June.

6. BBC (2005) 'Airbus pays price of A380 delays', 11 November.

7. Terry Macalister (2006) 'Airbus problems likely to continue, says BAE', *Guardian*, 14 September.

8. BBC (2006), 'BAE confirms possible Airbus sale', 7 April.

9. BAA plc has delisted from the London Stock Exchange and is now owned by Airport Development and Investment Limited, a company held by the Ferrovial Consortium. BAA owns and operates seven UK airports and provides over 1 million square metres of commercial accommodation for more than 900 retail organizations at its airports.

10. T5 represents a huge programme of construction works. It involves over 60 contractors, 16 major projects and 147 sub-projects on a 260-hectare site. The estimated cost is £4.2 billion. The projects will boost Heathrow's capacity by 30 million passengers a year. Many of the 60 aircraft stands are designed to handle the 550-seat Airbus A380s. The programme is being financed by BAA, and BA will be the sole tenant, transferring its operations from other terminals and consolidating its business into one building.

11. BAA T5 Agreement fact sheet.

12. www.baa.com

13. Apgar, D (2006) *Risk Intelligence: Learning to manage what we don't know*, Harvard Business School Press, Boston, MA.

Delivering improvements in risk management through measurement and assessment

Richard Archer and Alan Stanbra, DNV

Management adage

If you can't measure it, you can't control it.
If you can't control it, you can't manage it.
If you can't manage it, you can't improve it.

Organizations strive to improve the way they manage uncertainty. However, launching straight into improvement activities, without taking time to understand the current performance and capability of risk management, is unlikely to produce the desired results. 'Management by fact' is required for senior management buy-in and to ensure that investment is prioritized correctly.

All organizations seeking to implement or improve a system for risk management should first assess their current capability. For new systems, this is crucial so that existing informal good practices are not discarded. When existing systems are being improved, assessment enables future efforts to be targeted. Any improvement programmes that are developed without a sound understanding of the strengths and areas for improvement are likely to be wasteful.

There are two basic approaches to determine how well organizations manage risk. These are: 1) measurement (of past results); and 2) assessment (of existing capabilities that will deliver future results).

An assessment provides a vehicle and an opportunity for an organization to discover clearly its strengths and areas for improvement, from which improvement recommendations can be made. An assessment is also a vehicle for an organization to determine if its management systems are compliant with regulations, codes and laws, including, importantly for many UK organizations, the revised Turnbull Guidance.[1]

The assessment should cover more than just the risk management processes; to be comprehensive, the assessment needs to be at the system level.

For performance measurement and assessment, there are a number of good practice rules. Eight of these are listed below:[2]

1. Use a balanced set of measures – not just financial measures.
2. Make sure that you measure what matters to service users and other stakeholders.
3. Involve staff in determining the measures.
4. Ensure there is a combination of perception measures and performance indicators.
5. Use a combination of results and process/capability measures.
6. Take account of the cost of measuring performance on the indicators chosen.
7. Have a clear system for translating feedback from measures into a strategy for action.
8. Measurement systems need to be focused on continuous improvement.

In assessing the performance of management systems, there are five basic questions,[3] set out in Table 2.5.1. These are the same questions for any type of management system.

Management systems

A management system is a framework of policies and plans, approaches, structure, controls and behaviours. For the explicit management of risk, the risk manager often operates a dedicated management system integrated into the natural work processes of the organization. The explicit management and control of risks requires a robust structure. Such a management system defines the way risk management activities are organized around a 'plan, do, check and act' cycle.

A simple management system for risk management is shown in Figure 2.5.1.

The generic system has five main phases:

■ *Policy:* a statement of intent for managing risk. It explains why risk management is being carried out and depicts what success at a high level looks like.

Table 2.5.1 Basic questions for assessing the performance of management systems

Five questions	Referring to
What are you trying to do?	Have objectives and targets been set? For example, an objective of the approach to risk might be reduced insurance premiums.
How do you make it happen?	What risk management activities are carried out, at both the process and the system level?
How do you know it is right?	Does monitoring show that risk management delivers the expected outcomes?
How do you know it is the best way of doing it?	Are the risk management activities carried out good practice? Benchmarking is a common technique used to answer this question.
How do you know it is the right thing to do?	Are the objectives and targets of the management system appropriate? As the Cheshire Cat of *Alice's Adventures in Wonderland* reminds us, 'If you don't know where you are going, any road will take you there.'

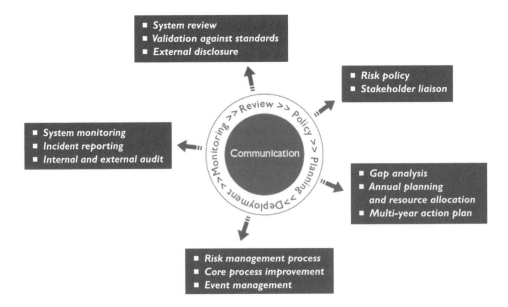

Figure 2.5.1 Management system for risk management

■ *Planning:* outlines the objectives and how success will be achieved.
■ *Deployment:* includes the development of the risk management structure and management system, carrying out risk assessments and the subsequent management of risks, and communication and monitoring.
■ *Monitoring:* the monitoring of the system, so that the review phase is based on fact.
■ *Review:* reviews the entire system, to draw out learning points and to drive continuous improvement.

It is important that risk management activities are embedded in the normal business practices of the organization. This is achieved by aligning risk management activities so that they support the business activities (as shown in Figure 2.5.2). Figure 2.5.2 is an overview of a risk assurance management standard[4] for both the risk management and the associated assurance activities (together called risk assurance).

Risk management and assurance activities are integrated increasingly. Together these disciplines form a systematic approach to the identification, analysis, control and reporting of risks, whilst also providing the assurance that the significant risks facing the organization are being managed explicitly.

The relative degree to which reliance is placed on 'competency' versus 'systems' will depend on the extent and categories of risks faced by the organization.

The benefits of management systems for risk management include:

■ Correct goals are set for the risk management processes.
■ Explicit risk management is carried out as desired.
■ Everyone knows his or her role and responsibility.

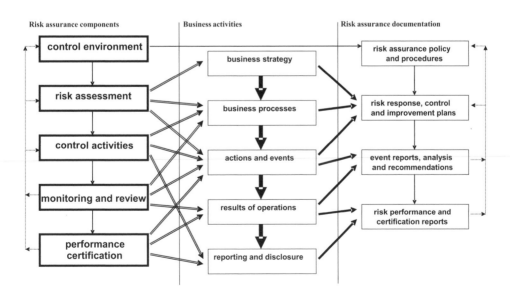

Figure 2.5.2 Risk assurance management system

■ There is total commitment from all levels.
■ Clear, measured performance requirements are set.
■ There is compliance with regulations and laws.
■ There is provision of assurance.
■ There is effective transfer of information.
■ Performance is continuously improved.

Measurement

The outputs of risk management should be assessed from two perspectives: 1) Does risk management support the ambitions of the organization, ie how successfully does risk management support the organizational objectives and stakeholder expectations? 2) Does risk management safeguard the organization, ie how successfully does risk management protect the organization while it achieves its ambitions?

Two types of factors should be used to measure risk management outcomes:

■ *Perception measures.* These are the key risk management outcomes desired, which are not always quantitatively measurable.
■ *Performance indicators.* These are the operational measures used to monitor and understand the risk management outcomes, and predict and improve future risk management outcomes. They are measured quantitatively.

The EFQM Framework for Risk Management,[5] an established framework that is used to measure the results of risk management, contains reference lists of perception measures and performance indicators for risk management.

The European Foundation for Quality Management (EFQM) measures results through five perspectives, as part of its RADAR score logic (which is explained in Table 2.5.2). The enabler-related aspect of RADAR is explained in the 'RADAR scoring matrix' section.

Table 2.5.2 EFQM measurement of results

Measuring results	*Referring to*
Targets	Have targets been met?
Trends	Are trends positive or negative? Is good performance sustained?
Comparisons	How does performance compare externally practically when benchmarked against 'best in sector' or 'world-class' performance?
Causes	Is the cause–effect link between enablers and risk management results clear?
Scope	Are the correct perception measurements and performance indicators being measured?

Excellent results for risk management can be defined as follows:

■ There are positive trends and/or sustained good performance for all risk management results over at least three years.
■ All risk management targets are achieved.
■ There are favourable comparisons for all risk management results.
■ Cause and effect are visible for all risk management results.
■ Risk management results address all relevant areas and activities.

However, measuring the results of risk management is complicated by the following factors:

■ Key business objectives can be influenced by multiple influences. This means that key performance indicators (KPIs) might be a poor measure of risk management performance. For example, profit is nearly always a poor measure of risk management. If profit increases, it is generally impossible to determine to what degree this might be due to better risk management. This mistake is often made in the desire to align risk management with the organizational objectives. Only focused measures and indicators that are free from the influence of other factors should be selected.
■ Variability means that events might occur or not occur owing to chance, and makes infrequent events difficult to monitor. It is not always possible to determine with certainty whether improvements are due to better risk management or to luck. Fault trees can be used to provide a better understanding of the likelihood of occurrence of infrequent events.
■ Organizations get better at presenting information. For example, if a risk profile is rising it is not always clear whether this is due to more risk being faced or to people just getting better at risk assessment.
■ Increased risk might be accepted to take advantage of associated opportunities.

When complications make measurement difficult, greater emphasis is placed on assessment.

The measurement of risk management can be integrated with the main performance measurement activity of the organization. If balance scorecards are used, targets for risk management performance can be set alongside the other targets.

Assessment

In designing an assessment, there are two core decisions: 1) Which assessment approach will be used? 2) Which knowledge set will it be assessed against? Together with improvement activities, these form the three interlocking elements of any improvement programme, for, without an assessment, improvements would not be targeted properly. Also, without the appropriate knowledge, any assessment would be baseless. After all, what the desired practice is must be known before it can be compared with actual practice. This interaction is shown graphically in Figure 2.5.3.

Figure 2.5.3 Project Management Institute Organized Project Management Maturity Model (OMP3)

Project Management Institute Inc., 2003. Copyright and all rights reserved. Material from this publication has been reproduced with the permission of PMI.

The main assessment approaches are:

■ protocol assessment;
■ risk maturity chart assessment;
■ RADAR scoring matrix.

Each of these is described below.

Protocol assessment

Protocols are used to carry out detailed, thorough and investigative assessments of the actual situation.

Protocols contain questions that determine whether the desired practice is being carried out. These questions are allocated scores and the assessor is invited to score each question during interviews with appropriate people. The scores provide clear results on which to base sound decision making. Guidelines and auditor instructions are provided to help constituent scoring. Protocols can be used 'off the shelf' using standard knowledge sets or can be developed on a bespoke basis.

Protocol assessment for each element and sub-elements provides:

■ scores;
■ details of any noteworthy efforts;
■ details of any areas for improvement;
■ details of any non-conformities.

Figure 2.5.4 Mocked-up assessment protocol

Figure 2.5.4 shows the appearance of a page of an assessment protocol.

Typical high-level scores from a protocol assessment are shown graphically in Figure 2.5.5. The bars indicate the scores for each element. Displaying the results graphically can help the communication of results and show where investment would be best targeted.

Figure 2.5.5 shows the scores from both measurement and assessment. This integration is common as it shows the entire picture.

In Figure 2.5.5, it is clear that investment in 'Strategy and policy' development is a priority. Resources could be directed from excessive expenditure on developing 'Partnership and resources', which exceeds the target set.

If questions are tagged, it is possible using software to generate protocols for an integrated assessment. For example, software can be used to generate a protocol that has all the questions tagged for risk management or ISO 9001. Integration avoids the need to repeat the asking of questions that are duplicated between different protocols, thereby minimizing the assessment burden.

Protocol assessments, being based on detailed evidence, are usually carried out when compliant. For example, protocols developed using the structure of the EFQM Framework for Risk Management[6] (see Figure 2.5.6) can be used to assess compliance with the revised Turnbull Guidance. The revised Turnbull Guidance requires that organizations carry out assessments of their system of internal control to determine if it is effective and as approved by the board. The knowledge for Turnbull compliance

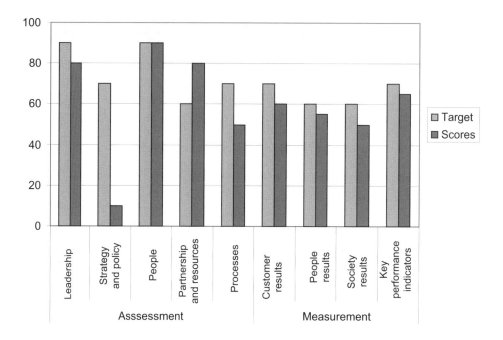

Figure 2.5.5   Example of high-level scores from a protocol assessment (and measurement)

can also be taken from the EFQM Framework for Risk Management, supplemented by questions from the appendix of the revised Turnbull Guidance.

Another example of an industry commonly using integrated protocol assessment is the major hazard industry. They regularly undertake assessments of their Health and Safety European Quality (HSEQ) management systems. Major incidents in such industries can result in multiple fatalities, major environmental pollution, significant repair and clean-up costs, irreparable reputation damage and the end of an organization's existence.

Risk maturity chart assessment

Risk maturity charts allocate capabilities for each element of the management system to a level of maturity. The charts usually read upwards from the bottom, ticking off the basic capabilities and stopping to score when the capabilities are no longer achieved.

Assessments using risk maturity charts are usually made during a dedicated workshop, although assessments can also be made as part of interviews. Unlike protocol assessments, however, risk maturity charts are scored based on perception (rather than evidence) and so are quicker to perform. Assessment workshops usually have a duration of a day.

Figure 2.5.7 is an example of a risk maturity chart based on the EFQM Framework for Risk Management.

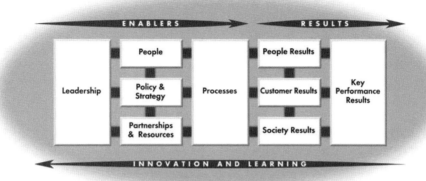

Note: The EFQM Excellence Model is a registered trademark of EFQM

Figure 2.5.6   The EFQM Excellence Model

As for protocol assessments, the scores from the use of risk maturity charts can be shown graphically as in Figure 2.5.8, which presents scores from a risk maturity assessment with the knowledge of the isrs7 HSEQ management system. The shaded bars show the average score rates of each process and the standard deviation shows the spread of opinion.

RADAR scoring matrix

This approach is the evaluation method used to score the European Quality award applications. RADAR stands for 'Results', 'Approach', 'Deploy', 'Assessment' and 'Review'. The first 'R' is for performance measurement. The remaining 'ADAR' is used for assessment.

The 'ADAR' is a continuous improvement loop. By scoring against each part of this loop, for each part of the management system, a comprehensive assessment is achieved.

With the RADAR scoring matrix (see Table 2.5.3), scores are given for the attributes of each of the 'ADAR' parts, for each part of the management system. Scores can be either quartiles or a percentage. Scores are only given when evidence can be provided to back up achievements. RADAR scoring matrices can be obtained from the EFQM (www.efqm.com).

The RADAR scoring matrix is scored against a set of knowledge that states what 'may be excellence'. This knowledge is not a prescriptive list but rather offers guidance to the assessor.

	Leadership	Policy and Strategy	People	Partnerships and Resources	Processes	Customer Results	People Results	Society Results	Key Performance Results
Level 5 ☐ Excellent capability established									
Level 4 ☐ Embedding and improving									
Level 3 ☐ Implementation completed in key areas									
Level 2 ☐ Implementation planned									
Level 1 ☐ Awareness/ understanding									

Figure 2.5.7 Example of a risk maturity chart

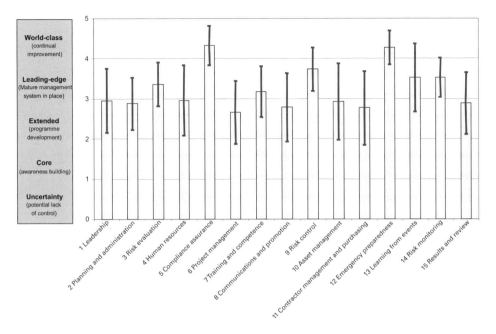

Figure 2.5.8   Example of risk maturity chart (isrs7) assessment results

Table 2.5.3   The RADAR scoring matrix

Element	Attributes
Approach	Sound Integrated
Deployment	Implemented Systematic
Assessment	Measurement
Review	Learning Improvement

Assessment programmes

For an organization to attain any real benefit from assessments they must be carried out in a planned systematic manner.

Assessment programmes/plans/schedules must be designed to suit the objectives of the organization and what it wants to achieve by the assessment process. Figure 2.5.9 shows the generic process flow for an assessment programme.

When considering the design of the assessment programme the following criteria must be considered:

- the complexity of the area, process or activity to be assessed;
- its importance to the organization;
- its size;
- previous assessment performance (if available);
- its impact on the organization if it goes out of control.

From the criteria above the frequency and depth of assessment are established. It could be decided, for example, to carry out small but frequent assessments by dividing the assessment up into sections or by focusing on the elements of the management system separately. Over a period of time the whole system (all elements) is assessed. Alternatively it could be decided to undertake a single comprehensive assessment once every one to two years.

The assessment programme must also take into account the assessor competency required to carry out the assessment, to ensure meaningful results, as well as the independence of the assessors to the area or process being assessed.

As time goes by, and with more assessment performance evidence available, the assessment programme should be changed based on the evidence obtained during the assessments. Whoever is responsible for the running of the assessment programme

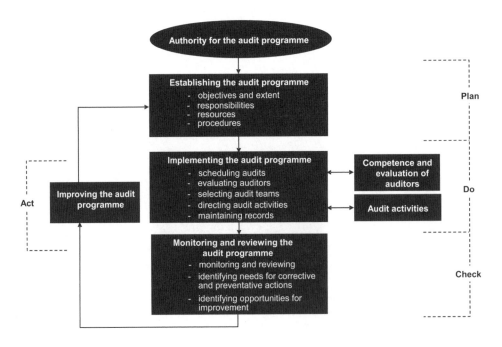

Note: ISO 19011: International Standards Organisation (2003), *Guidelines for Quality and/or Environmental Management Systems Auditing.*

Figure 2.5.9 Illustration of the process flow for the management of an audit programme (ISO 19011)

should evaluate each report and the associated findings. This person should look for systemic problems with potentially wider-ranging impact than would be seen during the actual assessment, whilst remembering that any assessment is a sampling exercise that may not always reveal the entire picture.

Assessor rotation is very important to ensure that complacency does not become an issue.

Summary

All management systems should be measured and assessed on a regular basis. Without this, management is managing by perception alone. If the management system is not working effectively or not as the board has approved, this needs to be rectified.

An assessment provides a vehicle and an opportunity for an organization to discover clearly its strengths and areas for improvement, from which improvement recommendations can be made. Improvements programmes that are designed without a true knowledge of the situation will not be effective. Assessments also determine if management systems are compliant with regulations, codes and laws.

Those wishing to carry out an assessment have two key decisions to make: what assessment approach should be used and which knowledge set will it be assessed against? If an inappropriate approach is selected, or if what is good practice is not known, the assessment will be poor. Assessments should ideally not be one-offs, but part of a coordinated assessment programme.

Notes

1. Financial Reporting Council (2004), *Internal Control: Guidance for directors on the Combined Code*, FRC, London.
2. Moullin, M (2004), Eight essentials of performance measurement, *International Journal of Health Care Quality Assurance*, **17** (3), pp 110–12.
3. Hoyle, D and Thompson, J (2001) *ISO 9000:2000 Auditor Questions: A real change in direction.*
4. Hopkin, P (2005) Risk assurance management standard.
5. EFQM and DNV (2005) EFQM Framework for Risk Management.

Keeping your reputation safe from risk

Kevin Taylor, Companycare Communications

Heritage can count for (almost) nothing

In modern business, brand and reputation count for an awful lot. As a result, companies spend serious amounts of income in an attempt to create brand power and to win the hearts and minds of their target audience. But, and this has never been more true, reputations that take a lifetime to build can be destroyed virtually at a stroke.

Of course, you don't have to look that far back to the days when a company's reputation was grounded on something rather more substantial, and less prone to the whims of fashion and a sometimes hostile media, than is the case for many of today's brands. Not too long ago, all the most famous names in business, the ones you implicitly trusted, were actually inventors: people you could associate with great achievements. Inventors like Ford, Marconi, Edison and Bell all helped create powerful companies trading on those achievements.

And when your invention has successfully changed the world, then maybe it's pretty hard to damage your reputation. But even in those very earliest days, Mr Ford did have to contend with the danger that his invention created.

However, times change and the speed with which a household name can now be built, put at risk and destroyed is quite breathtaking. And nobody is immune. Even those names with a heritage of achievement now need to invest both financially and intellectually to protect their brand and their reputation – as the Kodak case study so aptly demonstrates.

The power of the brand

Indeed, many of today's most powerful brands and companies have created their global success through the excellence and force of their marketing muscle. Yes, the product has to stand the test of the customer experience, but the brand creates desire and engenders the trust of the consumer.

In the sports and leisure industry, for example, Nike is a remarkable example of a company that grew from very small beginnings to a global success story in a remarkably short time. Nike is a company that is built on the strengths of its design and marketing expertise. Its advertising and public relations panache is second to none and connects it directly to its target audience in a way much admired, much copied, but rarely bettered.

But brand power also exists in the B2B world and can be just as powerful. Remember the old adage – nobody ever got fired for buying IBM; that is long-term brand power at work in the B2B environment.

However, what happens when a crisis hits a brand or a company? How do successful companies deal with the situation and move on without damaging the brand?

We all know the story of how the high street retail jeweller Gerald Ratner derided his own products at a 'private' city luncheon and subsequently found his comments all over the UK national media. Rather famously, Ratner reportedly called his own products 'crap' and at a stroke devalued the 'precious gift' experience at the heart of jewellery purchasing and caused shoppers all over the country to turn on their heels and head for another store.

Given the strength of the coverage and the severe nature of the crime, it is hard to know what his poor beleaguered PR adviser could have done to clear up the mess – the situation was immediately out of control. What is certain is that the name Ratner no longer features on Britain's high streets and that the brand was the victim of corporate reputation homicide. In fact, Ratner moved on by changing the names of all the stores and creating new high street names without the stigma of the 'crap' comment.

So – apart from changing your name or applying a gag to your loose-lipped chairman, as well as making sure you keep him away from the lunchtime Rioja – how do you cope with a risk to your reputation and the need to protect your brand from harm whatever the circumstances? And how do you cope with the bad times when they inevitably occur?

Preparation

As with many remedies, the secret is in the preventative actions you take beforehand, as well as the treatments you apply at the time. And the process starts some time before the crisis and the threat ever occur.

It begins with media and message training for anyone who could be a company spokesperson. And it's simply not good enough to test someone with a few easy lobbed questions. Do the process properly, work out the responses to the difficult questions and – this is really important – all the easy ones and then rehearse their delivery. Capture the responses on video and play it back. Let them see all their foibles of body language and performance and then work on establishing a persona and a method that allows them to feel comfortable and deliver on message, every time.

Formal presentations and media interviews rely on the same basic principle; the person giving the performance needs to be comfortable, confident and in control. If you are in charge of your company's brand reputation, your job is to ensure your spokesperson meets those basic criteria.

For example, you will be amazed how many senior executives of well-established companies trip up when asked to give the two-minute elevator pitch about their own company. Their grasp of the big picture is so complete, so all-embracing, that they find the focus required for a quick but wide-ranging answer to be beyond them.

CEOs of smaller companies, well versed through endless fund-raising meetings with venture capital companies, are much more adept at this process. The reason is simple – unless they can get that right they will not get funding and their project will be stillborn. You need credible, believable spokespeople who are calm under pressure and remain focused: people who can also distil the information required down to a very few salient points.

Once you have identified your 'go to' spokespeople, stick with them. If the chairman or CEO is not one of them, either keep him or her away from the front line or always pair him or her with one of your most accomplished performers. The chairman or CEO will soon pick up the process or go with the flow. Every company needs a drum beater, but it does not have to be the person at the very top.

Process

Having a good performer is one thing. Making sure you handle the situations as they occur is another. Putting process at the heart of the organization and ensuring consistency of response are essential if you are to ensure your PR effort – both proactive and reactive – supports and promotes your brand and its reputation.

A single point of contact for media enquiries is the start, ideally in-house and well known to your influential media. But every switchboard in every facility or every branch office should know one thing for certain – any journalist, calling at any time and asking for any person gets put through to the press office or media centre or whatever you choose to call your channel to the outside world.

If you are using a PR consultancy, they too will get calls. But they too should go to the centre that handles the process. Yes, you will need their help and advice and they can act as a gateway back to the media, but you must control the process internally.

And here's another rule for you. Answer every media question – every single one.

Always respond on time, within deadlines and with as much information as you can release. Offer interviews wherever possible. Establish a relationship with your key media – whether that is a reporter on the local weekly newspaper or a business editor on a national daily. Establish a relationship that says you, as individuals and as a company, are respectful, friendly, helpful and open. Should something go badly wrong, the fact that you have always treated the press well will come back and reward you at your time of greatest need.

Your willingness to help when journalists want something will also reward you when you want something from them in a positive way. When you have a good news story to promote, your past cooperation will ease the way. If your reputation is that you are simply a barrier to the media and never a help, then don't be surprised if your good stories end up in the 'recycling bin'.

There's another, much bigger, problem if all you are is a barrier to media enquiries and never a help. Media will stop coming to you. They will find another way into your company – despite your best efforts – and they will find a person who is prepared to talk. Almost certainly that will not be your preferred media spokesperson and it will almost certainly be someone who gives good insights to the company that you would rather were kept quiet but will keep appearing and be attributed to 'sources inside the company'.

So, if you do not control the simple route of enquiry between the media and the company, and also ensure that it is proactive and helpful at all times, then you are simply storing up trouble.

The difference is easy to explain. A good relationship with the media can minimize the impact of any given negative situation. A bad relationship can do the opposite and turn your molehill into a mountain.

Practice

The product recall is an excellent example of a situation where a company with good media handling skills can win the press over and manage a product recall with surprisingly little in the way of negative media comment.

In 2006, faults in some Sony laptop batteries caused problems not just for Sony but also for Dell and IBM/Lenovo who were using Sony battery packs. But the openness of the media handling, and the willingness of the companies to talk, coupled with superb technical support, minimized the negative impact.

This chapter was written on an IBM/Lenovo laptop potentially affected by the recall. With ready-to-hand support and guidance I was able to run a one-minute check on the machine, which then switched me to a website with advice about the installed battery and the next steps. Perfect customer care, and a crisis turned into a glowing reference.

Staying with the computer industry, back in 1994 we had the case of the Intel Pentium processor and the 'mathematical' error or flaw in the chipset, which if not actually denied at first was certainly disregarded. Any company that at first seeks to protect its reputation by denying its problems or attempting to minimize the risk by hiding the full truth puts its reputation at even greater risk when the reality is eventually and inevitably revealed.

Intel's supremacy in the market and the strength of its product enabled it to recover from the blip to its reputation that the fault and – more importantly – the initial cover-up had caused. It is how you react to the challenges that face your reputation that determine whether you survive whole or impaired. Intel realized in time the need to face up to the situation and then dealt with the consequences admirably and properly.

That is one reason why it was able to recover and continue to go from strength to strength. But that initial hesitancy also helped its competitors gain a foothold in the marketplace and broke a circle of trust with some of its key customers.

The strongest brands can come through the toughest situations with their reputation intact and undamaged – if they follow the rules and stay true to their company and brand values.

Case study: Kodak comes through with flying colours

George Eastman Kodak was one of the pioneers of photography and, in particular, family photography. In the world of photography the Kodak name is rightly revered and respected. But one simple mistake in an internet advert during the Christmas holidays put the company's family reputation at risk.

An advert for one of the company's digital cameras with a retail price tag of around £400 was mistakenly published on the internet for just £99. The mistake was quickly spotted and the advert taken down, but in the meantime hundreds of people took advantage of the mistake and ordered the bargain online – many of them dealers who recognized the price mistake and took quick advantage.

All of these orders were acknowledged by automatic e-mail response. However, legal advice was that this e-mail acknowledgement did not constitute a contract – just acknowledgement of a request for a product – and what's more the offer to sell the product could be withdrawn. In other words, legally, Kodak did not have to honour the sale.

With something like 500 orders for the camera, honouring the offer was the equivalent of writing off close to a quarter of a million dollars. Legal advice, and the initial realities of business, said that the offer to sale should be withdrawn.

The marketing team, and their PR consultancy, thought differently, however. In fact, through their constant monitoring of internet forums, they were soon able to advise management that the would-be purchasers were now beginning to get organized. A concerted media campaign was about to break with individuals agreeing, in online forums, to write letters and make phone calls to a sympathetic national media. The BBC's consumer *Watchdog* programme and the tabloid media were singled out for particular attention, and the threat to Kodak's reputation and brand were real and imminent.

This monitoring of the situation and the understanding of the wider commercial climate enabled the guardians of the brand to press their advice and win the day against the perceived legal position.

The result was that, although the *Watchdog* programme and the tabloids did cover the story, their take on it quickly changed. In fact, Kodak's reaction and decision to honour the mistake attracted widespread praise on air, in the tabloid press and in the specialist media.

By respecting and protecting the brand and its family values, Kodak was actually able to enhance its reputation. And if companies are judged on what they do when faced with a business and moral dilemma, Kodak passed with flying colours.

Three golden rules of reputation protection

■ *Honesty is the only policy.* Start with the truth and then work things out. Distortion is never the best policy, and owning up is better than covering up.
■ *Consistency through good and bad times.* Openness with the media when they are chasing you will pay dividends in all situations.
■ *Preparation is the key.* Have a crisis plan. Know your chain of command and who the best spokespeople are in a crisis situation.

3

Risk Issues in Operational Management

Understanding and managing operational risk exposures

David Breden, HSBC Operational Risk Consultancy

Introduction

Operational risk management has become a major topic of debate and discussion in the financial services industry in recent years. Major loss events have caused the downfall of historic financial institutions such as Barings – and the story of those events has made its way into popular culture by way of the film and the various books written by and about the perpetrator of those events, Nick Leeson. Such is the impact of such events that the world's regulatory authorities have begun to introduce regulation to protect financial markets and clients from the risk of bank failure as a result of operational errors. As I write, the Financial Services Authority in the UK is moving ahead with regulation based on European Union directives that will oblige financial institutions in Europe to hold capital in reserve to protect against the risk posed by operational risk. Other major corporate failings (eg Enron and WorldCom) have led US regulators to introduce Sarbanes–Oxley legislation to ensure that robust controls are in place to protect the integrity of financial statements.

Putting your risk management needs at the centre of our world.

At HSBC Insurance Brokers we strive to provide our clients with the confidence and certainty to pursue their objectives.
As one of the largest insurance broking organisations in the world HSBC Insurance Brokers has the depth of knowledge to analyse complex situations from multiple perspectives and develop innovative solutions that proactively meet the specific needs of our clients.
The Intelligent Alternative

Web: www.insurancebrokers.hsbc.com
Email: insurancebrokers@hsbc.com
Tel: +44 (0)20 7661 2511

With all this activity, it is tempting to assume that operational risk is a new phenomenon, but in truth this is not the case. The military, pharmaceutical companies, safety-critical industries and construction companies have all developed procedures to ensure that they manage their operational risk exposures successfully – and protect their clients, their personnel and the general public whose lives may be threatened should they fail. The financial world has also always managed operational exposures. In simpler times the signs of their actions were visible in the shape of security screens around cashiers, complex and extensive physical security, safes and strongboxes; and business managers tended to manage operational risk reactively, putting in place measures to prevent the repetition of risks.

In today's market, however, all industries are confronted with rapidly changing worldwide markets, meaning that flaws in systems, errors, omissions, frauds and other failures can be exploited continuously and with a speed that makes reactive management of risk ineffective and dangerous.

The nature of operational risk

Operational risk can be defined as: 'The risk of loss resulting from inadequate or failed internal processes, people and systems or from external events.'[1]

This definition covers a very wide range of diverse risks. We start with process failures, where a breakdown in the way basic tasks are performed leads to loss or has a negative effect on clients, staff or the public image. An example of such a risk might be the failure of airport security screening to detect the box cutters smuggled on to aeroplanes on 11 September 2001.

Closely connected with process failure are the failings associated with people. Human error is a factor in many operational events. We must add to this the risk of staff members acting dishonestly or deliberately ignoring or contravening the procedures laid down for carrying out a prescribed task. We must also consider the risk of employees going on strike or of key staff members leaving to join a competitor.

The next category to consider relates to the all-pervasive computer systems on which most businesses have come to rely. Fortunately, such systems tend to be reliable, for a feature of the modern world is that businesses have automated activities to manufacture more product or serve more customers. Few businesses would be able to revert to obsolete manual procedures and continue to maintain business levels if widespread system failure made this necessary.

The final category of operational risk relates to external threats caused by either natural events such as fire, flood or earthquake or malicious external attack such as the introduction of viruses into computer systems, hacking or fraud.

The characteristics of operational risk

The management of such a wide variety of risks presents a considerable challenge to business managers. Indeed, the characteristics of operational risk make this challenge even greater.

Context dependency

Operational risk is highly context-dependent. Businesses operating in different locations will have different risk profiles. Business premises in Holland will be exposed to flooding caused by rising sea levels, whilst a building in Mexico City, for example, is unlikely to flood, but will have a high exposure to the risk of earthquake. Unfortunately, context dependency extends much further than this. If managers look at the risks associated with the people they employ, they will be aware that the performance and reliability of every employee will be affected by events both within and outside the firm. A staff member with personal problems is likely to be distracted from his or her work and will be more error-prone than usual. If, as is very possible, a business manager is unaware of these problems, how can the risk be managed proactively?

The risk portfolio

The risk portfolio for operational risk is not limited. It is impossible to define with certainty the range of process failures or of human errors that may occur in a business. This feature can be seen most clearly in the continually evolving range of external threats that businesses face. As our businesses change and use new channels, so the risk of external attack changes. The internet has brought new opportunities for fraudsters that are being exploited with enthusiasm and are creating a wide range of possibilities associated with identity theft that would not have figured in a risk manager's list of concerns a few years ago. An interesting anecdote concerns the introduction of Chip and PIN credit and debit cards in UK banks recently. The measure was designed to make card fraud more difficult, but the immediate effect was that fraud increased as criminal gangs intercepted replacement cards issued by banks and sent through the post. We must anticipate that this trend will continue as the pace of change in delivery channels continues.

The size of exposures

The size of potential exposures to operational risk is beset with uncertainty. A simple keying error such as the addition of a zero to the amount of a £10 payment may cause insignificant loss. If, however, that additional zero is added to a more significant transaction, then the loss will be considerably greater. An identical error can give rise to a wide range of loss amounts. Therefore, it is unwise to ignore a small loss simply because of its size. It is preferable to explore the possibility that the loss could be more severe in other circumstances in the future.

Lack of data

Fortunately, most firms that remain in business do not suffer large volumes of significant events, but this also means that they are unable to draw on a full range of experience of all types of operational risk. This does underline the fact that firms cannot rely on a reactive management style. When a serious event occurs, it is likely to be unexpected, and if the firm has not explored a range of potential risks – that goes beyond those risks that have been experienced – then its management will be unprepared to manage the event.

Location of risk

Operational risk pervades all businesses. The only way to avoid operational risk is to close the doors of our premises, dismiss all personnel (whilst avoiding wrongful dismissal claims!) and cease all trading. If the choice is made to stay in business, then we need to recognize that every employee, from the security guard at the entrance of our premises to the chairman on the top floor, represents a risk and has a role to play in managing operational risk exposures.

Managing operational risk

Given the wide range of risks to be managed, and the unpredictability and uncertainty that surround these risks, the importance of building a proactive risk management structure capable of reaching all parts of the business is clear.

Policies, procedures and tolerance

As with all strategic issues, an operational risk framework will require leadership from the board and senior management. Without this leadership no operational risk framework can be successful.

The board will need to understand the key operational risk exposures that the business is subject to, and will need to reach a decision as to their attitude to such exposures. In bald terms they will need to weigh the gravity of the risk exposures that the business faces against the cost of managing, controlling or transferring those risks. They may decide that considerations of profitability mean that certain risks will be accepted as a cost of doing business and that, if these risks occur, the firm will have to bear the consequences regardless of their potential severity. Other boards will decide that risks must be controlled, accepting that this will impact on the bottom line.

In reaching their decision, the board will need to bear in mind the nature of their business and the consequences of error. As an example, an error committed by an airline pilot may lead to the death of passengers, whilst an error by a baggage handler may subject passengers to the inconvenience of a lost suitcase – certainly a less severe outcome. It is to be expected that policy will control the actions of the pilot with greater attention than those of the baggage handler. The board is also likely to be more tolerant of staff error than of staff fraud.

It will then be the responsibility of senior management to create procedures to implement the policy decisions throughout the company and to create a function responsible for the management of operational risk. This body should be independent of business areas to ensure that potential business/risk management conflicts are resolved by an independent party able to evaluate any issue with regard to the established policy.

Risk identification and assessment

Perhaps the most important element of any risk management process is the risk identification process. Failure to identify a risk will certainly mean that no action is taken to manage that risk.

The process for identifying operational risk will need to draw on a number of sources of information. The past experience of the company will be a key element but, as indicated earlier, this will need to be supplemented by other sources of information. These will include the experience of other players in the market (on the basis that it is cheaper to learn from the mistakes of others than your own), performance indicators from the business itself and changes in the environment. Most importantly, if the firm wishes to create a forward-looking operational risk framework, it will need to devise a way of accessing the knowledge of those with the closest working knowledge of operations, the staff.

Two main methodologies exist to access this knowledge: risk self-assessment and risk workshops.

A self-assessment process will enable the firm to reach out to all business units and seek their opinions on the main threats that the business faces. Most firms will provide staff with a checklist of key risk types, and will ask employees to evaluate exposure to these risks in terms of the probability of the event occurring and the maximum impact of the event if it should occur. It is good practice to ensure that employees do not think only in terms of monetary impact, but also take into account other factors such as the potential impact on customer service, on staff or on media attitude – all of which will have an effect on the business. Once the probability and impact of events have been evaluated, then the process will often be completed by an evaluation of the effectiveness of controls. If properly implemented, self-assessment should identify not only the expected risks within the business, but also potential areas of concern relating to weaknesses in processes, systems and products.

Risk workshops require more time and effort but have the advantage of being interactive and, if an experienced facilitator is used, may be more incisive. The aim will be to extract the same information as the self-assessment, but the facilitator will have prepared by looking at internal loss, incident and performance experience, and market experience so that key members of the unit staff can be challenged in their responses and assumptions.

Management and control

Once information has been extracted, then the challenge is to ensure that key risks and exposures are properly controlled.

In principle, management will need to decide whether the risks that have been identified are to be accepted, controlled or transferred in accordance with the underlying board policy. If a specific risk cannot be brought within acceptable limits then consideration must be given to withdrawing from the activity and avoiding the risk completely.

It is likely that the correct treatment will be guided by a scoring grid that will focus attention on potentially severe risks where controls are weak. Action plans can then be agreed to enhance controls or to minimize risk exposures.

The process will also highlight potentially high risks where strong controls are in place. All staff should be made aware of the importance of the controls and the impact if these controls fail.

Monitoring exposures

If operational risk exposures are constantly changing, then it is vital that we monitor these exposures. An operational loss database is a fundamental tool in this process. Such a database will contain information about internal operational losses and near misses.[2]

The database will contain full information on the circumstances and causes of the loss, the impact, the remedial action taken and the tracking of the recovery process. Analysis of trends and development of alternative scenarios, based on the actual event, will assist the firm in developing protective measures for the future.

A further method of monitoring exposures is to observe key risk indicators. These are performance measures that the business believes are indicative of higher levels of risk. Such measures might be higher levels of customer complaint, staff turnover or system downtime. Volumes may also be indicative of increased risk, as will higher levels of activity in volatile marketplaces. The objective is to identify higher levels of risk as they occur so that management can take action to prevent perceived levels of higher risk becoming tangible loss.

Transferring exposures

Many firms seek to transfer unacceptable exposures away from the firm, and the main technique for achieving this aim is to use the insurance market. It is possible to ensure a wide range of operational risks in the insurance market. In order to make the purchase of insurance effective, it is important to have due regard for the definition or risk tolerance and the risk identification and assessment process. Such an exercise will provide clear guidance on the limits to be insured and the appropriate level of deductibles.

It is also sometimes stated that outsourcing is an acceptable method for transferring risk. However, this is an error because, although it is possible to outsource an activity, the risk will remain within the business. The clearest illustration of this fact is that an error or omission by the service provider will impact on your clients. Regardless of any recourse you may have to the service provider, you will have to deal with the protests and issues raised by your clients and you will be exposed to the consequent loss of business. This means that, when activities are outsourced, the service level agreement must demand the same levels of performance as would be expected internally and must allow similar levels of monitoring and control.

Planning for contingencies

Detailed business continuity and contingency plans are the final element in a basic operational risk management framework. When a major event occurs, the presence of tested plans to deal with an emergency situation will provide added confidence that staff will respond promptly in a desired manner to guarantee minimal interruption to business.

Conclusion

Operational risk management is beset with the uncertainty of what events might occur and how serious their effect might be. In order to manage this uncertainty it is important for us to understand our business fully and to have identified potential scenarios that might affect our business.

This activity will enable business managers to use a basic framework to monitor and control exposures and to take action to manage the biggest potential threats to the business armed with the knowledge of the potential costs and benefits of their actions.

The views expressed in this article are the author's personal views and do not necessarily represent the views of the HSBC Group.

Notes

1. Basel Committee on Banking Supervision (2004) *International Convergence of Capital Measurement and Capital Standards: A revised framework*, June, Bank for International Settlements, Basel.
2. A near miss can be defined as an event where all normal controls have failed but the issue has been resolved without loss to the firm.

Origins of risk in the supply chain

Helen Alder, Chartered Institute of Purchasing and Supply (CIPS)

Whether it was the threat of avian flu, surges in energy prices, British Airways' debacle with its catering supplier or bra wars, recent events have laid bare the potential for risk in today's global and complex supply chains.

Despite an increase in awareness of the fragility and uncertainty of supply, strategies to deal with it are lagging behind. According to a 2005 Aberdeen Group benchmark study, more than three-quarters of the 180 global companies interviewed expected supply outages and disruptions to increase over the next three years. But fewer than half had procedures or systems to assess and respond to such risks.

Recent research by Cranfield University with the Chartered Institute of Purchasing and Supply (CIPS), AMR Research and supply chain consultants State of Flux all reaffirm this lack of strategic approach in supply risk management – an alarming state of affairs when risks in this environment are increasing.

In its 2005 *Supply Risk Management Benchmark Report*, Aberdeen groups risks into four areas:

- supply market risks;
- supplier risks;

■ regulatory risks;
■ supply strategy risks.

Factors that can affect supply markets include constraints in supply; increasing costs of commodities, energy or transport; threats from natural disasters and terrorist attacks; and delivery delays.

The number of risks that suppliers pose to buying organizations is manifold and can come as a result of anything from their profitability to their compliance with laws and ethical codes, production capacity, lead times and service levels.

A host of new regulatory requirements present additional considerations for purchasing and supply professionals. For US-listed companies and their suppliers, there is US corporate governance legislation such as Sarbanes–Oxley, as well as the revision of civil contingencies provisions (Civil Contingencies Act 2004), and the British Standard for business continuity (PAS 56 2003) in the UK. Regulation for environmentally responsible products such as WEEE and RoHS also requires companies to assess their supply chains more thoroughly.

Procurement 'best practices' that promise increased efficiencies and lower costs have also, unfortunately, brought with them risks. Low-cost country sourcing leads to longer lead times, threats of supply disruptions, security tariffs and currency issues. Outsourcing reduces visibility of supplier performance. And the damage to brand reputation sustained as a result of using suppliers with unethical employment practices has continued to hit the headlines over the past few years.

Practices such as supply base rationalization, just-in-time and lean principles have also made the supply chain more vulnerable to disruption. With less inventory in the supply chain, or fewer suppliers to call from, the impact of a supplier going to the wall in an earthquake, or even the impact of a late delivery, can have mighty consequences.

Implications of risk

As companies continue to rely on ever more complex and global supply chains, these risks will continue to increase. More than three-quarters of companies interviewed by Aberdeen envisaged an increase in risks over the next three years.

It is also likely that the implications of these risks will spread further than the domain of purchasing and supply. Seventy-nine per cent of the purchasing executives interviewed in the Aberdeen research thought supply outages would have an impact on customer relations, and 75 per cent envisaged an impact on company earnings and 73 per cent an impact on time-to-market cycles. Also, 56 per cent thought brand perception would take a hit.

With supply chain risk increasing and threatening a wider area of the business, its management is likely to emerge as a key business discipline and an important measure of competitiveness for business. Currently, however, progress towards a strategic approach to supply risk management is at an early stage.

The state of play

According to the Chartered Management Institute's (CMI's) 2006 *Business Continuity Management Survey*, 77 per cent of the 1,150 managers interviewed believe business continuity is viewed as important by their senior management teams. However, less than half say their organization has a business continuity plan (BCP) in place.

Aberdeen found that 55 per cent of enterprises benchmarked had no formal supply risk strategy in place and nearly half of companies said their companies almost always took a reactive approach to supply risk management once an issue had arisen.

Nearly one in five respondents of Cranfield University and CIPS's *Survey of Risk Management in UK Purchasing and Supply* (2005) reported that no major review of purchasing and supply risks had ever been undertaken to their knowledge.

The research also demonstrated that the high-profile coverage of security issues in the media was still having little impact on purchasing and supply management. Instead, factors creating concern revolved around internal business issues such as customer requirements and changes to business strategy.

Research by State of Flux provides further evidence of an insular approach to supply risk management. Of the European and US companies interviewed, more than half admitted to not having a bird flu risk management plan in place. And only one in five said they had consulted specialists in risk prevention. Instead, almost three-quarters were going to the media for information. And when the story stopped hitting the front pages, they mistakenly thought the risk had gone away.

'I don't think there is much use of the tools and intellectual capability in this space', says Alan Day, MD of State of Flux, who thinks purchasers should work with experts for guidance on risk. As an example, they work with insurance brokers that can provide risk statistics and build up probability cases of events such as earthquakes in Japan and inform them of what that would do to a supply chain.

Tackling supply chain risk

Assessing risk

One of the main reasons for this lack of preparedness, the Aberdeen research found, was a lack of formal metrics or systems to measure risks. And at the heart of any successful supply risk management strategy is assessment of the risk potential in the supply chain.

As AMR Research puts it: 'a supply chain risk assessment balances the probability of demand, the likelihood of reliable supply, the most effective allocation of resources, the probability of success of new product introductions, market conditions, and the opportunity costs of alternative decision paths' (AMR Research, *Supply Chain Risk Management Strategies*, Part I, 2005).

Businesses must consider where the risk is going to come from. Is it an internal risk, an external business risk or a risk in the supply chain? Is it from suppliers that are managed day in, day out, or is it from smaller suppliers at arm's length? What sort of risk is it? Is it a business continuity risk or a brand risk?

Organizations must consider all points throughout the supply chain where risk could occur and consider the potential impact of changes in cost, quality or availability of commodities, raw materials, energy and supplies. Key risk indicators to be aware of could include purchases that come from a single source, originate in potentially unstable countries or pass through vulnerable transportation bottlenecks. Supply risks that come as a result of political, tariff or weather issues should be built into costing models and decisions.

Key suppliers and commodities, or sources that present the highest risk, should be made subject to risk audits.

Once key risk areas have been defined and analysed, the organization can begin to develop contingency plans and start to remove risks from the supply chain.

Sourcing methods that balance performance and risk

Another key approach is to balance the demands of cost, efficiency and risk in the supply chain. Organizations may not want to sacrifice some of the cost benefits of practices such as just-in-time or low-cost country sourcing so will need to balance these systems against the risks they present.

This approach could involve monitoring dynamics in supply markets and adjusting the supply mix to fit, or using a mix of low-cost country and near-shore sources to ensure an element of predictable, shorter lead times and continual availability in the supply mix. Transportation routes can be changed to adapt to seasonal weather patterns such as hurricane seasons, and a buying strategy could lock in price for commodities where there is a high potential for cost increases.

Further tactics for building in flexibility and resilience include moving production among plants; using interchangeable, generic and fewer commodity parts; and employing tactics such as postponement. This is where the manufacturing process starts by making a generic product (such as a simple white T-shirt) that is differentiated into a specific end product (eg dyed according to a season's preference) as late as possible in the supply chain to enable production to cope with supply and demand uncertainties.

Communication with suppliers

For maximum impact, a supply risk management strategy must also be communicated with suppliers. And companies are also advised to collaborate with suppliers to overcome risks further.

The CMI's survey found that only 1 in 10 businesses with business continuity plans bothered to share them with suppliers. Further to this, only 7 per cent required all suppliers to have a plan and 7 per cent required it from outsource partners. (The CMI therefore suggested that purchasing offers a powerful lever for ensuring the adoption of risk management strategies across the supply chain if it required key suppliers and partners to have BCPs.)

Strong relations with suppliers can also have a positive impact on risk management. The risk of weak relationships was highlighted in the summer of 2005 when British

Airways operations at Heathrow Airport came to a standstill when ground workers staged a sympathy strike with laid-off workers at its core catering supplier, Gate Gourmet. A closer relationship with Gate Gourmet might have given BA more insight into how the company would react to its actions and the knock-on effect to its workers.

Buying organizations might also be required to help suppliers develop capabilities, remove unnecessary costs and reduce risk from the supply chain. 'Supplier improvement initiatives are critical in industries with sub-assemblies and products that are highly complex and are only available from a limited number of potential suppliers', said the Aberdeen report.

But the decision to collaborate with suppliers should not be taken lightly, say Timothy Mould and Edwin Starr from Accenture in *Supply Chain: Dangerous Liaisons* (2000). 'Some relationships are dangerous, others waste time and money, and only a few justify taking the risks demanded by fully integrated collaboration.' Collaboration, they explain, demands not only a commitment of resources but also the sharing of proprietary information. So while in some markets suppliers deserve attention and consideration, in others they may provide goods and services that require no more cooperation beyond timely payment of the invoice. In these situations there is no point in investing more than is necessary in the supplier relationship.

Technology

Aberdeen envisages leading solutions for investment for risk management within the next year to be for supplier performance management (SPM), spend data cleansing and analysis, and supplier and supply market intelligence services.

Web-based SPM systems allow organizations to track key business performance metrics of suppliers of everything from lead times to service levels, and to collaborate with suppliers to improve performance.

Supplier assessment services can provide third-party information on the financial, business and operational performance of suppliers, and supply market intelligence assesses future trends for commodities in both first and sub-tier suppliers.

Spending analysis solutions collect and analyse spend data and other vendor data to enable demand, supply and inventory planning and sourcing optimization.

However, there is evidence that few companies have yet grasped the true potential of technology to improve supplier quality, lead times and on-time delivery, and to reduce supplier crises.

Flexibility

A common feature of companies with a successful approach to supply risk management is flexibility, and companies that can engage with their employees, suppliers and customers quickly and consistently in a changing environment are likely to see positive results.

Part of this flexibility culture is being open and receptive to new approaches to risk management. Yet, at the moment, businesses are still harking back to the timeworn approaches to risk mitigation. According to the Cranfield research, 73 per cent of those interviewed were using fixed-price contracts with suppliers to mitigate risk, as well as close collaborative working with suppliers and dual sourcing. However, new approaches such as using simulation modelling, new technological solutions or outsourcing of high-risk activities were being used by a minority (3.6 per cent, 7.2 per cent and 17.1 per cent respectively).

But as the unexpected outcomes of recent risks have highlighted, companies need a more flexible and forward-thinking approach to cope with the surprises that risk can present.

When companies offshored their call centres to low-cost country sources, they did not envisage the problems incurred as a result of customers complaining about call centre staff in India who made shocked comments after processing large overdraft increases that were so alien to their culture.

As State of Flux points out, a business must be creative with its disaster planning, as problems won't necessarily erupt in expected places. 'Your factory in China may stay in operation while the port you use for shipping is suddenly shut down. So make sure you have plans – and back-up plans. These could include moving products through other ports, warehousing them in the country of origin, or closing down production.'

Companies need to think laterally and learn to link things up. And to do this, purchasing and supply professionals must come out of their functional silos and take a wider business view. Professionals need to set up company-wide risk management teams and learn to understand drivers in everything from CSR to finance, logistics to marketing.

One size does not fit all

The Cranfield study concluded that, when it comes to best-practice risk management in purchasing and supply, one size is unlikely to fit all. Analysis of how companies assessed and managed risk revealed a complex picture with distinct differences between sectors. For example, while recent disruptions to supply were a major influence in manufacturing, it was corporate responsibility risks that had the greatest impact in retail and the public sector. For financial services companies, it was changes in business strategy that drove change.

So before grabbing the nearest risk management tool such as total quality management or supplier rationalization, companies are advised to consider whether it is appropriate for their needs.

Conclusion

Before the purchasing and supply profession runs to the hills, far away from this terrifying picture of risk and threat, remember that risk is a fact of business: it is never going to go away and, more often than not, it is linked to opportunity. As an example, though low-cost country sourcing leads to longer lead times and increased risks in supply disruption, it also provides access to a reduction in material and labour cost.

And if risk management is embedded into all aspects of operations, it doesn't have to be seen as an extra expense. As the Aberdeen research highlighted, quite the opposite is the case, and companies with best-in-class supply risk management programmes were able to drive continuous improvements and outperform peers in key supply performance areas.

Syndication and supplier risk and the use of VSRD

Allan Gerrish, ICM Computer Group

Third-party business continuity services are not something you can afford to be vague about in a crisis.

Recent events have highlighted the fact that wide-area incidents are an increasing risk to organizations. Business continuity plans have historically concentrated on addressing incidents that just impact on the organization itself. However, where an event can affect neighbours, surrounding infrastructures, transport and communications there is the potential for the alternative facilities on which you rely in these circumstances to be impacted by the same incident.

Specific risks of syndication

In a review by the financial services regulatory authorities on the impact of the July 2005 bombings, some organizations raised concerns about the ability of syndicated business continuity service providers to meet their needs in the face of a wide-area event.

Much of this concern was a result of a lack of understanding of exactly what reliance could be made upon alternative workplace facilities. The FSA's Resilience Benchmarking Project stated: 'the lack of transparency over information on syndicated work area recovery is causing unnecessary confusion about how arrangements might be affected by multiple invocations'.

It goes on to say that 'recovery providers accept they need to be more proactive and open in sharing information, but firms also need to improve their understanding of risk management surrounding their recovery service arrangements'.

As a leading UK business continuity provider, ICM was very involved in this project, working on early drafts of potential risk transparency documents, which were based to some extent on FSA financial product disclosure documents.

Firms indicated the issues on which they would like more information, and ICM asked several clients to comment on our own risk disclosure. This helped shape our input into the benchmarking review.

Firms stated that they would like more transparency and openness from suppliers on matters such as syndication ratios, exclusion zones and the number of other clients who have purchased the same seats.

Providing this information is one thing, but another risk arises if it is not acted upon, so senior management need to understand the risks inherent in purchasing syndicated space. Syndication rates can change dramatically, changing the syndication risk over time. Therefore, an annual risk statement setting out how a risk profile might have changed from the previous year would state whether syndication rates for the seats bought have increased or fallen.

Following the benchmarking project, a transparency solution is now available. The Voluntary Supplier Risk Declaration (VSRD) is being promoted by the Business Continuity Institute as a potential industry standard, with the full support of the financial services authorities.

What are syndicated services?

The BCI defines a syndicated work area service as one where a subscriber pays for the use of accommodation in a recovery centre, provided that it is not already in use from a prior invocation by another subscriber.

However, this definition in itself highlights the primary risk: that the syndicated or shared service is already in use when you need it.

The BCI also defines two different bases on which the available resources may be allocated by a recovery supplier: 'first come first served' and 'equitable share'.

Resources allocated on a 'first come first served' basis mean that the first subscriber to invoke the service receives its full allocation of resources, and any remainder is available to subsequent subscribers. Resources allocated on an 'equitable share' basis are allocated in proportion to the resources subscribed to. For example, if two clients required 200 seats each in a 300-seat recovery centre they would be allocated 150 seats each if they both invoked at the same time.

Equitable share used to be effective; however, modern business demands, such as physical and network security, suggest that the requirements for data protection and confidentiality may well make this system impractical.

Don't gamble with your future

ICM is the UK's leading independent Business Availability provider, with nationwide services unrivalled for quality, functionality, geographic coverage and commitment to best practice.

Because ICM is also the only business continuity provider to have adopted the Voluntary Supplier Risk Declaration, recommended by the UK Tripartite Financial Committee, only ICM customers can be sure they are kept fully informed of syndication ratios and exclusion zones relating to their contracted services.

ICM has over 5000 workplace recovery positions, at 12 business continuity centres serving business communities throughout the UK. Plus, ICM's state-of-the-art datacentres, high availability & data replication services, mobile datacentre fleet, IT, email and telecoms recovery services, professional consultancy, planning, support and managed services all add up to the most comprehensive business availability portfolio solely dedicated to the UK market.

The extensive investment ICM has made in industry leading infrastructure facilities to provide these services, ensures its customers don't need to make huge investments themselves in order to secure their future.

To find out more,
call us on 08701 22 22 00 or
visit www.icm-computer.co.uk

the Business Availability group

Syndication ratios

It is important to understand exactly with how many people you are sharing the service. The BCI suggests that ratios between 25:1 and 40:1 are generally available, so that each seat in a recovery centre could potentially be sold up to a maximum of 40 times.

However, the Financial Services Authority review following the events of 9/11 found that some firms had bought access to services that had already been sold between five and 60 times; so it seems that there is a fairly broad range in practice.

ICM has been using a standard ratio of 25:1 for several years. This figure has arisen from a combination of actual invocation experience, financial modelling, some science, the published professional standards and our intention to have the capacity for regular client testing of all assets up to twice a year: thus 25:1 for around 50 working weeks in a year (excluding Christmas holidays).

Voluntary supplier risk declaration – an example

The declaration form itself is driven from the client's risk site, ie the actual building that is covered by the contracted recovery site. The fundamental question is whether the recovery centre chosen continues to be a viable alternative to the client site at that moment.

In the example provided, a client office in High Wycombe is being covered by ICM's Thames Valley business continuity centre.

Part 1 of the form (see Figure 3.3.1) states the current operational state of the centre. Apart from some general information about the set-up of the centre, it also includes some specific information, including the distance between the centre and the client site.

A question that needs to be considered is whether they are too far apart or too close. There is no definitive answer, but the client needs to use the information to consider the consequences.

Also necessary for consideration is the information on the number of other sites supported from this centre, as at the review date. In the example, 37 client sites account for the 2,796 seats that have been sold in total. At 25:1 over 250 seats in the centre, this indicates that only 45 per cent of the syndicated capacity has been taken, or a syndication ratio of around 11:1.

Client risks

Part 2 of the VSRD form (see Figure 3.3.2) explains the nature of the service, which will be either syndicated, as in this example, or dedicated, which means that it is not available to any other clients.

The current syndication rate is presented in the form, which in this case is 11:1.

Additionally, with business continuity service providers, it is important to know exactly how they count client sites for subscription purposes. ICM counts any

Customer Name :	
Contract Reference:	DR9999 (2222/001)
Client Site	
High Wycombe	
Buckinghamshire	
HP	

Review date:	25 April 2006
Recovery Site	
ICM London Thames Valley Recovery Centre	
Boundary Road	
Loudwater	
High Wycombe	
Bucks	
HP10 9PN	

ICM continually monitors the risk profile of services supplied to clients. As a subscriber to our services you will receive a Voluntary Supplier Risk Declaration at commencement of your contract and an updated Declaration every subsequent year on or around your contract anniversary. This important information enables our clients to regularly evaluate the risks associated with outsourced services against their appetite for such Risks. A traffic light system has been used to highlight the risk status and areas of potential concern

RECOVERY SITE STATUS

Office Size:	12,500 square feet	**Dedicated Seats**	0 at review date
Secure Recovery Suites:	4	**Syndicated Seats**	250
Workplace invocations in last 12 months:	0	**Dealing Positions**	0
Total number of risk sites supported (1):	37	(1) Each client, based at a defined post code per risk site, is classified as a full subscriber on a 1:1 basis.	
Client site distance to Recovery Site	3.9 miles.		
Total contracted Seats:	2,796	(2) Calculated as a multiple of the number of syndicated seats by the maximum ICM syndication limit per seat (as stated below).	
Centre utilisation (2):	45%		

Figure 3.3.1   Voluntary supplier risk declaration (VSRD) form, Part 1

CLIENT RISK STATUS

Risk with Explanation	ICM Statement	Current Position At Review Date
Service Basis A syndicated service is shared with other subscribers and may not be available in the event of multiple invocations by other clients	The nature of the service contracted is a Syndicated (Shared) Service.	To mitigate risk, syndicated services are provided to monitored exclusion zone & subscription rates as disclosed below
Service Allocation The method by which your contracted services are allocated if there are competing demands.	Syndicated services are available on a 'first come first served' basis whereby legitimate invocations are allocated resource in the order in which they are received (time logged).	None in past 12 months
Syndication rates The number of times each item of equipment or workplace position (seat) can be sold to different clients risk sites	Each asset may be sold up to a maximum of 25 subscribers per asset. Each subscriber will be located in an agreed exclusion zone area.	11:1 (workplace positions & PC's)
Exclusion zones and contention Outside agreed exclusion zones there is the possibility that clients may compete for syndicated services if there are multiple invocations.	Within 250m of the above address Within 250-500m Within 500-1000m	0 x contention 0 x contention 0 x contention
Alternative ICM Sites Alternative Recovery Centre available in case primary site is unavailable	Other sites may be made available on a reasonable endeavours basis only, subject to availability and outside of the Agreed SLA.	Wapping RC (630 seats 38.9 miles) Romford RC (1,715 seats 40.5 miles) Sevenoaks RC (310 seats 49.6 miles)

Figure 3.3.2 Voluntary supplier risk declaration (VSRD) form, Part 2

client site under contract against the syndication ratio. However, it is possible for a different interpretation to be made if a recovery centre is being contractually sold as a secondary or tertiary back-up to the principal recovery site. For example, sites could be considered 'half'-sites if they are less likely to be utilized. ICM believes that such interpretation hides the actual contractual rights that multiple clients have over these syndicated assets.

To clarify, some organizations may have nine clients with full rights to an asset and four with so-called half-rights, and would therefore consider this as a ratio of 11:1. ICM would count this example as having a ratio of 13:1, owing to there being 13 discrete client sites subscribed to the asset, regardless of the nature of the subscription.

Exclusion zones

Syndication normally has an associated exclusion zone. This is the distance around the client site within which the recovery supplier will not resell the client's resources to another potential customer.

As an example, ICM will typically not sell the same syndicated service to anyone within 250 metres of an existing subscriber. It is important at this point to clarify that we are talking about not selling a new client the *same* seat as an existing subscriber; several clients can be within 250 metres of each other, but not be sold the same seat within a sufficiently large recovery centre.

This is an important concept when producing risk declarations. ICM clients may negotiate wider exclusion zones based on their own assessment of shared service risk.

Exclusion zones and contention

Outside the agreed exclusion zones there is the possibility that clients may compete for syndicated services in the event of multiple invocations. This is an area where ICM's implementation has moved away slightly from the BCI model.

Originally, the VSRD form looked only at how many other clients were within the range bands. This could be a sizeable number, particularly in city centres.

ICM believes that the real issue is competition, that is, if all other clients with seat claims in these bands invoked at the same time, the site would be beyond its capacity. As already stated, this fear was raised specifically by financial service firms in the wake of the 7 July 2005 bombings.

As a simple example, if five clients were all within 250 metres but everyone had 50 seats, then a 250-seat centre would be large enough in overall capacity. However, if six clients within 250 metres of each other have 50 seats each and all invoke simultaneously, then they will be in jeopardy.

ICM's risk management systems act to avoid any such contention up to 250 metres. Above this distance contention is monitored. However, it may still occur in such a large geographical area; an exclusion zone radius of 1 kilometre encompasses an area of over 3 square kilometres.

ICM believes contention is a more effective measure of syndication risk than the original client site count alone.

With bands of 250 metres, being extremely accurate on the locations of client sites and recovery centres is critical. ICM discovered that postcodes were not accurate enough to determine the necessary exclusion zones and contention figures, so an Ordnance Survey grid system was adopted. An internet link on the VSRD takes the client to an online map that accurately pinpoints their relevant client risk site.

Alternative sites, invocations and testing

An important risk mitigation is access to alternative sites to the principal alternative site. The VSRD form indicates the location and capacity of other, nearby business continuity centres.

Unless contracted, an alternative site would potentially only be made available on a 'best endeavours' basis if the primary business continuity centre were fully occupied when needed. Clients have no contractual right to such sites, and those that did have contractual rights would have priority if they invoked, but the supplier would accommodate them if at all possible.

Part 3 of the VSRD form (see Figure 3.3.3) recognizes the need to communicate if another client has invoked facilities that are available to other subscribers. This is an immediate information requirement that changes the risk profile significantly.

It is now well established that untested recovery facilities cannot be relied upon; therefore a section on the form documents what testing is under contract and what has been used.

Accountability

ICM's managing director of business continuity holds himself personally accountable for the data provided in ICM's VSRD, so, while there is always the possibility of error, ICM accepts responsibility for the consequences of any client decision that is made as a direct result of any such error on ICM's part.

Summary

To summarize, suppliers must consult with customers regarding the clarity and effectiveness of the VSRD information, whilst recognizing that consistency is key to regular comparison and review.

While ICM is happy to be the vanguard of this transparency initiative, we believe that it must become an industry standard in order to succeed, and we are therefore keen to see how other suppliers are addressing the issue.

SLAs (Service Level Agreements)	
Adherence to contracted SLA's	SLAs as stated in contract
Invocation Notification	
Making clients aware when equipment or workplace positions they have syndicated rights to have been invoked	Workplace - E-mail with 24 hours of invocation
Testing Contractual	
Client contracts contain adequate test days	2+ days per annum minimum 4+ days per annum recommended	Standards met None in past 12 months 2 days on 1 site under contract.
Testing Actual	
Test days used in last 12 months.	Total client test days	None undertaken

ICM have used a grid reference map system to position the client site above. This enables us to accurately calculate other risk sites near your location and the distances to alternative ICM Recovery Centres. You can use the link below to confirm the specific location used. Just cut and paste the link into your Internet Explorer or other internet browser.

http://www.streetmap.co.uk/newprint.srf?x=398480&y=297954&z=1&ar=Y&searchp=newprint.srf&mapp=newmap.srf&dn=848&ax=398480&ay=297954

On behalf of ICM I warrant that the information is correct as at the review date above.

Michael Osborne, Managing Director - Business Continuity

Figure 3.3.3 Voluntary supplier risk declaration (VSRD) form, Part 3

Conclusion

In order to maintain awareness of the risk issues involved, senior management must insist upon an annual risk statement from their supplier. As mentioned earlier, this sets out how their risk profile may have changed since the previous year, including whether the syndication ratio has changed. Suppliers should be issuing these statements on commencement of the contract and on every anniversary. Clients must in turn assess their syndication risks at least as often.

As mentioned previously, suppliers can only provide and explain the information; it is the client's business continuity management who should act on it. But senior management within the client organization must remain accountable for deciding the cost/risk balance inherent in purchasing syndicated services.

Businesses must ensure that they obtain the information they need to remain certain, not vague, about the third-party business continuity services upon which their company's very survival relies.

Quality risk

Ian Hodgskinson, LRQA

The current multimillion-dollar quality assurance industry grew out of a poor perception of UK industry's ability to produce quality goods, which was presenting a threat to its survival. Over the last 30 years there has been a focus not only on identifying issues that create a risk to quality, but more importantly on measuring, analysing and managing them to create measurable improvement in performance and consequent reduction in risk. But despite this focus it appears that industry remains poor at getting to the root of quality problems, and few companies seem to be able to get to grips with quality risks. Also, whilst financial risk is a key agenda item in any board meeting, it is rare to see quality risk as a regular point of discussion, and many have difficulty obtaining an accurate financial expression of quality costs. So is quality risk management not seen as a key element of business strategy?

It is easy to forget that, only 30 years ago, few business executives in the West were prepared to listen to a risk of high quality standards being achieved in Japan having an impact on their business. The ability of Japanese industry to focus on accuracy and achieve incredibly consistent results was not on the agenda of Western manufacturers. So what happened to our car makers, our electronics industry and those East German high-quality cameras?

The Japanese story of the 1980s is a demonstration of how a focus on reducing quality variances to the customer significantly reduces perceived quality risk and changes expectations for everyone. An example was in the manufacture of steel ships' plate. When specifying thickness of ship plate, in addition to the required thickness to support the vessel, corrosion in service must be taken into account. In European steel mills, lack of control of thickness pushed production to the top limit of thickness tolerance – reducing the risk of being below the minimum by aiming for maximum thickness. But the Japanese steel mills had a capability to roll within much tighter tolerances and regularly produced plate accurately to the minimum thickness, so saving material and money. The result was a change required to thickness specification as corrosion tolerance was now too small. This had a devastating effect on European steel and raised perceptions of Japanese steel production quality to an unprecedented height.

Supply chain risk

Quality risk is a costly element of the business if not effectively managed, and in most organizations its management leaves much to chance. Some organizations deliberately choose to tolerate their current quality on the basis that provided the product is fit for service someone will buy it, and very high quality requires very high prices, which can make the product unattractive. Whilst this is possibly true, it is usually the case that this low-quality market sector is very competitive, driving down already low prices.

Other companies have chosen to transfer their risk and move their manufacturing to suppliers in low-cost countries, becoming project managers rather than manufacturers. It is amazing how many high-quality global brands are no longer made by the original company, and even stranger to find the country in which the product is made. Managing contractors is not an easy task, and maintaining quality in a separate organization must be achieved through indirect control, which has many new difficulties. It is interesting that the Japanese are today facing this very issue, where their own labour costs are forcing manufacture to move to cheaper countries. Maintaining product quality in branded goods made outside Japan is a major issue.

Managing quality risks

Quality risks must be recognized, analysed and managed. The problem is that many companies have difficulties in identifying their quality risks, and quality planning does not seem to be based on risk analysis. Almost a million companies across the world have decided that quality should be managed through a management system developed to comply with the popular ISO 9001 standard.

In this standard, each organization is required to identify a number of improvement targets and set in train an improvement programme to achieve specific objectives in a reasonable timescale. The targets are to be specifically drawn from a quality risk assessment of the gap between customer expectation and current performance. Operating the quality management system will generate reliable data on progress, allowing management to monitor quality performance in the business against obvious key performance indicators.

With such a clear mechanism it would seem obvious that the starting point is to analyse the impact of quality risks on the key stakeholders of the business and determine the means by which those risks will be mitigated. In some cases they can be eliminated by changing the process, or managed through process controls that determine specific key performance indicators to measure process control effectiveness. In other words, the management system is planned to address the quality risks the company wishes to manage, and in return deliver reliable metrics on risk-based performance indicators.

However, evidence from third-party certification bodies assessing the systems seems to show two major issues. First, many companies have great difficulty in establishing the gap between customer expectations and current perception of performance – or at least they claim this to be the case. And (perhaps as a consequence) it is difficult to get senior management commitment to the improvement programme and to raise quality issues to board-level discussions. The so-called 'quality manager' is left to get on with it.

Yet there is no question but that it is far less expensive to continue to serve existing customers rather than constantly to have to win new ones. And it is equally clear that satisfied customers stay with their traditional suppliers (sometimes even when there is a price advantage in moving). So it is interesting that the key management performance indicator tends to be 'how much money', not 'how much quality'.

Understanding the customer need

Let us consider some of the factors that present a risk to quality and that should be at least subject to analysis if not prime candidates for improvement targets.

The most important issue is the level of understanding of what the customer expected to get as a result of placing a contract with the supplying organization. This may seem obvious, but it is amazing how much misunderstanding can exist. In business-to-business contracting, it is usually necessary to buy something because you cannot make it yourself or do not know how to do it. So the buyer (the specifier) is not the expert on what is wanted; rather the buyer's expertise is on what is needed – and the two are quite different.

There are many examples of differences about what the purchaser expected the supplier to understand from the purchase specification that have genuinely been totally overlooked or misunderstood. Suppliers can easily be deluded into thinking that what they see as important about the product is the same as what the customer sees as important. But this is a dangerous assumption, and managing the risk means actually finding out what really matters to the customer – some effective early communication, not simple euphoria about winning a great contract.

In the growing business of outsourced facilities management, large organizations are moving from internal controls to having the need for a specification of the controls to be applied by the facilities manager. This is an immediate test of the organization's knowledge of what it actually currently controls and how that is achieved. On the other side of the contract, facilities managers know that tiny differences in price can lose huge contracts, so they study the specification closely to ensure they do not inadvertently oversupply. Not surprisingly the outsourced service is often rather different to the internal controls, and some differences can become high-profile media issues.

— INCREASING CONFIDENCE IN YOUR FUTURE

Too much of today's risk management is an exercise of going through the motions of standards compliance, with little demonstrable impact on the business revenue, relationships or reputation.

What's more, too many management systems fail to deliver the confidence management needs about how well it's meeting stakeholders' expectations; to know that its key business risks are under control and to let them feel secure that they can manage the future in today's uncertain world.

With management systems playing a more critical role in business success than ever before, it's never been more important to demand more from your systems' assessor.

This is why at LRQA our approach is different. LRQA's risk management support - Business Assurance - is designed to help you ensure that your systems are driving down critical risks and delivering real improvements in the eyes of your critical stakeholders.

Business Assurance is our approach to management systems assessment. It focuses on developing effective and efficient management systems - giving your business the confidence it needs to thrive and grow. By understanding your business and your goals, we're able to

Lloyd's Register Quality Assurance is a member of the Lloyd's Register Group

LRQA
Measure the Difference

"Assurance: The quality or state of being *safe*. A *belief* in one's powers."

work with you to accurately pinpoint the key areas that need to improve, helping you turn risks into opportunities and weaknesses into strengths.

With Business Assurance, you can feel confident about your future.

Contact us

+44 24 7688 2373
enquiries@lrqa.com
www.lrqa.com

How knowledgeable are the senior management team in understanding the critical controls that underpin the quality of the company's outputs, and what key performance metrics do they use to measure quality?

Even when there is good understanding of what the customer wants, there is the challenge of internal communications. Most of the problems that have been identified through assessment of ISO 9001 systems have their source in internal communications systems. It is surprising how many companies seem to think that the complex requirements agreed with a customer can be adequately communicated to the manufacturing units through simple standard forms. When errors occur it is more likely to be a result of poor instruction than lack of competence.

Establishing capability

Internal communications problems increase in complexity as large organizations spread their manufacturing across different countries with different languages and cultures. And where the instruction is no longer internal, but to a subcontracted manufacturing organization with its own view of what the ultimate customer may have needed, communication systems become very stretched. Internal quality issues must always focus on the effectiveness of the communication of what it was intended should be done. The question is whether better systems might have prevented money from being wasted, and the additional costs of putting it right, not forgetting that the delivery is now probably going to be late.

Is the board interested in the effectiveness of the operational IT systems? Does it even know the cost of rework (often concealed from the financial systems and lost in work in progress)?

The second area of potential concern is ensuring that what you promote as the functionality of your product is matched by the capability of your equipment and the people who create it. Related to this is the question of whether the claims of features of your service are seen as of value by the market. Will you delight the customer or create dissatisfaction if you fail to deliver these extras? Who is responsible for matching the quality perception the organization seeks to create with the investment in people, equipment and product offerings to support it?

In some organizations this does not seem to be considered as a senior executive responsibility. Indeed lack of clarity regularly results in managers throughout the organization making their own decisions and not surprisingly being inconsistent. So a question is how clear is the quality strategy of the organization and, if it is not very clear, is that because the service strategy is equally unclear?

Finally, what happens when it goes wrong? Every company has disasters but the clever ones really understand the causes by fostering an open no-blame culture. Although the cause of a problem is bound to end in a specific area, it is rare for it to be the result of a deliberate plan to get it wrong. But, unless the culture is right, the organization will never determine the true cause and so cannot learn.

Risk management requires that the organization can learn from errors and through that improve organizational competence and reduce the risks. But for the right culture to be in place the right management decisions must be taken and the right responses made when difficult situations arise. Culture in all organizations is driven by the behaviour of top managers. 'If that is what they want, that is how we will respond' is a natural human reaction.

So when the board discusses a disaster that has had serious financial consequences (perhaps the only reason it has been raised at the board), how is it handled?

The importance of management systems

Quality risk is real and it is only ignored at your peril. Unmanaged quality risk is just as likely to cause the demise of a business as unmanaged financial risk. So why is there not equal focus by the board? Perhaps the answer is that there really is focus on quality risk but undertaken in a different guise. Of course, a board is interested in revenue and most are interested in growth. Major customer losses will come to the attention of the board if only as a result of their impact on revenue and the potential for the need to cut costs. Major issues with current contracts are also increasingly brought to the attention of individual non-executive board members by senior managers of the customer or even the customer's client. But an agenda item on quality risk reduction is rarely a feature of normal board meetings.

So how can quality risk be elevated in importance? Quality management systems have traditionally been designed around standard criteria. In fact the basic criteria may well be valid in most situations since quality issues are usually the result of problems in sales, subcontract procurement, manufacturing planning and works instructions, measurement or final inspection. But issues for individual organizations are not generic. There is a real problem that for many organizations defining a system against generic requirements has created something that does not reflect that company's quality risks. This is a problem because senior managers do not see the relevance of the controls of the ISO 9001 system to the commercial risks created by quality problems. Quality system data are often completely ignored when decisions are taken to address quality risks.

In many organizations there are two distinct management systems, the one needed to maintain the ISO 9001 approval – necessary to stay on the bid list for new contracts – and the system used to run the company, where quality risks have a true business dimension. These systems must be brought together and that is the responsibility of both the company and the certification body that provides the ISO 9001 certificate.

All the data needed to manage quality risks are available in a company operating an effective quality management system, but in many cases lack of focus from senior management results in important messages being lost in a barrage of information. Senior managers must be much clearer on what is important and the key indicators of change in risk. There must be a better understanding that these indicators are not the same as the financial indicators most senior managers feel greater comfort in debating. Perhaps more management teams should spend time with their quality professionals rather than simply delegating all quality issues to people with no authority to manage the root causes.

Effective management of quality risk is essential to provide shareholder confidence of a sustainable business. Luckily this is as yet not recognized by shareholders so that share prices do not yet seem to be influenced by the effectiveness of management systems.

Critical engineering and risk management: avoiding complacency

Paul Saville-King, Norland Managed Services Limited

Introduction

The ever-increasing demands of customers, combined with the need to sustain competitive advantage in a global economy, have driven a pace of change that today's business has never experienced before. Challenges of 24/7 accessibility, speedier service and the drive for lower costs mean significant technology and communications investments are necessary to stay ahead. Add the result of global terrorism, the failure of trusted household names such as Enron and WorldCom, and the proliferation of international regulations such as Basel II and Sarbanes–Oxley, and the landscape is vastly different. These changes are further centralizing the role of technology in corporate strategy and increasing a company's dependency on information and communication systems, and the engineering infrastructure that supports them. One does not have to look too far for evidence that this is affecting the world of facilities management in the design and day-to-day operation of increasingly complex buildings.

However, it appears widely unrecognized by risk managers and boardrooms just how much risk there is for business disruption caused by the engineering infrastructure. At a recent 2006 business continuity seminar there was not one agenda item relating to operational risk in an engineering infrastructure sense, and the hall of exhibitors had a notable absence of engineering service providers. This is the second year that this has been the case. One could assert that this is a failure of the 'risk industry' to recognize the potential for the immediate and the catastrophic impact associated with infrastructure failure.

This omission combines with the relatively high probabilities of such disruption happening in heavily technology-dependent businesses with traditional maintenance approaches. It appears that boardrooms sit in relative comfort, thinking that the engineering aspects of their operational risk profile are the most tangible and controllable risks they face. This is not the case. If your business is dependent on technology for communications, IT for its core business activity (for example Amazon) then you may be at increased risk. Take Reuters, which according to media reports was offline for 10 hours and unable to provide the market data that is their core product following a power outage. Share prices suffer from engineering complacency and under-investment, and the traditional mechanical and electrical services tender process drives out costs by encouraging savings in the most intangible yet critical elements of service design. Engineers' holidays and training are simple examples; these may be easy short-term savings for hungry contractors eager for new business but they will expose the client to long-terms risks associated with increased staff attrition and low levels of critical engineering competence.

As with business continuity planning (BCP), investment banks are leading the way in managing their critical engineering systems. Banks are also adept at planning to meet the future challenges posed by increasing infrastructure complexity, even in the face of the common conflicts between IT and facilities management departments. Building owners and management should network with facilities staff and executives from this group to add a new perspective on engineering risk management and battle to convince core business leaders that these 'cost centres' require continued levels of significant investment, even in the face of competitive cost pressures.

Combine the above challenges with the increased 'risk awareness' that now permeates boardrooms, and what you get is a new horizon for the management and audit of 'operational risk'. A study by the Chartered Management Institute (CMI)[1] found that 70 per cent of respondents had concerns about IT systems failures and 64 per cent had concerns about communications failures. Actual disruptions followed a similar trend with 41 per cent of IT disruptions and 25 per cent of communications disruptions. Only 6 per cent of respondents to a BCI survey[2] selected loss of power as their biggest threat, but this is understandable in the current 'terror-focused' geopolitical context.

Why is critical engineering and risk management (CERM) important? Simply put, no power or cooling = no communications or IT = no business. The question then is: 'What can I do to avoid catastrophic failure of my engineering infrastructure and the resulting impact to my business?'

Extensive data analysis[3] has demonstrated that around 90 per cent of catastrophic business-critical impact related to human or process error and not to the design of the infrastructure at all. Unfortunately for some, especially those of an engineering disposition, concentrating on the less tangible softer elements of managing risk takes people out of their comfort zone.

Industry estimates vary wildly about the actual costs of downtime and there are tangible and intangible elements of this to consider. According to Gartner research, the costs of downtime include:

1. productivity loss;
2. revenue loss;
3. damaged reputation;
4. impaired financial performance.

In financial terms alone, downtime for a brokerage/trading institute can run at around $6.4 million per hour.[4] That equates to over $100,000 per minute. The London Chamber of Commerce found that 90 per cent of businesses that lost data in a major disaster were forced to shut down after two years.[5]

Without doubt Sarbanes–Oxley has spread its tentacles into many areas of operational risk but it seems not yet to have made a material difference where this risk is of an immediate and dramatic systemic nature (through the engineering infrastructure). A traditional mechanical and electrical maintenance services partner may not be equipped – or have the right culture and awareness – to deliver adequate risk protection, especially in the softer elements that produce the most significant risks. In some respects the industry as a whole is still 15 years behind the risk management and banking sectors, although some pioneering companies are attempting to change the industry.

A structured approach to mitigating engineering risk is recommended. The five fundamental pillars (see Figure 3.5.1) of critical engineering and risk management cover the most important aspects of this approach, namely:

■ focus;
■ consistency;
■ compliance;
■ visibility;
■ learning and improvement.

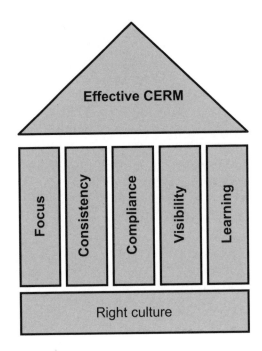

Figure 3.5.1   CERM pillars

The five pillars

Focus

Focus relates to the need to concentrate specifications, systems and processes on activities completely aligned with reducing or eliminating risk from the critical engineering infrastructure. Examples in this respect would include challenging the norms around traditional key performance indicators (KPIs). Traditional maintenance specifications often have measures around completed maintenance tasks or reactive tasks completed on time. In reality this is often misaligned with the activities critical to keeping the customers' core business operational. Many organizations include uptime specifications within service provider contracts (such as 99.999 per cent availability) when this is recognized by industry experts[6] as impossible, even with a system-plus-system design. What does this achieve except to cause conflict between customers and supply partners even when the intent is correct? Surely, it is far better to include measures and KPIs that reflect the inputs or levers that will influence the maximization of uptime. Examples include many of the softer elements of service provision such as specific CERM competencies, staff motivation and levels of proactive scenario training delivery. These softer aspects pose measurement challenges, and this may be why historically many service providers and facility operators have hesitated to challenge ambiguity and define them more adequately.

Additionally, CERM best practice would recommend that the areas critical to the customer's core business are identified in a joint working group (for example the data centre or trading floors) and as a result critical engineering paths are mapped holistically. This should be in terms of geographic location, systemic interconnectivity and security/accessibility. Once completed, this review allows for a complete realignment of the planned preventative maintenance (PPM) system to focus activities on those elements of the path that are most effective for risk mitigation. This should involve new ways of working and perhaps the introduction of technologies such as hand-held units or tried-and-tested non-intrusive maintenance techniques. Around 90 per cent of existing maintenance systems can be modified without any major cost or disruption to the business.

Consistency

Consistency relates to the consistent application of 'hard earned' local knowledge, tested systems and procedures. At its most basic level, this provides a platform for measurement and benchmarking across geographic regions or even between client groups. At the more complex end of the spectrum, consistency alludes to the need to ensure that tacit knowledge[7] is transferred between team members, across boundaries and at its ultimate between homogeneous customer groups. This requires a time commitment that many incorrectly judge to be a poor investment.

Primarily, this pillar relates to the need to have consistent core processes that have passed resilience tests and deliver effective risk management from an engineering perspective, for example evolving traditional permits in use in facilities management and mechanical and electrical engineering to a system specifically designed for authorizing works relating to critical equipment and areas, thereby reducing potential risk significantly. These principles seem simple but in practice are rare in most maintenance operations.

Another essential control mechanism is the software change permit. Some senior managers have lost their jobs through failure to control the software aspects of what would otherwise have been a straightforward maintenance or project activity. In one example an 'old' revision of software – accidentally installed – on an uninterruptible power supply (UPS) protecting hundreds of trading positions caused an immediate and unplanned shutdown despite rigorous prior change management approvals. This one event cost hundreds of millions of dollars of lost revenue for an investment bank. A software control permit not only forces clarity about 'the what' and 'the when' but it also forces consideration about contingency measures and fall-back positions should things not go according to plan.

Compliance

Compliance relates to the need to ensure that critical engineering activities and measurements, and the critical processes that support them are effective. It is more than auditing although this is an essential element. It is more about stakeholder assurance and, when combined with adequate visibility, provides managers and board members with peace of mind. Traditional audit processes focus on antiquated elements of performance, usually around financial processes, statutory maintenance compliance and performance against traditional service level agreements (SLAs). This approach is not 'critically aligned' and should be prioritized for change.

Compliance must also pick up important 'noise', which may or may not contain essential information that could prevent a future business impact. Examples include the implementation of a critical incident reporting system, which records not only detail of actual business impact but records – and more importantly encourages – the reporting of near-miss data. Most near-miss recording systems fail to differentiate those events that result in a business process change or improvement, despite this being a key ingredient for generating enthusiasm and buy-in from the engineering team.

Visibility

Visibility concerns the ability of the management team to focus on delivering or supporting the core business through having peace of mind about engineering risk. This is made possible through the accurate reporting of critical engineering exceptions and potential threats that would otherwise need to be 'mined' out of the daily furore. An example of this is the CERM risk register, which not only records current and future risks relating to the engineering infrastructure (such as design issues, union strikes and potential fuel supply shortages), but also includes a success register for risks that have been systematically eliminated. This demonstrates a progressive and unrelenting 'war on risk', especially if the unfortunate should happen and difficult questions are asked by shareholders or board members. Technology has an important role to play here, and sophisticated yet simple dependency modelling systems can facilitate effective traffic light analysis – via a web browser – of the status of all systems, processes, system capacities and competencies no matter how large or globally dispersed a company is. This is probably the most important aspect of CERM, and serious thought and investment are essential to have adequate and effective levels of visibility.

Learning and improvement

Learning and improvement demonstrate CERM as being a dynamically evolving concept. Events happen despite the best systems in the world and, apart from a reliable CERM incident response team, your service provider or expert should ensure that effective lessons-learned exercises are carried out. Structure this to reflect the McKinsey 7S model with headings of systems, structure, strategy, staff, shared values (culture), skills and (management) style. These headings provide useful insight into the concept that these elements act in harmony (or not) and that one cannot focus only on the 'hard' elements such as systems and processes. 'Soft' elements such as management style, skills, CERM strategy or 'culture' are just as likely to be complex root causes of system failure and far harder to eliminate.

The sharing and leverage of local knowledge also fall under this category. This is more difficult than it seems, and a technological solution for knowledge management will not solve the problem. Again, the 'soft' elements of critical engineering such as a risk-aware culture, CERM competencies and varied communications mediums are far more effective in this regard.

Culture and behaviours

It is clear that you can have the best systems, technology and processes in the world but, without the right culture and behaviours in the first place, these processes will be poorly applied at best, and at worst deliberately disregarded. There are several 'levers' that can be applied to driving the right behaviours and culture required for critical environments as follows:

- stringent recruitment and selection in the first place based on required behaviours, not just experience and qualification;
- correct launch and communication of the need for a more robust approach to critical engineering and risk management;
- constant communication of progress and the establishment of clear metrics;
- formal training on systems and processes;
- appraisal alignment incorporating risk mitigating/highlighting behaviours;
- 360 appraisal feedback from suppliers, customers, management and peer workers;
- celebration of successes, no matter how small they seem at first;
- reward and recognition, both formal and informal;
- formal knowledge-sharing programmes.

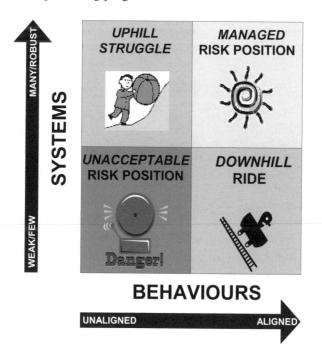

Figure 3.5.2 Risk evaluation matrix

A new model

Although the elements above are intended to provoke thought and evaluation of your current approach, it is important to select a service provider that recognizes the redundancy of traditional maintenance and is willing to work closely with you to implement a completely new model. What should be clear to you is that it is not enough to rely on systems and processes – it is the culture that counts.

This takes time, and when implementing a new CERM model – depending on the starting point – it can take up to two years to change to the desired state. Systems alone can be implemented by a proficient operator in as little as three months.

The model shown in Figure 3.5.2 provides a framework for you to assess your risk position in relation to behaviours/culture versus systems/processes. The right approach to CERM is not a collection of isolated systems and processes but a cohesive collation of many elements in a new model.

Five steps to peace of mind

The following are five recommended steps, based on the above, which when followed will reduce your exposure to engineering infrastructure risks:

1. Be clear what you want to achieve and set SMART targets.
2. Choose a CERM-aware partner.
3. Realign your maintenance model (five pillars).
4. Drive hard on the 'soft stuff'.
5. Review formally and audit on a regular basis.

Notes

1. CMI (2005) *Business Continuity Management*, CMI, London (440 respondents).
2. Business Continuity Institute (BCI) in conjunction with IMP Events and sponsored by Hitachi Data Systems, 13–18 March 2005.
3. A live online database of Norland Managed Services customers – CERM*View*™.
4. Meta Group (2000) *IT Performance Engineering and Measurement Strategies: Quantifying performance and loss*, October, Meta Group; Fibre Channel Industry Association.
5. London Chamber of Commerce and Industry, *Disaster Recovery: Business tips for survival*, LCCI, London.
6. Uptime Institute.
7. Tacit knowledge is that which enters into the production of behaviours but which is not ordinarily accessible to the consciousness.

Consolidating operational risk

Odd Andersen, DNV

Operational risk is defined as 'the risk of loss resulting from inadequate or failed internal processes, people and systems or from external events'.[1] Although this definition comes from the banking sector, it is applicable to most industries and organizations.

The upside of effective operational risk management is that it can contribute to competitive advantage through more stable operations, improved stakeholder confidence and trust, improved compliance and better governance. Many organizations are trying to realize these benefits and have initiatives to establish a framework for coherent and effective company-wide risk management.

Whereas tools for measuring and aggregating some classes of risk, eg market risk and credit risk, are highly developed, operational risk is multidimensional. A key challenge in managing operational risk challenge is simply that the level of risk frequently is *not known*. The question is then: how do we assess and consolidate operational risk?

The short answer is that some operational risk can be quantified, eg project time and cost, but other risks are difficult to quantify, eg the business effect of insufficient firewalls in IT systems or insufficient internal controls. This chapter will discuss measuring and consolidation of operational risk through two specific examples: 1) How do we measure project risk and consolidate project and programme risk? 2) How do we describe the overall risk of the organization?

Measuring project risk and consolidating project and programme risk

Projects are everywhere. In this context, a programme is defined as a 'group of projects'. From this it is clear that the number of risks may be large, and it will be a challenge to consolidate these risks to keep track.

Important risk factors in a project/programme can be meaningfully measured and consolidated. This is best done by presenting a probability density for the quantifiable objectives (time, cost), supplemented if necessary by risk matrices for risks against non-quantifiable objectives (performance). There are three steps in this process:

- *Use a common programme/project planning tool throughout the organization.* The single most important task is to establish clear and common objectives for risk analysis. In projects, the objectives are typically time, cost and performance. The objectives will set the direction and scope for risk identification. For quantitative analysis on time and/or cost, the programme should use a common planning tool, eg MS Project, to describe duration, dependencies and critical path, both within a project and to other projects across the programme.
- *Quantify uncertainty on individual activities.* The next step is to estimate the uncertainty with regard to time (duration) for each activity on or close to the critical line. This is typically used by asking qualified personnel, eg the project manager, for the 'most likely' duration, the 'best-case' duration (P_{10} is frequently used) and finally the 'worst-case' duration (often P_{90}). In labour-intensive projects, cost is primarily a function of duration. In capital-intensive projects, the uncertainty in cost estimates should be addressed separately.
- *Calculate and present aggregate risk.* Once the common/integrated plan is established and the uncertainties are quantified, it is possible to quantify the aggregate risk. This is done by either statistical calculations or Monte Carlo simulation, using dedicated, off-the-shelf software. For each project – and for the entire programme – the result can efficiently be presented as in Figure 3.6.1, which shows the probability (the y-axis) for project/programme completion within a given date (the x-axis).

This quantitative approach will also take correlations (positive and negative) among activities into account. This approach can also handle both estimate and event (discrete) uncertainties.

In most projects and programmes, the quantitative analysis of time or cost gives sufficient information for assessing risk and can point to adequate measures. However, in some programmes there might be a need for a supplementary analysis of non-quantifiable risk. We will address this in the next section.

Describing the overall risk of the organization

The overall risk picture at a corporate level is obviously more complex than the programme risks. Programme risk is important, but is still a subset of the overall

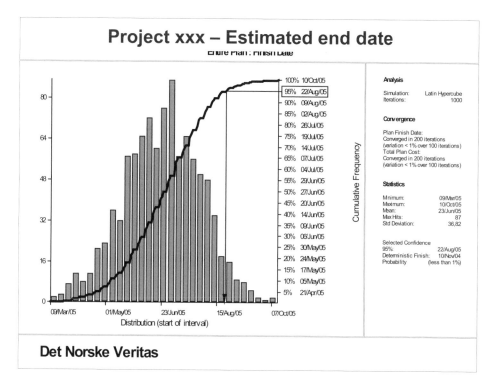

Figure 3.6.1 Probability density for project end date

corporate risks. Both the number and the diversity of risks are higher at a corporate level. Additional risks can include political, strategic and reputation risk to name a few.

The short answer to the question of how to consolidate operational risk is that there is no generally established and accepted way meaningfully to consolidate non-quantified risks. However, by careful manual effort it can be possible to establish a useful representation of the aggregate risk picture. One good way of doing this is by presenting risk in one matrix for each objective.

There are three steps in the process for a qualitative (or semi-quantitative) analysis:

■ *Establish a common risk management 'language'*. This includes defining the relevant objectives and – for each objective – the scale for probability/frequency and a precise definition of the consequence. For a listed company, there will typically be two overall objectives: 1) a financial objective, eg market value, profits or cash flow; and 2) a qualitative objective, eg reputation or 'quality of services/products'. This is illustrated in Figure 3.6.2. At any level, the number of objectives should be limited to as few as possible. More than three to four objectives can introduce unnecessary complexity. To ensure relevance, there can be different objectives

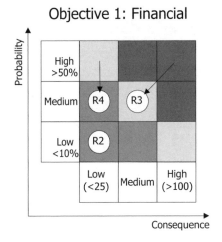

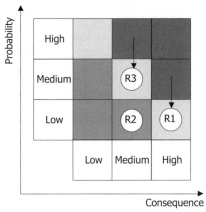

Figure 3.6.2 One risk matrix per objective

at different levels of the organization. The typical objectives for a programme/project are time, cost and performance. The objectives for an IT department can be confidentiality, integrity and availability of data and systems. It is clear that both the objectives and the scales for consequences and probabilities must differ to be relevant for different functions of the organization. To summarize, there is a need for a common, clearly defined hierarchy of objectives.

■ *Identify and evaluate risks.* After a common framework of objectives and definitions of consequence and probability is established, risk can be qualitatively assessed and mapped into the matrix. This will raise a number of questions related to the formulation of risks – the level of abstraction, etc – but this will not be discussed here.

■ *Manually consolidate risks into a meaningful aggregate risk picture.* Qualitative data cannot easily be aggregated or compounded. There are a number of complicating factors:

  – The *correlation* among qualitatively formulated risks is not clear. Risk can add up linearly, or exponentially – or they might cancel each other out.

  – The *'translation'* of a risk at one level, eg the risk of reduced availability of computer systems, to a risk at a higher level, eg to objectives like financial performance or quality, is not straightforward. This translation can only be approximate.

  – Another challenge is the *aggregation/consolidation* of risks to a manageable number. In our experience it is difficult for one person or function (eg the board) to relate meaningfully to and manage more than 10 to 15 risks. The aggregation of risks to a manageable number requires abstraction and can be an art as well as a science.

  – The *formulation* of risks is a challenge. The risks should both adhere to the MECE (mutually exclusive, collectively exhaustive) principle and be formulated at the same level of abstraction.

Given these challenges, presenting a complete, qualitative risk picture is difficult. However, it is still our experience that it is possible, by being aware of the challenges, effectively to aggregate and present a relevant picture of risks at the corporate level. Even though the consolidation does not give a numerical value of aggregate risk, it has three important benefits:

1. *An identification of the risks.* The explicit identification, assessment and display of operational risks in the matrix will in itself increase risk awareness.
2. *A ranking of risks.* This can be an important input when prioritizing risk-reducing initiatives.
3. *A tracking of how key risks 'move' in the matrix over time.* This will show if risk-mitigating actions reduce probability or consequence.

This chapter has only scratched the surface...

We will use the opportunity to refer to the components that DNV argues must be in place to establish efficient risk management in any organization, as shown in Figure 3.6.3.

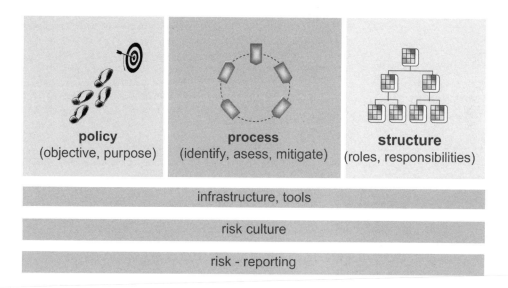

| policy | process | structure |
| (objective, purpose) | (identify, asess, mitigate) | (roles, responsibilities) |

infrastructure, tools

risk culture

risk - reporting

Figure 3.6.3 Components of a risk management system

A warning

The future comes too fast, and in the wrong order.

(A Toffler)

The two questions discussed in this chapter are often critical in making risk management operational, but still relate to only three of these components (risk policy, risk process and risk reporting).

The term 'risk management' and the discussion above can give the impression that – given enough analysis – it is possible to get a sufficiently complete picture of the future. This is wrong and misleading. Think of attempts to predict the oil price, the impact of Napsters, the al Qaedas, stock market bubbles and so on. So given the limitations of risk management, the ability to *respond* must be developed.

There is an important distinction between risk, which is quantifiable, and uncertainty, which is not.

The objective for risk management is not to predict the future. A better question to ask, since we cannot predict the future, is what is the best we can do now?

Note

1. Basel Committee on Banking Supervision, 2001.

Managing the sticks and the stones: bouncing back from a crisis

Elisabeth Lewis Jones, Liquid Public Relations Ltd

Companies and individuals often experience a roller coaster ride in popularity. They seem to be able to move from 'hero' to 'zero' in record time, especially in today's 24/7 news environment.

As the public becomes more 'media savvy' and as the world gets smaller, they expect individuals, companies and organizations to behave in a particular way. They demand for them to act responsibly and can easily form pressure groups or cry '*Watchdog*' in order to bring an organization to heel.

It doesn't have to be a major incident that can impact hugely on an organization. A change – either internal, for example a new managing director, or external, such as a fluctuating stock market – can have dramatic effects on the well-being of an organization and how it is perceived by the outside world.

A simple comment posted on to a trade website about the security of online bank accounts had worldwide repercussions for Barclays. This small item was picked up by a journalist just surfing the web and was catapulted on to the front pages of newspapers across the globe, resulting in a major loss of confidence in Barclays' online business.

Although change can happen on a very regular basis, the message is not one of doom and gloom. With careful management and communication of a change, and especially a crisis, directors can put away their lucky horseshoes and four-leaf clovers.

In the immediate aftermath of a crisis or change, directors need to move away from hands-on management, step back and take a long, hard look at their business. Having a strategic overview of their organization is crucial if the company is to acknowledge the change and move forward. For many, this is easier said than done. It takes a brave person to criticize openly an organization he or she works in – perhaps even heads up.

For the public relations professional, crisis management is all about three main areas:

1. reducing the loss of a client base or market share;
2. maintaining or enforcing a positive company image or profile;
3. using the current crisis experience to improve the market share, image and performance of the organization.

The last area is important for the post-crisis life of a business if it is to continue to trade, grow and, importantly, bounce back. There are many examples of companies from Pan Am to Ratners that have failed to achieve this.

The aftermath

Managing an actual crisis well is crucial. From those earliest moments the tone for the event and the recovery from it can be set.

Once the flurry of media activity has gone and the holding statements and crisis manual have been filed away, many would argue that the real work has to start.

Today, crisis management goes hand in hand with corporate culture. It is one of the main reasons why an organization can suffer a crisis and one of the main cures too.

In the case of certain landmark crises, for example Perrier, BSE/CJD, British Midland or even the Paddington rail crash, it is believed that they were defined by the culture of the organization and the attitude of their senior managers.

As part of the aftermath, evaluation is important. The Chartered Institute of Public Relations' toolkit enables companies to look not just at the media relations activity but also at the wider impact of the incident. From hits to the website and calls to customer service teams to tracking footfall into a store, the CIPR guide encourages companies to think about the wider implications of the crisis and where it has had the greatest impact.

Although a review of the press coverage is important in the aftermath of a crisis situation, it is wise not to focus on every word and headline but to think about tomorrow's story and how to rebalance the negative coverage.

An integrated approach

Change also allows organizations to step back and look at their stakeholders. From understanding how stakeholders were affected in a crisis, how they were communicated to during the incident and then how dialogue can be developed with them again in a more positive, proactive light, organizations can start to communicate to their key stakeholders in a far more effective and efficient manner.

Considering stakeholders is a key part of looking at the real needs of a business. Through thinking about customers, prospective customers, suppliers, advisers, staff, government bodies, influencers, trade unions, etc, their needs can be assessed (see Figure 3.7.1).

Many argue that in the aftermath of a situation the most important stakeholder is the internal audience – the staff. Their ability to understand the situation, implement change and rise to the challenge is crucial.

A demoralized workforce will only lead to a downward spiral of navel gazing, ill feeling, resentment and, at best, poor performance. Ill-informed staff can create rumours, adverse speculations or even critical comments in the media.

A stakeholder example: By considering all stakeholders an integrated approach can be developed, allowing communication to all.

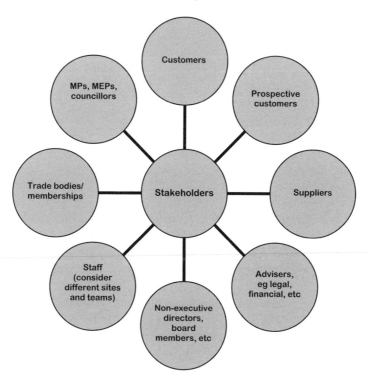

Figure 3.7.1 A stakeholder example

Company culture

When organizations do not fully identify the cause of a crisis, they can allow the potential for failure to continue or to incubate. Often the result of management activity, problems can be left untreated for years. The poor health and safety processes, lack of operational training and inefficient customer service can all be simple, unnoticed or unevaluated causes that one day may have the potential to create an industrial accident, contaminated product or *Watchdog* investigation.

In public relations, effective crisis management is not just about contingency planning but also about identifying management culture and the process of crisis incubation.

An external consultant may be better at taking an overall view. When in-house there can be a reluctance to identify a problem for fear of scapegoating and the stigma and trauma attached to people involved in the event.

Positive changes can only happen if the management perceives that changes need to be made – especially if the problem challenges an organization's core beliefs or industry.

A crisis can bring the problem to the top of the agenda. Therefore, management have to take serious steps to correct the issue and re-examine their business as a whole. It is this process that often enables companies to bounce back from a crisis stronger, bigger and better than they were before.

A survival strategy

When bouncing back from a crisis, careful planning is essential. Negative stories need to be outweighed by positive outcomes and visible improvements. When appropriate and considering internal and external influences, there is also much to be gained from keeping quiet during the aftermath too.

During the dry summer of 2006, the water companies, even the well-performing ones, kept their heads down. They left the publicity stunts and high-profile campaigns alone and concentrated on their corporate offering and stakeholder communication. They realized that raising their heads above the parapet would not be constructive for them or the industry.

For organizations having undergone a crisis or change, a simple SWOT analysis can be an effective way of looking at how to turn threats into opportunities and weaknesses into strengths. Out of this a survival strategy can be developed. It will need to address the four key areas of:

1. *Image.* In a global marketplace with modern technology and processes it is often only the image of a company that can set it apart from its competitors. Image is fascinating when you look at mobile phone companies. They largely offer the same products, services and tariff packages – but it is really only how they're branded that makes them distinguishable by the consumer.
2. *Stakeholders.* As already mentioned, the stakeholders are very important. These are the people – the staff, customers, creditors, insurers, etc – with whom a company or organization engages or hopes to have a future relationship for its own benefit.

3. *Income generating/fee earning.* This relates to the part of the business that generates income and cash flow, in other words the tasks that achieve the goals and objectives of a commercial organization.
4. *Non-fee earning/support.* These activities help to support the achievement of the goals and objectives but they do not provide value by themselves. This area relates to administration, marketing, customer service, etc.

When a crisis happens one or more of these four key areas may be damaged. In public relations we think of them as four walls to a room (see Figure 3.7.2). When a crisis hits, the organization needs to react in order to reduce the damage and recover the wall before it falls and impacts on the other areas. The saggy floor to the room is made secure and alternative facilities are put into action along with recovery plans in order to return the wall to its pre-crisis state.

Now imagine that the floor to the four walls illustrates performance. An organization's performance will obviously dip in the area that has been damaged. In order to recover the dipping floor, the level of the floor will need to be raised; in other words, performance will have to increase.

This increase in performance doesn't just happen to the area that has been damaged; the other walls also need to improve in order to help support the damaged wall. This increased performance can have a huge benefit to the company.

Staff working together to help support the damage can provide an increase in morale, improvements in systems and more efficient processes. Intense efforts made during a crisis, such as working around the clock, are unlikely to be maintained, but any improved focus on stakeholders, an organization's image, extra effort in delivering

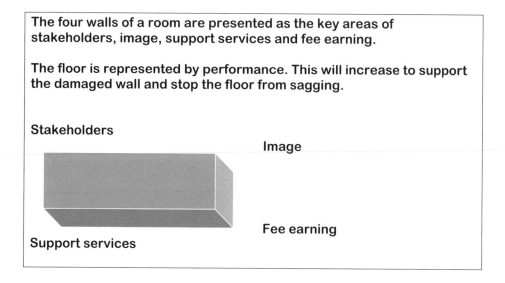

Figure 3.7.2   Survival diagram

services and support and a search for innovative solutions to prevent the loss of market share may leave the organization with a better than pre-crisis performance level.

During the BSE/CJD crisis many of the large beef abattoirs diversified. They used their packing plants to package a wide range of meats, they worked with retailers to produce a range of products for consumers and they realigned their distribution network to carry other chilled and frozen goods – not just beef.

Bouncing back

In the post-crisis period, a common-sense approach is needed. From evaluating activity, looking at an organization's culture and managing the stakeholders, the bounce-back process can begin.

The process does not happen overnight but a company can recover slowly. It is often beneficial if an organization looks at developing and maintaining a wish list. These should be items that members of an organization or business would like to change should the opportunity arise.

There are no rules for the wish lists – they can include a new office, new designs for facilities and products, staffing procedures, and changes to operational processes and even location. By encouraging departments and/or teams to look at their wish lists, an organization can listen to one of its stakeholders and look to embrace change as appropriate. Even if the wish list consists of small items, they can still impact on the corporate culture. As with all activity, it is important that the wish list changes are both clearly measurable and identifiable.

A wish list is important not only for looking at solutions but for galvanizing a team and increasing morale. It can also highlight new skills and strengths within a team or of an individual that may have gone unnoticed prior to the crisis or change.

Increasing skills

A crisis also allows an organization to increase the skills of its members through training. Having evaluated any crisis gaps within a team's or individual's knowledge, they can be pinpointed and rectified. It is important to remember that simple crisis management skills can be utilized on a day-to-day basis, helping to improve efficiency across an organization. Examples include time management training, communications, information management and stress management.

Out of this also comes the need to develop experts rather than 'jacks of all trades'. A crisis will highlight weaknesses and show where resources are needed. Having an expert on board will increase knowledge, working practices and efficiency in that area – again having a positive knock-on effect on the business.

Communication

A change can be a great catalyst for looking at how stakeholders are communicated with. From staff to the media, organizations can look at how information is disseminated and the most efficient and effective way of doing so. Different audiences will need different channels of communication, and a crisis can be useful in highlighting which channels work and which don't.

Communication is key both during and after a crisis. The smooth flow of information can position an organization as being in control and taking positive action.

During the BSE/CJD crisis, communication of the situation happened over a number of weeks as the story unfolded. In order to keep staff within Europe's largest beef abattoir briefed and to make sure that they read and understood the latest information, the method of delivery was constantly changed. This kept the news fresh and maintained interest at a time when it was all too easy to delete the endless updates and e-mail messages.

Communication channels out of hours are just as important. It is very rare that a situation happens between the working hours of 9 to 5, Monday to Friday. More often the situation happens at weekends or in the night, when the main people are away – which can exacerbate the crisis and increase its profile.

Image

When bouncing back from a crisis, careful consideration needs to be given to the image of a company. If the 'strap line' or the current identity portrays something that the company, post-crisis, is not, then the image will be seen as being inconsistent and even fraudulent and manipulative.

It is often sensible, when looking at the image and external perception of the company, for organizations to drop a specific advertising campaign or promotion in the short term. Cadbury's, responding albeit slowly to the salmonella scare in chocolate, pulled their sponsorship of *Coronation Street* on ITV during the announcement and investigation.

Managing an image after a crisis is not easy. Within the 24/7 media culture and with clever viral marketing, identities can be altered and 'witty' e-mails can be sent around the globe without being policed.

Keeping a watchful eye on an identity and a brand is difficult, especially within a global organization, but after a crisis or a change organizations need to develop an image that reflects their self-perception and objectives and this needs to be matched by the perceptions of the outside world.

Bringing the crisis to an end

When bouncing back from a crisis it is often important to draw a line under a situation, so that the organization can, at last, acknowledge what has happened and move forward. Depending on the crisis, this needs to be handled sensitively. It could be an anniversary, a celebration or a ceremonial act or service. It could be remembering people lost, the setting up of a trust or a remembrance garden. By having an actual act it can help signal an end to a particular situation and help people to recover.

A crisis can be the end for some companies and it can be the making of others. The way an organization responds to a situation can enable it to address its own weaknesses and to rebuild a stronger, more focused and more successful business.

No crisis management manual will address the post-crisis situation. Nothing can predict how stakeholders will respond to a change or an incident, but careful communication and a realistic view of the situation can enable organizations to manage the sticks and the stones and bounce back.

4

Risks for Financial and Corporate Managers

Risk without reward

Richard Coello, ACE European Group

How insurance can and should play a part in mitigating the operational risks faced by funds and fund managers

Operational failures in the fund management sector

It is not often one comes across genuinely surprising statistics; however, over the last few years, the fund management sector has produced two that are noteworthy.

According to Capco Research, 50 per cent of hedge fund failures in 2005 occurred because of operational events rather than investment risks.[1] Perhaps more amazingly, in research carried out by the Bank of New York over 2004, institutional investors cited outstanding risk management (41 per cent) as the main factor in deciding the fund managers to which they allocate mandates, with a further 37 per cent citing operational and infrastructure excellence. On the other hand, transparency of investment process was chosen by only 11 per cent of investors.[2]

These surveys show that investors want to see their portfolio managers understand operational risks and take steps to reduce these risks.

The history of the fund management sector is littered with high-profile examples of operational failures. There has been split capital trust mis-selling in the UK, where products advertised as low-risk ended up sustaining large losses to investors owing to substantial cross-holdings and leverage. More recently in the United States, the late trading scandal rocked the mutual fund sector, with allegations of fund managers allowing favoured institutional investors to benefit from trading on funds after the daily pricing close. In both cases, substantial costs were incurred by fund managers in dealing with claims for damages from investors and investigations from regulators. These are just two examples of negligence, mismanagement and fraud that highlight the need for improved operational risk mitigation in the fund management world.

Recent developments suggest that the risks faced by this sector will continue to rise, perhaps even accelerate. On 1 February 2006, the SEC implemented new rules requiring the examination and registration of almost all hedge fund advisers in the United States. In simple terms all advisors with more than 15 investors or with a lock-in period of less than two years were subject to such requirements. While the federal Appeals Court subsequently overruled the requirement in June and there is presently a moratorium allowing the SEC to come up with alternative arrangements, there is little doubt that regulation will become the norm, and advisers continue to prepare for greater scrutiny voluntarily.

New regulations and controls

The Federal Reserve, in the working group formed after the collapse of Long Term Capital Management in 1998, is also looking at the controls and procedures of hedge funds. In a May 2006 speech about the working group's findings, the Fed's chairman, Ben S Bernanke, stated: 'In particular, good risk management should link the availability and the terms of credit granted to a hedge fund to the fund's willingness to provide information on its strategies and risk profile. Our supervisors are pushing banks to clearly link transparency with credit terms and conditions.'[3]

Similar burdens for the European fund sector come from the recent Capital Requirements Directive and the Market in Financial Instruments Directive (MiFID) in 2007. Stuart Campbell, a fund management consultant at KPMG, suggests some funds will struggle with the requirements for better oversight and control: '[Fund managers] may have to think again if they believe they have left the red tape of investment banking behind them. If the regulator doesn't like what it hears, it can impose additional capital on you.'[4] MiFID will require appointments in compliance and development of a code of conduct. Firms have until January 2008 to comply with the new rules on risk control.

The risk of litigation

From an investor risk viewpoint, we will surely see levels of retail investor litigation rise in the UK owing to the changes in rules governing self-invested personal pensions (SIPPs), given the more exotic investment strategies now available to such vehicles. Hedge fund and derivative instruments can be used, property funds can be accessed and so on. Very much more the domain of institutional or high net worth individual investors previously, such structures will see a growth in individual pension money.

The same applies to real estate investment trusts (REITs). Gordon Brown's April 2006 Finance Bill set out the rules governing these proposed vehicles, which aim at providing property-owning entities with a similar tax-free status to that of their counterparts in the United States, so long as certain income distribution and gearing rules are complied with. Few argue access to these alternative investments is a bad thing for investors, but clearly the broadening of investment choices for unskilled investors brings a new dynamic to the risks faced by those managing and explaining such new products.

As Richard Wood, an associate investment director with Rensburg Sheppards, says:

> As with all new things, there are risks... Liquidity of property (or lack of it) is always an issue, although this will be mitigated to some extent by the number and diversification of properties held by the REIT. And with any property-related investment, the investor will be subject to the usual risk that the income and underlying value of the investment could be subject to change depending upon the behaviour of the UK property market.[5]

The impact on returns

Returns too are under pressure, with the private equity sector being an excellent example. Recent studies show that as of August 2006 the amount of unutilized committed cash in private equity and venture capital funds worldwide could buy up every company on the FTSE and on NASDAQ. This will inevitably lead to more competition for deals, and thus higher acquisition costs being paid, forcing fund managers to look at other ways of reducing cost and improving returns. To this extent, even investment risks can create operational risks.

So we can see across the industry – from the importance of risk control to regulation, from exposure of funds to retail investors, from pressure on returns and from rising levels of litigation – that operational risks represent potentially the most important issue in the establishment and ongoing management of funds. To this end, investment in compliance infrastructure, good information technology and a general focus on the importance of a risk management culture from senior management down are essential to the running of funds today.

Professional and managerial liability insurance

Part of this process can and perhaps should include the purchase of a comprehensive professional and managerial liability insurance product. Many elements of the above scenarios, whether they be damages sought as a result of loss to investors or defence costs for innocent directors, are insurable through the purchase of just such a policy.

The advantages of such a policy are numerous:

■ The cost of the insurance is generally deemed a 'reasonable cost' and therefore can be cross-charged to the fund, just like advertising or administration costs.
■ Insurance is often seen as a signal to investors and regulators that risk management and protection of investors are taken seriously and are part of the culture of the organization. Indeed, prudent institutional investors regularly demand the purchase of such a policy.

- The policy can be adapted to cover the fund manager and funds separately, with their own 'towers' of insurance, so that the needs of the various stakeholders (directors on the one hand, investors on the other) can be met.
- The level of understanding with regard to this sector from an insurance standpoint is ever improving, resulting in more appropriate levels of premium, excesses and broader terms.

Insurance carriers in this area have been slow to catch up with the realities faced in this industry, not just in terms of providing the right pricing for their potential insureds, but also in terms of offering clear and meaningful coverage. However, this has changed and companies like ACE European Group have been at the forefront of developing new ideas to improve the coverage offered, taking account of the latest developments.

Pending EU directives and their impact

For example, fund managers now face the advent of the 2004 Undertakings in Collective Investments in Transferable Securities Directive (otherwise known as UCITS III) across the European Union. UCITS III represents in itself a broadening of the investment possibilities in Europe. The regulations allow collective investment schemes to operate freely throughout the EU on the basis of a single authorization from one member state.

A collective investment fund may apply for UCITS status in order to allow EU-wide marketing. The concept is to create a single market in funds across the EU. With a larger market the economies of scale will reduce costs for investment managers, which can be passed on to consumers. Throughout Europe approximately 5 trillion euros are invested in collective investments. Of these funds about 70 per cent are UCITS compliant and will be subject to the new rules.

UCITS III consists of two directives. First, Directive 2001/107/EC (the Management Directive) seeks to give investment managers a European 'passport' to operate throughout the EU, widens the activities that they are allowed to undertake and introduces the concept of a simplified prospectus, which is intended to provide more accessible, comprehensive information in a simplified format to assist in cross-border marketing.

Second, Directive 2001/108/EC (the Product Directive) aims to remove barriers to cross-border marketing by allowing funds to invest in a wider range of financial instruments. Under the new directive, it is possible to establish money market funds, derivatives funds, index-tracking funds and funds of funds as UCITS.

The ultimate success of UCITS III is dependent on the way in which each member state implements the directives. In Luxembourg, Circular 02/77 was issued with a view to putting in place specific rules for investor compensation in the event of net asset value miscalculations, including a strict liability rule for the payment of such compensation. This can have a specific impact on the type of insurance cover needed by fund managers in this domicile – for example, cover can be extended to pick up potential costs of correction incurred as a result of special audits or recalculations, and furthermore policies have been designed so as to allow quick mitigation of an error (by removing the usual requirement of prior insurer consent to a settlement). We can see from these extensions that insurance cover is attempting to reflect the pace of current developments.

The rise of regulatory or governmental investigations is also a cause for concern. However, the cost of attending and potentially defending against any investigation alleging wrongful actions can also be covered by such an insurance. It is common for regulators to investigate any allegations of wrongdoing quickly, and the costs of defending such actions can be substantial.

Timothy Spangler, partner at Berwin Leighton Paisner LLP, outlines the position:

> Enforcement actions and investor lawsuits have been steadily on the rise. In the United States, the SEC filed more than 20 enforcement actions against hedge funds in 2005. The FSA has also begun proceedings against hedge funds and their portfolio managers under the new market abuse regime.
>
> A regular review of the systems and controls of a hedge fund will enable the directors (as well as the investors) to identify and adequately address unacceptable risks. However, no matter how comprehensive the procedures or how frequent the review exercise, some risk will inevitably remain. Directors of hedge funds, therefore, should consider the desirability of two different types of liability insurance: directors' and officers' liability insurance (D&O) and professional indemnity insurance (PI).[6]

These types of insurance are two of the main coverages on offer in a comprehensive investment management liability product.

Whatever the needs or pressures, policies can be tailored to suit such demands, and there are a number of highly skilled brokers in the insurance market able to negotiate these changes and push for the best possible terms.

One could argue that, with the furious pace of intrusion into this area by due diligence reviews, regulators and exchanges, it is simply common sense for the directors of a fund or fund managers to ensure they obtain some form of insurance protection. It is certainly an oddity that, in almost all other respects, portfolio managers are outstanding at hedging out unknowns and analysing out financial concerns – but when it comes to operational failures there continues to be a blind spot. Given the protections offered by the latest insurance solutions this is an unnecessary gap – and, after all, there is no reward to running such a risk.

Notes

1. Hedge Funds 101 and 102 Conference, Harvard Club, New York, February 2006.
2. David Aldrich and Marina Lewin, 'The seven habits of highly effective hedge funds', Bank of New York, December 2004.
3. Bernanke address, Federal Reserve Bank of Atlanta, Sea Island, GA, May 2006.
4. *Financial Times* Fund Management supplement, August 2006.
5. 'A good REIT of return', www.newbusiness.co.uk, July 2006.
6. 'Liability insurance for hedge funds', *Hedge Week*, May 2006.

Top priorities for internal audit in a changing environment

*Robert B Hirth, Protiviti, USA and
Carmen M Rossiter, Protiviti, Canada*

In response to new challenges, changes and expectations within the business environment, internal audit functions are striving to provide greater value as a key component of the organization's governance framework. Internal audit has emerged as an independent, objective assurance and consulting activity designed to add value and improve an organization's operations. Effective internal audit functions help organizations to accomplish their business objectives by bringing a systematic, disciplined approach to evaluate and improve the effectiveness of governance, risk management and control processes. This emergence needs to continue evolving, developing and changing to meet the dynamics of the business world.

Drawing from the Institute of Internal Auditors' International Standards for the Professional Practice of Internal Auditing and our experience with leading internal audit functions, we provide 10 strategic priorities that we recommend every public and private company – along with every government-sponsored and not-for-profit organization – employ in its internal audit function, whether it is in-house, co-sourced or outsourced.

Raise the bar – live up to heightened expectations

Regulatory reform and a changing business environment underscore the growing importance of effective governance, risk management and control. Internal audit plays a key role as an essential pillar of the governance framework, working with management, the board of directors and the external auditors. As a result, internal audit functions are being upgraded and given greater visibility and responsibility in organizations.

Internal auditors have long sought greater prominence for their roles, but increased focus and attention bring with them the responsibility to deliver on heightened expectations. Internal audit functions must respond to the demands of their new environment and the evolving needs of their stakeholders by raising the bar and moving to the next level.

By revisiting their methodology, processes and practices to focus on the right things, internal audit can provide unique insight and deliver 'real-time' value to their organizations. Internal audit functions are refining risk identification and assessment capabilities to enhance risk-based auditing to align with organization-wide priorities, and are providing assurance and advisory support where it is most needed. Moreover, internal audit is aligning its activity with key business risks, recognizing that the audit universe should cover the full spectrum of the organization's major risks and activities. Audit coverage is being expanded to include governance, entity-level controls, fraud, new business initiatives and a more comprehensive approach to information technology, security and other pervasive and/or high-risk areas. Most important, internal auditors are learning to deal with change – they are monitoring constantly their organization's risk profile and incorporating flexibility in the audit plan.

Effective internal audit functions also are re-emphasizing the basics of risk and control by adopting generally accepted risk or control frameworks as cornerstones to guide their work. Sarbanes–Oxley compliance also has reinforced fundamental skills in documentation, walk-throughs and testing with more disciplined narratives, flow charts and risk/control matrices. Testing is recognized as an essential step to validate the operating effectiveness of control, with sample sizes being adjusted to more realistic levels to provide assurance based on the rigour of statistical concepts. Internal audit functions also are formalizing issue ranking and tracking mechanisms, recognizing that control deficiencies need to be prioritized and cannot be left to linger until they degenerate into bad news or disaster.

The practice of internal auditing is continuing to evolve to address heightened stakeholder needs and expectations. Internal audit functions are raising the bar and moving to the next level to provide greater value to their organizations.

Revisit the charter and reporting relationship – validate purpose and position

Today's directors and senior management have greater accountability for governance, risk management and control. They are relying on internal audit to assist with these responsibilities and, as a result, are revisiting and rethinking their expectations of the role of internal audit. Overall, we are seeing greater demands and heightened expectations of internal audit, with a growing focus on core assurance activities as a primary value driver.

The purpose, authority and responsibility of internal audit – as well as the nature of assurance and consulting activities provided to the organization – should be articulated clearly in a charter validated with senior management and approved by the audit committee. Given changes in shareholder expectations, internal audit functions should ensure their mandate is revised and aligned with the requirements and value perceptions of their stakeholders. Ideally, the internal audit charter should be formalized as a corporate policy, subject to annual review and approval by the audit committee. This will ensure the charter properly reflects the authority, responsibility and accountability assigned to the internal audit function and that it clearly articulates functional and administrative reporting relationships.

Reporting relationships are being revisited where the ownership for internal audit is being elevated to senior management and the audit committee level. To be effective, internal audit must be both independent and objective in the performance of its work. To achieve organizational independence, the chief audit executive should report to a level within the organization that allows internal audit to fulfil its responsibilities. Internal audit should be free from interference in determining the scope of internal auditing, performing work and communicating results.

The Institute of Internal Auditors' (IIA) International Standards for the Professional Practice of Internal Auditing Practice Advisory 1110-2, Chief Audit Executive (CAE) Reporting Lines, states that: 'The IIA believes strongly that to achieve necessary independence, the CAE should report functionally to the audit committee or its equivalent. For administrative purposes, in most circumstances, the CAE should report directly to the chief executive officer of the organization.'

Interestingly, in a 2005 survey of members of the IIA from Fortune 1000 companies, three-quarters of the nearly 300 respondents said that their organization's internal audit functions report functionally to the audit committee.

Internal audit acts as the 'eyes and ears' of the audit committee and company management by providing independent objective assurance on the state of governance, risk and control in the organization. This 'dual reporting' is sensitive and requires delicate balance since the CAE is both a member of management and the leader of an independent group expected to report on management's risk and control stewardship of the organization.

The CAE should be positioned for success with an appropriate place on the company's organization chart and a mandate that clearly addresses purpose, authority and scope.

Rebalance internal audit activities – focus on risk and stakeholder expectations

Sarbanes–Oxley and similar legislation have introduced measures to restore investor confidence and the integrity of financial reporting. These requirements have significantly affected management, audit committees, external auditors and the interaction of these groups. These new requirements also have had an impact on internal audit functions, as many stepped up to help their companies meet the challenges of complying with these new regulations. This diverted internal audit efforts to assist management in addressing other business priorities.

As Sarbanes–Oxley and other corporate governance laws have been enacted, internal auditors responded promptly to educate their management and audit committees on new internal control reporting requirements and to assist their organizations in scoping these compliance projects, providing guidance and often going beyond what some might think to be the normal role of internal audit. They assisted with, or in some cases even led, documentation and design evaluation efforts, and executed much of the operating effectiveness testing and remediation required to help ensure their organizations would pass the first-year internal control audit. As efforts and resources were channelled to the immediate task of compliance, internal auditors increasingly were pulled away from their normal duties. In many instances, internal audit activities in other high-risk non-financial areas were cancelled or deferred.

Recognizing this, some internal audit departments are beginning to 'reprioritize' and 'rebalance' their activities. They are refocusing on risks encompassing the full spectrum of organizational objectives, including coverage of the reliability of financial reporting, the efficiency and effectiveness of operations, and compliance with applicable laws and regulations, as articulated in the COSO Internal Controls – Integrated Framework.

In a survey conducted by Protiviti in July and August 2005, almost three-quarters of respondents at public companies reported that a rebalancing initiative was either under way or in the planning stages at their companies. Most organizations planning to rebalance said this would occur within the following year or so. High-performing internal audit functions are aligning their activities to stakeholder expectations and prioritizing their activities to areas of greatest risk and opportunity to yield the most value for their organization.

Internal auditors diverted their efforts to Sarbanes–Oxley compliance out of necessity to help their organizations. It is now time to re-evaluate internal audit activities, with a focus on stakeholder expectations and risk-based auditing.

Communicate – sharpen dialogue with senior management and the audit committee

Communication is a key determinant of a successful internal audit function. The CAE must be kept informed to stay abreast of the business, strategic plans, new developments, initiatives, events and transactions. Internal audit must have 'a seat at the table', acting as a trusted adviser without participating directly in the management process in order to preserve independence and objectivity.

Most importantly, internal audit must communicate effectively with management and the audit committee to support them in the discharge of their governance and stewardship responsibilities. Pertinent information must be identified, captured and communicated in a form and time frame that are appropriate to the recipient. Clear, concise, forthright, relevant and timely communications – oral and written – are critical to the role of chief audit executive. The IIA Practice Advisory 2060-2 Relationship with the Audit Committee is clearly defined: 'In large part the overall effectiveness of the CAE and audit committee relationship will revolve around the communication between the parties. Today's audit committees expect a high level of open and candid communications. If the CAE is to be viewed as a trusted advisor by the committee, communications is the key element.'

Effective communication requires effort on all sides – not only should internal audit foster dialogue with senior management and the audit committee, but the audit committee should welcome and facilitate ongoing communication, while also providing the chief audit executive direct access.

Act as a change agent – facilitate positive change

Nothing is more constant than change itself – especially in our fast-paced environment. Internal auditors need to be alert to change and the speed with which major risks can evolve and the momentum they can achieve if left unattended.

New risks often wreak havoc in organizations through the element of surprise. Greater vigilance is required to identify new risks, assess their exposure and ensure that the company is responding in a manner that is consistent with its defined risk appetite and tolerances. Internal audit cannot manage risks directly, but it can play a role by maintaining a flexible audit approach and a dynamic audit plan to address the emerging risks of today as well as potential future risks. Effective internal auditors want to be where the risks and action are.

Beyond the ability to cope with change, the true measure of performance for internal audit is the ability to effect and facilitate organizational change that fosters continuous improvement and gradual progression up the risk management continuum. The true worth of internal audit is not measured in the weight of after-the-fact recommendations, but in the ability to provide just-in-time advice and influence positive change that adds value to the organization. In today's marketplace, change management is a core competency that successful companies need to develop in order to stay on top.

Internal audit should be at the forefront of positive change by recommending and facilitating the process of aligning people, processes and technology to achieve improved sustainable performance. Internal auditors should be both the guardians of established policies and procedures, and the champions of positive change and continuous improvement.

Drive efficiency – 'work smarter'

Spending on internal audit is increasing as organizations realize the value-added contribution internal audit can bring in establishing, maintaining and improving governance, risk management and control across the organization.

General data on current internal audit spending is provided annually by the IIA Global Auditing Information Network (GAIN) reports. For example, according to GAIN's 2005 study, large companies ($30 billion or more in annual revenue) spend an average of more than $15 million a year on internal audit activities, and more than $12 million a year on their external audits. Smaller companies – annual revenues of $1 billion to $5 billion, for example – spend an average of $1.5 million on internal audit and $1.3 million on external audits every year.

This and other research and information provided by GAIN represent well-established, reputable data that offer average internal audit cost based upon revenue ranges, with additional information available by industry. Although these are estimates, they provide valuable benchmarks on internal audit spending. Keep in mind that the actual level of expenditure may vary among companies based on the size, nature and complexity of the business.

While internal audit budgets are on the rise, internal audit leaders are nevertheless being asked to do much more with far less. To achieve this, internal auditors are revisiting their methods, processes, practices, capabilities and technology support to enhance efficiencies and 'work smarter'.

In our experience, efficiency gains are typically available from the following:

■ first and foremost, risk-based auditing connecting the risk profile of the enterprise to the internal audit plan;
■ dynamic risk identification and assessment capabilities to support a robust, comprehensive and ongoing risk assessment;
■ standardization of methods, approaches and repeatable activities;
■ utilizing self-assessment techniques to increase coverage and efficiency;
■ leveraging technology, tools and techniques to increase productivity;
■ knowledge sharing and supporting databases;
■ focused analytics, performance measures and risk indicators to facilitate desk auditing and focus follow-up activities;
■ teaming effectively with outside parties in meaningful co-sourcing relationships;
■ continuous monitoring and auditing;
■ developing guest and virtual auditor programmes; and
■ effective personnel deployment and proactive management of staff utilization.

Today's internal auditors must strive for ongoing improvement to meet increasing demands while managing expenditures in order to contribute positively to the organization's value equation.

Build talent – attract, develop and retain the best

Amid the changing regulatory climate and increasing demands for performance and efficiency, internal audit leaders are challenged in attracting, developing and retaining the resources they require to deliver on their new mandate.

Our era of regulatory reform has highlighted resource and experience shortages in accounting, finance and auditing. In many cases, compliance activities were delegated to already lean departments, which had been targeted for cost-cutting measures during the downturn that preceded corporate reform. With the reform-driven spike in demand for talent along with emerging business growth opportunities, more companies have realized the need to step up their recruiting efforts and offer more competitive compensation and benefits packages for internal audit as well as accounting personnel.

The overall demand for accounting, finance and audit professionals is unlikely to lessen significantly, as there will be an ongoing need for companies to meet regulatory requirements and emphasize governance. Demographic forces also will keep demand high. As baby boomers begin leaving the workplace, the enrolment in university accounting programmes is now rising after years of decline, but it will take some time for graduates to gain the experience needed to fill certain positions.

A more complex business environment also has created the need for specialized expertise to assess new risks and address areas of complex business auditing. The complement requirements of internal audit functions are changing. Internal audit leaders need to perform a comprehensive skills assessment to identify gaps to be filled by additional talent or flexible staffing arrangements such as strategic co-sourcing relationships.

Continuous education and staff development are also critical to enhance capabilities. While not required or mandated specifically, it is now considered best practice for internal auditors to possess and maintain professional designations that are directly relevant to the practice of internal audit. Leading internal audit practices are encouraging and rewarding personnel to attain specialized designations and accreditations including certified internal auditor (CIA), certified information systems auditor (CISA), certified fraud examiner (CFE), certified public accountant (CPA), chartered accountant (CA), certified management accountant (CMA), certified general accountant (CGA) and others. Supplemental training is also required to meet requirements for continuing professional education (CPE) and further professional development.

Most importantly, effective leadership is critical to high-performing internal audit functions – starting at the top with the CAE to set the tone, elevate the stature of the functions and preserve the independence and objectivity required to effectively fulfil the internal audit mandate. The chief audit executive must not only 'mind the store' and manage the function, but also possess the vision, foresight and drive to lead the function in raising the bar and moving to the next level in a world of constant change.

To deliver effectively on their mandate, internal auditors need to ensure they have both the quantity and the quality of resources they require. The success of an internal audit function will be driven, in large part, by its people and their capabilities.

Participate in the profession – embrace the IIA Standards

Internal audit is a self-governed profession through the Institute of Internal Auditors promulgating a Professional Practices Framework that includes mandatory guidance in the form of a Code of Ethics and International Standards for the Professional Practice of Internal Auditing (IIA Standards). As a fundamental requirement, internal auditors should comply with the IIA Standards. In addition, they should be active in the profession at the international and local chapter levels, and contribute to the development of the practice of internal audit.

Internal audit is evolving as a respected profession separate and distinct from external audit, bringing added opportunity to demonstrate its fullest potential to add value to the organization.

Strengthen quality processes – focus on continuous improvement

Internal auditors should practise what they preach to the company. The IIA Standards require ongoing and periodic assessment of the entire spectrum of audit and consulting work performed by internal audit, including an ongoing internal quality assurance process with periodic reviews and an external quality assessment by a qualified independent reviewer every five years. In other words, internal audit should take steps to ensure its activities undergo quality assessment.

Assessments of quality programmes should include evaluation of the following:

■ compliance with the IIA Standards and Code of Ethics;
■ adequacy of the internal audit activity's charter, goals, objectives, policies and procedures;
■ contribution to the organization's governance, risk management and control processes;
■ compliance with applicable laws, regulations and government or industry standards;
■ effectiveness of continuous improvement activities and adoption of best practices; and
■ whether the auditing activity adds value and improves the organization's operations.

Many internal audit departments already comply or are in the process of complying with these requirements and are now looking beyond mere compliance to benchmark themselves against leading practices to foster continuous improvement within the function. Other internal audit functions realize that, for whatever reason, the function needs to change substantially from its current structure. In these cases, internal audit functions and their audit committees take a 'transformational' approach, working with outside advisers to redirect and reorganize to meet current reality, expectations and needs.

Quality also is highly relevant to the external auditors. Internal audit operates as a key element of the organization's control system. In addition, auditing standards specifically acknowledge the ability of external auditors to rely on the work of others, such as a competent and objective internal audit function. Senior management and the audit committee should seek feedback from the external auditors and their viewpoint on the performance, competency and objectivity of the company's internal audit function, including the level of coordination with the external audit firm and the degree of reliance the firm places on internal audit's work.

Assessments and feedback promote continuous improvement to strengthen quality within the function. The chief audit executive should share the results of external and internal quality programme assessments with their various stakeholders, including senior management, the audit committee and external auditors.

Measure performance – add value

Gone are the days of internal audit as a forgotten sleepy place. The reality of today's business environment is that internal audit, like other functions in the organization, is responsible for contributing to the success and performance of the enterprise and will be held accountable for results.

What gets measured gets done. Appropriately developed performance measures help to drive results, performance, quality and continuous improvement. Strong internal audit functions have processes for measuring their own performance with a balanced scorecard of measurements focusing on cost, quality and timeliness.

To be effective, performance measures should be aligned directly to stakeholder value drivers. These will vary among organizations but could include measures such as audit plan accomplishment, cycle time, recommendations accepted, control breakdowns or deficiencies in areas recently reviewed by internal audit and customer satisfaction.

Examples of performance measures for internal audit could include:

■ *Quality:*
  - customer/process owner satisfaction scores from auditees;
  - audit committee and management evaluation scores;
  - external audit evaluation score from company's external auditor;
  - upward feedback scores on chief audit executive and internal audit managers from internal audit staff;
  - percentage of internal audit staff with CIA or other relevant certifications;
  - performance evaluation scores on internal audit staff;

- control breakdowns/deficiencies in areas recently reviewed by internal audit;
- internal control scorecard results by major area within the company;
- results of internal and independent quality assurance reviews.

■ *Cost:*
- percentage of fully loaded internal audit cost as a percentage of company revenues and assets;
- actual and average cost per internal audit project;
- average cost per internal auditor;
- cost per audit hour in total;
- cost per audit hour based upon actual audit work only, excluding administration;
- travel costs of the internal audit function and average cost per trip;
- training costs and training cost per auditor;
- technology licensing costs and other outside costs;
- costs related to use of outside resources.

■ *Timeliness:*
- report cycle time from completion of fieldwork to issuance and finalization of report;
- budgeted hours versus actual hours by individual audit;
- percentage of audits called for in the audit plan that are not yet complete;
- unresolved/incomplete recommendations from prior audit reports;
- average length of audit assignment in person hours or weeks;
- major risk areas not audited in the last year;
- ageing/status of open, unresolved audit findings (especially those beyond their due date).

■ *Other:*
- degree of reliance on internal audit work by external auditor;
- turnover rates;
- percentage change rate in the annual audit plan;
- percentage of assets, revenues, locations, business units, etc covered by the internal audit plan;
- linkage of key risks to specific skills of the internal audit team;
- degree of IT-related audit work to total audit effort.

Leading internal audit functions have well-developed scorecards of selected measures that are agreed upon with senior management and the audit committee. They measure the internal audit functions' success and constantly re-evaluate their effectiveness. Top-performing internal audit functions are committed to quality, value and satisfaction, using balanced scorecards to assess their contribution in quantifiable and measurable terms.

Conclusion

Given current regulatory reform and the changing business environment, the future for internal auditors has never been brighter. As the expectations of stakeholders rise with regard to internal audit's performance, internal auditors will benefit greatly by employing the 10 strategies detailed in this chapter. In addition, as the role of internal audit continues to evolve, the opportunity exists to take internal audit functions to the next level to improve the effectiveness of governance, risk management and control in the organization, which will create true value enterprise-wide.

Regulatory risk – senior managers, systems and controls in financial services firms

Penny Sanders, KSB Law LLP

A recent series of disciplinary cases has made clear the Financial Services Authority's (FSA) expectations of firms' systems and controls under current rules. On the basis that it is always easier to be wise after the event, two of them will serve in this chapter as useful case studies.

Senior managers of all firms should be aware of the risks, including firms in the Contact Centre that are rarely visited by the FSA. Should they be aware of these two decisions and review their internal systems and controls accordingly? The ARROW II risk model (see page 194) is a good starting point.

Case study: The risks (1) – L Limited (fined £63,000)

L is a regional firm of IFAs. The FSA found that the firm's failings resulted from serious systemic weaknesses in its systems and controls and its senior management arrangements. L failed to maintain a clear and appropriate apportionment of significant responsibilities amongst its senior managers. Many of the senior managers were not aware of their responsibilities.

Senior management had failed to demonstrate to the FSA a sufficient understanding of the firm's regulatory obligations.

One of the more serious aspects of the case was that L had been unaware of the failings, which were only discovered as a result of the FSA's visits rather than through the operation of its systems and procedures.

Breaches of the FSA Rules were as shown in Table 4.3.1.

Table 4.3.1   Breaches of the FSA Rules

FSA Rule	Description of breach
SYSC 2.1.1R and SYSC 2.2.1.R	Failure to clearly and appropriately apportion significant responsibilities amongst its senior management and adequately monitor and control its business.
	Failure to record the roles and responsibilities of senior management and have clear and appropriate reporting lines.
SYSC 3.1.1R and SYSC 3.2.6R	Failure to implement systems and controls adequate for the nature, scale and complexity of its business for training and competence, approval and communication of financial promotions and internal complaints handling.
	Failure to have a suitably tailored compliance manual.
	Failure to implement systems and controls in relation to the provision of management information and to counter the risk of financial crime.

During the period in question, L had registered approved persons who held the controlled functions of director, apportionment and oversight officer, compliance oversight officer and money laundering reporting officer respectively.

However, the weakness lay in the fact that L had apparently not applied adequate focus to apportioning responsibilities amongst its senior management, particularly in the areas of training and compliance. There were no clear and appropriate reporting lines. Such as they were, they were confusing and uncertain. Furthermore, the relevant management responsibilities were not communicated to staff within the firm.

Senior management themselves were confused about their responsibilities and roles, and the FSA found that this had led to a failure to apportion responsibilities effectively and poor maintenance of systems and controls.

Some simple procedural steps might have prevented the failure, subsequent fine and damaged reputation:

- Keep a record of the responsibilities of senior management.
- Include these arrangements in job descriptions.
- Document roles and responsibilities in organizational charts and diagrams.
- Where functions are shared or divided ensure the division is clear and well understood.

The board of L only began to have regular board meetings in June 2004, notwithstanding that it had been incorporated in 1999. Although board members maintained that compliance-related matters were discussed on an informal and *ad hoc* basis, the FSA found that, since June 2004, no formal compliance reports or papers had been reviewed.

L had no arrangements in place to ensure that adequate and regular management information was provided to the board for the purposes of business oversight. The only regular report to the board was of the profit and loss figures. Furthermore there were no arrangements in place to ensure that delegated responsibilities were being performed adequately. Regulatory and compliance issues were not reported to the board and, on the few occasions when limited information was produced, it was neither reliable nor timely.

Systems and controls were not reviewed on a regular basis because of a lack of any proper apportionment of responsibilities, and senior management roles were not understood. Consequently, L was unable to identify, quantify and manage regulatory risks. Its senior managers were probably unaware of compliance risks.

L failed to appreciate the requirement for senior management to review its approach to treating customers fairly (TCF) and, as a result, no TCF policy had been formulated.

The FSA's TCF initiative needs to be considered and documented in a structured manner. Some practical matters to be considered concerning staff remuneration, management information, complaints handling and how to embed TCF into strategic change are outlined in the following sections.

Staff remuneration

A structure that is heavily commission-driven for sales staff can create risks, which need to be effectively managed. A failure to manage and control the risks inherent in particular remuneration structures can threaten a firm's ability to treat its customers fairly.

Pay is only one form of incentive: promotion, recognition and other non-monetary rewards can influence behaviour.

Issues to consider:

■ How are sales staff remunerated? Do you manage risks arising from setting up incentives to encourage staff to meet particular sales targets?
■ How to set targets and rewards for non-sales staff. This includes senior management, marketing, customer service, complaints handlers, compliance and middle management. They can all have an impact on TCF.

Management information

Senior management needs to ensure that it has access to appropriate management information (MI). In the context of considering whether TCF is embedded in your business, there may be a need to review some current MI. A review may be necessary both in terms of coverage and in terms of delivering the right information to those responsible for different aspects of TCF. The exercise should be proportionate and cost-effective.

The effectiveness of MI systems will be one of the issues FSA supervisors expect to discuss with firms in the context of supervisory work on TCF.

Some issues to consider:

■ Does current MI cover areas that are relevant to TCF?
■ Identify adequate performance measures to track delivery of TCF.
■ Identify changes that will be effective in closing the gaps.
■ Can information already available within the business be used more effectively and, if not, what other information is available and how can this be obtained?
■ Make sure that MI is filtered and distributed to appropriate audiences within the firm including those responsible for different aspects of TCF.

Complaints management

Complaints handling is seen as a key role in consumer protection. In the FSA's view, complaints received should also be a valuable indicator of the effectiveness of a firm's systems, pointing to problems in the firm's operations that need to be addressed.

The number of cases referred to the Financial Ombudsman Service and subsequently upheld in favour of the customer will often be key indicators that management can refer to when assessing the effectiveness of complaint handling arrangements.

Some issues to consider:

- Encourage staff to consider complaints positively.
- Make sure there are appropriate incentives for staff to treat complaints fairly.
- Encourage staff to recognize expressions of dissatisfaction from customers as complaints and to record them appropriately in the firm's system.
- Allocate sufficient resources to deal with complaints efficiently.
- Track complaints trends in a timely manner so that you can respond quickly if, for example, volumes suddenly increase.
- Consider whether you put up any unnecessary barriers, making it difficult for customers to complain.
- Ensure that complaints are fully and fairly investigated and, if the review of complaints involves potential conflicts of interest, these should be managed properly.
- When communicating with customers make sure that materials are clear and concise, avoiding unnecessary 'legalese'.
- Make sure the firm learns lessons from complaints data.
- Does senior management exercise control over complaints handling?
- Consider whether the firm remedies the root cause of complaints, in order to prevent similar problems recurring.

Managing strategic change and taking account of TCF

The FSA appreciates that management needs to be able to pursue profitable new business opportunities but, when considering possible strategic change, firms should start considering the implications for TCF at an early stage.

Issues to consider include assessing how TCF can be taken into account when:

- entering new markets – in terms of either customers served or products/ services offered;
- undertaking mergers or acquisitions and disposals involving some or all parts of the business;
- cost-cutting or implementing operational improvement activities such as outsourcing or staff cutbacks;
- implementing major new systems affecting customers or products;
- changing business status, such as taking advantage of depolarization.

The FSA expects firms to protect consumers from potential detriment during major change by considering TCF 1) at the business case development and assessment phase and 2) during the planning and implementation period, and monitoring the impact of change.

It is worth noting the matters which reduced the level of fine that the FSA would otherwise have imposed on L:

■ L engaged a consultant to review its compliance arrangements and systems. L provided the FSA with a copy of the consultant's report and indicated that it was willing to implement the recommendations contained in the report and remedy the inadequacies that it had identified.
■ Shortly after the FSA investigation had commenced, L amended its financial promotions procedures so that an external review of all promotions would be carried out by the compliance consultant prior to L's own final approval.
■ Two of L's employees agreed to undertake industry training, approved by the FSA, in relation to the apportionment and oversight requirements, financial promotions, training and competence and compliance.
■ The FSA found no evidence that L had deliberately breached the FSA Rules and Principles.
■ There was no evidence of customer detriment.

L cooperated fully with the FSA and quickly agreed the facts of the case and settled the matter. In fact by agreeing to settle at an early stage, L qualified for a 30 per cent reduction in penalty, reducing the fine from £90,000.

Case study: The risks (2) – Mr N

Mr N was a director of a firm that provided financial advice to a customer base of some 10,000 individuals, serviced by 30 financial advisers operating from different bases around the United Kingdom. The firm specialized in the sale of investment products, mostly to retired individuals, and was actively involved in the selling of structured capital at risk products (SCARPS), which became commonly known as 'precipice bonds'.

The firm eventually went into voluntary liquidation. The liquidator estimated that the value of outstanding claims against the firm from customers was potentially over £1.3 million if all complaints against the firm were successful.

Mr N personally held the key controlled functions of director, apportionment and oversight officer, compliance oversight officer and money laundering reporting officer. As well as being personally responsible for these roles, he also held a managerial post.

The FSA considered that it should have been obvious to Mr N that he was unable to carry out all of his duties properly, especially in the light of the wide geographical spread of the individual advisers.

Mr N failed in his personal responsibilities by:

- Not sufficiently scrutinizing the advised sales of SCARPs from a compliance perspective.
- Not visiting the firm's advisers in their offices. He often met up with them in hotel rooms and the advisers selected the files he was to review.
- Not adequately investigating the 'own account' activities of one of the firm's advisers who was promoting and selling to customers 'investments' in which he had a personal interest. Mr N received customer complaints and eventually did take action, but the FSA found that it was insufficient.
- Failing to implement comprehensive complaints handling procedures and to keep clear, accurate records.
- Failing to provide the firm with an internal compliance manual that met FSA standards. This led to a transfer of the burden of dealing with complaints against the firm to the Financial Ombudsman Service and customers themselves.

Mr N failed to reach the standards set by the FSA's Statement of Principles for approved persons.

In particular his conduct breached the following Principles:

- Principle 2: Use adequate skill, care and diligence when carrying out a controlled function.
- Principle 5: An approved person carrying out a significant influence function must take reasonable steps to ensure the business he or she is responsible for is organized and controlled effectively.
- Principle 6: Use due skill and diligence in managing the business of the firm.
- Principle 7: Take reasonable steps to ensure the business of the firm complies with the requirements and standards of the regulatory system.

As a result of these personal failings, Mr N was prohibited from carrying out any controlled function involving the exercise of significant influence over any authorized firm. In other words he was prohibited from occupying any senior management position in a firm carrying on regulated activities. The ban was for two years.

There is a clear message in both these case studies. Senior management is ultimately responsible for ensuring firms meet FSA standards, and the case of Mr N shows how the FSA will hold an individual senior manager liable for the failings of the firm where they are his or her responsibility.

ARROW II visits

For relationship-managed firms, the FSA has officially launched its ARROW II supervision and has published its Risk Assessment Framework paper. This moves the supervision of firms towards risk-based supervision. Each relationship-managed firm will have its own risk score, which is a combination of impact and probability. More specifically:

The risk to the FSA's objectives set out in the Financial Services and Markets Act 2000	is equal to	the impact of the problem if it occurs	×	the probability of the problem occurring

Firms that are assessed as being low-impact will rarely be subjected to firm-specific risk assessment work, reliance being placed by the FSA on the remote monitoring of the information submitted by the firm.

For firms that are assessed as anything other than low-impact, the FSA will conduct regular assessments of risks within the firm. The frequency of assessments will be once every one to four years, depending on the risk profile of the firm.

The FSA will adopt three different supervisory approaches:

■ *Full Arrow.* This will involve a full risk assessment of probability, covering all business and control risks. Supervisory teams will have a discretion to investigate any areas and issues during the assessment as they think fit. Elsewhere in the FSA, there will be a validation procedure that will have the task of ensuring proportionality. Following the assessment, risk scores will be communicated to the firm in an ARROW letter.
■ *Arrow Light.* This risk assessment will have a reduced scope. It will only cover certain core areas and sector-important issues unless another clearly identified significant risk is identified.
■ *The Small Firm.* 'Small Firm' is an expression used by the FSA Firm Model to describe low-impact firms that do not have a specific relationship manager at the FSA appointed to them. They are instead dealt with through the Firm Contact Centre. No regular assessments are carried out at these firms. However, they are subject to thematic reviews and to specific risk mitigation work that might be triggered by submitted returns or information from third-party sources such as the Financial Ombudsman Scheme.

All firms, particularly relationship-managed firms, should spend the necessary time in understanding the new FSA risk-based approach and should prepare for the new-style supervision visits.

The FSA has the following helpful advice for firms preparing for an ARROW risk assessment:

- The pre-visit information request will give a good indication of what is likely to come up in the assessment.
- Simple explanations of the firm's abbreviations, for example, can help understanding and save time.
- Take a look at the FSA's Financial Risk Outlook and Business Plan, which are published annually and can be found on the FSA website. These indicate the areas that the FSA will focus on. Conduct a gap analysis to reveal how your business measures up.
- Make sure you read 'Dear CEO' letters and keep up to date with what sector leaders are focusing on, as sector priorities can influence supervisory priorities.
- Keep in touch with your relationship manager if you have one and avoid presenting him or her with surprises.
- Brief staff who are likely to be interviewed, making sure they have a clear understanding of the FSA's aims and objectives. If it would be useful, hold mock interviews.
- Agree with the FSA before the visit whether note takers will be appropriate and from which area within the firm.
- It may be beneficial to hold an internal debriefing meeting with your own staff who have been interviewed, after the visit, to discover what issues have been focused on.
- Bring key documents to interviews such as management information, strategic documents and organization charts.

The Markets in Financial Instruments Directive (MiFID)

Finally, no consideration of regulatory risk can be complete without an eye to the future. The future, in this instance, is the implementation in UK law of MiFID in November 2007. In general MiFID will cover most, if not all, firms currently subject to the Investment Services Directive ('any [firm] the regular occupation or business of which is the provision of investment services for third parties on a professional basis') plus some that are currently not. This will include:

- investment banks;
- portfolio managers;
- stockbrokers and broker dealers;
- corporate finance firms;
- many futures and options firms;
- some commodities firms.

The FSA believes that holding senior management to account is key to achieving the desired corporate culture.

This focus is reinforced by the advent of MiFID, which introduces the additional concepts of 'senior personnel' and the 'supervisory function' for investment firms.

In implementing MiFID, the FSA will define senior personnel as anyone who effectively directs the business of the firm, including the board.

The supervisory function will be defined as any function within the firm that is responsible for the supervision of its senior personnel.

Responsibility of senior personnel

The firm must ensure that senior personnel and, where necessary, the supervisory function are responsible for ensuring that the firm complies with its obligations under MiFID.

In particular, they must assess and periodically review the effectiveness of the policies, arrangements and procedures put in place to comply with the firm's obligations under MiFID and take appropriate measures to address any deficiencies.

Conflicting priorities – best practice in conflict management

Graham Massie, Centre for Effective Dispute Resolution (CEDR)

Preface

The quality of canapés offered at law firm receptions has increased significantly in the last couple of years. And so has the quality of conversation – at least to the extent that I don't have to define mediation or explain who CEDR are as often as I used to. But what hasn't changed, particularly when I'm talking to business people – to finance directors, chief executives and chairmen/women, rather than simply to lawyers – is what happens when I move into sales mode:

'So, tell me about your business – do you get involved in many disputes yourself?'
'Oh no, we don't really have disputes. It's not really my area as our lawyers deal with that sort of thing.'
'Really? So do you have any conflict in your organization?'
'Oh yes, conflict – we have lots of that.'

And 9 times out of 10 the non-verbal answer is even clearer – a thin smile and a resigned look as I see the other person recall an argument, a difficult colleague or most often a simple reality of business life.

So what's going on here? When Sun Tzu's *Art of War* is required reading at all of the leading business schools, why is it that business managers shy away from the word 'dispute'? It's certainly not because they don't have any – or because it doesn't have any impact on their business.

A universal condition

Conflict is a fact of life even in the best-run organization. It goes under many names – disagreement, disharmony, dispute, difficulty or difference – but the results of mismanaged conflict are the same: at best unwelcome distraction from a heavy workload; at worst damage that may threaten the very future of the organization.

On the other hand, conflict can be productive, with a healthy disagreement often fuelling the cauldron of debate from which new ideas and innovation emerge. Conflicting views can lead to debate and refinement of solutions, or can act as an impetus for further information gathering, leading to more informed decisions.

So the challenge for management is to realize the benefits of creative tension without straining relationships to breaking point. From an unhappy customer to a disgruntled director, business can have the challenge of conflict come from any direction – and, just as with all other aspects of risk management, the goal is to maximize the benefits whilst minimizing the downside and avoiding, or at least surviving, the catastrophic.

Poorly managed conflict costs money, creates uncertainty and degrades decision quality.

Furthermore, it pervades an organization's activities, its effect can be significant but is usually unmeasured, and no one is really designated to deal with it.

The cost of conflict

In November 2005 a research project by CEDR and law firm CMS Cameron McKenna gathered data from lawyers and business people involved in over 300 separate business disputes. We identified nine possible adverse consequences of business disputes:

- effects on company reputation;
- exposure in the public domain;
- effects on company morale;
- effects on personal reputation;
- damaged business relationships;
- lost customers;
- increased staff turnover;
- failure to meet targets;
- missed opportunities.

We surveyed the extent to which each may have been significant. Remarkably, this revealed that, in 80 per cent of the disputes surveyed, at least one (but frequently more) of these consequences was described as being 'significant' or 'very significant' to the business.

I'm not sure I agree with the late business guru Peter Drucker, who coined the phrase that 'You can't manage what you can't measure', but what I would say is that, if you aren't trying to measure something, it's a pretty good indicator that you aren't even trying to manage it.

Yet one of the problems with corporate conflict is that the majority of the costs fall through the cracks of management responsibility. The in-house lawyer may be accountable for the legal costs of disputes, but even here financial management leaves a lot to be desired – the 2005 Fulbright & Jaworski Litigation Trends Survey reported that 43 per cent of corporate lawyers are unable to budget adequately for litigation costs.

And yet the costs of conflict are huge. A 2006 study by CEDR has revealed that conflict costs British business some £33 billion a year – and, of that amount, less than a fifth relates to legal fees whilst the vast proportion can be categorized into three broad categories:

■ damaged relationships;
■ tarnished reputations;
■ lost productivity.

Damaged relationships

Because of the way that most of us behave in conflict situations, disputes cause damaged business relationships, which in turn can lead to breakdowns in previously fruitful customer or supplier relationships, or to increased staff turnover.

And even where conflict does not result in a parting of the ways, its effect on day-to-day business efficiency can be debilitating. One of the universal symptoms of conflict (and, generally, one of its most common causes) is a breakdown in communications – just as spouses who are having a row tend not to talk to each other, managers and business colleagues fail to communicate so well when there is tension or conflict in the relationship. And this behaviour can lead to failures to communicate vital information, possibly leading to missed opportunities and/or some key inputs to a decision being either suppressed or ignored.

Tarnished reputations

Evidence of our historical love of conflict as a spectator sport can be found in the ruins of the Colosseum, but today's corporate combat can be tracked from the comfort of your armchair, courtesy of the media.

However, you don't have to read too many news reports of corporate disputes to conclude that they really are 'a plague on both houses', with even the winner's reputation often tarnished by what is revealed during the course of the battle. Whether it's the publicity about the harassment or discrimination case that harms both employer and claimant equally, or the professional negligence claim that reveals shortcomings on both sides, exposure in the public domain is frequently damaging to both personal and corporate reputations – damage that is usually described in the language of the brand or public relations consultants, but is often most visible in reductions in stock market value. In fact, have you ever heard of an organization whose public reputation has been enhanced by reports of its involvement in a significant dispute?

Lost productivity

A 2003 survey by accountants BDO Stoy Hayward[1] identified the personal impact of disputes on senior management, with 46 per cent admitting that their stress levels increased, many (24 per cent) losing sleep over a dispute, and almost one in five even suffering from decreased motivation towards their own business.

Other forms of lost productivity are also commonplace in business conflict – CEDR's research shows that a typical £1 million value dispute will burn up over three years of line managers' time in trying to sort it out – that's time that takes them away from their real jobs, creating a cost of conflict that far outweighs the legal fees involved (see Figure 4.4.1).

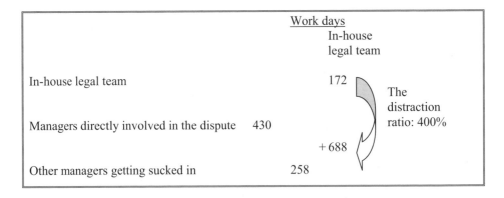

Figure 4.4.1   Time spent on a typical £1 million-plus dispute

This distraction cost is one of the key hidden costs of corporate conflict. As our research shows, manager time is four times that of in-house counsel involved in a dispute, which means that 80 per cent of the cost of conflict comes out of line management budgets. And since engagement in conflict isn't a line item in most managers' budgets, this means that the cost comes through in the form of reduced time available for other priorities.

Is there any good news?

Of course, conflict isn't all bad. And in fact some of the healthiest companies have some of the most intense discussions: '…all the good-to-great companies had a penchant for intense dialogue. Phrases like "loud debate", "heated discussions" and "healthy conflict" peppered the articles and interview transcripts from all the companies.' Jim Collins *Good to Great* research[2] of top management teams, has found that the more productive ones were able to manage conflicts without getting involved in personality conflict, treating conflicts as opportunities for collaboration to achieve the best solution for the organization as a whole.

Conversely, when a separate research team[3] studied a group of business failures arising from highly unsuccessful strategic decisions, they found a remarkably consistent pattern of stifled debate, with negative opinions or adverse information discounted as unhelpful.

Developing a conflict management strategy

So what is business doing about addressing these risks? Well, the typical cocktail party conversation cited would suggest that they're not doing much beyond resigning themselves to the inevitability of it all. And perhaps the reason for this is that business people aren't very comfortable in dealing with conflict in their day-to-day roles. This isn't that surprising when we consider the limited training most have had in this area – a recent CEDR survey of over 600 business people revealed that only 37 per cent regarded themselves as being adequately trained to cope with business conflict.

Furthermore – or, more likely, because of this lack of training – managers also revealed themselves to be significantly conflict averse. Over a third of managers (35 per cent) would rather parachute-jump for the first time than address a performance problem with their work colleagues, whilst just under a third (27 per cent) would rather shave their head for charity – and some (8 per cent) would rather live on 'bush tucker' bugs for a week.

However, the fact that many are doing nothing about this problem, or feel uncomfortable in dealing with it, doesn't mean that nothing can be done. CEDR has been in the business of effective dispute resolution for over 15 years. And in that time we've worked on many thousands of disputes, acting as neutral mediators assisting over 1,500 negotiating teams every year. Whilst helping clients get themselves out of conflict situations, we've learned a lot about how they got there in the first place, what mistakes they made along the way and what they could have done better.

We've now synthesized the lessons of our dispute resolution experience and have developed a package of consultancy and training solutions to help organizations improve the way they manage conflict, whether internally or with outside stakeholders, customers, suppliers or business partners.

These solutions won't make conflict go away, but they will help organizations manage conflict more efficiently and effectively – cutting the cost of conflict.

How to get there

Typically, the six key elements of a strategy for making conflict management a core competency in an organization are:

- developing conflict literacy;
- measuring conflict styles;
- building conflict management skills;
- developing team-working approaches;
- creating options for conflict resolution;
- embedding a conflict management culture.

Developing conflict literacy

Some theoretical background and a common language about conflict are required to help organizations think effectively about the causes and consequences of conflict.

Firstly, an organization needs to have a clear understanding of what it means by conflict. This isn't just a question of open warfare – as the earlier cocktail party conversation reveals, a lot of conflict occurs on an informal and sometimes covert level. It's important also to remember that conflict isn't necessarily bad.

Secondly, a lot of conflict arises – or escalates – as a consequence of how people behave in difficult situations. Life experience causes all of us to acquire preferences and habits of how to respond to conflict and we tend to use these over and over again. Individuals and organizations can have different conflict styles, each depending on the extent to which they place emphasis on two key areas: their own needs/agenda (the outcome); and the relationship with the other person.

Different terms may be used by different authors, but broadly individual styles can be divided into five categories:

- *Competing:* focusing on achieving your own concerns above all else.
- *Accommodating:* the opposite of competing, sacrificing your own concerns for the benefit of the other person's.
- *Avoiding:* not wanting to pursue either your own or the other side's needs, and in fact you'd rather not be involved in the conflict at all.
- *Compromising:* this approach seeks the middle ground, partially satisfying your own concerns and partially satisfying the other's.
- *Collaborating:* both assertive and cooperative, this approach tries to problem-solve to find a solution that fully meets the interests of both parties.

Each of these labels carries emotional baggage, leading most of us to think of some as good behaviours and others as bad, or weak. However, in conflict management, these characterizations are inappropriate – each style has its place in certain circumstances, and each causes difficulties in others. There is no universal 'right answer'.

Measuring conflict styles

As with much development work, the key to implementing change is first to understand where you are now. Hence, diagnostic tools can be used to assist individuals determine their own preferred conflict style, thus making explicit what might previously have been unconscious habits and assumptions about the best way to handle conflict situations. These tools can also be used to establish a pre-action baseline, and results can generally be aggregated to form an impression of the overall culture of a team or organization.

Building conflict management skills

Whilst each person will have a default behaviour, we are not locked permanently into that mode, and appropriate training can help individuals to modify their behaviour to suit particular circumstances. Furthermore, by understanding and recognizing the conflict styles of others, we can implement appropriate strategies to communicate with them. Additional communication and creative problem-solving skills training also add to the portfolio of conflict competencies.

Developing team-working approaches

Although enabling individuals to modify their conflict management styles will have some impact in mitigating team-level conflict, additional work will most likely still be required at a team level to make sure that established team cultures are not overwhelming and that an appropriate collective strategy is adopted.

For example, a collaborative style is generally accepted as being the most effective approach for dealing with task-based conflict, that is dealing with differing views as to the best way to achieve agreed objectives. A strategic management team may need high levels of disagreement to facilitate the critical evaluation of decisions, but an unmoderated competitive approach may lead to dissatisfaction and relationship conflict as well as suboptimal decision making.

Creating options for conflict resolution

It is important that a conflict management system provides options for all types of problems for all people within the organization, and a 'one size fits all' strategy is unlikely to be workable beyond a very narrowly defined area of conflict. Generally, therefore, a comprehensive system will provide for a range of entry points and for a variety of options, both rights-based and interest-based, for addressing conflict.

One of the most important options involves providing an outlet for situations where direct discussions between key individuals are unable to resolve a problem. Mediation, the intervention of an impartial third party with neither decision-making authority nor the power to impose a resolution, has proven to be a highly successful method of resolving even the most intractable deadlock.

> Mediation is a flexible process conducted confidentially in which a neutral person actively assists parties in working towards a negotiated agreement of a dispute or difference, with the parties in ultimate control of the decision to settle and the terms of resolution.
>
> (Centre for Effective Dispute Resolution – CEDR)

It also has the advantage of being quick and cost-effective when compared to alternative recourse mechanisms such as arbitration, litigation or, perhaps worst of all, significant unresolved conflict.

Key facts about mediation

- Over 70 per cent of cases settle at mediation, with a further 20 per cent settling within the following weeks, after parties have seen and explored the other side's position.
- Of those companies that have used mediation, over 77 per cent said it was quicker, over 78 per cent said it was more effective and almost 80 per cent said it had reduced their anticipated legal costs.
- Business cases mediated with CEDR in 2005 had an average dispute value of over £1.5 million, or a total figure of well over £1 billion.
- 2005 saw the 11,000th case referred to CEDR.

Embedding a conflict management culture

As with any change management project in an organizational setting, implementation of a conflict management programme requires activity at a variety of levels. It's not enough simply to build protocols and provide training; leadership needs to come from the top such that open communication and effective conflict management become embedded in the culture of the organization.

Conclusion

Conflict is part of working life but it is how we deal with it that is important. Effective management of conflict can reduce the amount of time and money spent in trying to sort out a problem, reduce the damage it could cause to those involved and enable decision makers to make smarter choices earlier on. There aren't any silver bullets, but a lot can be done, and it's time that business woke up to the wastage that lack of proper conflict management causes.

Notes

1. BDO Stoy Hayward (2003) *Commercial Disputes Survey*, BDO Stoy Hayward, London.
2. J Collins (2001) *Good to Great: Why Some Companies Make the Leap . . . and Others Don't,* HarperBusiness, New York.
3. S Finkelstein (2003) *Why Smart Executives Fail*, Portfolio (Penguin Putnam), London.

Warranty claims – managing common risks on the sale or purchase of a business

Andrew Cromby, KSB Law LLP

Introduction

Whether a business is large, medium-sized or small it will always be, to some extent, in a state of flux. At any particular time a business is either growing or becoming smaller. The illusion that it is possible to maintain a *status quo* in business is just that – an illusion. The reality is that the route to success is growth and, conversely, unsuccessful businesses are likely to 'downsize'. It is therefore unsurprising that virtually all businesses find themselves, sooner or later, either purchasing or selling a business. The vehicle for that business might be a private limited company, a public limited company or a business run as a partnership. Whatever its nature, a number of common problems occur, time and time again, when the sale or purchase of a business takes place.

Inevitably, it seems, in order to get the deal done it becomes necessary to ramp up the pressure on either the purchaser or the seller (and more often both) so that negotiations, due diligence and completion of contractual documents are shoehorned into a relatively short period.

As a consequence of this it is common for issues simply to 'get lost' or become overlooked in the negotiations. Sometimes sufficient attention is not given to what is considered to be, at the time of sale, a minor issue. This might, for instance, be completing due diligence on a warehousing inventory system to check that it is accurate and up to date. Whatever the actual oversight is, the risk, which ought to be apparent from the balance sheet or from the documents and information produced on due diligence is overlooked and lies dormant, waiting to be the subject matter of a claim – most likely by the purchaser – after the dust has settled and once the new business has commenced the process of integration into the purchaser's group.

Warranty claims

Typically such claims are made as 'warranty claims' – being based on warranties as to the good standing or financial status of the company or business being purchased by the seller. Time and time again a number of problems in relation to the making or defending of such claims rear their heads. Typically these revolve around exclusion clauses found in the sale or purchase agreement that attempt to limit the liability of the seller. If properly drafted those exclusions can make it extremely difficult for a purchaser successfully to make a claim.

Anyone involved in selling or purchasing a business will not necessarily be involved in the drafting or otherwise consider the scope of limitations on making claims (or their ability to defend such claims), perhaps leaving this in the hands of their legal team. This is, however, an area that needs to be considered very carefully. The scope of the limitation clauses contained in sale and purchase agreements can dictate whether claims will stand or fall. A prospective purchaser or seller should make time to consider whether the exclusion clauses in the sale and purchase agreement will help or hinder them in the future.

Standard exclusion provisions

Capping liability and de minimis

It is standard practice for sale and purchase agreements to contain a limitation as to the overall sum that may be claimed by a purchaser post-sale, whether this is in aggregate or in respect of each individual breach of warranty. It is also equally common for there to be a threshold level below which claims cannot be made. Always give careful consideration to whether claims should be dealt with in aggregate or on an individual basis when determining whether the relevant level has been reached.

Whether it is preferable to aggregate claims or keep them separate depends on whether you are interested in raising or lowering the level at which claims can be made.

In fact the *de minimis* provisions are usually considered by most clients with their lawyers, fairly carefully. This is absolutely vital. A *de minimis* provision should never be considered as a 'boilerplate' clause that requires moderate tinkering. It can be a real boon in preventing unwanted litigation or, conversely, in permitting claims to be made when they might otherwise be barred.

Limitation periods

This is one of the commonest areas where difficulties arise for purchasers who wish to make claims, when it emerges that the agreement that they have signed provides for a short 'limitation' period within which claims must be commenced.

Under English law a claim for breach of contract can be brought, in most cases, within six years of a breach of warranty. In certain cases (where an agreement is signed as a deed) that period is extended to 12 years. Other limitation periods can also apply, but the starting position for two parties entering into a legally binding agreement is that they have six years to sue each other if there has been a breach of that agreement.

It is, however, entirely possible for the parties to shorten the period within which any claims must be brought – to say one or two years. If a company is acquiring a large group, or part of a group, then it is quite possible that matters revealing the existence of a claim will not become apparent for some considerable period.

An example already mentioned above is the situation where the purchaser of a warehousing business finds that errors exist in the stock-keeping system. One of the greatest dangers to purchasers who wish to make claims (and one of the greatest boons to sellers who hope to avoid them) is that the 'bible' of documents completed at the conclusion of the transaction, which contains the sale and purchase agreement setting out the relevant limitation period within which claims must be brought, is usually ignored. The more minor terms of the agreement reached are quickly forgotten. The bible usually finds its way into the hands of the purchaser's company secretary who quickly forgets what the relevant limitation period is.

Sometime later (perhaps months, in some cases years) a potential claim rears its ugly head. It is *essential* that, as soon as any potential claim becomes known of, the relevant limitation period is checked. Often, as the extent of the claim begins to become apparent, one or more of the parties will adopt a 'sit back and see' approach waiting to ascertain whether a full-blown claim emerges. If time is in hand, this is fine. If time is short, this is completely unacceptable and could jeopardize the status of any claim. To the seller, of course, delay is almost always a very good thing and if it is possible to enter into dialogue with a dissatisfied purchaser this can work to the seller's advantage – particularly if close to the cusp of a limitation period.

The name of the game for the seller is to keep the purchaser talking – make it feel that the problem will be resolved and that there is no need to pursue the legal option.

Purchasers, on the other hand, should usually stop time running as soon as possible. Often this is as simple as serving a notice under the agreement and does not necessarily mean that court or arbitral proceedings will need to be commenced – although watch out for an obligation to commence formal proceedings within a set time after service of the notice. Alternatively a suitably worded waiver by the seller of its right to rely on a defence of the expiry of a limitation period may equally well preserve a purchaser's position – provided it fits within the contractual framework.

One of the biggest risks to the purchasing business is that one of the company officers will take the view that there is time aplenty to make the claim and, as a result, time is frittered away until a claim becomes time barred.

Notification of claims – the mechanics of notification

This is another potential pitfall for claims under sale and purchase agreements. Hand in hand with the limitation period within which a claim must be brought walks the provision in most sale and purchase agreements that claims or potential claims must be notified to the seller as soon as possible and, in some cases, within a fixed time, in any event. In effect this is another way of decreasing the time available to make a claim and, for all practicable purposes, has identical risks (or advantages) to those set out above on limitation.

One of the commonest scenarios is for a partially informed company representative, who has peripheral awareness of the terms of the notification clause, to give what he or she considers to be a valid notice when, in fact, the terms of the notice provisions have not been complied with. Typically this might be because the notification is given by fax or e-mail when delivery by post or some other physical means is specified – or vice versa.

Typically such notices might be served by a company's secretary or responsible officer directly because 'time is short', thus putting the potential claimant under a double whammy of pressure – not only is limitation about to expire, but the knee-jerk reaction to 'serve a notice' (which subsequently emerges as an inadequate notice) may well mean that all hope of making the claim is lost, because there is no time to get it right the next time.

Most sale and purchase agreements provide for a specific mechanism for notification of claims. Typically an agreement's notification clause provides for:

■ where the notice is to be given – for instance at a company's registered office or at a party's solicitors;
■ how the notice is to be communicated – by hand, fax, e-mail or a combination of these and perhaps other methods;
■ whether any specific information is to be included in the notice.

Getting any of these wrong could result in an invalid notice being served. If time is short, getting the notice right the first time may be critical to the preservation of the claim.

Practical points to remember

■ Ensure that company secretaries or those responsible for fielding or giving notices have copies of all relevant sale and purchase agreements and other transactional documents readily to hand.

■ Request from your lawyers a schedule of limitation periods for all agreements. This work can often be undertaken during the course of the transaction itself, failing which any solicitor will be happy to review the provisions of the sale and purchase agreement and provide a brief note on what is required, if he or she is only asked to do so. Although this may seem like unnecessary work, the benefit of staying informed about the mechanisms for making and resisting claims, etc are self-apparent when a potential claim arises.

Case study

The purchaser of an automotive supply company has given a warranty that all stocks comply with an audited spreadsheet. It subsequently emerges that the spreadsheet in question is completely inaccurate, with a potential claim for, say, £2 million. This becomes apparent during the course of the first year after the sale of the business. The limitation period provided for in the sale and purchase agreement is 18 months. Towards the end of the 18th month a notice is served by the purchaser's company secretary. The notice is addressed to the wrong individual at the wrong address and is sent by e-mail but not by fax or by hard copy, as provided for in the sale and purchase agreement.

Subsequently the error becomes apparent, but the time for service of the notice has now expired and any claim in respect of this breach of warranty has become time barred.

Post-notification matters

After notification, be alert to the possibility that further action may need to be taken in relation to the claim to promote its continued existence. The following are possibilities:

■ It may be necessary formally to commence proceedings by way of court action or arbitral proceedings.

■ The claimant may have to consult with the defendant as to the way in which the claim might be passed on to a third party. Failing to do so could jeopardize the validity of the claim.

■ It may be necessary to invite the defendant to take on an active role as claimant in associated third-party proceedings.

■ If the recipient of a claim, always consider notifying insurers to make certain that any existing insurance cover is not lost.

Conclusion

Ignorance of the general rules relating to the making of warranty claims (as provided for in the sale and purchase agreement) can prove to be expensive. Missing the deadline for making a claim could be the last thing a business executive does – before being sacked. Set out below is a procedural table drafted from the perspective of a potential claimant – but equally valid as an *aide-mémoire* for a potential defendant. This does not (and cannot) have universal applicability – but it is a good place to start when a claim emerges from the haze of the corporate distance.

Warranty claim checklist

1. Is there potential for a claim?
2. Where are the relevant documents and agreements?
3. What is the deadline for the claim? Bear in mind that limitation periods for tax claims are often longer than six years.
4. Should insurers be notified?
5. Should notification be made to the seller?
6. If so, to whom does the agreement say that it should be made?
7. Where is the notification to be delivered?
8. How is it to be sent?
9. What proof can be obtained that notice has been given? This should be carefully preserved.
10. After notification of the claim, what further action should be taken? Does the agreement provide that the other side be consulted regarding the claim, etc? Is there a deadline for instituting formal proceedings, etc?

Taxation risk

Louis Cooper, Chiltern plc

Tax risk management and tax internal controls are now increasingly on the agenda of senior management and the board. Tax is a significant cost for many businesses and must be well managed. Any residual risk in the company's tax position should be understood and properly controlled.

Tax risk management is not necessarily about minimizing risk. Businesses make a profit from taking risks, and a 'no risk' strategy is not cost-effective or right. Taking risks is as important as reducing risk. A company's policy on tax risk management will determine:

- the value that can be achieved by taking risks;
- the costs that can be saved by reducing risks;
- the resources needed to manage both the upside opportunities and the downside risks.

Taxation risk has come to the fore both in the UK and internationally, principally in the United States, during the last few years.

HM Revenue and Customs in the UK

HM Revenue and Customs (HMRC) in the UK was created in April 2005 with the merger between the Inland Revenue and HM Customs and Excise. It was envisaged that HMRC would: 'through **better risk management**, more flexible use of resources and customer focus, reduce the burden on those who comply with their tax obligations and deal effectively with those who do not' (*Financing Britain's Future*, 2005).

HMRC's new Large Business Service has set out a range of key business processes that provide a framework for delivering taxation services. One of the essential processes is 'managing risks', and the concept of 'risk reviews' is the cornerstone of the new compliance process.

Risk reviews will be used to assess the level of confidence HMRC has in a company's tax compliance and will involve an open discussion between the company and its HMRC 'client relationship manager'. HMRC will use these reviews to:

■ increase their understanding of the business;
■ target 'interventions' on the areas of highest risk;
■ refine risk assessments by sharing perceptions of current risk factors;
■ identify and work through any problem areas.

Risk reviews are seen as being more than an annual event and should be part of an ongoing process to manage risks.

HMRC is seeking to develop coherent and effective risk assessments across all taxes and regimes in order to:

1. get the best return from their resources;
2. identify companies with non-compliant tax systems that display perceived non-compliant actions and behaviours; and
3. switch 'intervention resources' to those that do not fulfil their tax obligations.

Risk reviews will be comprehensive in outlook and will cover three main risk areas:

1. generic risk factors (including: size, structure and complexity of the business; tax governance; use of avoidance arrangements and schemes; strengths of underlying systems; legal complexity);
2. sector-specific risks (depending on industry sector issues and benchmarking against other similar companies);
3. unique business risks (individual risks relevant to the company and its trade).

HMRC is looking to be more proactive and more 'customer' focused in its dealings with companies and it will be seeking real evidence of effective governance processes and controls, particularly in respect of tax risk management strategies and policies. This is the challenge for UK businesses.

US regulatory framework

Although the majority of UK companies are not subject to the regulatory framework in the United States, it is beneficial to have some awareness of current developments, as often there are some common themes that are relevant to UK corporates. In the area of taxation risk there are two main areas of interest: Sarbanes–Oxley section 404 reporting and FASB Final Interpretation No. 48 (FIN 48).

Sarbanes–Oxley section 404 reporting

There has been a lot of dialogue in respect of the mechanics and merits of section 404: Internal Control over Financial Reporting. A review of the recurring areas of material weakness during the past two years shows that 'tax accounting' features as one of the top five financial accounting issues, and this has resulted in a number of companies being given an adverse audit opinion in their section 404 audit report.

There are a number of reasons why taxation has featured as an area of material weakness, and these have included the following:

■ Segregation of duties in tax is typically weak, with a lot of reliance placed on one or two key individuals.
■ Tax processes and procedures are often not documented and are not always subjected to detailed internal review routines.
■ The preparation of tax computations is usually a year-end exercise and any issues with the process cannot be easily rectified and retested before the accounts are signed off.
■ Areas of tax can be very subjective or judgemental and in the past have often lacked supporting documentation as evidence of decisions made. There is also a lot of reliance on estimates, which are not always tied back to final settlements with the tax authorities.

Based on the issues identified above, companies are now looking to work smarter. They are seeking to address growing tax risks by improving documentation processes and enhancing resources and technical capabilities, whilst developing more appropriate controls and using IT systems and software to help increase efficiency.

FIN 48

In July 2006 the US Financial Accounting Standards Board (FASB) published its *Final Interpretation No. 48: Accounting for Uncertainty in Income Taxes (FIN 48)*. Although principally of relevance to US companies, FIN 48 will have application for both: 1) UK subsidiaries of US companies; and 2) UK companies that have a primary or secondary US reporting requirement, under US GAAP.

The primary focus of FIN 48 is to recognize and measure the taxation liabilities associated with tax positions taken by an enterprise where there is a material degree of uncertainty regarding the final outcome. This is a responsibility of the management of the company. FIN 48 requires an objective and impartial appraisal of the tax position of an enterprise, resulting in comprehensive disclosure in the financial statements.

The provisions of FIN 48 will have a profound impact upon many US and international companies, especially in ensuring that they have the internal processes in place to discharge management's responsibilities.

Consequently, there is a need to understand the risks associated with 'uncertain tax positions' and to put in place the appropriate systems of internal control. As with section 404 reporting there is a strong emphasis on documentation to support key decisions and to evidence review procedures.

A framework for taxation risk management

There are a number of common elements to the new focus on taxation risk. However, this should not be viewed in isolation, and taxation risk management should be a subset of a company's overall risk management framework.

An example framework is set out in Figure 4.6.1. This shows the essential building blocks, starting from an understanding of how stakeholders in the business define value and using this as the key driver for the company's enterprise-wide risk management systems.

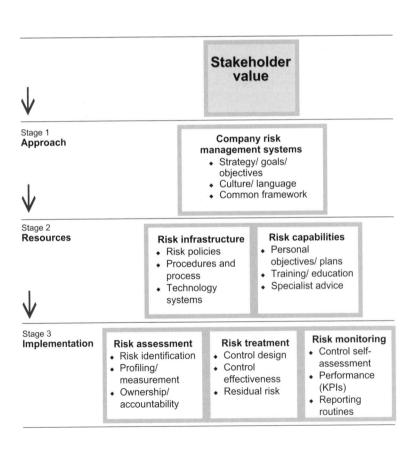

Figure 4.6.1 Risk management framework

Taxation risk management should be considered in respect of the 'Resources' and 'Implementation' stages of the framework.

Risk infrastructure

More emphasis is now placed on documentation and, within the company's overall policy on risk management, there needs to be some detail on how taxation should be covered. A formalized approach to recording tax-related procedures and process information is critical, and some companies are looking to IT systems to help ensure that a consistent approach is followed. This would seem to follow the new demands of HMRC in the UK and the US IRS requirements.

Risk capabilities

Access to well-trained and qualified staff has also been an issue for many companies, especially where there is no in-house tax team. The new focus on independence and auditor ethics has reduced the reliance on support that can be provided by a company's external audit firm.

The US Sarbanes–Oxley experience has indicated that the internal control activities provided by staff need to be improved, as there are often too few people in finance teams and their all-round skill set is weak. This has led to specific training and education on risk matters, or to companies seeking specialist advice and support, through partnering or outsourced arrangements.

Risk assessment

In assessing risk there are a number of types of risk that are relevant to tax. A summary of the main categories, with some practical examples of application, is given in Table 4.6.1.

Risk treatment

As part of the documentation process controls need to be linked to the identified tax risks. Key controls should be tested to ensure that they are the best controls, in terms of both design and effectiveness. This is a new approach as in the past taxation – both direct and indirect – has just been 'done', either at the year-end or as part of specific quarterly routines, very much in isolation.

Companies should now consider the internal controls they have over all areas of tax. Key points to consider include:

∎ Is there linkage/interaction with other areas of the business?
∎ Are there any segregation-of-duties issues?
∎ Is there a control owner with appropriate responsibility and accountability?
∎ Are review and monitoring routines evidenced as completed?
∎ Is a particular control activity reliant on another control?
∎ Are there controls where tax-related processes are outsourced?
∎ Is the control automated or manual?

Table 4.6.1 Main categories of risk and examples of application

Risk category	Background	Example
1. Transactional risks	Tax risks and exposures associated with specific transactions undertaken by the company. The more complex or unusual the transaction the higher the risk. Highest-risk transactions are those that happen for tax purposes, such as tax-driven reorganizations.	The key risk associated with individual transactions is the failure to implement properly specific actions that have been planned and agreed, especially where the tax result depends on a particular sequence of events.
2. Operational risks	Underlying tax risks in the routine everyday business operations. Different types of operations will have different levels of tax risk.	Operational risk has increased with more focus by companies on connected party cross-border product sales and services. Increased globalization can also bring an increase in the risk of inadvertently creating a taxable presence in a particular country of operation.
3. Compliance risks	The risks associated with meeting an organization's tax compliance obligations. This relates to the preparation, completion and review of an organization's tax returns. Issues include the costs associated with this work and the attitude to any potential tax penalties.	Compliance risks are those implicit in the processes and procedures adopted by the company to prepare and submit tax returns, as well as responding efficiently and effectively to any enquiries or issues raised by the relevant tax authorities.
4. Financial accounting risks	The risks surrounding the management of the tax figure in the accounts. A 'no surprises' approach has led to more risk-averse and conservative views with the resulting discussions on over-provisioning with the auditors.	Tax figures also appear in cash flows, budgets and investor relations material and not just the accounts. More focus on this area has also come from the work undertaken to support US section 404 Sarbanes–Oxley reporting requirements and more will be needed with the new FIN 48 measures.

Table 4.6.1 Continued

Risk category	Background	Example
5. Portfolio risks	Portfolio risk concerns the overall aggregate level of risk when looking at transactional, operational and compliance risks as a whole and considers the interaction of these risk areas. The question may be about what would be the impact if all areas of tax risk went wrong at the same time.	Individual transactions may be below the 'risk threshold' but when a number of transactions are combined the cumulative position may not be acceptable.
6. Management risks	A more general tax risk is the actual management of each of the areas previously outlined. Very few companies have a formalized tax risk management policy. The real risk is under-managing the area because of a lack of skills, resources or time.	The importance of managing tax risks has led to more time and resources being spent on the management of tax-related processes and procedures.
7. Reputation risks	Reputation risk concerns the wider impact that might arise from an organization's actions if they are carried out in the public domain or inadvertently become a matter of public knowledge. Companies are also under pressure to pay tax that is in accordance with the letter and spirit of the law and doing anything different could have an impact on the company's wider reputation.	The impact on a company could be high where, pursuing a tax issue through the courts, other information on the company's activities or practices are released that result in a change in perception of the company in the eyes of its customers, suppliers or employees.

Risk monitoring

Much attention is now given to regular monitoring and reporting routines. The emphasis here should be on timing, presentation, authority, and linkage to other mainstream financial and non-financial procedures. There also needs to be a degree of performance measurement from a personal, team and overall business perspective.

Tax shouldn't be taxing...

The overall enterprise-wide risk management systems of the company should help to shape the management of taxation risk; tax risk is one of many risks faced by the business. The essential requirement is to ensure there is the right level of formality around the processes and procedures adopted for identifying, assessing and managing specific taxation risks.

The critical success factors for taxation risk include:

1. Provide clear roles and responsibilities for tax activities.
2. Recruit staff and retain advisers with the appropriate tax and accounting technical skills.
3. Develop comprehensive and consistent tax reporting packages.
4. Undertake regular reviews and reconciliations of all tax accounts.
5. Document each stage in the tax process, on the assumption that it will be reviewed and challenged by a third party.

Managing business risk through contractual schemes of liability

Christopher Parr, KSB Law LLP

Introduction

Never put all your eggs in one basket; but consider putting all your liabilities into one contract. In terms of risk management, the contract document is the best receptacle for all the potential liabilities that might arise in connection with the performance of that contract. That is better than leaving some risks lurking about outside the document waiting to catch a party if and when it defaults. This all-inclusive approach creates a 'scheme of liability', and this chapter will examine the prime elements of such schemes.

Price and risk are bound together: the higher the risk, the higher the price. There is no sense in taking a high risk for a low reward. If the liability and risk aspects of the contract are not addressed in the agreement, then how can anyone know whether the price is an adequate compensation for the liability and risk being assumed, or whether the potential risks and liabilities are ruinous?

Any company that allows its executives and other employees to enter contractual arrangements that do not deal comprehensively with the risks inherent in the underlying transaction is negligent in its duty to its shareholders. The company is allowing these deal makers to gamble with the company's assets.

By dealing with risk and liability in a scheme-based way, companies should be able to reap considerable benefits:

- reduced insurance premiums;
- more accurate pricing;
- purchasing managers should be able to make more informed and price-sensitive acquisitions because they can better assess the risk that they are taking for the business;
- product and service designers should be better able to produce lower-risk products and services because they are taking time to examine the risks and the protections that can be put into place to reduce either the chance of the risk arising or, if it does arise, the effects it has.

All of these elements should drive the business to produce better and more cost-effective products or services, which in turn should allow the company to perform better; and all of these elements are derived from the discussion of risk and liability.

The potential list of issues is long and detailed. However, we will consider the following broad categories of risk and liability that a business should consider when preparing its standard-form contracts and/or negotiating bespoke documents for particular deals:

- quality;
- quantity;
- time;
- payment.

We will consider the nature of the risks involved and the primary solutions that can be deployed to deal with the different parties' concerns and interests.

With regard to the latter point, it is inevitable that the respective parties will have different and essentially opposing views on each element. One will want to take little or no risk while the other will want to have as wide and deep a set of rights to claim as is possible.

This chapter does not deal with risk and liability arising in consumer contracts. The law provides the consumer with a range of rights and remedies. Those who sell directly to consumers should know that, if their product or service causes loss or injury to a consumer, then they have little or no defence.

Finally, we must note a material difference between the legal approach to contract and tort liability. Generally, damages for breach of contract are intended to put the injured party where it would have been had the breach not occurred. Damages in tort (eg negligence) are intended to compensate the injured party for the loss that it suffers as a result of the (negligent) act.

English law will allow contractual damages for a wider range of losses suffered or incurred by the injured party than are available in tort claims. The parties to a contract have had the chance to negotiate its terms. They are assumed to have assessed the risks and rewards inherent in the arrangement. As a result, the courts are ready, within reason, to accept the terms of the contract as a true reflection of the parties' positions.

In tort, the parties must prove a breach of the duty of care and then they must prove that the damage they claim to have suffered flowed from that breach and was reasonably foreseeable. The rules and technicalities mean that a party might not be able to recover at all, or may only be able to recover part of its real loss.

Quality of performance – products and services

This is fundamental to any normal commercial contract: what is the quality that is expected or the quality that is being paid for? In relation to most goods, the qualitative distinctions are clear, and price is fixed accordingly. The parties can see whether the thing that is delivered is the same as the thing that was ordered. However, other contract deliverables are less easy to categorise. For example, a production plant is a complex thing and the concept of 'quality' is harder to define; but defined it must be or the supplier can get away with poor quality and still expect to be paid in full.

In this case, the broad answer to the question lies in the inputs, outputs and maintenance of the plant. Any production plant is, in effect, a cake maker. Therefore, the ingredients will have a direct effect on the products. For both parties, a clear and precise specification of these things, including utilities and other consumables, is critical.

The output of the plant is equally critical and deserves equal attention. In fact, it is typical for the parties to spend a disproportionate amount of time on output compared to other aspects of the contract because they both see their commercial interests as being directly related to what is produced. The plant seller will sell it on the basis of, for example, 'It makes the best cakes in the world.' The buyer will buy the machine or plant for exactly the same reason. As a result, they are fixated by the cakes and will tend to forget that cakes are the sum of their ingredients.

The plant seller should not promise that the plant will deliver a quality or style of output that is not possible or that can only be achieved 'if lucky'. If the plant can only produce particular grades or styles, then the seller should make that clear. If the buyer wants particular characteristics in the products, then it should make that clear too.

The parties must also understand whether the buyer is buying something that it has chosen or something that the seller has recommended or designed for a purpose. If you go into a hi-fi shop and buy a stereo, you are the best judge of your own needs. If you choose a model and then find that it fails to please, that's your problem. On the other hand, if you get an expert to specify the best kit for the job and it fails to meet expectations, there may be a duty on the expert to put things right.

In commercial contracts, it is critical that the parties address this issue. If the seller is selling, for example, bulk chemicals, then the buyer should be expected to make its decision of its own risk. Typically, the buyer will not reveal its process or recipe so that the seller cannot possibly know whether or not the chosen product is the right one. In those cases, the seller will be taking a huge risk if it gives a 'fitness for purpose' warranty or commitment.

The seller might take the risk on a generic purpose such as 'for food use' or 'suitable for use at temperatures above X degrees'. These are aspects of the product that the seller can control and, indeed, should be happy to represent as characteristics of its product. Elements of performance over which the seller has little or no control should be excluded, in clear and specific terms, from the contractual obligations.

Clearly, there is another side to the coin: the seller might hold itself out as a bespoke supplier. In that case, the buyer should ensure that the seller puts its money where its mouth is. If the seller claims that its product will do a particular thing, then the buyer should ensure that the risk is with the seller if that proves to be untrue.

The elements of the foregoing principles are:

- *Raw materials* – specify exactly, for example by referring to chemical compositions that are verified before input, or to a range of tolerance, for example 'not more than 10 per cent, but not less than 3 per cent, water content'.
- *Utilities* – specific rates of power or flow.
- *Volumes* – not more than X tonnes or less than Y tonnes per period.

The keys are verification and testing. The contract negotiators should work very hard to create objective, testable compliance standards.

The parties must also consider the ramifications of failure to perform or to deliver. There are some clear options here. The thing might be:

- totally useless and should be rejected;
- not totally useless but less valuable than it would have been;
- only a little below its specified performance level and so, for all practical purposes, 'as specified'.

These aspects of performance should be addressed in the scheme of liability.

In case one (totally useless), the seller should be required, ultimately, to take the thing away and make everything good, as if performance had never occurred. (The buyer may still be entitled to additional compensation for other losses incurred as a result of the failure. We will come back to that later.) However, the seller deserves the right to be allowed to put right the defects. Probably, it represents the best result for both parties. The buyer gets what it ordered – a plant that works as required – and the seller has minimized its loss because it can be paid in full for the fully functioning equipment. Of course, the seller will have incurred costs in undertaking the repairs, and the buyer may have a claim for losses suffered during the repair period, eg because production was stopped or reduced.

The seller should avoid being required to keep on trying to the death. It is reasonable for a supplier to state in the contract that, in effect, it will make (say) three attempts to rectify the problem and then, at its option, elect to stop and take everything away and make good. There may be other, consequential liabilities to meet in that case, but if the total risk exposure has been capped then this may be a much smaller negative effect than otherwise would be the case.

In case two (not up to standard but still usable), the seller should negotiate a discount on the price as opposed to an obligation to take the plant away and make good. Within set limits, the buyer should be happy with this concept because it gets nearly what it wants and pays a corresponding price.

If the plant was supposed to produce 100 tonnes per hour but, after three attempts to rectify the defect, it can do only 80 tonnes per hour, then the seller might stop spending money on rectification and accept a discount on the total price. The discount might be pro rata or on some other basis. Of course, the parties must agree on 'How bad is bad?' In this context, they may allow that the 'price discount remedy' will be applicable if the plant is performing at between 95 per cent and 75 per cent efficiency. Any less than 75 per cent may be just too bad to be of any use to the buyer. Any more than 95 per cent efficient may be, for all practical purposes, 'as good as anyone could reasonably expect'. In that case, the third category of performance is applicable.

In case three (as good as reasonably possible), the seller will argue that the plant is, for all practical purposes, 'as specified'. The performance might be at 96 per cent of the absolute guarantee, but in the circumstances that is a negligible difference off 100 per cent. The seller will argue that the buyer should be happy and should pay the full price.

This is not to say that the seller should not try to make the plant meet the 100 per cent guarantee figure and it is not to argue that the buyer should simply accept that the target will not be reached. However, it is to argue that the parties could spend more trying to squeeze the last 1 per cent or 2 per cent from the plant than that 1 per cent or 2 per cent is worth.

What if the plant performs at over the guaranteed level? Is that worth a bonus? It might be, if the seller can use the additional production.

Services

Performance standards for services are harder to quantify and measure because of their more subjective nature. However, there are some basic concepts that can be used to help the process.

The parties must decide whether the services are to deliver a specific result or simply to contribute towards a result. For example, commissioning an architect to design a house should lead to the delivery of a design of a house. There will be issues about whether it is a nice house, the right house or a house that the client actually wants to live in. However, the basic deliverable is a concrete, objectively verifiable object – a design.

Alternatively, a person might be engaged to help negotiate a deal. Some concrete deliverables might be required here. However, we are interested in the intangible aspects of the services. The person concerned might turn up, speak for hours on end, take notes and, generally, work in the negotiation team. Whether the negotiation is 'successful' is not necessarily relevant in this type of service.

In planning the contract, establish whether it will be a 'contract for results' or a 'contract for performance'. In the former case, the buyer should spend time defining the required 'results'. Those results should be described in concrete terms with objective, measurable elements created around them to allow the parties to demonstrate that the required standard has or has not been met.

In contracts for performance, the task is much harder. The performance will have to be defined more in terms of (for example): hours spent on the work; place of work; reports produced; other paper outputs produced; and meetings attended.

The key, in all cases, is to create objective milestones against which performance can be measured.

The parties, particularly the services provider, should also consider the absolute standard at which they will be judged, for example the standard of:

■ a first-class supplier?
■ a reasonably skilled supplier?
■ a supplier who has similar experience in similar tasks or circumstances?

This is important for both parties because, particularly if litigation or arbitration is instigated, the third-party judge will seek an objective standard against which to measure the actual performance as delivered. The parties will help themselves greatly if they pre-agree that standard.

Quantity delivered

Quantity is much easier to deal with in contracts. There is no ambiguity in the statement 'Deliver 100 units.' However, just as in the case of quality, the parties might not want to face the stark reality of this clarity. If the seller only delivers 99, does it really want to accept the risk of rejection of the whole lot?

But, how short is 'too short' when it comes to short delivery? The answer depends, of course, on the nature of the supply. One wing is not terribly helpful if the order for the plane was 'two wings'!

However, in less clear cases, perhaps a 10 per cent under-delivery should be dealt with by way of price reduction rather than the draconian option of an all-or-nothing, accept-or-reject provision.

As with quality and services, quantity and services do not sit well together. There will be some easy examples of quantifiable services – three nights' performance at Covent Garden or one report on traffic flow on the M25. However, if the service requires a receptionist to turn up for a week on a temporary assignment, apart from the number of days on which he or she actually turns up, it is hard to quantify the rest of the performance.

Ultimately, the parties should take the time to try to ensure that, to the extent sensible and reasonable, they agree some measurable performance criteria so that, with minimum argument, they can assess whether the contract has been performed as required.

Time for performance

'Time is of the essence' is a classic phrase. The default position in English law is that time is *not* of the essence unless expressly agreed. Therefore, if time is critical to the contract, the parties had better say so.

What are the real issues?

First, the buyer may really want the contract performed on or by an exact time. In the case of 'just-in-time' performance, this has become a clear concern. Inventory and raw material management are huge commercial issues in business, and holding quantities of stock 'ready' is not efficient. Large manufacturers like to see the next batch of raw material rolling into the yard just as the last batch is entering the production process. A late delivery might cause the process to stop. In some cases, that means that the whole process train must be cleaned out and worked on before production can restart. That can cause huge losses and costs, which the purchaser will seek to recover from the supplier. Equally, an early delivery may be a problem because the purchaser has nowhere to store it. If the purchaser is running on the edge with production it will not have overspent on storage capacity. A lorryload of raw material may just have to sit in the road or yard waiting. At worst, it will be turned away and told to come back only at the allotted time.

Time is not always critical and sometimes it is not even very important. However, in most commercial contracts, the parties should discuss and agree timetables.

Second, if time *is* of the essence, then lateness will be taken as a breach of condition and so the other party may have a right to rescind the contract and seek damages (as opposed to just seeking damages, without rescission). This is a serious difference in effect. Rescission requires the party not in breach to be put back, as nearly as possible, into the position it would have been in had the contract not been performed at all. In addition, the party can sue for damages on the basis that it has not had the performance to which it was entitled.

In many contract structures, lateness is dealt with, at least at the first level, by the use of liquidated damages (LDs). Under English law, LDs must be a 'genuine pre-estimate of the loss' that one party will suffer as a result of the breach of the other party. LDs must not be a 'penalty'. That is, they must not be held over the head of a party to frighten it into performance.

However, the party claiming the LDs need not show that it has actually lost that sum. Provided that the court accepts that the LDs amount is a genuine pre-estimate of the loss, the LDs are payable, even if the actual loss is much less – or much more.

As a result of this principle, LDs should be negotiated carefully. In the case of delay, it is reasonably normal to see provisions that allow the party not in breach to recover X per cent of the contract price for each hour, day, week or month, etc by which the contract event is late. Normally, there is a cap on the total amount of LDs that can be recovered. That prevents the late party being bled to death as its delay eats into the contract price, and perhaps beyond it. However, the cap can work against the 'innocent' party such that it is suffering terribly because of the delay but is not, ultimately, compensated for its losses. For this reason, LDs may be combined with other remedies, eg the right to claim 'normal' damages, if the delay continues beyond a set time.

Payment for performance

A sale is a gift until it is paid for, and many would argue that payment is the most vital part of any contract. But payment clauses are often inadequate. Agreements are written with 'Payment 30 days net' as the sum total of the payment provisions. What does that mean?

If payment is not clearly and definitively expressed, then there is a serious risk that there is no contract at all. A court might decide that the agreement is void for uncertainty because the parties have failed to express the price clearly. Certainly, the judges will not draft additional provisions to give certainty where there is none.

When considering price clauses, the parties must pay attention to the realities of both the deal and the world. For example:

- Phased payment – be clear about the phases and the 'trigger' points for payment. Ask questions about the process and work through examples. Even add examples to the contract as annexes to help those who come later to understand exactly what was intended.
- Whenever the passing of time affects a contract, the parties must play the 'What if…?' game to ensure that they have considered the most likely and most obvious contingencies.
- Consider currency rate fluctuations and who is to carry that risk.
- Consider the cost of raw materials, services and labour in the contract. Ten years ago, no one would have foreseen the 'carbon tax' or some of the other green levies that are now imposed. Who expected oil to rise so far in price? Who was ready for the rise in gas prices? All these things can have a material, adverse effect on the economics of a contract and, to the extent reasonably possible, all should be addressed and provided for.

Conclusions

This chapter has advocated a schematic approach to risk, liability and reward and the use of all-encompassing, written commercial contracts. It has done this for some clear and sound reasons:

- The parties can know and understand what risks they are taking in entering the deal.
- The seller can price its goods or services according to clearly expressed and understood potential exposures.
- The buyer, which typically is assuming the risk of poor, bad or no performance, can assess its side of the deal and can take insurance or look for an alternative lower-risk or better-priced supplier.

- The parties generally should be able to control and manage their risks more accurately because they will have spent time considering and negotiating them.
- If an event occurs for which one party seeks compensation or some other remedy, a well-written and well-thought-out contract will save time, cost and energy because a reading of its provisions should show, clearly and simply, what the parties agreed would happen in such cases.
- It is easier to advise senior management on a schematic risk profile than have to try to explain how different aspects of law will or might work to change the liability being accepted in the deal.

5

Risks in Innovation and Expansion

Risk management in innovation

Clare Farrukh, James Moultrie, Rob Phaal, Francis Hunt and Rick Mitchell, Centre for Technology Management, Institute for Manufacturing, University of Cambridge

Introduction

Innovation is the activity of managing from idea to launch, ie invention plus commercialization. Risk management is an important consideration because innovation is inherently risky, with possible failure in both technical and commercial stages. This chapter looks at managing innovation risk in two ways: 1) mitigating risk within an innovation project by reviewing potential hazards and taking action; 2) minimizing investment risk for one or more innovation projects by evaluating the technology potential and using managerial flexibility. Both avenues are considered here in practical terms by giving examples of possible tools that companies can use to manage innovation risk more effectively.

Managing risk within an innovation project

Two approaches are considered here: 1) overall risk assessment approach; 2) specific approach to predicting failure modes (FMEA).

Risk assessment

The aim of this approach is to help focus attention on areas of uncertainty and highlight inaccurate, incomplete or out-of-date information.

Description

Product development is full of risks and uncertainties, whether technical, market or organizational. Many of these can be resolved in the early stages of the project – the fuzzy front end – by searching for information or conducting pilot studies. Others will remain throughout the project as design and development proceed.

Rather than just crossing fingers and hoping that it will be 'all right on the night', it makes sense to draw up and maintain some form of register of risks, and plan activities to reduce significant risks as quickly as possible.

This simple method can be used to assess and prioritize risks, on the basis of their probability of occurrence and severity of impact on the project.

Method

- *Draw up a list of potential problems.* Make a list of all the 'unknowns' or other issues that could impact on the project. This could be done during a team brainstorm session.
- *Assess probability and impact.* For each issue, rate the probability of occurrence and severity of impact as either high, medium or low.
- *Derive a risk 'score'.* Score 5 for high, 3 for medium and 1 for low. The risk score is then derived by simply multiplying severity times probability. This will produce a number in the range 1 to 25.
- *Prioritize each issue.* Each issue can now be categorized by shade. Priority should be given to dark 25s and dark 15s. See Figure 5.1.1.
- *Assign responsibility.* If the risk is due to absence of information, assign someone to find out. Look out for high-risk issues that may occur downstream. What can be done now to reduce that risk?
- *Continue to update the list on a regular basis.* Make sure that positive action is being taken on the major risk items. Add new risks to the list as they become apparent.

Failure mode and effects analysis (FMEA)

The aim of this tool is to enable potential errors or faults to be predicted during the early design stages.

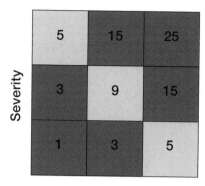

Figure 5.1.1   Risk assessment matrix

Description

Many companies use FMEA as a central pillar of their design process. FMEA provides a structured approach to the analysis of root causes (of failure), the estimation of severity or impact, and the effectiveness of strategies for prevention. The ultimate output is the generation of action plans to prevent, detect or reduce the impact of potential modes of failure. In a nutshell, it encourages the design team to consider:

∎ what could go wrong;
∎ how badly it might go wrong;
∎ what needs to be done to prevent or mitigate the problem.

FMEA emerged from the US military in the late 1940s as a tool to improve the evaluation of reliability of equipment. Its benefits quickly became apparent and it was adopted by aerospace industries and NASA during the Apollo programme in the 1960s. It was later taken up by many of the larger automotive companies, including Ford in the 1970s. It has since become a core tool in product development in many organizations and is recommended as a part of an organization's quality management system.

The basic logic can be applied at a number of levels, including organizational issues, strategy issues, product design issues, production processes and individual components. Typically, it is used to analyse either a product design or a production process:

∎ *Product or design FMEA.* What could go wrong with a product while in service as a result of a weakness in design?
  – Carried out during the early stages of a design project.
  – Tends to assume that the product will be produced to the required design specifications.

– Aims to reduce reliance on process controls and inspection to overcome limitations in the basic design and, thus, there is a need to consider the technical and physical limitations of the manufacturing and assembly processes.

■ *Process FMEA.* What could go wrong with a product during manufacture or while in service as a result of non-compliance with specification or design?

Typically, the information is collated and presented in a tabular format, as shown in Figure 5.1.2.

Method

1. *Level of analysis.* The analysis can be carried out at a project, product, system, subsystem or component level. It is important to be clear about the level at which the current analysis is taking place. A hierarchical organization of analysis enables the design team to drill down to detail where appropriate.
2. *Date and prepared by.* To record who was involved and when the analysis took place.
3. *FMEA number and reference information.* Clear numbering is important, to enable the team to trace an analysis from system to component level. It may also be important to reference any important test results, documents or drawings here.
4. *System/component/function.* The specific name or number of the element or issues under study.
5. *Potential failure modes.* The manner in which a component, subsystem or system could possibly fail while being used. Here the design team must be creative in seeking ideas for all potential modes of failure. Ask open and general questions: How can it fail? Under what conditions? What types of use? etc.
6. *Potential effects of failure.* For each mode of failure, what will the likely effect be? How will the failure affect different stakeholders? What will be the likely outcomes if the system or component fails? Provide as detailed a description as is necessary of the potential impact of failure. An individual failure mode may have many possible effects.
7. *Severity rating.* Each failure effect can be judged for its potential seriousness. Typically, this is done by scoring the effect on a 1 to 5 (or 10) scale. This value should be discussed and negotiated by all members of the team. A team may wish to define for itself the severity to go with each score. Below is a suggested scheme:
   Rating criteria
   – 5 (9–10) with potential safety risk or legal problems – potential loss of life or major dissatisfaction;
   – 4 (7–8) high potential customer dissatisfaction – serious injury or significant mission disruption;
   – 3 (5–6) medium potential customer dissatisfaction – potential small injury, mission inconvenience or delay;
   – 2 (3–4) the customer may notice the potential failure and may be a little dissatisfied – annoyance;
   – 1 (1–2) the customer will probably not detect the failure – undetectable.

FMEA worksheet

Project: ① Product: System:		Date: Prepared by: ②									FMEA Number: Reference documents: ③	
System/ Component/ Function	Potential Failure mode	Potential effect(s) of failure	Severity	Critical?	Potential cause(s) of failure	Occurrence	Current design controls	Detection	Risk Priority Number	Recommended action(s)	Responsibility & completion date
④	⑤	⑥	⑦	⑧	⑨	⑩	⑪	⑫	⑬	⑭	⑮

Figure 5.1.2 FMEA worksheet

8. *Critical?* A column is provided to enable the rapid identification of potentially critical failures that must be addressed (eg safety issues, sales issues, etc).
9. *Potential cause and mechanisms of failure.* Each failure mode will have an underlying root cause. Thus, it is important to spend time to establish the potential root causes or mechanisms of failure by asking 'What is the likely cause of the failure mode?' Possible causes could include: wrong tolerances, poor alignment, operator error, component missing, fatigue, defective components, maintenance required, environment, etc.
10. *Occurrence ranking.* It is also necessary to consider the likelihood of the potential failure occurring. Here, a 'probability' assessment is made by the team and scored on a 1 to 5 (or 10) scale. Possible occurrence ratings (you can define them in other ways) are shown below:
Rating criteria
   – 5 (9–10) very high probability of occurrence;
   – 4 (7–8) high probability of occurrence;
   – 3 (5–6) moderate probability of occurrence;
   – 2 (3–4) low probability of occurrence;
   – 1 (1–2) remote probability of occurrence.
This section is critical in the FMEA procedure, and each of the responses categorized as very high or high should be considered and addressed.
11. *Current design controls.* Are there any design controls that aim to reduce or eliminate the potential failure? These could include labels, barriers, instructions or total redesigns. Other controls could include prototyping, evaluation or possibly market surveys.
12. *Detection rating.* The final rating aims to establish how 'detectable' the potential fault will be. Will it be instantly noticeable or will it not be apparent. In addition, how likely is it that the controls listed will enable the detection of the potential failure? Suggested ratings on a scale of 1 to 5 (or 10):
Rating criteria
   – 5 (9 or 10) zero probability of detecting the potential failure cause;
   – 4 (7 or 8) close to zero probability of detecting the potential failure cause;
   – 3 (4, 5 or 6) not much likelihood of detecting the potential failure cause;
   – 2 (2 or 3) good chance of detecting the potential failure cause;
   – 1 (1) almost complete certainty of identifying the potential failure cause.
If the FMEA is being carried out at a 'project' level, then it can be beneficial to consider this value as 'reactability'. Will it be possible to react to the failure rapidly enough to reduce its impact sufficiently?
13. *Risk priority number (RPN).* It is likely that the team will have identified many possible failure modes and effects. Each one needs to be assigned a 'risk priority number' to enable the prioritization of mitigating action. The RPN is simply the product of the severity, occurrence and detection ratings:
RPN = Severity rating × Occurrence rating × Detection rating, perhaps more easily remembered as: RPN= S×O×D.
The RPN value gives an indicator of the design risk and, generally, the items with the highest RPN and severity ratings should be given first consideration.

14. *Recommended actions.* Follow-up is essential and actions to reduce the impact or likelihood are essential. These actions should be specific and preferably measurable. Attention should be given to actions that address the root cause and not the symptoms.
15. *Responsibility.* Finally, all actions should be clearly allocated (to an individual, department and/or organization) and a clear deadline given.
16. *Additional columns if wanted.* Some FMEA users add additional columns to record the actual actions taken or keep an update on the status of actions. It can also be a good idea to revise the RPN value following the corrective action. This enables full traceability between potential problems and the outcomes of actions.

Managing the risk of innovation investment

Three approaches are considered here, based on work carried out within the authors' recent research project 'Business appraisal of technology potentials':

■ value roadmapping;
■ decision trees and options thinking;
■ portfolio management.

Value roadmapping (VRM)

The aim of this tool is to provide a way of exploring the value potential of early-stage (and hence inherently risky) technology, when traditional cash flow projection methods are not appropriate.

Description

Technology roadmapping was originally developed by Motorola in the late 1970s to support integrated product-technology strategic planning, using a simple graphical representation to align market requirements, product evolution and technology development. See Figure 5.1.3.

The roadmapping approach has been subsequently adopted (and adapted) widely in industry, at both the company and the sector level, to support a variety of strategic goals. Roadmaps take a variety of forms, although perhaps the most generic and flexible is based on a time-based multi-layered architecture. Such roadmaps support integrated strategic planning, and are more appropriately called innovation, strategic or business roadmaps.

The value roadmap (VRM) concept builds on CTM's experience with roadmapping, focusing on the need to explore the value potential of key company technologies, particularly in the following situations: early-stage R&D, where traditional valuation techniques such as net present value (NPV) or return on investment (ROI) are not appropriate; and 'technology push', where new opportunities are sought for existing technological capability. Both of these situations are characterized by a desire to explore a broad 'opportunity space', in a divergent process that starts from understanding technology capability, in terms of current state-of-the-art and future development.

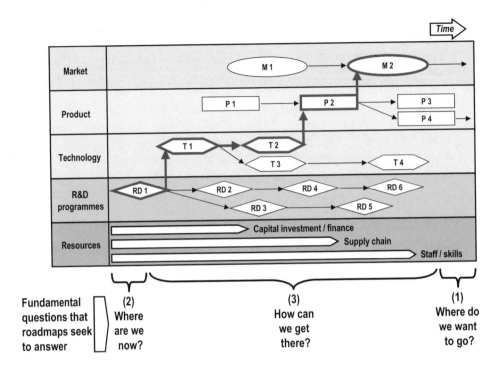

Figure 5.1.3   Typical product-technology roadmap

The VRM aims to provide a framework for supporting technology evaluation and valuation (to explore, communicate, calculate, maximize and manage value). The workshop-based approach is designed to explore the value potential of technology (emerging technology or 'push' situations) and to improve the design of the technology development programme (to reduce risk and increase flexibility, using options-based thinking). Starting with a VRM workshop, roadmapping methods can support the business case for research and technology, qualitatively and quantitatively (in financial terms), when the technology reaches a higher level of maturity (closer to market), providing a consistent framework that can be used to link technological and commercial perspectives throughout the technology life cycle. See Figure 5.1.4.

Method

The VRM approach has been configured to be as efficient as possible, focused on a multifunctional half-day workshop, with the following aims:

■ to provide a structured framework for mapping and exploring potential value streams based on the selected technology, for either 'early stage' or 'technology push' situations, where the route to market is not clear;
■ to identify focused opportunities to follow up;
■ to support the process of managing technology for value in the firm, providing input to technology strategy, planning, exploitation, etc;

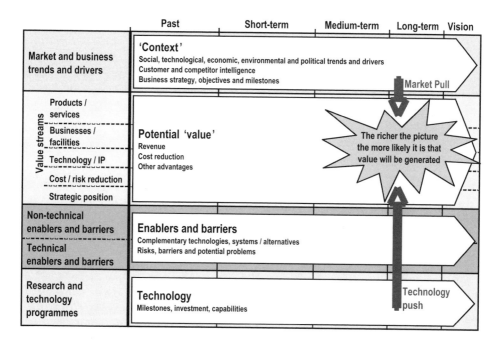

Figure 5.1.4   Value roadmapping template

■ to support communication between technological and commercial functions in the business.

Together, the horizontal time axis and the vertical architecture (or layers) provide a canvas for the brainstorming of ideas by a mixed group of commercial and technical people.

The VRM 'architecture' includes the following layers:

■ *Market and business trends and drivers.* These are the drivers that focus on external market trends such as social, economic, environmental, technological and political drivers and internal business factors that influence the development of products and technology in the area of interest, including strategic milestones and goals.
■ *Value streams.* Value streams are the sources of future revenue and savings: products, services, business/facilities, technology/IP, cost/risk reduction, strategic position. All of these value streams relate directly to the generation of cash revenue, except for 'strategic position', which includes all non-financial factors that provide a foundation for future revenue generation.
■ *Enablers and barriers.* Enablers and barriers are the technical and non-technical challenges and risks, together with complementary assets and actions needed to exploit the potential value of the technology or capability.

■ *Technology capabilities.* The technology capabilities are the underlying technologies that are the result of the technology investment decision.

The VRM time axis is the key feature of the value roadmap that links the short-, medium- and long-term perspectives for all of the layers. This is an important element as it links current technology investment to longer-term aspirations, providing a forward-looking 'radar'.

Decision trees and options thinking

The aim of decision trees and options thinking (see Figure 5.1.5) is to weigh up the risks and benefits of uncertain technology investments, so that a better understanding of the potential value of the investment is obtained.

Description

The term 'real options' is used to describe a range of ideas. Three of these are as follows:

■ *options thinking:* being aware of the value of informed managerial flexibility;
■ *decision tree analysis:* quantifying the value of choices given a range of different possible outcomes;
■ *real options valuation:* adapting mathematical models from the financial markets.

Each of these is described in more detail below.

Methods

■ *Options thinking.* A fundamental idea behind so-called options thinking is that uncertainty can be good. This is so if a manager has the flexibility to amplify the

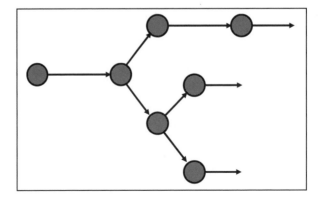

Figure 5.1.5   Options thinking and decision trees

benefits if things turn out well and minimize the negative effects if they do not. An example would be an inexpensive research project to find out if a technology is feasible – if it is, the manager can invest heavily to reap the benefits and, if not, he or she need incur no further costs. The argument is that options thinking provides a more realistic assessment than (the naïve use of) discounted cash flows, which makes risky projects look unattractive. Applied at the strategic level, various authors classify the types of options, eg options enabling future growth, options to defer investments, options to stage investments, options to expand or contract operations.

■ *Decision trees.* Decision tree analysis attempts to quantify options thinking. It classifies possible future outcomes, eg a research project failing, producing a reasonable result or producing an exceptionally good result. It then ascribes probabilities to these outcomes by some means, eg past data on similar projects or expert opinions. This can be done for a series of events, eg the research project and then the market launch, and from these a tree of outcomes can be constructed. Next decision points need to be inserted and the optimal decisions chosen to maximize the expected value. This approach can be extended into one of Monte Carlo modelling where probability distributions are assigned to variables such as 'market size' and then simulations run using software (eg Crystal Ball, @Risk). A criticism commonly levelled at decision tree analyses is the reliability (and meaning) of the probabilities.

■ *Real options valuation.* Real options valuation is the term usually used for mathematical evaluation techniques inspired by the modelling of options on the financial markets. Particularly well known is the model known as the Black-Scholes equation. This model assumes that the price of an asset on the stock market can be modelled as a type of random walk. It then derives a price for an option on this asset, eg the right to buy a share in three months' time at a guaranteed price. It does this by constructing an instantaneously risk-free portfolio, ie one whose value is not affected by variations in the price of the asset, and then arguing that this portfolio must have the same price as other risk-free assets. There are recognized to be a number of issues about applying real options valuation. In particular representing price movement realistically, deriving the value of an asset that has no equivalent currently being traded and estimating the volatility parameter. It can be queried to what extent a continuous-time stochastic model is likely to be more accurate than a simple decision tree. In addition the loss of intuitive understanding of the model may significantly undermine the value of the technique for non-expert users. It has been argued that the 'lumpy' nature of information release in projects makes decision trees a better model than commonly used random walk processes. In addition and previous use of the Black-Scholes model for past investment decisions has been reviewed and it has been suggested that in some situations important model assumptions did not hold. In general (and obviously) the financial modelling approach described in this section will be useful if the model is a good fit to the situation being modelled. For example, if it is possible to distinguish market risk and technical risk and where the main risk is market risk, then real options models seem appropriate.

Summary

The term 'real options' is used to describe various ideas, but the common essence of all of them is that uncertainty is not necessarily a bad thing. Incorporating uncertainty into calculations is not always readily accepted by managers, but if it is done well it should lead to better understanding of the value of an investment.

Portfolio approaches

The aim of portfolio management is to ensure that a sensible set of innovation projects is supported by the company, for example balancing risk against reward.

Description

Portfolio management is a decision process where a business's list of active new products and R&D projects is constantly updated, reviewed and revised. In this process, new products are evaluated, selected and prioritized; existing products may be accelerated, killed or deprioritized.

Method

Selecting a portfolio is in theory merely a question of optimizing profitability within constraints of resources and timing. Well-proven mathematical techniques are available for doing this but, as several authors have observed, they are seldom used in practice. There are two key reasons for this. The first is that the financial information required for the analysis is often incomplete or unreliable, especially in the early stages. The second is that the selection process tends to be hidden by the mathematics. Managers cannot readily review or justify the results, nor amend them to take account of factors not explicitly included in the calculations. In practice there is therefore a preference for more transparent techniques:

■ *Evaluating single projects.* Any portfolio management process must start with an evaluation of the potential worth of each of the projects under consideration. The simplest method is a basic income and expenditure calculation. More realistically a discount factor is applied to the incomes and expenditures taking account of the cost of money to the organization, to give the net present value (NPV) of the project. A measure of the robustness of the profitability may be obtained by calculating the break-even point – the time before the project first achieves an overall profit after initial expenditures – or the internal rate of return (IRR), which is the discount rate that would reduce the NPV to zero. Clearly, a short time to break-even or a large IRR implies robust profitability.

Risk and uncertainty may be included in financial calculations in a number of ways. For a project that is expected to proceed in a single phase without decision points, risk can be included by multiplying the expected income by the probability of success. The costs of the project are unaltered so the result is a reduction in the forecast of net present value, NPV. New product introductions, however, usually proceed in a number of stages with decision points in between. There may also be branches where the project could take one of several directions, as represented in decision trees. Clearly, the possibility of failure in an early stage reduces not only the probability of the income but also the probability of expenditure in the later phases. If this is included, the correct valuation is higher than it would have been if the project had been planned as a single phase. Arguably this is the value of management action at the decision points.

It has been suggested that competing projects should be valued by separately calculating the possible upsides and downsides of each one in relation to a benchmark and weighting them differently according to the organization's appetite for risk.

Thus

Project Value = Upside – (R × Downside)
where R is greater than 1 (>1) if the organization is risk averse
and less than 1 (<1) if not risk averse.

This approach appears to have promise for comparing project values more rationally than by using the long-term averages. However, it is not clear how factor R is to be calculated, especially as it must depend on the magnitudes involved (individuals and organizations are usually less willing to gamble for very high stakes than for low ones).

∎ *Scoring methods.* Financial analysis suffers from the fundamental problem that the data required may be unavailable, or of dubious quality, especially in the critical early stages. For this reason many companies prefer to replace, or at least supplement, the data with a scoring method. In this, projects are assessed and scored according to a range of criteria regarded as predictors of success. For example, scores may be given for unique product features, size of market, the ability to leverage the company's core competences, etc, as well as the planned cost and profit. The criteria may be very broad, reflecting what is known in general about success criteria for new products, or they may be industry- or company-specific. The sum of the scores against all the criteria represents the overall merit, or potential value, of the project. A simple selection of projects can be done by ranking them according to value for money or for effective use of critical resources.

∎ *Multiple projects.* The portfolio must also be balanced in other ways. For example, a spread of projects over time is desirable: no company will want all its projects to come to fruition at the same time, with nothing planned before or after. The portfolio must also reflect the company's general strategic intent, ensuring that sufficient resources are allocated to strategically important businesses, markets or technologies. This may be achieved by simply allocating a certain proportion of innovation spend (known as 'strategic buckets') to particular businesses or types of project. Alternatively the company may draw up a strategic roadmap stretching several years ahead and use that to ensure that the longer-term orientation of the business is adequately served by the selected projects.

The balance of risk and reward across the portfolio must also be considered. High-risk projects should not necessarily be avoided if the potential payback is good enough and provided they are accompanied by some low-risk opportunities.

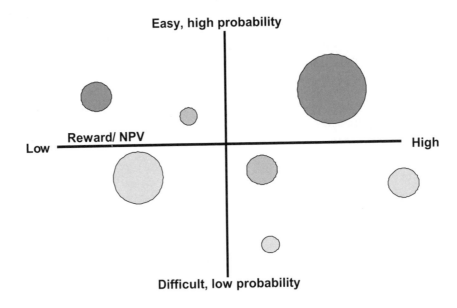

Figure 5.1.6 Risk–reward 'bubble diagram'

The risk–reward profile of a portfolio may be displayed on a two-dimensional diagram with risk and reward (however quantified) as the two axes (Figure 5.1.6). Such displays are often called 'bubble diagrams'. Managers can use them as an aid to ensure that the portfolio is not inappropriately biased in one direction or the other. Many authors advocate the use of checklists to ensure that all relevant aspects of value and risk are captured.

The size of the bubbles can represent the expenditure required and colour can even be used to show how close each project is to fruition. The bubble diagram is merely an aid to understanding the portfolio, not a decision-making tool in itself. Generally a mix of low-risk projects will be desired, balancing a few higher-risk opportunities, but it is left to management judgement how they are to be balanced. Other applications use ellipses, with the axes showing the uncertainty in reward and in risk in the technical phase (the risk dimension being reserved for the commercial risk).

Further reading

Boer, FP (1999) *The Valuation of Technology: Business and financial issues in R&D*, Wiley, New York

Cooper, RG, Edgett, SJ and Kleinschmidt, EJ (2001) *Portfolio Management for New Products*, 2nd edn, Perseus Books, Cambridge, MA

Goffin, K and Mitchell, R (2006) *Innovation Management*, Palgrave, Basingstoke

McDermott, RE, Mikulak, RJ and Beauregard, MR (1996) *Basics of FMEA*, Quality Resources, Cambridge

McGrath, ME, Anthony, MT and Shapiro, AR (1992) *Product Development: Success through product and cycle-time excellence*, Butterworth-Heinemann, Boston, MA and London

Phaal, R, Farrukh, C and Probert, D (2001) *T-Plan: Fast start to technology roadmapping*, Institute for Manufacturing, University of Cambridge, Cambridge

Stamatis, DH (2003) *Failure Mode and Effect Analysis: FMEA from theory to execution*, ASQ Quality Press, Cambridge

Trigeorgis, L (1996) *Real Options: Managerial flexibility and strategy in resource allocation*, MIT Press, Cambridge, MA

Wheelwright, SC and Clark, KB (1992) *Revolutionizing New Product Development: Quantum leaps in speed, efficiency, and quality*, Free Press, New York and London

Wilmott, P, Howison, S and Dewynne, J (1995) *The Mathematics of Financial Derivatives: A student introduction*, Cambridge University Press, Cambridge

Political risks

Stephen Capon, ACE Global Markets

Introduction

The private political risk market was almost extinct less than 15 years ago but today political risk has rarely been more topical. This chapter will provide some background on the private insurance market and its capabilities while also examining why political risks should be a critical element within the risk management process.

Shaping the private market

A brief history

The market was really founded in the late 1970s. However, by the early 1990s the commercial market had almost vanished under the impact of:

■ Iraq's invasion of Kuwait;
■ conflict in the former Yugoslavia;
■ the break-up of the USSR;
■ losses sustained by insurance groups from storms and a range of other events;
■ lack of capital from reinsurers;
■ the decision of some primary players to deploy capital to other business lines.

As a result, the global capacity per risk is estimated to have fallen to a mere $50 million.[1]

However, Lloyd's and AIG continued to write the business and in the mid-1990s new capital entered the market, for example ACE Ltd, Exporters Insurance Corporation, Sovereign Risk Insurance (now a wholly owned managing agency of ACE Ltd) and Zurich.

By 2000, the political risk market had record capacity and subsequently showed resilience in the face of falling investment returns and rising claims between 2001 and 2003. This period saw significant capacity retrenchment not only as a result of political risk-associated losses such as Argentina, Zimbabwe, Cuba and the Dominican Republic but Enron, WorldCom, the World Trade Center towers, etc. Figure 5.2.1 clearly demonstrates the impact of the downturn in the cycle but also the commitment of core players.

To put Figure 5.2.1 in a little more context, it is estimated that the gross notional exposure of the global private political risk insurance market is now in excess of $100 billion, and it currently insures risks in up to 140 countries and territories around the globe.

So in 2001/02, despite even worse corporate results than in the previous downturn, three things had happened:

■ Unlike the early 1990s significant capacity remained in the market.
■ The tenors of risks underwriters were willing to underwrite continued to be far longer than in the early 1990s.
■ The market was writing and continued to write private sector default and insolvency risks in emerging markets.

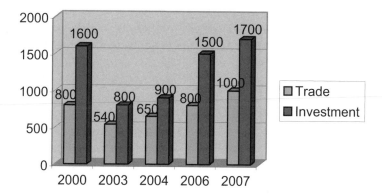

Trade and Investment Capacity Any One Risk

Figure 5.2.1   Market capacity 2002, 2003 and 2004

These facts suggest:

■ There is now a core of institutions with a real commitment to the class in the long term.
■ The insurance product/solution has become an integral part of risk management for leading international banks, exporters, contractors, engineering groups and multinational corporates.

So what had caused this seismic shift?

1. Development of economic capital at risk models within banks and the need to lay off risk to other risk takers.
2. The expansion of FDI flows to emerging markets and the gradual reduction of donor support and commercial lending.
3. The huge growth in global trade, which today is estimated at around $20 trillion of which about 25 per cent originates in or is destined for emerging markets.
4. The development of co-insurance and reinsurance relationships with the Multilateral Investment Guarantee Agency and export credit agencies.
5. Insurers sought higher-yielding business opportunities as investment income began to stagnate.
6. Investment by insurers in skilled and experienced professionals and supporting infrastructure.
7. The fact the market has had a significant number of opportunities to demonstrate its ability and willingness to pay claims: 1994, 1997, 1998 and 2001–06.

Product offerings

Table 5.2.1 gives an overview of the various perils that can be typically covered, while Figure 5.2.2 gives an indication of their application. Policies are bespoke, with insureds able to choose from the broad menu to ensure the protection provided matches their specific needs.

Today the term 'political risk insurance' often, rather confusingly, covers not only the traditional political perils associated with investment in or exporting to foreign markets but also protection from the default or insolvency of private sector suppliers and buyers, or banks, in emerging markets.

Arguably the two biggest developments in the past five years have been:

1. The extension of the product to cover private bank/corporate default and insolvency risk with tenors of up to five years and for some market participants seven years.
2. The increased tenors of coverage available:
   - Multinationals tend to avail themselves of three- to five-year protection for their overseas assets.
   - Exporters, contractors and engineers will, in general, use the product for pre-shipment risks and protection from wrongful calling of bonds up to seven years.
   - Payment protection from government default will vary depending on the risk

Table 5.2.1 The perils

Investment insurance perils	Trade insurance perils
Confiscation, expropriation and nationalization, and deprivation	Unilateral contract repudiation by a government buyer or supplier
Currency inconvertibility and transfer risk, wilful destruction by the host government, deprivation of collateral	Non-payment by a government buyer
	Non-honouring of payment instruments by state-owned banks
Non-repossession of an asset	
	Non-honouring of guarantees issued by state-owned or state-controlled institutions
Where *appropriate the policy could be extended to cover:*	
Selective discrimination	Currency inconvertibility and exchange transfer restrictions
Forced abandonment	
	Export or import embargo
Forced divestiture	
	Licence cancellation
Political violence	
	Frustration of the contract due to war or civil war, government law or decree
War and civil war	
Non-honouring of an arbitration award	Arbitration award default
Non-honouring of a guarantee	Wrongful calling of guarantees (private and public)
Import/export licence cancellation	
Import/export embargo	
Operating licence cancellation	
Business interruption	

rating of the country but for the better risks will generally be five to seven years but in some cases the market can cover up to 10 years.
- Lenders' protection on project financings tend to be available from five to 10 years, but the market can cover up to 15 years.

Figure 5.2.3 shows how the aggregate market capacity breaks down by the maximum tenor or terms of the risk.

	TRADE			INVESTMENT				
BUSINESS SECTOR	TRADE FINANCE	COMMODITY TRADE FINANCE	EXPORT FINANCE	MOBILE ASSETS	FIXED INVESTMENT	PROJECT FINANCE	CROSS-BORDER LOANS	CAPITAL MARKETS
RISKS	Contractual default by government obligors

Political force majeure

Non-honouring of L/Cs issued by government banks

Unfair calling of on-demand bonds

Bank-confirmed L/C facilities for government and private issuing banks | Non-payment/non-delivery by government obligors

Non-honouring of confirmed L/Cs issued by government banks

Confiscation of mobile assets | Contractual default by government obligors

Political force majeure

Non-honouring of MOF guarantees

Unfair calling of on-demand bonds | Confiscation of contractor's plant and equipment and associated perils

Non-repossession of leased assets

Confiscation and associated perils of stocks | Expropriation

Inconvertibility

PV/WAR

Concession cancellation

Embargo

Business interruption | Expropriation of borrower/ project

Inconvertibility

PV/WAR

Non-honouring of guarantees

Arbitration default

Concession cancellation | Expropriation of borrower

Inconvertibility

PV/WAR | Currency inconvertibility |
| APPLICATION | Short-term export contracts | Short-term structured commodity transactions | Short-/medium-term export contracts (buyer/supplier credits) | Overseas contractors /construction/ engineering Leasing and finance Commodity traders | Equity investors | Non-recourse project loans | Lenders' interests | Capital market bond issues (144A) |

Figure 5.2.2   Application of the product suite

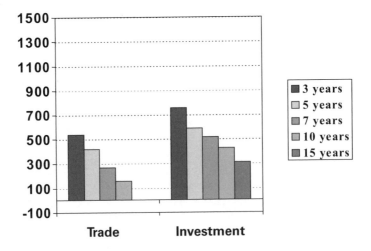

Figure 5.2.3   Market capacity by risk tenor

What next?

Basel II

Several international banks have been utilizing the private insurance market for at least a decade. While this has had no regulatory capital benefit these banks have taken the decision that in terms of their own internal risk models there is a benefit in utilizing political and trade credit insurance. It improves internal risk adjusted returns.

However, with the advent of Basel II these products can provide regulatory capital relief. This is true for securitizations but also for traditional trade finance and even commodity and project finance.

A range of underwriting companies firmly believe that insurance policies qualify as 'guarantees' within the meaning of Basel II while not actually being unfunded risk participations and/or unconditional on-demand guarantees.

The precise benefits accorded to an institution will ultimately be for negotiation between it and its national regulator, but a number of insurers have already engaged with leading international banks to assist in this process.

Tenors and credit risk

Effectively most of the work on tenors has already been undertaken over the past three years with a range of insurance providers now able to cover credit risks up to five years. Given that the market functions on the understanding that it is assisting trade finance there seems little scope to take tenors longer.

For project finance the majority of the market can support risks of up to 10 years but there are a few providers who can go to 15 years. However, coverage remains restricted to political perils and does not, as yet, cover commercial risks. There is every chance that over the next few years the market will move to providing comprehensive protection albeit on a very selective basis.

The appetite for credit risk remains firmly focused on trade-related transactions with strong underlying documentation and clear recovery opportunities. However, the market has become much more responsive to exporter and importer needs and structured transactions including a wide range of commodities.

Capital

Traditionally capital for this market has been provided by a small group of reinsurers. However, hedge funds and alternative risk transfer vehicles are becoming increasingly interested in supporting this market. On the one hand this should increase competition and lower capital costs and assist in growing capacity, but on the other hand it raises issues with regard to the stability of the enlarged market and to the impact of potential excess capital upon risk returns. These developments mean that assessing the commitment of your insurance provider to this product as well as its credit standing becomes more important.

However, the role of alternative markets for new capital should not be overstated. There is, it is suggested, a strong and committed core of insurers and reinsurers to support the future of the product. Furthermore, it is actually very complicated for capital markets to provide a product that would seamlessly meet the needs of a primary underwriting company in the way reinsurers can. For example, the triggers in the credit default swap market do not match those in a credit insurance policy. As regards nationalization or political violence, there is not currently an alternative risk transfer vehicle, although it is not inconceivable that one will be developed. There is then the issue of the return demanded by investors in such vehicles versus the costs associated with traditional reinsurance structures. It is anticipated that many alternative risk transfer options will prove far too expensive. Such developments have potential implications for credit ratings of primary insurers in terms of 'reinsurance' recoverables.

Currency depreciation

Some segments of the market are already providing depreciation protection but the market remains split and this is unlikely to change any time soon. Insurers have no way to hedge such risk without entering into potentially complex and expensive structures. The general opinion is that banks remain in the best position to provide such hedging protection and insurers should stick to providing protection related to losses directly resulting from clearly defined political events.

A discretionary spend?

Global trade flows are estimated at $20 trillion per annum of which about a quarter are imports and exports to and from emerging markets. Foreign direct investments in emerging markets rose from $202 billion to $399 billion between 2003 and 2006. Yet, political and trade credit risk insurance is perceived as a 'discretionary spend'.

Are emerging markets simply no longer risky?

At a recent event attended by risk managers from both corporates and financial institutions it was interesting to hear that there was a view that a range of major emerging economies were now perceived as much stronger and more stable. Yet in the past five years the private political risk insurance market has paid out over $1.5 billion. It is estimated that less than a third of this was in relation to Argentina. There have been claims in Brazil, Venezuela, Belize, the Dominican Republic, Cuba, Tajikistan, Russia and Zimbabwe. Claims have involved currency inconvertibility and non-transfer, expropriation, and sovereign and quasi-sovereign and private sector defaults.

High commodity prices have encouraged a range of governments across the globe to reconsider contractual arrangements with investors, eg Russia, Peru and Guinea. In others an increasing sense of socio-economic injustice and patriotism, if not nationalism, has swept radical leaders to power, eg Bolivia and possibly Ecuador. There have been political violence in Nigeria, riots in Hungary, concerns over the creation of parallel governments in Mexico and a coup in Thailand.

Socio-political factors such as the environment, education, healthcare, employ-ment, etc are all at play and are factors that feed into the rich tapestry of political risk. Economic development and globalization increase social and institutional stresses within transition economies. Sudden and unexpected change is a reality. Change can be brought on by social and intellectual movements, doctrines and creeds, economic policy and mismanagement and even natural disasters including pandemics. All can interrelate with political and credit risks to disrupt supply chains, wipe out corporate profits and destroy value.

I would venture that there are sufficient examples of institutional vulnerability, and political and economic mismanagement and uncertainty, and even instability, to make many risk managers and executive boards reconsider their ongoing capabilities to identify, measure, manage and mitigate such risks.

Clearly, perception of risk varies depending on where you are viewing it from physically, philosophically and in terms of past or future. Historical experience does indeed inform but I believe it is very dangerous to assume that because it is informative it is predictive.

The nationalizations and expropriations of the 1960s and 1970s gave way to more currency inconvertibility-led losses in the 1980s and 1990s. With the Asian crisis and then more specifically Argentina we have seen the development of 'creeping expropriation'. The theory espoused is that outright nationalization is effectively a thing of the past and currency inconvertibility-related losses are also in decline. In future, apart from terrorism, it is 'creeping' expropriation, eg government interference with tariffs, royalties and taxes, that impacts upon the commercial viability of the investment.

Yet exchange controls at various levels can be instigated and maintained for years, with access to hard currency being manipulated for political purposes, eg Venezuela. Furthermore, Argentina's apparent success with rescheduling its international and domestic debt has certainly set a precedent. It is doubtful that Nigeria would have been quite so bold or had so much success at the Paris Club and now we wait to see whether Ecuador will follow. Arguably, the belief in the cost of defaulting in terms of global integration, lack of access to funds and, in the case of Ecuador, the limited savings in relation to annual payments and the current account may be misplaced in certain situations. One needs to really understand what the political and domestic social gains may be as well as the costs. Sometimes the cost/benefit may in fact indicate that there are sound reasons to introduce currency controls, default and/or nationalize/expropriate when looking from a domestic political perspective.

Currently, US foreign and economic policies are probably the greatest risks we face. Should the United States continue to block certain foreign entities from acquiring US assets those investors will look for alternative assets, quite possibly in another currency. These are 'political' decisions, which can impact on financial market confidence, liquidity, exchange rates, global growth, etc.

The knock-on impact of surgical air strikes on Iran would be significant. Terrorist attacks would probably increase and oil prices could go over $100 per barrel. The impact that this would have on the global economy (consumer demand, supply chains, input costs, risk appetite and funding) would be significant.

Recent research undertaken by the Economist Intelligence Unit (EIU) and sponsored by ACE, IBM and KPMG involving about 150 corporations around the globe showed that almost 40 per cent of respondents were investing 'significantly' more in emerging markets. It also showed that they felt that risks had only increased slightly and that rewards still outweighed the risks. However, only 25 per cent of respondents confirmed that they were spending significantly more time on political and operating risk management in emerging markets. Furthermore, the EIU research also appeared to indicate significant complacency among risk managers and executives over the risks associated with investing and/or doing business in emerging markets. The reason for saying this is that the research suggested that the vast majority considered a wide range of political and operational risks before formally investing, while in fact less than a third of respondents undertook any ongoing monitoring of these risks. This is certainly upheld by the experience of the private political risk market. In general ACE's experience with investors is that at the initial point of investment they are well prepared and have undertaken appropriate due diligence, and its perceptions of the risks vary little from those of the investors. However, when a policy comes up for renewal ACE finds that there is often a gap in the parties' perceptions of the risks and that this is often due to differences in monitoring processes.

Of particular note was the fact that while a large proportion of respondents had pulled out of investments at the due diligence stage over a quarter had actually pulled out of investments during their life span – generally a very costly decision. If the risks were being truly monitored, measured and managed on an ongoing basis it might be that this number would be much smaller.

In recent years there has been a noticeable increase in the dialogue between corporate risk managers and political risk underwriters. There is a realization by risk managers that while insurers may not be providing protection for a range of direct operational risks (eg intellectual property rights, etc) they do have a long history as a market of taking a very wide range of risks in emerging markets, and as a market they are a useful source of practical knowledge and risk assessment. Insurers are increasingly seen as partners in assessing, monitoring and managing risk.

Conclusion

Politically related risks remain substantial and can impact on a business in a variety of ways. While engaging national and local government and communities in the host country will remain critical to managing the risks, the issue is how you predict future changes. Risk profiles are changing ever more rapidly. Greater integration increases contagion risk and arguably reduces the effectiveness of a portfolio approach unless you can measure risk correlations. Increasingly risk managers are using a range of tools to plan, manage and mitigate politically related risks. An increasingly common one is to carry out scenario analysis, possibly even adopting formal scenario plans. Another tool is to have semi-annual business interruption audits that highlight what local, regional or divisional management believe are the critical risks they face over the next 12 months and possibly beyond. Framed correctly these surveys can be an extremely effective way of monitoring changing environments and the risk profile over time.

Insurance policies do not provide a perfect hedge to all risks in emerging markets, but the market has considerable knowledge and expertise, and substantial capacity and appetite to build long-term partnerships with investors and financiers.

Note

1. Per risk is the definition for both global and underwriter specific capacity. It refers to the maximum line that can be underwritten on any one contract or risk.

China: counterfeiting and brand protection

Neil Miller, CSI–Commercial Security International Limited

Introduction

The number of commercial organizations on both sides of the Atlantic that have established supply and outsourcing relationships together with those in discussions with potential third parties in South-East Asia, specifically China, indicates there is a significant upward market trend and cost-effective benefits in this area. As a result, the strategy is now high on the corporate agenda and board strategies around the world. This strategy appears essential if you wish to remain competitive and increase your net and gross margins – missing out may cost your business.

The People's Republic of China (PRC) is quite clearly too large to be ignored. The PRC has changed its environment in recent decades, with a general switch from socialism to capitalism; it has become an emerging market in its own right. This will continue and in addition become more appealing for new and established multinational companies as it has an increasingly large, educated and cost-effective labour availability, cheaper distribution logistics and established manufacturing platforms.

However, experience shows that taking advantage of cost-effective labour, cheaper logistics and less regulated jurisdictions does not come without risk. Perhaps these are inevitable in the eagerness for better margins and profitability.

All risk managers should be aware of the usual supply chain risks involved in dealing with any foreign third party, issues such as language barriers, time zone differences, labour strikes, shipment turnaround, customs disruptions, environmental and political risks, etc, all of which delay responses, affect productivity and reduce profit margins.

However, instead of analysing these points in depth, this chapter aims to examine the inherent risks encountered specifically in the PRC in terms of intellectual property and brand, which inevitably are being infringed at some point, either in or by your supply chain. Below are also some preventative measures that should be considered to assist in protecting your brand.

Intellectual property risk

Intellectual property (IP) is the property or assets held by an individual or business in the form of patents, trademarks, copyrights, registered designs, etc, which includes products ranging from luxury goods, sportswear, fragrances and automobile parts to electronics and consumables.

IP assets being passed off by individuals, businesses or other third parties as their own can damage the brand owner's reputation, often resulting in lost opportunities and the loss of existing and potential business customers. Thus the financial impact and share value are diminished. More importantly, though, is the cost of rebuilding these losses and brand reputation.

The PRC has a huge domestic consumer market, mixed with less regulated legislation and ease of trans-border trade; intellectual property is often overlooked in an organization's risk management plan.

Businesses forming relationships with third parties in the PRC should consider placing IP protection high on their agenda before entering into any third-party contractual agreements. It is often a lack of awareness of regional risks that causes long-term difficulties.

The numbers

A recent survey conducted by an industry association based in Beijing, the Quality Brands Protection Committee, provided a comprehensive overview of the risks experienced by over 140 multinational companies concerned in IP infringement, and highlighted especially the impact of counterfeiting.

Over 70 per cent of the companies stated that their counterfeiting problems remained the same or had even worsened, which highlighted the size of the risk. Of the companies involved, 60 per cent also stated that counterfeiting is one of the top five business risks they face in the PRC markets.

This risk will continue to grow in South-East Asia. The European Commission recently reported that 71 per cent of counterfeit goods entering the EU originated in Asia, with 54 per cent from China alone.

Traditional and internet infringements

There are two major issues surrounding IP infringement in the PRC, traditional infringements and internet infringements.

Traditional infringements include innate problems such as counterfeiting, parallel imports, factory overruns, and trademark and patent infringements. These forms of traditional infringements are well known to brand owners and enforcement agencies, as outlined in the case studies below.

Case study: Factory overruns

A well-known sportswear company contractually licensed a third-party factory in the PRC to manufacture T-shirts and polo shirts. The company was extremely pleased with the quality of the products and valued its cost-effective decision to outsource the contract; however, after a period of time the Chinese factory recognized that excess cloth, labels and swing tickets were available and began to manufacture identical but surplus shirts. This surplus soon became available in discount stores and markets and was offered on sale over the internet, evidently damaging the sportswear company's brand and profit margins.

Case study: Parallel trading

A UK plc outsourced its electrical manufacturing requirements to a respected Chinese operator in Beijing. After a long contractual period of over three years, the Chinese company requested whether it could be the official distributor in South-East Asia, to which the UK plc agreed. It was not until a year later that a record profits statement was released by the PRC distributor that the plc became suspicious. After an investigation, the UK plc found that their 'lower-priced' products for the South-East Asian market were being shipped back to the UK, a higher-priced market, with the diverter pocketing the price difference.

Many brand owners experience these problems and their markets are being flooded with parallel imports. Diversion jeopardizes the exclusive relationships that brand owners seek with their authorized distributors overseas, interferes with their ability to promote products in certain markets and leads to loss of market share.

Local rules...

In most Western countries patent information is publicly available on the internet. Chinese companies with the basic technical and manufacturing capabilities have started to replicate and register identical products in the PRC and have secured patents as their own. A major pharmaceutical organization learned this lesson when it entered the South-East Asian market with a revolutionary drug and discovered that Chinese scientists had already patented the active ingredient there and were selling it.

Counterfeiting in particular is not unique to China, but is still evidently a massive problem, and in recent years it has been difficult to implement enforcement strategies.

The counterfeiting of registered and trademarked products:

■ poses threats to consumer health and safety;
■ deprives legitimate businesses of revenue;
■ demises the brand owner's reputation and client loyalty;
■ often financially supports criminal and terrorist organization activity and fuels global money laundering;
■ significantly reduces national and international employment;
■ causes consumers unknowingly to commit offences under the Proceeds of Crime Act 2002.

Those who produce these counterfeit products are able meticulously to reproduce logos, packaging and even serial numbers in order to fool buyers, suppliers and distributors. However, these organized criminals cease to pay close attention to detail when it comes to product testing and safety, often with fatal consequences.

Aviation and automobile infringements: a danger to consumers?

In the past, counterfeit parts were mainly non-safety items such as upholstery and body parts. However, as outlined below, it is now common to find engine, brake, steering and suspension parts on the market:

1. Fake brake linings often take up to five times longer to bring a vehicle to a complete stop. They have in the past been found to be made of compressed wood chips and cardboard.
2. Counterfeit windscreens are usually made with untoughened glass and shatter on the slightest impact.
3. Imitation parts often disintegrate within a year of use.
4. Counterfeit alloy wheels are made of cheap and non-durable aluminium, which crack easily.
5. Counterfeit transmission fluids, antifreeze and coolants (often dyed for appearance) are made up of ingredients that erode engine parts rather than serve their intended purpose.

Current communications, notably the internet, are becoming a tool for illegal and IP infringement acts, such as the selling of counterfeit product, usually at low cost, but also of low quality (including online auction houses such as eBay, etc). These kinds of sites are making it far simpler for counterfeit products to infiltrate a global market, causing a devastating decrease in the demand for your genuine product.

---

eBay – a threat to your brand?

It is believed that eBay has 94.9 million users, 9 million of whom are registered in the UK, and on any given day there are millions of items listed across thousands of categories. At any one time, eBay estimates there are 1 million items for sale from UK sellers alone.

Put all this into context and, in terms of assessing the risk to your brand, reputation and market share and of overall loss in potential revenue, then I believe there is a significant problem, especially as these goods can be sold online, at any time and anywhere.

Most investigators and brand protection officers, dare I say it, have a life and deserve the weekends to themselves. However, did you realize that most illicit sales of counterfeit, stolen and grey-market goods are placed on eBay at 6.30 pm on a Friday night and sold for a profit before the brand protection officers come back to work at 9 am Monday morning?

Internet service providers who are protecting websites selling infringed goods are becoming more anonymous, nearly impossible to trace and difficult to regulate. Even if you succeed in forcing a domain or ISP to cease trading, another one enters the industry with even less traceability.

IP protection recommendations

To reiterate, any company that is looking to exploit a supply chain or third party in these jurisdictions must understand the hazards involved and put in place as much protection as deemed necessary. Your company should also be perceived as being proactive in terms of investigation, enforcement and prosecution, as this will deter any potential infringers.

Due diligence into third-party suppliers, manufacturers and distribution agents in any foreign jurisdiction, not just the PRC, must be carried out to help prevent long-term problems relating to the infringements against your intellectual property. Our advice for companies entering into these contractual agreements is to strongly consider the following points:

∎ Establish whether your brands can be registered in the PRC before releasing information about your product or marketing your product.

- Register your brands in neighbouring jurisdictions such as Hong Kong, Taiwan, Indonesia and Macau; this will prevent others registering your marks to use on products that consumers may confuse with yours.

- Select a reputable and experienced international law firm that specifically has a Chinese office or partner with first-hand experience of intellectual property-related issues.
- If necessary, develop and register a Chinese-language version of your product.
- Ensure that your registered rights are up to date, paid and renewed on a regular basis.
- Creating and retaining an organized paper trail is essential. Sign and date all notes relating to IP meetings, notes and decisions.
- Consider joining relevant trade associations such as the Quality Brands Protection Committee, IFPI and the Anti-Counterfeiting Group for support and advice.
- Make sure all confidentiality agreements are in place.
- Consider visiting trade shows to check that your vendors are not exhibiting counterfeit or surplus products.
- Regularly perform on-site supplier evaluations and factory/product audits.
- Conduct regular screening of your suppliers.
- Each potential supplier should be required to produce a detailed plan of disruption awareness.
- Identify potential outcomes and test your contingency plans.
- Train and educate personnel to improve the security culture and informed decision-making capabilities.

Recent enforcement legislation

The risk of IP infringement in the PRC began to be addressed as the Republic joined the World Trade Organization in December 2001 and agreed to implement the Trade Related Aspects of Intellectual Property (TRIPs) Agreement, which sets down minimum standards for copyright and related rights.

In addition, the Ministry of Public Security in the PRC commenced a new enforcement campaign in 2004, which allowed the national police to accept, investigate and report on the results of IP enforcement work. As a consequence of this campaign, the number of criminal arrests and prosecutions for IP-related offences has multiplied, but is still far from that which is necessary to bring counterfeiting and piracy under control.

Conclusions

Although IP legislation and enforcement agencies are improving slightly, we strongly recommend that companies identify and protect their IP assets before entering into third-party agreements, as this will minimize the risk of infringement. Once these assets have been identified, due diligence, factory audits and extensive background checks are an absolute necessity.

Find a trusted Chinese partner, as risks related to IP infringement are greatly reduced. However, this can only be achieved through extensive due diligence into prospective supply chain partners, suppliers, distributors and customers.

The measures described above will assist your company to develop the comfort of security. However, there will always be those seeking new ways of circumventing the protection techniques. It is recommended that you remain aware and vigilant of the problems and, before embarking on a strategy of marketing or business in this jurisdiction, put into effect as many of these preventative measures as possible.

Expanding by acquisition – managing the unknown and undisclosed risk

Alena Watchorn, HSBC Insurance Brokers

Every year companies spend billions of pounds expanding their assets by acquiring other businesses. In the second quarter of 2006 alone, the value of UK M&A transactions totalled £3.5 billion.

Acquisitions are not for the faint-hearted. They are inherently risky and, for many buyers, minimizing these risks can be fundamental to the enlarged group's future prospects. Stories such as the 2005 acquisition of Unwins (see box, page 266) just prove that buyers cannot be too careful.

Known risks will be disclosed by the seller, leaving the buyer to weigh up whether to proceed or not. However, how can buyers assess and protect themselves against undisclosed and unknown risks? The obvious problem with such risks is that a buyer has no idea of how these could impact on the strength and value of the business.

Assessing the risks

The first crucial step is to make sure that such risks are properly managed. A good starting point is to take an in-depth look at the business to be acquired by conducting a thorough due diligence process.

Companies should try to extract as much information from the sellers and management of the target. They should also employ experienced professional advisers to conduct a thorough due diligence exercise covering legal, financial and tax matters. The legal due diligence should cover all relevant areas, including corporate standing, contract risk, intellectual property rights, employment, pensions, environment, real estate, IT and data protection, insurance, litigation and regulatory compliance. The review should obviously focus on these areas that are critical to the business operations, eg intellectual property rights in a software business.

This process should highlight contingent exposures, and where further information or investigation is required in order to pin down as far as possible those risks. In today's international business environment, advisers from other relevant jurisdictions should also be retained at an early stage to assist the due diligence exercise.

Some of the areas of investigation may be less obvious than others. Legacy issues such as unresolved disputes or litigation may pose significant difficulties in the future, even if currently dormant. Relationships with key customers or suppliers should also be explored to establish their robustness.

Environmental issues have never been so high on the agenda and liability in this area can be extremely significant. Some businesses are obviously more exposed to such liability than others, but buyers should never be complacent. What may appear to be a low environmental risk, such as a hotel business, could turn out to be a major problem if it is discovered that the hotel was built on an old gasworks or petrol station site.

Although all businesses face some generic risks, unknown risks can have an obvious connection with the company's business or sector, but can also be a complete surprise, for example a buyer of a potato farm being sued for infringement of intellectual property rights in connection with the design of a potato-grading machine that it had adapted and was selling as its own product. In the sale process, a buyer may have overlooked this area as being insignificant or unrelated, but the subsequent litigation could be a nasty surprise.

In public company transactions, which account for the vast majority of the big deals that hit the headlines, much of the information about the company should be in the public domain. However, a larger volume of deals involves the sale of private companies. Sellers of private companies are not under such obligations of disclosure and they may not be too keen to provide full information, particularly where the buyer is a trade buyer and competitor or where some disclosures may impact on the price. The exposure under warranties given to the buyer does focus the minds of the sellers on the disclosure process and aids the buyer in getting full information on the business and its value.

The warranties and disclosure process against them thus become the tools to allocate the unknown and undisclosed risk.

Warranty protection – risk allocation and transfer

Most agreements for the sale and purchase of private companies will have warranties from the sellers (or management), which can give a buyer protection in the event that matters undisclosed or unknown at the time of the sale arise in the future. Faced with these exposures, sellers are usually strongly motivated to disclose as much information as possible in order to limit their liability to the maximum extent. However, sellers can only disclose what is in the scope of their actual knowledge, and information can be lost or simply forgotten or the wrong people can be asked the wrong questions. In addition, there is always the risk of fraud or a seller deliberately withholding information.

The negotiation of warranties is all about allocating the risk between seller and buyer. In general, the known disclosed risks are borne by the buyer and catered for in the price set for the target. If buyers are unwilling to accept such risk, they may seek a specific indemnity from the seller. The unknown and undisclosed risks are generally borne by the seller, unless the buyer has not managed to negotiate sufficient warranty protection. This is where the legal minutiae of the wording of warranties become vital in allocating the risk. Therefore a poorly or hastily drafted warranty can expose gaps in a buyer's protection.

All too often it is the last-minute, late-night warranties or those that are just 'glossed over' as they are not seen as relevant to the business that result in a claim.

The effects of an unknown risk 'coming home to roost' are amply illustrated by the following examples.

AWG vs Morrisons

In September 2000, AWG bought Morrisons for £263.3 million from its shareholders including two former executives of Morrisons. In February 2003, AWG launched a £130 million lawsuit against two former directors alleging that the March 2000 accounts were inaccurate. Such claims were vigorously denied by the former executives. Whilst such litigation is a costly affair, according to the media AWG felt that 'they had a duty to their shareholders to seek to recover losses which they had sustained'.

Unwins

In 2005, Unwins was acquired by DM Private Equity for a reported £32 million; however, nine months later the business collapsed. The press reported that the buyers claimed to have discovered a £13.2 million black hole in the business's finances and its advisers had identified 'gross accounting mistreatments and errors' dating from 1999 to 2005. A short statement from the joint administrators at KPMG, appointed by HBOS, the main secured creditor of Unwins, announced that 350 branches had to be put out of business with the loss of over 1,400 jobs.

A buyer is therefore well advised to conduct a thorough and probing due diligence process and negotiate the warranties. But regardless, some undisclosed and unknown risks may remain (although hopefully minimized). If buyers or sellers want to transfer the residual unknown risks, insurance is one option.

Risk transfer

Seller and buyer may allocate the risks between them, or they may agree to leave a pot of money in escrow to cater for known or unknown risks. Whilst this offers the buyer some security, the seller is unable to realize the full proceeds and is exposed to risk on the cash left in escrow and thus does not transfer the risk. Insurance is an alternative that is rarely considered and, although heavily dependent on the specific circumstances of each deal, can be very effective at unblocking a deadlocked deal.

Although a buyer may feel it is getting adequate protection, will the seller have enough assets to meet a warranty claim a year or more after completion? Or does the buyer really want to claim against its own management for an unknown issue? The seller on the other hand may be completely comfortable with assuming the unknown and undisclosed risk: perhaps it has been involved in the business for a lengthy period, or operates from one site, or the sale may represent less than 10 per cent of its assets and therefore the risk is not material to its ongoing business.

In today's business environment, mergers and acquisitions often involve institutional investors who are unwilling to assume residual risk or leave money on the table and want to protect their funds from the rogue deal. In addition, directors are ever more conscious of the need to demonstrate to shareholders that they are protecting their interests, so giving warranties and having adequate protection are considered vital.

Therefore, insurance is increasingly being considered in transactions as a tool to transfer the unknown and undisclosed risks as part of the parties' risk management strategy in the acquisition process. For a buyer, warranty insurance can top up or enhance the level of protection available to the buyer either by increasing the level of cover or by adding the security of having an 'A'-graded insurer to recover from in the event of a claim, rather than private individuals or a financially insecure seller. However, such policies are not a panacea and will still rely on the underlying disclosure and due diligence process. Insurers are acutely aware that, if such processes are not conducted properly, or where the seller is clearly withholding information from the buyer, then the risk of a claim is significantly increased.

Occasionally, having an insurance policy in place may be a condition imposed by those financing the deal. Even with high-value warranties in place, banks and other financial institutions may refuse to sign on the dotted line unless all fronts are covered, and insurance is just one of the tools available. This may be due to the seller's lack of financial security behind the warranties or due to the buyer's need to have security and control over such protection.

For example, on commercial property transactions involving the development of brownfield sites, financial investors are often insisting on environmental insurance in addition to environmental warranties and indemnities as they begin to appreciate this can be utilized not only to protect their investment but to enhance the value and opportunities for selling on the site.

Competitive advantage

In a time when bidding processes are extremely competitive, buyers may be tempted to compromise their normal protection against unknown and undisclosed risks.

Competitive tenders, particularly in Europe, tend to involve multiple bidders including both trade buyers and private equity firms. Sellers' advisers control the sale process, and access to information can be restricted at the initial stages until the bidder becomes preferred or successful. In assessing the bids from buyers, whilst price is clearly a key driver for any seller, any bidders that seek a large escrow fund for protection or full warranties up to the deal value can find themselves at a disadvantage. The bidders are therefore caught in a difficult situation in formulating their bid, weighing up the need for protection against the desire to be the preferred bidder. Buyers that show a little edge and lateral thinking can put themselves ahead of the game.

In any auction process, careful consideration by bidders and their advisers should be given to the sensitivities of the sellers in formulating the structure of the bid. If the seller is a holding company that is disposing of a non-core business that is marginal to the underlying operations, then price is likely to be a prime focus and the giving of warranties to the buyer may not be an issue. However, if the target is owned by private equity houses or is owned by a disparate group of shareholders with little or no involvement in the running of the business, the giving of warranties to protect the buyer from unknown and undisclosed issues is likely to become a sensitive issue.

While buyers could just rely on their due diligence exercise rather than seeking warranties from the sellers, this gives little or no protection for the residual unknown and undisclosed issue. An alternative approach is to seek warranties from those sellers and/or management, but cap the liability at a low amount (eg 2 per cent of deal value) and then seek buyers' warranty insurance to top up the level of protection. For the seller that is sensitive to leaving funds in escrow or assuming the residual risk through warranties, this can be seen as an attractive proposition compared to the alternative bids. For the buyer, rather than compromising its protection for the unknown and undisclosed risk it can make its bid more attractive provided that the cost of insurance is commercially viable.

For the known risks identified during due diligence, the bidder and seller will still need to consider how to manage these risks in the normal course of negotiations. Typically, indemnities and escrows are the main ways in which such risks are allocated, but more specific insurance products can also be considered, eg specific environmental insurance attaching to a site, or specific indemnity insurance. The latter can be particularly useful in low-risk, high-impact situations where the seller refuses to accept that the risk is significant, owing to remoteness, but the buyer is concerned of the financial impact in the unlikely event it occurs.

Buying a company will never be risk-free. Any buyer also has to consider the post-deal risks and assess the cultural and process integration of the company and its business prospects and forecasts. However, by carrying out an effective due diligence process, assessing all risks (known and unknown), considering other protection options such as insurance and finally taking the plunge, the residual risks are likely to be much more manageable should the 'perfect fit' acquisition turn out to be a little more problematic than the buyer anticipated.

6

Employment and Human Relations Issues

Management fraud – your boss is involved

Sean Holohan and John Cassey, Protiviti

At work, you've been uneasy for some time. For the last few months, you've been noticing some strange patterns and behaviours: odd transactions with third parties that you've never heard of, for services that are vague and unconnected to your company's business; last-minute deals with little or no paperwork; what's more, nobody in the finance department knows anything about them.

You ask a few questions, but draw a blank every time. Except... one person's name keeps coming up – your line manager. Your worst nightmare has just come true!

So, what do you do? As a conscientious employee, you don't feel it's right to ignore your concerns. But every time you ask someone about the transactions, they tell you: 'You'll have to ask Steve about that' or 'That's Steve's contact' or 'Steve's the only one that knows about that' or 'That's one of Steve's funnies.'

So, why don't you go and ask Steve about his funnies? Well, it would be difficult to describe Steve as a people person. He has a habit of flying off the handle when under pressure and scrutiny, which isn't very often. He's a successful manager, regularly exceeding growth targets and, as a result, he's well liked by senior management.

You have an idea – the employee handbook you were given when you joined the firm, several years ago. It must say something in there about what to do in situations like this. Maybe there's somebody nice in HR who will listen. You find your handbook and search – 'If you have a grievance or concern, you must raise it with your line manager, who will give guidance.' Arghhh!

You turn to someone in HR for help: 'You need to follow the guidance in the employee handbook', they say.

You look again and find that there's a whistle-blowing hotline administered by internal audit, but it isn't clear whether they would treat your call in confidence or whether you could call them anonymously. The telephone number given is an internal line. Who would answer the call? Could they trace the caller? Would they tell Steve?

What follows is a true story, and Steve could easily happen to be the CEO referred to below.

An insurance company, a subsidiary undertaking of a larger company, administered the receipt of premiums and payments of claims for insurance business on behalf of a number of insurers and Lloyd's syndicates. It arrived at a position where its accounting system was so deficient that it led to a significant number of outstanding unallocated premium receipts of around £1.5 million. These premiums could not immediately be reconciled and paid to the correct insurer, and nothing was done to rectify the situation. Neither the existence nor the true origin of these funds was disclosed to the insurers involved, which meant they were unable to make a claim against them.

It was arbitrarily decided by the chief executive officer of the insurance company to retain the funds in an escrow account, where they were allowed to sit and gain interest over a three-year period, in the hope that no claim would be made against them.

Subsequently the CEO, instead of resolving the situation equitably by paying the premiums to insurers in proportion to the percentage of risk taken by them, decided to transfer the funds from the escrow account into the company profit and loss account without reference to his own board. He instructed a junior member of his accounts team to transfer the funds and post them as income from normal administration fees. His rationale for this was to increase the profitability of the company at the year end, thereby triggering larger bonus payments to certain members of the board including himself.

However, one of the board members learned that this had been done and raised his concerns with the CEO, who advised him to say nothing. Not satisfied with this response, the board member then brought it to attention through the company whistle-blowing scheme, which was administered on a somewhat informal basis by an internal audit committee headed by general counsel of the parent company. The whistle-blower quite rightly believed this was a misappropriation of funds that effectively belonged to insurers.

General counsel thought he could resolve the problem by informing the CEO of his wrongdoing, and instructed him to reverse the transfer and to make proper efforts to reconcile the funds with the relevant insurers. The particular board member who had made the complaint was named and exposed by general counsel in conversations with the CEO. This caused irresolvable friction between him, the CEO and other board members who were looking forward to an increased bonus. The board member's position within the company became untenable and he resigned without taking the matter further.

This occurred in a subsidiary undertaking of a very large international company and it highlights problems that can be encountered when senior management and their legal advisers are involved in a cover-up, and the manipulation and abuse of their own whistle-blowing policy.

The CEO probably tried to rationalize his position by claiming that there was no one individual entity that could be identified as a claimant to the funds, rather than acknowledge that the company accounting system was deficient. By applying the objective test of what a reasonable person would have done in the circumstances, the CEO's deceptive manner in misrepresenting the true state of the accounts could have left him exposed to criminal and civil action. By hiding and disguising the funds as he did, he could also have been in contravention of money laundering regulations.

General counsel, believing that he had the best interests of the company in mind, failed to realize the seriousness of the allegation and breached a confidential disclosure given in good faith by a trusted employee. He could also have been guilty of 'tipping off' the CEO (in this case) contrary to money laundering legislation.

The board member who raised this issue in the first place was badly let down by the highest management. Had the whistle-blower taken matters further and reported it externally to the Financial Services Authority and police, financial penalties or possibly worse might have followed; the integrity and reputation of the company and its parent would have suffered.

In a business world now governed by compliance and accountability, it is no longer acceptable for management to behave in this manner. It exposes their company to risk of prosecution and a loss of shareholder confidence.

It is not uncommon for some unscrupulous companies to deliberately exploit staff whom they know to be financially vulnerable or whose employment status could be placed in jeopardy. Examples of this are foreign workers on temporary work permits dependent upon their employer's sponsorship, those with a family and sole income in areas of high unemployment or those whose background may make them difficult to employ elsewhere, such as those with a history of bankruptcy or a previous, undisclosed criminal conviction.

Financial investigators in Protiviti's integrity risk team have investigated many cases in which vulnerable employees were coerced by a senior manager, often against their better judgement, to submit false information or figures in order to suppress losses, cover up inadequate procedures or misrepresent the efficiency of an operation to keep to pre-agreed key performance indicators to avoid penalty charges, often with disastrous results. In one particular case a well-established company deliberately recruited vulnerable staff to facilitate a serious fraud, knowing that they were unlikely to complain or refuse orders. If they did, they were told in no uncertain terms that their continued employment would be 'reviewed'.

This is why an effective whistle-blowing policy must be available to all staff from the most senior to the most junior; information received must be sensibly evaluated and acted upon in order to avoid, at the very least, damage to staff morale and the loss of decent and honest employees.

So what is considered best practice for reporting suspicions of fraud and how is this regulated? An effective whistle-blowing policy is a vital tool for uncovering management fraud. In the United Kingdom, the Public Interest Disclosure Act 1998 protects employees from detrimental treatment or victimization from their employer if, in the public interest and acting in good faith, they expose what they genuinely believe to be wrongdoing or malpractice at work.

To be protected, an employee needs to reasonably believe that malpractice in the workplace is happening, is about to happen or has happened. The type of malpractice covered by the law includes criminal offences, failure to comply with legal obligations, threats to health and safety, damage to the environment and a deliberate act to cover up any of these.

A whistle-blowing hotline should be made known to all employees and vendors, and have a dedicated number available 24 hours a day, 365 days of the year, together with an e-mail address, fax and postal address. Ideally it should be operated by an independent third party with specially trained interviewers who have multilingual skills, if necessary.

There should also be a system to ensure that distribution of information from the hotline is made to the appropriate individuals within the company depending on the nature of the allegation. Allegations involving senior management should be directed to the head of the audit committee without referral to management or other personnel.

Recent surveys undertaken by some of the large accounting firms, the Chartered Institute of Management Accountants and various government bodies all come to similar conclusions. Broadly speaking, the following conclusions were reached:

■ Almost two-thirds of organizations participating in the various surveys had been defrauded in the previous 12 months. Almost 1 in 10 suffered more than 50 frauds.
■ Eighty per cent of the worst frauds were committed by employees, nearly one-third of them by management.
■ The largest frauds with the most catastrophic results were committed by senior management or those with a high level of fiduciary responsibility.
■ Only 30 per cent of assets lost or stolen as a result of fraud had been recovered.

A survey of convicted workplace fraudsters, *Learning from Fraudsters*, published by Protiviti in 2006, confirms some of these findings, namely that the fraudsters occupied positions of trust and senior management, that they rarely felt threatened by anti-fraud measures such as audit and that none were caught as a result of their organizations' whistle-blowing policies.

The survey focused on identifying methods of making fraud more difficult for fraudsters to perpetrate, one of which was to increase the chances of detection. Policies such as an effective whistle-blowing process, together with strong ethical attitudes and fraud awareness, act to increase the chances that fraudsters will get caught by colleagues who are the eyes and ears of the business.

So before your organization finds itself on the receiving end of some adverse publicity or litigation as a result of a whistle-blower turning to the press or other external parties as a cry for help, ask yourself, would you be confident that you and your colleagues could safely and easily report any concerns to the appropriate personnel? If not, then now is the time for action. If yes, well, you're better prepared than most.

Ten tips for reporting fraud:

1. Be prepared to support your allegations with evidence that could include documents, observations, corroboration from other witnesses and diary notes of events. Keep a confidential written record, with dates and times, of anything suspicious.
2. Keep copies of any documentation that you submit in support of your allegations. If relying on original documents, keep them in a secure place and ensure that they are not damaged, altered or compromised in any way as this might affect their admissibility as evidence.
3. Concerns should be reported to the relevant line manager, orally or in writing. Specify if the matter is to be treated in confidence.
4. If unable to raise the matter with the direct line manager, for whatever reason, raise the matter with the head of department or head of human resources.
5. If unable to adhere to the above procedures, or the matter is so serious that the matter cannot be reported to the above persons, report it to the head of finance, the head of the audit committee or even the CEO.
6. If uncomfortable with any of the above or anonymity is preferred, report concerns using the approved whistle-blowing procedure. This will involve following the public interest disclosure policy, which will set out the designated persons approved to receive public interest disclosure reports and the processes that will subsequently follow.
7. Whistle-blowers should be prepared to substantiate the allegations raised since malicious and unfounded allegations should not be tolerated and could result in disciplinary or legal action.
8. When making a disclosure anonymously, possibly by letter, it is essential that as much detail as possible is given relating to suspicions. This will assist investigators to understand the nature of the problem and those thought to be involved. Be specific and include documentary evidence if possible.
9. The independent charity Public Concern at Work has lawyers who can give free confidential advice at any stage on how to raise concerns about serious malpractice at work. In the absence of a whistle-blowing facility, it would be worth consulting this charity for guidance.
10. The police are unlikely to take action without sufficient evidence, a formal complaint and a statement of loss. They will not be able to act on suspicion of wrongdoing without first substantiating the information through other sources. Public Concern at Work can advise on this option.

Disability risk assessment of your premises

Caroline Summerfield, KSB Law LLP

Executive summary

The outlawing of discrimination against disabled people is at the heart of the disability discrimination legislation. The duties were imposed by the Disability Discrimination Act 1995 (as amended by the Disability Discrimination Act 2005) (DDA) and its subordinate regulations.

What the DDA covers

Part 1   Defines disability
Part 2   Employment
Part 3   Provision of goods, facilities and services
           Disposal or management of premises or land
           Private clubs
Part 4   Education
Part 5   Transport

The duties imposed by the DDA on businesses were imposed in three stages:

- *Since 2 December 1996 (1996 Duty)* ('less favourable treatment unlawful'):
  - unlawful for service providers to treat disabled people less favourably for a reason related to their disability;
  - unlawful for landlords and other persons selling, letting or managing premises to treat disabled people less favourably for a reason related to their disability.
- *Since 1 October 1999 (1999 Duty)* ('reasonable adjustment to the manner in which service is provided'):
  - service providers must change a practice, policy or procedure that makes it impossible or unreasonably difficult for a disabled person to make use of their service;
  - auxiliary aids or services should be provided if these would enable or make it easier for a disabled person to use the service;
  - service providers must provide a reasonable alternative method of making their services available to disabled people where a physical feature makes it impossible or unreasonably difficult to make use of the service.
- *Since 1 October 2004 (2004 Duty)* ('reasonable physical adjustments to your premises'): service providers are obliged, where a physical feature makes it impossible or unreasonably difficult for a disabled person to make use of a service, to take such steps as are reasonable in all the circumstances to adopt one of the following courses of action:
  - remove the feature;
  - alter it so that it no longer has that effect;
  - provide a reasonable means of avoiding the feature;
  - provide a reasonable alternative method of making the service available.

No equivalent duty is imposed to make reasonable adjustments in relation to premises on landlords, or those selling, letting or managing premises. Their duty as from 2 December 1996 has been not to treat disabled people less favourably for a reason related to their disability.

The risk for businesses is that it is now unlawful to discriminate against staff or customers on the grounds of their disability. In this chapter we will examine the risks for businesses where their premises fail to comply with the standards now expected from service providers when dealing with disabled persons. These duties are set out in Part 3 of the DDA.

A risk assessment in the form of a disability access audit of your premises is the essential first step for compliance with your obligations under Part 3 of the DDA. Your first port of call should be the Disability Rights Commission (DRC), an independent body set up by the government to help secure civil rights for disabled persons, and established under the DDA and responsible for issuing the *Code of Practice – Rights of Access, Goods, Facilities, Services and Premises* on 27 May 2002. Although this does not have mandatory authority, it contains detailed guidance and is likely to have strong persuasive authority for the courts when interpreting your obligations under Part 3 of the DDA. The DRC came into operation in April 2000. In addition to its statutory duties and advisory and educational roles, the DRC has enforcement powers, which include:

- Power to conduct formal investigations.
- Power to serve non-discrimination notices. These operate like stop notices and will require further occurrence to cease. The DRC may request an action plan from the service provider, but if this is inadequate the DRC may apply to the county court for an order. As an alternative to taking enforcement action the DRC may enter into an agreement with the service provider.
- Power to act in relation to persistent discrimination.
- Power to provide assistance.
- Power to issue codes of practice.
- Power to act as a conciliator in the case of disputes.

What is a service provider?

A service provider is anyone who provides goods or services to the public or to a section of the public, whether in the private or in the voluntary services. It does not matter if the services are provided free of charge. Since December 2005, Part 3 of the DDA has applied to private clubs where the club:

- has 25 or more members;
- has a constitution that regulates the admission of members and admissions are carried out in such a way that the members do not constitute a section of the public;
- is not a trade organization, eg a trade union.

Health and fitness clubs, despite their use of the term 'club', are not private clubs for the purpose of the DDA, but are treated as general service providers and thus subject to the pre-existing duties imposed in 1996, 1999 and 2004, referred to above.

What is a physical feature?

Under the Disability Discrimination (Services and Premises) Regulations 1999 anything and everything to do with a property, whether fixed or not, temporary or permanent, is a physical feature. The term 'building' is also widely defined, as it means an erection or structure of any kind, so this will include temporary stands. From a practical point of view therefore, a physical feature will also include steps, stairways, kerbs, exterior surfaces, parking areas, building entrances and exits (including emergency escape routes), internal and external doors, gates, toilets and washing facilities.

What is impossible or unreasonably difficult for a disabled person?

No definition is given in the DDA of what is meant by the phrase 'impossible or unreasonably difficult'. However, when considering if services are impossible or unreasonably difficult for disabled people to use, service providers should take into account whether the time, inconvenience, effort, discomfort or loss of dignity entailed in using the service would be considered unreasonable by an able-bodied person who had to endure similar difficulties.

What is it reasonable in all the circumstances for the service provider to do?

Guidance, albeit of a non-statutory nature, is given in the Disability Rights Commission Code of Practice (*Rights of Access, Goods, Facilities, Services and Premises*, 27 May 2002), referred to above. Although, as has been noted, this does not have statutory authority, it is likely to have persuasive authority for the courts when interpreting Part 3 of the DDA. The 2002 guide provides that what is a reasonable step for a particular service provider to take will depend upon all the circumstances of the case. It will vary according to:

■ the type of the services being provided;
■ the nature of the service provider and its size and resources; and
■ the effect of the disability on the individual disabled person.

If therefore there are no steps that the service provider, having considered the issue thoroughly, could reasonably be expected to take in order to make its services more accessible to a disabled person, the service provider is unlikely to be in breach of the law if it makes no changes to its premises. However, such a situation is likely to be rare. It is more likely that the service provider will need to make a reasonable adjustment to the manner in which it provides the service.

Can a service provider justify less favourable treatment or failure to make reasonable adjustments?

Under the DDA, in certain circumstances this is permissible on the following grounds:

■ health and safety;
■ the disabled person lacks the capacity to understand a particular transaction that a service provider offers;
■ it would prevent the service provider providing the service to the general public;
■ a lower standard of service enables the service provider to provide the service;
■ the disabled person is charged a higher price for the service because the service provider needs to tailor the service individually to the disabled person's requirements;
■ the service provider cannot provide the service without fundamentally altering the nature of the service provided.

Dealing with access to your premises

Since 1985, building regulations in England and Wales have required reasonable provision to be made for disabled people to gain access to non-domestic buildings. Part M of the Building Regulations, often referred to as Approved Document M, has been revised over the years and sets out certain minimum standards for disabled access to buildings. The latest version of Approved Document M, which came into force on 1 May 2004, applies to:

■ the access to and use of new buildings;
■ the access to extensions to buildings other than dwellings;
■ the access to existing buildings other than dwellings undergoing a material alteration or change of use;
■ the sanitary conveniences in extensions to buildings other than dwellings;
■ the sanitary conveniences in dwellings.

An issue therefore facing many service providers is what to do about past alterations to their premises that may not now comply with the latest version of Part M of the Building Regulations. A 10-year exemption was introduced by the Disability Discrimination (Providers of Services) Adjustment of Premises Regulations 2001, but this only applies to work undertaken after 1 October 1994 and then only to the extent that such work complied with matters covered by the 1992 and 1999 editions of Approved Document M. The 10-year exemption runs from the 'due date' and, although the 2001 Regulations do not stipulate how the 'due date' is to be established, it is likely that in the majority of cases this will be the date upon which the service provider was able to make use of the physical feature introduced by the alteration. Where industry standard forms of construction contracts are used, this will be the practical completion date. You should therefore work on the basis that the 10-year exemption period commenced from the date upon which the installation of the feature was completed or, where the physical feature is installed as part of a larger project, from the date upon which the works to that part of the project were completed.

An access statement should be provided prior to start of the proposed works and accompany the plans deposited with the building control team of the local authority. This should assist the building control officer when determining if the works proposed will make 'reasonable provision' for access to the building and the services provided within it for disabled persons.

Are your premises exempt from Part 3 of the DDA?

Education establishments and the means of transport are excluded, but in the case of transport not the infrastructure, eg a bus station. However, do bear in mind that there are other statutes that may apply, for instance in the case of access to public buildings, places of accommodation and entertainment, universities and schools, where practical and reasonable access must be provided.

In addition, manufacturers and designers of goods are also excluded because they are not providing services directly to the public. However, if they do provide services directly to the public then they will have duties under the DDA, eg a manufacturer of self-assembly furniture that sells directly by mail order. The issue here would be the accessibility of the design of the self-assembly furniture for assembly by a disabled person, not accessibility of the manufacturer's premises.

What happens if the duty to make reasonable adjustments is not complied with?

A service provider must comply with the duty to make reasonable adjustments in order to avoid committing an act of unlawful discrimination. A disabled person is able to make a claim against the service provider if the service provider:

■ fails to do what is required;
■ makes it impossible or unreasonably difficult for that person to access any services provided by the service provider to the public; and
■ cannot show that such a failure is justified in relation to the disabled person.

Claims can be brought by disabled persons both in conjunction with and independently of the DRC. The DRC can grant assistance to an individual who wishes to bring proceedings under the DDA. Such assistance is discretionary, and the DRC will consider if the case raises matters of principle, and whether or not it is reasonable to expect the applicant to proceed unaided.

The use of access audits

In order to demonstrate whether or not you might need to make physical alterations to your premises and/or the manner in which you deliver your services to accommodate the needs of your disabled customers the first step is to carry out an 'access audit' of your premises, which should deal with the following:

■ identifying existing physical and communication barriers to access;
■ examining the access needs of users;
■ assessing the impact of these on features of historic, architectural or archaeological interest or their setting;
■ devising solutions that reconcile access and conservation needs.

Special considerations apply when dealing with listed buildings. The DDA does not make unlawful any act done in pursuance of another statutory obligation. The obligation, therefore, not to discriminate against disabled persons is subordinate to other enactments, and to the conditions or requirements imposed by such enactments, which might conflict with the DDA. Therefore, there is no obligation to make alterations to premises where planning or similar permissions for the works cannot be obtained or, even if planning consent to the alterations can be obtained, if the adjustments required are unreasonable – perhaps because they involve excessive expense or radical alterations to historic buildings.

The nature of the use of the building and its type, function, scale and ownership will be critical factors in formulating an access audit, and care must be taken to ensure that, in each case, the proposed solution meets the long-term needs of both property and user. Large historic buildings that are in daily use, such as town halls, libraries and museums, may have more extensive access requirements than smaller country houses that are open to the public on an irregular, discretionary basis. Churches and cathedrals will need to meet the needs of regular worshippers as well as secular visitors. Archaeological monuments, such as hill forts, ruined abbeys and castles, will require especially sensitive treatment and in some cases physical access may need to be restricted on safety or structural grounds. Where physical access is restricted, supplementary interpretive material can help to create an informed and enjoyable visitor experience for disabled persons.

In drawing up the access audit it will be necessary to evaluate suitable access devices to ease movement at level changes. This can include:

■ passive devices, eg ramps and handrails;
■ mechanical devices, eg passenger, platform and stair lifts;
■ temporary and managed solutions.

All permanent devices will impact to some degree upon architectural details such as plinths, column bases, staircases, ironwork and door openings. It is important that these features should not be disturbed, obscured or altered if they contribute significantly to the property's special character or design.

Where a permanent intervention is not practical or because of conservation requirements, cost or other constraints, a managed temporary solution using staff to erect and remove a portable ramp can be used to avoid the danger of visual clutter. This may be preferable in smaller properties that are too sensitive to sustain alterations.

Checklist of issues

■ Familiarize yourself with the Disability Discrimination Act 1995 and 2005.
■ Familiarize yourself with the Disability Discrimination Code of Practice 2002.
■ Familiarize yourself with Part M of the Building Regulations (as revised).
■ Consult an access auditor, chartered surveyor or solicitor.
■ Consider whether compliance may be effected by alterations to business practice rather than by physical alterations to the premises, as this may be the more cost-effective solution.

Occupational pension schemes – risk versus reward

Emma Watkins, ACE European Group

Introduction

Over the years, UK employers have seen the gradual transformation of pensions from a 'best endeavours' gratuity into a binding contractual promise. This has never been more pertinently demonstrated than by the recent court determination preventing KPMG cutting payments to its scheme members rather than making good a significant shortfall, even though the trust deed and rules appeared to allow it to take this course of action.

Add to this the ream of pensions law that has been introduced in recent years and it is safe to conclude that the UK pensions market (particularly in respect of defined benefit (DB) schemes) is the most legislated pensions environment in Europe.

The recently published Department for Work and Pensions White Paper 'Security in retirement: towards a new pension scheme' congratulates the Pensions Act 2004 on introducing 'improved security and confidence for occupational pension scheme members'. Indeed, much of the Pensions Act and the powers given to the Pensions

Regulator help protect members' benefits and promote good administration of work-based pension schemes, but at what cost to the employer? It goes on to state that the Finance Act 2004 'swept away the complexity of many separate tax regimes, replacing them with a single, flexible regime based on the simple concept of a lifetime allowance'. Whilst strictly speaking this is true, those involved in 'tax simplification' may agree that this is one of the greatest misnomers yet invented. The combined effect of this new legislation is to make it more expensive to run occupational pension schemes, whilst simultaneously disincentivizing those key to managing them: the employers and trustees.

This has been further complicated by a number of economic factors. The value of pension funds has fallen in line with stock markets, and income has decreased owing to changes in tax laws, coupled with a decline in interest rates and dividend yields. At the same time, liabilities have been creeping upwards, with falling annuity rates and increases in life expectancy. Demographic changes in the workforce have also had an impact, with increases in the number of women (with their longer life expectancy) in pension schemes.

The resultant deficits and move towards greater transparency have put trustee actions firmly into the limelight and pensions on to the boardroom agenda. Consequently many companies are now looking to limit the potential risk associated with their occupational pension schemes.

The migration from defined benefit to defined contribution

Closing DB schemes is not a new concept. Debenhams, Rentokil and Harrods are many in a long list of schemes to have closed their doors to new employees and, in some cases, future accrual. According to research by Watson Wyatt, four out of five FTSE 100 companies now provide a defined contributions (DC) scheme for at least some of their employees. However, while DC pensions work for employers, they themselves have mixed views on whether DC meets the needs of employees. A workshop held by Watson Wyatt found that around 78 per cent of polled senior HR and benefits managers believed that, as a basic design concept, DC can meet the pension scheme needs of employers either extremely or fairly well. However, only 42 per cent thought that DC can meet the needs of an individual employee at least fairly well, with 35 per cent saying that employees' needs could only be met 'with difficulty'. Thus, more paternalistic employers may not be rushing to consider the migration to a DC scheme and instead will see the recruitment and retention benefits of a well-communicated DB scheme.

Alternatives exist and include managing the costs of DB schemes through benefit changes (eg reducing accrual rates, increasing normal retirement ages) or introducing or increasing member contributions. Other possibilities include more innovative risk-sharing and hybrid schemes, such as career average revalued earning schemes and cash balance plans.

Nonetheless, evidence dictates that the cultural shift from DB to DC is inevitable. That said, the process of achieving this, particularly for a company with a history of DB, remains difficult. There are a number of potential pitfalls that could give rise to a claim against the trustee or an employer, which need to be considered in order to be avoided. These include:

- *Scheme amendments.* Closing a scheme to future accrual usually requires a formal amendment to the scheme's documentation. As a result both the employer and the trustees need to ensure that they have the power to implement the proposed changes. The trustees also need to take particular care when exercising the power of amendment as they need to ensure that they balance the concerns of the employer with members' interests. Consequently trustees should fully explore the possibility of any viable alternatives first.
- *Consultation.* The consultation regulations brought in by the Pensions Act 2004 impose a requirement that no listed changes (which include closing a scheme to new members or future accrual) should be made until the legislative requirements have been complied with. Employers and trustees need to ensure compliance to avoid fines being imposed, but should also view this process as a way of ensuring that proposed changes are properly communicated and discussed to reduce the possibility of challenges being brought by disgruntled members at a later date.
- *Age discrimination.* Whilst there are no clear answers at this stage to the impact of the age regulations on closing DB schemes to new members or future accrual, employers and trustees should be aware of the potential impact. Ideally, legal advice should be sought before progressing down a path that may later be determined to be discriminatory.
- *Contracts of employment.* Changing pension scheme entitlement may have employment law consequences depending on how the contracts are worded. Employers have a couple of options to achieve their desired result, but trustees may have difficulty in agreeing to freeze future accrual if they become aware of employees challenging any change to their terms of employment.
- *DC investment return.* Once the transition has been completed, an area of potential risk is that of claims being made by members whose retirement income is considerably less owing to poor investment performance. Whilst this is a largely untested area, it would be prudent for employers and trustees to ensure that members are fully aware of the risks of DC arrangements and, in particular, those related to investment, including the need to get independent financial advice.

Trust versus contract arrangements

If an employer decides that it wishes to set up a DC scheme, it needs to consider whether this should be a trust-based or a contract-based arrangement.

Smaller employers will view the cost efficiencies potentially offered by contract-based arrangements more favourably. In such an arrangement, the employer does not meet the administration costs, and the requirements to govern and regulate the scheme fall to the insurance provider. Thus, if the worst was to occur members could look for redress through a claim under contract against the pension provider.

Larger, more paternalistic employers may wish to provide reassurance to their employees and, therefore, are more likely to set up a trust-based arrangement, with a trustee board in place to act in the members' best interests. In addition, trust-based schemes allow employers and trustees to monitor the standard of administration and investment performance, and the trustees may play a part in communicating to members when it is appropriate to review their contributions or to consider their investment choice. There are also certain tax advantages to trust-based schemes due to the trustees' discretionary powers, eg death-in-service benefits will not attract inheritance tax in a discretionary trust.

Finally, trust-based schemes may be the most obvious choice when replacing a DB scheme, as a trustee board will already be in place and its presence may provide a level of continuity to members.

The trustee professional

Becoming a trustee can no longer be viewed as an interesting pastime. Trustees look after the pension savings of millions of people, choose to back or sack some of the most talked-about fund managers and can exert a vast amount of influence in company mergers and acquisitions. They are fast becoming some of the most important people within the business world. However, being a trustee can often be a thankless task in an increasingly complex industry.

The role of trustee has expanded significantly over the years, with the pressure increasing further by the trustee knowledge and understanding requirements introduced by the Pensions Act 2004. The code of practice published by the Pensions Regulator sets out the scope of knowledge required and gave existing trustees until 6 October 2006 to comply with the regulations. Whilst the guidance document is not a legally enforceable document, regulatory bodies and the courts will take compliance with the document into account when considering whether the requirements have been met in, for example, a maladministration claim. Thus, trustees need to consider how they meet these requirements and document their conformity (eg training logs).

Conflicts of interest have always been an area of risk for pension trustees. However, a combination of scheme deficits and changes in scheme funding legislation, which have increased the number of areas where trustees and the employer need to reach agreement, has brought this issue into much sharper focus. A pension scheme trustee is obliged to act in good faith and in the best interest of members. A company director owes similar loyalties to the employer. Thus, it is not difficult to see that in certain situations the company director who doubles up as a trustee could fulfil his or her duties to the company but at the same time be failing in his or her duties to the scheme members. If a conflict arises, resignation and therefore loss of good skills and knowledge from the trustee board could be too high a price to pay. In order to mitigate the risk this poses, trustee boards need to have decided on alternative strategies that could be adopted in the event of conflict for a trustee.

It comes as no surprise therefore that choosing the right trustee is crucial and with the requirement for one-third member-nominated trustees this has never been more important. Selecting trustees who are reliable, competent and trustworthy is vital. However, it is typically the case that the individual most suited to the position is the one who knows the onerous responsibilities and personal liabilities that attach to the role. Thus, trustee boards and employers need to ensure that they communicate that support is in place and the various protections available to these individuals when embarking on the process of recruitment.

Managing risk in an ongoing scheme

One of the new requirements under the Pensions Act 2004 is that trustees need to develop and implement a system of internal controls that promote good trustee governance. These controls must be sufficient to ensure that the scheme is administered and managed in accordance with the scheme rules and the relevant legislation. The Pensions Regulator has recommended that trustees may wish to follow a risk assessment approach based on the Turnbull Report, including:

- *Identification of clear objectives.* The Pensions Regulator suggests that the trustee's objectives should include safeguarding the assets of the scheme, maintaining suitable funding levels, ensuring that members receive the benefits to which they are entitled and ensuring that the scheme operates within the law and in accordance with the scheme's trust deed and rules.
- *Identification and prioritization of risks against objectives.* A facilitated risk workshop can assist in this, where trustees rank risks in terms of the significance to the scheme and the likelihood of it happening. Risks can then be rated in terms of impact and the full results collated in a risk register.
- *Analysis of high-priority risks and controls.* Risks that have been rated as highest-impact should be analysed further. This involves looking at each in turn and the processes that surround it, including controls that are currently in place.
- *Development and implementation of adequate future controls.* Once the output of the risk assessment has been considered, the trustees are in a position to agree what controls are appropriate going forward. This can then be formalized into a clear action plan, including who is responsible for putting the controls in place.

The experience of corporations in implementing these types of procedures is that this can re-engage individuals who manage this wide range of risks. For this reason, the new internal controls requirement should not be seen as another paper-filling exercise but rather be enthusiastically embraced as it can bring comfort to not only trustees but also the sponsoring employer and members, not to mention the Pensions Regulator.

Trustee protection

Trustees who breach their increasingly complex responsibilities may place their personal assets at risk or, in certain circumstances, find themselves liable for civil and criminal penalties. Employers can also bear the brunt of disgruntled pension members' claims where they have endeavoured to balance their paternalistic approach with the business's needs.

Add to this a generally more litigious society, scheme members becoming more aware of their pension rights and the ever-increasing profile of pensions in the news and it is easy to understand why scheme sponsors are thinking twice about whether the risk–reward ratio is appropriate. So what protections are available?

Companies can help reduce the liability exposure of trustees by the incorporation of exoneration and indemnification clauses in trust deeds. However, sentiment has begun to swing against sole reliance upon such provisions because their successful operation usually entails a financial loss to someone, be that the employer or the fund itself. For example, successful application of an indemnification or exoneration clause can result in a loss to the pension scheme and thus, indirectly, to its beneficiaries. And an indemnity offered by an employer is only as strong as the company's financial ability to pay. Furthermore, it is difficult to ensure the wording of such clauses covers every conceivable eventuality.

Outsourcing some or all of the pension scheme's functions can help transfer some of the risk. However, trustees seeking contribution from other professionals involved in a claim may be faced with different limitation periods that could expire prior to the claim being brought against the trustees, leaving them to face the music alone.

Thus, at a time when legislation and litigation continue to increase, pension trustee liability insurance should be considered as a useful additional protection. However, it should not be seen as a replacement for properly trained and informed trustees diligently carrying out their duties in line with the requirement of trust law and other legislation.

Work-related stress – a hazard that organizations should not ignore

Allison Grant, KSB Law LLP and Caroline Raymond, Stress in Perspective

Introduction

Three of the key messages from the Health and Safety Executive (HSE) concerning work-related stress are:

- Work-related stress is a huge occupational health problem facing Britain today, inflicting a heavy toll in terms of both financial cost and human suffering.
- The law requires organizations to take action with regard to work-related stress.
- There are many potential benefits from taking action.

The HSE is recommending that where possible organizations take a proactive approach to work-related stress rather than a reactive one. In other words, take action to remove the causes rather than treating stress after it has occurred.

The HSE is keen to work with organizations to help them address the issue of work-related stress. Evidence of this is the actions they have taken recently. For example they have issued:

- practical information on how to draw up a policy for stress;
- guidance on how to risk-assess for stress;
- information on how to achieve successful rehabilitation of staff who have been off work with stress;
- case studies showing what action organizations have taken.

Recognizing the need for a yardstick against which organizations can measure their progress in tackling work-related stress, the HSE published Management Standards in November 2004. The Management Standards are designed to encourage employers, employees and their representatives to work in partnership to address work-related stress throughout the organization and help simplify risk assessment for stress.

The Management Standards are based on a continuous improvement model featuring a benchmarking tool to help managers gauge stress levels plus guidance on how the results can be used to start a dialogue with employees to identify problem areas and develop practical solutions. The Management Standards are not in themselves a legal requirement but demonstrate how employers can discharge their existing legal obligations. Information about the Management Standards, and how they can be implemented, can be found on the HSE website, www.hse.org.uk.

In an attempt to achieve a significant reduction in the incidence of work-related stress the HSE is currently working specifically with volunteer organizations from five key sectors that have reported the highest incidence of work-related ill health. These sectors are: health, education, central government, local government and financial services.

Although most of the current HSE activity will be addressing issues in these five key sectors it should be noted that the HSE will also be working with other employment sectors. The aim is to develop a community of 'centres of excellence' or 'management standards champions'.

The purpose of this chapter is to:

1. review what is meant by the term 'stress';
2. assess the potential benefits from taking action to manage stress effectively;
3. explain your legal responsibilities in respect of work-related stress;
4. review the elements of an effective corporate strategy for work-related stress;
5. suggest who should be involved in executing such a strategy; and
6. give advice on how best to make the strategy work in order that organizations can reap the benefits.

What is meant by the term 'stress'

In its current guidance the HSE makes clear the difference between stress and pressure and defines work-related stress as:

> The adverse reaction people have to excessive pressures or other types of demand placed upon them. This makes an important distinction between the beneficial effects of reasonable pressure and challenge [which can be stimulating and motivating and give a 'buzz'] and work-related stress, which is the natural but distressing reaction to demands or 'pressures' that the person perceives they cannot cope with at a given time.

Examples of other definitions supporting and expanding on the above HSE definition include:

- 'Stress occurs where demands made on individuals do not match the resources available or meet the individual's needs and motivation... stress will be the result if the workload is too large for the number of workers and time available. Equally a boring or repetitive task which does not use the potential skills and experience of some individuals will cause them stress' (Trades Union Congress).
- Stress is 'That which arises when the pressures placed upon an individual exceed the perceived capacity of that individual to cope' (Confederation of British Industry).

These definitions illustrate the now accepted view of work-related stress as being that which occurs when individuals are in a position where they perceive either 1) that they do not have the necessary resources or skills to carry out a specific task or tasks or 2) that they are not sufficiently challenged by the task(s) allocated to them.

It is important to keep in mind two important points: 1) 'pressure' and 'stress' are *not* one and the same thing; 2) stress is something anyone can suffer from and is not something that only happens to 'wimps'.

Common causes of work-related stress

The Health and Safety Executive booklet *Tackling Work-Related Stress: A manager's guide to improving and maintaining employee health and well being* identifies seven broad categories of risk factors for work-related stress, as shown in Table 6.4.1.

It should be noted that although the HSE considers 'culture' to be a potential area of risk it is not included in their Management Standards as the HSE believes any problems within this area will be corrected if the other six areas of risk are managed effectively.

Common effects of stress

Common effects of stress for organizations are:

- a rise in levels of absenteeism;
- increased staff turnover;

Table 6.4.1 Categories of risk factors for work-related stress

Category	Risk factors
1. Culture	Lack of positive response to stress/health concerns. Lack of staff involvement. Poor communication. Lack of consultation and participation in decision making. Lack of support. Long working hours/lack of rest breaks.
2. Demands	Lack of challenge and pressure. Exposure to violence/aggression. Work overload. Poor physical environment. Lack of training. Lone working. Fast pace of work.
3. Control	Low or lack of control over task design. Non-participation in decision making.
4. Relationships (interaction)	Bullying/harassment. Low levels of support. Violence.
5. Change	Changing market demands. New technology. Restructuring.
6. Role	Role conflict. Role ambiguity.
7. Support, training and factors unique to the individual	Lack of adequate training. Mismatch between person and job. Lack of support/feedback. Lack of constructive advice.

- increased recruitment costs;
- increased insurance premiums;
- poor public image;
- underperformance;
- low staff morale;
- low productivity;
- increased mistakes;
- low staff commitment.

Common effects of stress for the individual include physical signs, for example:

■ stomach disorders;
■ headaches;
■ muscle tension;
■ acute tiredness;
■ sleep disorders;
■ increased colds/flu;
■ skin disorders;
■ chest pains;
■ high blood pressure;
■ eating disorders.

Common effects of stress for the individual also include mental and behavioural signs, for example:

■ being irritable and short-tempered;
■ low self-esteem and self-confidence;
■ being more prone to accidents;
■ being aggressive;
■ feeling unable to cope;
■ lack of interest in life;
■ withdrawal;
■ relationship problems.

The above examples are only some of the possible signs. Stress can manifest itself in a whole manner of different ways depending on the individual.

Research has indicated that constant exposure to stress may result in serious illness, either mental or physical. Serious physical illnesses that have been linked to stress include:

■ asthma;
■ depression;
■ coronary heart disease;
■ cancer.

The potential benefits from taking action

An effective stress management strategy can achieve the following benefits:

■ reduce the cost of sick pay, replacement cover and recruitment;
■ strengthen the employer's position with regard to employers' liability insurance;
■ reduce the likelihood of claims being made against them for breach of the duty of care and improve defences against such claims;

- improve the overall morale and commitment of employees;
- improve relationships amongst the staff;
- improve relationships with customers;
- improve and streamline the design and management of existing working conditions; and ensure that the organization complies with health and safety legislation.

The law on stress

The legal reason for taking action is that the law imposes a duty on all employers to ensure the health and safety of their employees. Under the Health and Safety at Work Act 1974 employers have a general duty to ensure, so far as is reasonably practicable, the health of their employees at work. This includes taking steps to make sure they do not suffer stress-related illness as a result of their work.

Similarly, employers must take account of the risk of stress-related ill health when meeting their legal obligations under the Management of Health and Safety at Work Regulations 1999.

Regulation 3 recognizes that every employer must make a suitable and sufficient assessment of risk to the health and safety of its employees.

Regulation 4 recognizes that every employer must introduce preventative and protective measures. The introduction of a stress policy is recommended, as are the education and training of both employees and managers.

Regulation 5 states that every employer must make and give effect to such arrangements as are appropriate for the effective planning, organization, control, monitoring and review of the preventative and protective measures. Employers are therefore required to set up an effective health and safety management system to implement their health and safety policy that is appropriate to the hazards and risks. Importantly every employer is also required to ensure that its employees are provided with such health surveillance as is appropriate having regard to the risk to their health and to safety that is identified by the assessment.

It is important to remember that all employees have responsibilities under the Health and Safety at Work Act 1974. Section 7 of the Act states that employees at work have a duty to avoid knowingly putting themselves or others at risk through their own acts or omissions, and to work safely, use protective equipment provided by the employer, cooperate with the employer's reasonable instructions intended for health and safety purposes, and report anything at work that might be a risk to themselves or others.

An approved Code of Practice and Guidance accompany the 1999 Regulations to ensure so far as possible that employers understand their obligations and furthermore understand how to implement them. A copy of the Code of Practice is available from the Health and Safety Commission.

An employer does not have to avoid all possible risks but only those that are reasonably likely to occur.

Whilst the Health and Safety at Work Act established a duty that every employer must ensure, so far as is reasonably practicable, the health, safety and welfare at work of all its employees, in addition to which the 1999 Regulations imposed a need to carry out risk assessment and introduce preventative and protective measures, there is no exact statutory law specific to stress except for requirements on employers to assess the risks of stress for expectant, new and nursing mothers and young people. There is also no formal legal definition of stress.

This leaves us to rely on the courts to consider the legal aspects of work-related stress, which were first brought to general attention by the 1995 High Court decision in *Walker* v *Northumberland County Council*. In that case, the High Court ordered a county council to pay damages to an ex-employee on the basis that, as employers, they had a duty not to cause him psychiatric damage by giving him too much work and/or insufficient back-up support. The council had dismissed the employee on grounds of ill health.

On the facts of the particular case, which included the fact that Mr Walker had had previous stress-related work problems, the court decided that the council had not performed its duty properly. It was reported subsequently that Northumberland County Council had decided not to appeal and agreed damages at £175,000 (*The Times*, 27 April 1996 re Walker case).

In February 2002 the Court of Appeal in *Sutherland* v *Hatton* overturned three stress cases in an attempt to establish a consistent framework across the legal system for dealing with stress-related personal injury claims. All the cases concerned employees who had suffered psychiatric illness that they alleged was caused by stress at work. Among the guidelines put forward by the Appeal Court judges were the following statements:

■ The threshold question is whether this kind of harm to this particular employee was reasonably foreseeable.
■ There must be an injury to health that is attributable to stress at work.
■ Foreseeability depends upon what the employer knows (or ought reasonably to know) about the injured employee.
■ The employer is entitled to assume that an employee can cope with the normal pressures of the job unless it knows of some particular problem or vulnerability.
■ For the duty to act to be triggered, the signs of impending ill health must be clear enough for any reasonable employer to appreciate that it needs to take action.
■ The employer is only required to take such steps as are reasonable in all the circumstances.

Perhaps more importantly than establishing specific propositions, this case provides a comprehensive analysis by the Court of Appeal of the legal position in this type of case. The judgment also notes that stress claims are multiplying 'due to developing understanding in two distinct but inter-related areas of knowledge', psychiatric illness generally and the nature and extent of occupational stress.

The *Sutherland* ruling had a mixed reception. Some believed it could lull employers into a false sense of security and others that it had not emphasized the necessity for risk assessment by employers.

In respect of claims in negligence, since the *Sutherland* Court of Appeal ruling other cases have arisen demonstrating that the courts do, in fact, expect employers to exercise care in favour of an employee who is known to be prone to stress-related illness. In the case of *Morris Young* v *The Post Office* in 2002, the court found that the Post Office had been negligent by not taking sufficient trouble to monitor that an employee, who had suffered two breakdowns, was not exposed to conditions that he found stressful. The Post Office had mainly relied on the employee telling them that he was still finding problems at work after his return. The court found that this was not an acceptable excuse and ruled that, although he had not been heard complaining about stress, it was plainly foreseeable that there was a risk of recurrence upon his return to work. This case is noteworthy because it shows the very high level of care the courts (a county court and the Court of Appeal) expect employers to exercise in favour of an employee who is known to be prone to stress-related illness. Mr Young won compensation of over £90,000 from the Post Office even though he had returned to work voluntarily after a nervous breakdown.

In 2004 the House of Lords expressly approved the general statement of the law set out by the Court of Appeal in *Sutherland* (above) – see *Barber* v *Somerset County Council* (2004). However, in *Barber* the House of Lords put increased emphasis on the duty of employers to be on the lookout for signs of stress in their employees and to keep themselves abreast of developing knowledge of occupational stress and protective measures that can be taken to alleviate it. Alan Barber is a former teacher who was awarded £91,000 for loss of earnings plus £10,000 for pain, suffering and loss of amenity in a claim against Somerset County Council for work-related stress that led to depression and early retirement. He regularly worked 60 to 70 hours a week, and the pressures of an OFSTED inspection did not help. Somerset County Council, encouraged by its insurers, won on appeal to the Court of Appeal but, on the facts, this judgment was overturned by the House of Lords on 1 April 2004 and his damages were reinstated (albeit reduced by some £30,000).

The House of Lords was of the opinion that it was important to look at the point at which an employer's duty to take action was triggered, what action that should have been and whether it would have done any good. A claim will therefore succeed when the indications were plain enough for any reasonable employer to have realized that it should do something about it and did nothing or did too little.

The emphasis is that employers should be both reactive and proactive at an early stage and should not ignore any symptoms or any information that in any way puts them on notice that an employee is in trouble.

The House of Lords rejected the argument that was put forward by the Court of Appeal that, before an employer is under a duty to take steps to do something in order to prevent injury, the onus is on the employee to complain. The House of Lords made clear that the risks of occupational stress place a duty on an employer to organize a system of work to manage it.

The House of Lords cited the passage of Swainwick J in *Stokes* v *Guest, Keen and Nettleford (Bolts & Nuts) Limited* (1976) as representing the best statement of general principle as to the duty of care by an employer to its employees: 'The overall test is still the conduct of the reasonable and prudent employer, taking positive thought for the safety of his workers in the light of what he knows or ought to know.'

In the further case of *Hartman v South Essex Mental Health and Community Care NHS Trust* (2005) (when the Court of Appeal were deciding six appeals on the issue of an employer's liability for psychiatric injury suffered by employees owing to the pressures or stresses of work) the Court of Appeal took into account the guidance laid by themselves in *Sutherland* and also considered the decision of *Barber*. In *Hartman* the Court of Appeal re-emphasized that liability for psychiatric injury caused by stress at work is in general no different in principle from liability for physical injury. Therefore it is foreseeable injury flowing from an employer's breach of duty that gives rise to this liability. The mere fact that an employee suffered stress at work and that the employer was in breach of duty in allowing that to occur does not mean that the employer is liable to the employee.

Recent Court of Appeal cases have applied the guidance in *Sutherland*:

- *Bonser v RJB Mining (UK) Ltd* (2004). The Court of Appeal specifically held that a person claiming damages for psychiatric illness caused by stress at work must prove not just that it was reasonably foreseeable that overwork would lead to stress but also that the employer should have been aware that the stress would result in illness (applying *Sutherland* above).
- *Harding v The Pub Estate Co Ltd* (2005). This case highlights the critical element of foreseeability, particularly in relation to first instance breakdowns. Harding was an experienced pub manager working in a rough area of Manchester. He suffered a heart attack, which he alleged occurred because of stress caused by work. He was successful at trial and the employer appealed. The Court of Appeal allowed the appeal, primarily on the ground that the employer was not given a sufficiently clear warning of the impending ill health. Harding had made several complaints to his employers but these were primarily about the environmental factors (the clientele and the neighbourhood) rather than his health.
- *Vahidi v Fairstead House School Trust Limited* (2005). Mrs Vahidi worked as a teacher in the reception class at Fairstead House School. An inspection report in 1997 was critical of the teaching methods in the reception class. Mrs Vahidi found it difficult to cope with the required changes and suffered a serious breakdown. On her return to work, the school put in place support mechanisms for her. Despite the additional support, she had a relapse and did not return to work thereafter. The Court of Appeal upheld the first instance decision to dismiss the claim. The first breakdown was not foreseeable. The second breakdown was foreseeable but was not caused by a breach of duty by the school. The school foresaw the possibility of further mental illness and put in place a support mechanism to try to prevent this. Mrs Vahidi was unable to satisfy the court that the school had failed to take reasonable steps.

Further noteworthy cases are *Donachie v Chief Constable Gtr Manchester Police* (2004), and the separate case of *Simmons v British Steel* (2004). Both cases show that the employer has to take the employee 'as he finds him'. The fact that the particular employee has, for example, an unusually low pain threshold or is particularly susceptible to problems is bad luck on the employer as the 'egg shell skull' defence does not work in this context.

According to *Cloisters Case Analysis UKHL 13* the principles that now seem to apply to workplace stress are:

- An 'autocratic and bullying style of leadership' which is 'unsympathetic' to complaints of occupational stress are factors that Courts can take into account in deciding whether there has been a breach of duty.
- Once an employer knows that an employee is at risk of suffering injury from occupational stress, they are under a duty to do something about it. This duty continues until something reasonable is done to help the employee.
- Employees who complain do not need to be forceful in their complaints and need not describe their troubles and symptoms in detail. After all, they may be suffering depression, for example, making it more difficult to complain. Their complaints should be listened to sympathetically.
- Certified sickness absence due to stress or depression needs to be taken seriously by employers. It requires an inquiry from the employer about the employee's problems and what can be done to ease them. They should not be brushed off unsympathetically; nor should they be handled by sympathising but simply telling him or her to prioritize their work without taking steps to improve or consider the situation further.
- A management culture that is sympathetic to employees suffering from occupational stress and 'on their side' in tackling it, may make a real difference to the outcome. Monitoring employees who are known to be suffering from occupational stress is mandatory. If they don't improve, more drastic steps may need to be taken to help them. Temporary recruitment may be required. Although this will cost money, it will be less costly than the permanent loss through psychiatric illness of a valued member of staff.

Discrimination

The *Sutherland* case concerns claims in negligence (in the courts) and is not concerned with claims under the Disability Discrimination Act or any other legislation (which would be dealt with by an employment tribunal). A 'stress claim' is likely to take one or more of three possible forms: a personal injury/negligence claim for damages in the courts (as was the case in *Sutherland*) or a constructive dismissal or disability discrimination claim at an employment tribunal. The law on work-related stress, for instance in the context of a disability discrimination claim, has the criteria for such claims prescribed by the Disability Discrimination Act and the case law that is relevant to such claims.

It is clear that foreseeability is often a key element in stress claims. With psychological injury the risk may be hidden from the employer and therefore not foreseeable. However, if the employee alleges that any depressive illness has been caused by unlawful discrimination or harassment at work, the employee can choose to bring a claim in the employment tribunal rather than the civil court. It is established law that a tribunal award for discrimination can include damages for personal injury (including psychiatric injury): *Sheriff* v *Klyne Tugs Ltd* (1999). There is no need for the claimant to prove foreseeability in a tribunal claim for discrimination. The claimant need only demonstrate a causal link between the act of discrimination and the injury. A depressive illness might amount to a disability within the meaning of the Disability Discrimination Act 1995 depending on the duration and severity of the depression. Employees may bring claims in the employment tribunal if they are subjected to any detriment or dismissed because of the disability. Employers will also have a duty to consider what reasonable adjustments they could make to remove any substantial disadvantage faced by a disabled employee.

The elements of an effective strategy

Traditionally employers have taken a reactive approach to stress management but for many businesses this has proved ineffective, costly and risky. The best practice is to take a more proactive stance employing a *stress management strategy* consisting of primary, secondary and tertiary levels of intervention as follows:

■ *Primary.* The primary intervention is concerned with identifying the possible causes of stress plus the level of risk to individuals and the organization as a whole. This will be achieved through the process of risk assessment. For the primary level of intervention to be successful it is important that all staff involved in the initiative, plus the management, are:
   – fully conversant with the issue of work-related stress;
   – properly informed as to why action is being taken;
   – committed to taking action;
   – clear about their role in the initiative.
   A stress policy (together with relevant supporting procedures) should be drawn up at this stage. A model stress policy, if required, is available on the HSE website.
■ *Secondary.* The secondary intervention sets out to improve the overall situation in the workplace by implementing the recommendations identified in the risk assessment.
■ *Tertiary.* This stage deals with the treatment and rehabilitation of those individuals who have suffered ill health as a result of stress. Support schemes are usually employed at this stage.

Naturally the methods used to meet the employer's legal duties regarding stress will vary enormously from organization to organization. It is therefore vital that they be undertaken with reference to the individual needs of each particular organization.

Who should be involved

It can be useful to review the needs and roles of the following staff groups.

Senior management team

For any stress initiative to be successful it is imperative that the senior management team is committed to taking action and give their support to any planned initiatives. To achieve this it is important that:

1. They are made aware that they have legal responsibilities to take action to prevent work-related stress. This should include an introduction to the HSE Management Standards.
2. They understand what is currently meant by the term 'stress'. Often senior managers mistakenly believe that pressure and stress are one and the same, some even believing that stress is good for employees. Such beliefs can result in a reluctance to take steps to prevent stress in the workplace.
3. They recognize that there are substantial benefits to be gained if they give their commitment and support to well-thought-out and effective stress management initiatives within their organization.

Steering group

To ensure that any initiatives to manage work-related stress are implemented effectively, a steering group should be formally set up. Its task should be to plan, oversee and facilitate the management of work-related stress initiatives as a whole.

It is important that all of the key decisions made by the steering group are recorded and documented and for the group to meet on a regular basis to review progress. It is likely that the steering group will be responsible for the development of the stress policy and the supporting procedures.

Health and safety, occupational health and human resources departments

It is important that these three departments recognize their own individual roles in the management of work-related stress and both cooperate and work together to ensure that effective action is taken.

Managers

Managers have a key role to play. They can often spot problems at an early stage and, if equipped with the necessary skills, can take appropriate action to correct the situation. Unfortunately they can also be a source of stress if their management style is not appropriate. It is important that they are equipped with the skills to:

■ manage their staff effectively;
■ understand the legal implications of stress in the workplace and be equipped with the necessary skills to ensure that they are doing everything to comply with the law to ensure the health and safety of their staff;

- be capable of conducting ongoing risk assessments for stress by, for example, using the Management Standards approach;
- address and, where possible, correct any problem areas identified by the risk assessments;
- recognize any signs of stress in their staff;
- know how to approach an employee exhibiting signs of stress and listen *properly* to what the employee is *really* saying;
- be aware of the need for record keeping;
- recognize that they are not failing if they themselves are unable to help an individual but instead have to pass him or her on to someone more qualified to help – failure to do this could only compound the problem and could increase the number of individuals experiencing stress;
- manage their own stress;
- *take the issue of stress seriously and work with their employees to manage it effectively.*

Employees

Employees, and their representatives, have an important role as the law requires that all employees:

- avoid knowingly putting themselves or others at risk through their own acts or omissions;
- work safely, use protective equipment provided by the employer and cooperate with the employer's reasonable instructions intended for health and safety purposes;
- report anything at work that might be a risk to themselves or others.

To meet these requirements it is important that employees, and their representatives, have access to information about what stress is and 1) understand what they can do to manage their own stress effectively and 2) work in partnership with their managers to prevent, where possible, work-related stress occurring.

A key message from the HSE is that employees and managers should learn to work together in tackling the issue of work-related stress.

Making the strategy work and reaping the benefits

The important thing is to be practical, devise a realistic policy and strategy to manage work-related stress and work in partnership with employees.

The stress policy, and supporting procedures, should be drawn up and agreed at an early stage. It is advisable to have the policy and procedures in existence prior to the commencement of any training initiatives. All members of staff should receive a copy of the stress policy and supporting procedures.

It is crucial to ensure that everyone involved understands what is meant by the term 'stress' and recognize that preventative action will benefit all employees and the organization as a functioning unit.

Stress is a very sensitive subject for many people and it is important that any initiatives take this into account before being introduced. All initiatives need to be planned carefully and, where appropriate, the staff kept fully informed.

When assessing the risks of work-related stress it is important to get the starting point right. There are four key issues here:

1. Whoever is involved in conducting risk assessments for stress needs to be competent to assess this type of risk.
2. Work-related stress is the harm or injury that can occur as a result of occupational stressors. These stressors – not their effect on the individual – are the 'hazards' that need to be identified in Step 1 of any risk assessment.
3. Even though individual stress responses to a particular stressor may vary from one person to another, this does not preclude something from having the potential for harm. If there is a potential for harm, the risk of the harm occurring must be assessed and controlled.
4. The harm or injury resulting from occupational stressors can affect both physical and mental health and can involve both health and safety. It may also vary with the level, duration or frequency of exposure.

Risk assessment forms for stress should be easy to complete and reflect 1) the five-stage risk assessment process as recommended by the HSE and 2) the Management Standards. Appropriate risk assessment forms, with clear guidance on how to complete them, should be completed, for example when:

■ a member of staff has been off work with stress;
■ a member of staff has reported that he or she is experiencing stress;
■ a manager thinks that a planned activity has the potential for stress.

It is most important that any vulnerable groups are taken into account when risk-assessing for stress.

Remember also not to rely on just one measure of work-related stress. Instead an overall picture should be formulated using data from several sources.

In the event that the decision is made, as part of the risk assessment process, to carry out a stress audit it is important to keep in mind that a successful audit demands complete confidentiality. Reassurance should be provided for all those who participate in the process that any information they provide will be treated in strict confidence. It is clearly difficult for respondents to answer honestly if they feel there is a possibility that they may be identified and that their superiors may see their responses and judge them harshly. Therefore to obtain a reliable result, a reputable outside agency is often employed to carry out the audit. Ideally a stress audit should be designed specifically for an organization's culture and philosophy as opposed to using an 'off the shelf' stress tool.

It should always be kept in mind that tackling stress is a management issue. Managers have a key role to play in the effective management of work-related stress and it is critical that 1) they are equipped with the necessary skills to manage work-related stress and 2) they both communicate and work with their employees in respect of such an initiative.

It is also vital that anyone carrying out stress management training for managers is fully conversant with HSE best practice and has undergone formally recognized training in the field of stress management. Thoroughly check credentials when selecting an external trainer for such training courses and always ask for evidence of qualifications and written proof of previous successful training. This is particularly true in respect of stress management training for managers as there are many people these days jumping on the 'stress bandwagon' and claiming to be trainers when in fact their professional knowledge is very limited and their understanding of organizational cultures is minimal. There are frequent instances of courses being run for managers where they learn little if anything about their responsibilities for stress and how to carry them out. Instead they are entertained with stress balls and biodots and encouraged to engage in deep breathing!

Ask yourself these questions:

- Are you carrying out risk assessments for stress?
- Are you implementing the HSE Management Standards for work-related stress?
- Has your organization an effective stress policy in place?
- Has your organization effective stress management procedures for both managers and staff in place?
- Are your managers undergoing training that helps them to prevent stress amongst their staff and not just attempting to cure it once things have gone wrong?
- Are your employees aware of what stress really means and equipped with the skills to help manage any stress they may experience?

Tackling work-related stress effectively can bring many benefits to employee and employer alike.

Disclaimer: *The information in this chapter is for guidance only. It is not an authoritative statement of the law. KSB Law LLP cannot accept responsibility for use of the information. You should always take professional advice on any specific legal matter.*

Age discrimination – protect your business

Allison Grant, KSB Law LLP

Yes, it will affect you

The Employment Equality (Age) Regulations 2006 came into force on 1 October 2006. The new legislation prohibits age discrimination on the basis of actual or perceived age.

The new legislation does not concern just old people; it covers young and old alike throughout their working lives. It will cover both employment (which includes recruitment) and vocational training. It is also relevant to both the private and the public sector and every organization.

Skills, experience and the ability to do the job are what is important, not someone's age.

Therefore, employers will need to adopt *age positive practices*. It is essential that employers familiarize themselves, particularly management and those involved in the recruitment process, with the terms and provisions of the new Regulations. It is also essential that employers review their employment policies and procedures to ensure that they are compliant. Failure to do so could be expensive: compensation for age discrimination is uncapped.

It does not take long for the consequences of not complying to bite. Take the example of the Republic of Ireland where allegations of ageism now make up 19 per cent of Ireland's formal discrimination claims. Defending their cases is proving highly costly for employers. However, it does not have to be this way – *just be prepared*.

What the new legislation prohibits

The Regulations prohibit both direct and indirect discrimination, harassment and victimization.

Four categories of discrimination are unlawful:

- *Direct discrimination.* Where actual or perceived age is used as a reason for different treatment in a comparable situation this will amount to direct discrimination if it is not objectively justified.
- *Indirect discrimination.* Where a policy or practice disadvantages a certain age group, it will be indirectly discriminatory unless it is a 'proportionate means of achieving a legitimate aim'.
- *Harassment.* Harassment occurs when someone's dignity has been violated or he or she has been subjected to an intimidating, hostile, degrading, humiliating or offensive environment. The court will look at both subjective and objective viewpoints, including the employee's perception and whether it is reasonable to consider the offending conduct as having that effect.
- *Victimization.* Victimization is less favourable treatment of someone caused by something done by that person in connection with the age regulations. To put it another way, victimization happens in two stages. Firstly, a person takes an action or makes a complaint under the Regulations about age discrimination. Secondly, that person is treated less favourably because of the action that he or she took.

Justification

The Regulations differ from other types of discrimination legislation in that both direct and indirect discrimination can be justified under the Regulations.

To justify age discrimination the employer will need to show that the less favourable treatment, provision, criterion or practice is a proportionate means of achieving a *legitimate aim*.

Direct discrimination may pursue a legitimate aim for reasons such as health and safety, encouraging and rewarding loyalty, and training requirements.

The discriminatory treatment will need to be *proportionate* even if it does pursue a legitimate aim. Therefore, an employer seeking to rely on justification will need to provide clear evidence in support of its actions. Economic factors alone will not be a sufficient reason.

As with other areas of discrimination, it is not only individuals who harass who are at risk of facing claims – there is also a vicarious liability upon the company that employs them. It is not enough for companies to claim that comments or actions were unauthorized. To avoid liability firms must show that they have taken all reasonable steps to prevent harassment, that staff are aware that harassment will not be tolerated and that a complaints (grievance) process is in place for staff who feel that they have been harassed.

The following sections cover the employment relationship from recruitment to termination. All parts of the employment relationship are affected by the age discrimination laws. Employers must adopt an action plan in the form of a series of checks to ensure their policies and practices do not open the door to grievances and age discrimination claims.

Recruitment

It will be unlawful for an employer to discriminate against job applicants and employees on the ground of age both on recruitment and during employment (ie promotions). What this means is that it will be *discriminatory unless justified* to specify minimum or maximum recruitment ages, to prefer applicants from a particular age group for work and even to require a particular level of experience or qualification.

There is an exemption for employers with respect to the recruitment of older workers. It will not be unlawful to discriminate against job applicants whose age is greater than the employer's normal retirement age (or, if there is none, the default retirement age of 65) or who would, within a period of six months of applying for employment, reach that age.

Employers are advised, if they have not done so already, to put in place an action plan to take account of the following:

- Amend your equal opportunities policies to reflect the new legislation, ie update your equal opportunities policy to include age. You can start by inserting a statement that your organization does not discriminate on the basis of age.
- Hold training workshops for your staff, in particular human resources and managers, on the impact of the new law. Understanding the law and applying the law to the workplace are vital.
- Recruitment material should avoid references to age or age ranges unless employers can show objectively that it is appropriate and necessary to apply an age criterion to a job. Take care with the wording of advertisements. Avoid words that could imply age, such as 'mature', 'youthful', 'modern', 'senior', 'recent graduate' or even 'experienced'. If you use graduate schemes, avoid criteria such as 'under 25'.
- Does any qualification requirement have a discriminatory effect? Can you justify a requirement for a particular level of experience or a particular age?
- Start monitoring for age – in terms of recruitment and retention or turnover of staff.

In Ireland it was held that Ryanair's advertisement for a 'young and dynamic professional' was discriminatory, even though it was argued that 'young' had been used to indicate a state of mind rather than an actual age. Ryanair was fined IR£8,000.

Promotion

Promotion criteria should be *age neutral*. They should focus on competency and skills, rather than factors such as length of service or the age of the individual.

Unless it can be justified, businesses should remove artificial barriers to promotion such as maximum and minimum ages.

The ages of those applying for, and receiving, promotion should be monitored. Check that all staff have access to training and promotion opportunities.

Service-related benefits

Providing benefits based on the length of service of an employee is *potentially discriminatory*, although the Regulations do contain some exemptions. For example, a length-of-service criterion for awarding benefits will be allowed if it is for five years of service or less. An employer may also allow a length-of-service criterion for awarding benefits where it reasonably appears to the employer that there will be a business advantage from rewarding loyalty and the benefit is awarded to all of the employees who meet the length-of-service requirement and whose circumstances are not materially different.

The following checks are recommended:

■ Review your length-of-service benefits to check whether these have an adverse impact on staff with more than five years' service. If not, no further action is needed; the general exemption will apply.
■ If staff with more than five years' service will be adversely affected by a policy, eg extra holiday is awarded to staff with six years' service, consider if this fulfils a business need. If there are good reasons for the policy, the exemption should still apply. Keep a note of the reasons, and review them regularly. If the policy does not reflect a business need, the exemption will not be available, and the policy should be amended.

Enhanced redundancy pay

For a payment to qualify as an 'enhanced redundancy payment' and be permissible under the Regulations it must be based on the *method of calculating statutory redundancy pay* (SRP). Therefore, a scheme that pays double SRP will be permissible but a scheme that pays all employees a multiple of their salary based on their years of service will not be permissible as it does not follow the SRP model of calculation.

When an organization is faced with redundancies it is recommended that the following are considered:

■ Is there a selection criterion that recognizes 'last in first out'? If so, make sure this is not discriminatory.
■ Check that your redundancy policy does not have potentially age-discriminatory aspects, eg is the multiplier based on age?

■ Does the redundancy pay calculation mirror the statutory scheme? If so, no further action should be necessary as the calculation will be permissible.
■ If an enhanced redundancy scheme does not mirror the statutory scheme, can the scheme be objectively justified? If so, record any justification.
■ Amend the redundancy scheme if it does not mirror the statutory scheme and the scheme cannot be objectively justified.

Retirement

The Regulations provide a *default retirement age of 65*. Enforced retirement below age 65 will generally be unfair dismissal (unless it can be shown to be a 'proportionate means of achieving a legitimate aim').

It will generally be lawful to require an employee to retire on or after his or her 65th birthday, provided that the prescribed procedure set out in the Regulations is followed. Therefore although the Regulations prohibit discrimination on the grounds of age, the dismissal of an employee by reason of retirement is lawful provided the employer complies with the retirement procedure. The Regulations amend the Employment Rights Act 1996 by adding a new section so that 'retirement' becomes the sixth potentially fair reason for dismissal.

In assessing the risks associated with dismissing an employee at age 65, regard must be had to the Regulations, which provide *set procedures* for meetings, appeals, notifications and deadlines. The existing statutory dismissal procedure will no longer apply to retirement dismissals. It should therefore be possible to dismiss a member of staff fairly and without age discrimination at age 65, assuming a proper procedure has been followed. The procedure is complex and requires the employer to notify an employee of retirement between six and 12 months in advance.

An employee can request to continue working beyond the age of retirement, and again the Regulations state the procedure to be adhered to. The employer must inform the employee of his or her right to request to continue working. The employer has a 'duty to consider' the request but is not obliged to accept it.

A retirement dismissal *will arise* where:

■ there is no employee normal retirement age, the employer complies with the 'duty to notify' and the dismissal takes effect on or after the employee's 65th birthday and on the intended date of retirement;
■ the employee's normal retirement age is over the age of 65, the employer complies with the duty to notify and dismissal takes effect on or after the employee's normal retirement age and on the intended date of retirement;
■ the employee's normal retirement age is below the age of 65 (and is not unlawful because it is objectively justified), the employer complies with the duty to notify and dismissal takes effect on or after the employee's normal retirement age and on the intended date of retirement.

The chances of employers successfully relying on a retirement dismissal are greatly increased if they operate a lawful retirement age, follow the duty to notify procedures and terminate the employee's employment on the retirement date. Human resources should check if their employees' retirement age, if less than 65, is objectively justified, diarize their retirement dates accurately and notify employees at least six months before their retirement.

Scenarios that *cannot* amount to a retirement dismissal include the following:

∎ There is no employee normal retirement age and dismissal takes effect before the employee reaches the age of 65.
∎ There is an employee normal retirement age and the employer complies with the duty to notify but the dismissal takes effect before the employee's intended date of retirement.
∎ There is an employee normal retirement age (whether above or below 65) and dismissal takes effect before the employee reaches that age.

Please note that the above scenarios are not exhaustive.

The government has produced transitional provisions in relation to employees who have been given notices for termination by their employer before and after 1 October 2006 but whose effective date of termination is before 1 April 2007 (six months after the regulations came into force). These provisions may be summarized as follows:

∎ If an employer fails to comply with its duty to notify, a penalty of eight weeks' compensation is payable to the employee.
∎ If an employer dismisses an employee short of his or her notice period entitlement, it is automatically deemed to have breached the duty to notify and a penalty of eight weeks' pay is payable.
∎ In both cases, the employer remains under a continuing duty to notify the employee right up to his or her effective date of termination.
∎ The employee must exercise the right of request at least four weeks before his or her termination date or four weeks after at the latest.

The transitional provisions aim to ensure that, if employers deliberately dismissed employees before the axe fell on 1 October 2006, they remain under an obligation to go through the retirement procedures if retirement is contemplated. Employers who have already given their employees notices for the termination of their employment on retirement grounds must therefore ensure that they discharge their duty to notify on or after 1 October 2006 and deal with any right to request in a timely manner.

In addition to an organization's need to familiarize itself with the relatively new procedures that now govern dismissals at the age of 65, an action plan to cover the following should be put in place, if you are to avoid and reduce the risk of an age discrimination claim:

∎ Review your contracts of employment. If the normal retirement age is below 65, consider whether this is justified. Keep a written record of any justification.

■ Ensure that systems are in place for identifying staff approaching retirement age and notifying them in accordance with the time limits.
■ Amend your written internal policies to reflect an employee's right to request working beyond requirement age and set out the procedure to be followed.

There are statutory grievance procedures under which an employee wishing to complain of age discrimination must first submit a statement of grievance to his or her employer. Therefore, any employee who brings a claim relating to the right to work beyond his or her normal retirement age without going through the statutory grievance procedures will face the risk of a tribunal reducing his or her compensation by at least 10 per cent and up to 50 per cent.

To protect your business and to manage the risks brought into the workplace by the age discrimination laws you must act now!

This chapter is by no means a comprehensive guide. It is recommended that employers seek advice on the impact of the age discrimination laws and that they have regard to a checklist that will ensure their policies, procedures and practices are not discriminatory and so are not unlawful.

Disclaimer: *The information in this chapter is for guidance only. It is not an authoritative statement of the law. KSB Law LLP cannot accept responsibility for use of the information. You should always take professional advice on any specific legal matter.*

7

Areas of Risk in IT Management and Usage

Information risk management

Mike Madgin, DNV

Introduction

Senior management may have considered information risk management, particularly information security, as unnecessary and a cost overhead. The aim of this chapter is to look at why information risk management is now on the board agenda and how it can contribute to driving competitive advantage.

Businesses increasingly operate in a fast-changing environment; they are required to adapt continuously to change, remain competitive, ensure smooth and secure customer transactions and remain profitable. This means they are often completely reliant on electronic processing of information to meet more demanding productivity and efficiency objectives, as well as comply with corporate governance. They therefore have to review regularly:

■ the way they operate;
■ how to keep costs down;
■ ways to achieve enhanced efficiency; and
■ how to support best-practice governance.

Information risk management evaluates the management, system and user controls, including IT and technical controls, to make sure that information remains private and is complete, accurate and available as needed. Thus information risk management is an integral part of the continual improvement process. The scope and coverage of risk management is shown in Figure 7.1.1.

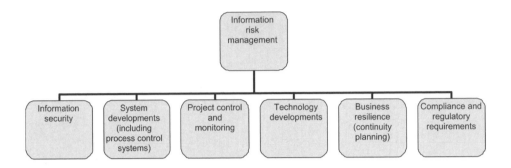

Figure 7.1.1   Elements of information risk management

The focus on improving cost-effectiveness is driving organizations to streamline their management structures and business processes. In addition, rapid technological developments, in particular the emergence of e-commerce and supply chain application systems, are enabling businesses to place greater reliance on their own and their customer and supplier systems. This requires essential integration between different business functions, which gives rise to the emergence of new risks. Management require simple, yet thorough, processes and effective preventive and detective controls operating in a cost-effective environment. They do not want complex and complicated processes or numerous disjointed and incoherent controls that add to cost and risk. Effective information risk management can help organizations achieve these objectives through aligning the IT strategy with the business strategy, developing efficient control procedures, reducing the risk of control failure and maximizing the cost benefits of an organization's investment in new computer systems.

Business drivers

The DataMonitor UK IT Priorities Survey, conducted in association with ZDNet UK and Butler Group, is an ongoing research programme. Respondents were asked to indicate the primary motivation behind each of their selected priorities. Overall 47 per cent of projects were motivated by the need either to increase user productivity (25 per cent) or to improve the competitiveness of the organization (22 per cent). This emphasis on IT as a contributor of value, rather than purely as a cost saver, was borne out by the high ratings given in areas such as the development of web applications, workforce mobility and business intelligence. The third most popular motivator was managing risk (19 per cent).

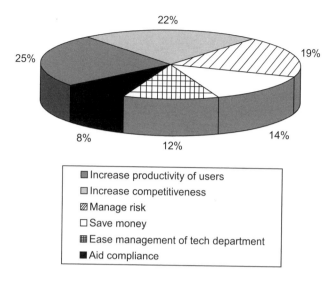

Figure 7.1.2 Distribution of motivators in managing risk

The overall distribution of motivators in the DataMonitor UK IT Priorities Survey is shown in Figure 7.1.2.

IT risk in a changing business environment

Information technology is a key enabler of business strategy and it helps companies to build and integrate solutions as well as achieve cost-effective efficiencies. Information risk management enables management to align their business and technology strategies, achieve the planned cost efficiencies and ensure there are no unexpected and unwelcome surprises, which could affect their reputation, lead to loss of confidence in their services or products or result in financial loss.

As a result it has become an important issue on board agendas. Management want to create a business environment that is secure and that manages and mitigates risks in a cost-effective way.

Many threats to the use of IT are well known. However, technology continues to advance at considerable speed, with the result that new threats continually emerge, some of which could be highly aggressive.

Examples of information threats facing businesses are shown in Figure 7.1.3.

System developments

There has been rapid growth in the use of smart card technology in the development of secure systems. Use of integrated chip card technology is a complex area and one that has become an essential requirement in large electronic trading systems, credit card systems, access control systems at refineries, laboratories, etc and substantial security architecture developments (eg motorway toll systems). This means that

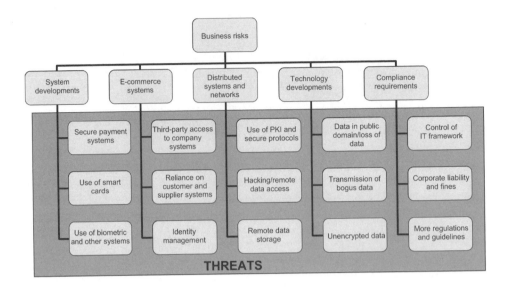

Figure 7.1.3   Information threats facing businesses

risks associated with a secure architecture component, as well as with biometric and identity management systems, need to be identified and assessed.

Businesses are reliant on e-commerce and complex enterprise-wide systems (eg SAP, Oracle and internet systems) and want assurance that their business-critical systems are secure. This means that complex system risks need to be identified and assessed.

Enterprise-wide systems typically operate over an organization's network, and potentially serious risks are emerging, which could affect the resilience of the network, as well as the integrity and confidentiality of data transferred. Banks and insurance companies, in particular, will want to ensure all customer information is secured properly. The growth in the implementation of open systems and the spread of wide/ local area networks give rise to the emergence of complex risks, which need to be assessed and mitigated.

In addition to business-critical systems, the general public are now increasingly reliant on safety critical systems. If these systems malfunction there may be potential loss of life resulting in severe financial penalties for the organizations concerned. Management want confirmation that the systems have been developed in a well-controlled environment, are safe and reliable and conform to international standards and regulations.

Process control and health and safety environmental systems

Oil and gas, transport and engineering multinationals rely considerably on a wide variety of process control and health and safety environmental systems. These systems are intrinsically linked to potentially dangerous processes that could place human life, property and the environment at risk. Management want assurance that the risks are being assessed and that the systems are secured appropriately.

Project control and monitoring

The national and computing press frequently report that major IT projects are delivered late and considerably over budget, mainly because of poor project management and lax cost control. Recent examples include slippage of implementation of the police national intelligence system to 2010 (16 years after it was proposed) and warning signs appearing about the national programme for IT in the NHS, the world's largest IT project. This programme has a history of delays and its basic technical viability has been questioned. The government and senior management want to know whether there are any significant project risks that could affect the implementation of new systems, in particular whether the project will be delivered on time and within budget.

Technology developments (eg mobile devices)

Today, it is very common for companies to provide mobile devices for their staff, eg 3G mobile phones, PDAs and BlackBerries. Anticipated benefits will include improvements in productivity as employees can work on important projects while travelling or at other corporate sites. According to research firms, in many large enterprises about 20 per cent of the workforce have a company-provided mobile device. It is highly likely that mobile devices will be more regularly lost or stolen and this will be very damaging if they contain confidential or customer information. This could severely damage confidence internally and with third parties. Management need to be confident that the risks linked to the use of mobile devices are being identified and assessed.

In addition to distribution of 'competitive edge' mobile devices, other devices are now widely available that could also pose serious security risks. Use of USB storage devices, cameras and iPods could enable confidential data to be downloaded or copied quickly and taken off-site by unauthorized personnel. Management need to be aware of the risks from these devices so they can take necessary steps to secure both the integrity and the confidentiality of data stored on mobile devices, as well as take end-point security measures.

Business resilience

Considerable media coverage has focused on the potential effects of pandemic flu, terrorist activity in major financial centres, and environmental disasters (eg the Buncefield fire). These events have heightened companies' awareness of their reliance on people, systems and networks and the need to reduce the risk to their business through effective recovery planning.

Compliance and regulatory requirements

The high-profile collapses of Enron and WorldCom have triggered a wave of new legislative and regulatory requirements, especially Sarbanes–Oxley. These requirements, combined with Basel II guidelines and International Financial Reporting Standards, mean that multinationals and banks, in particular, have been required to review and improve their overall control framework. It is highly probable that more regulations and guidelines will emerge in the years ahead, adding to corporate governance requirements.

These examples are by no means exhaustive. Businesses need to adapt to change but remain competitive and profitable; this means that new information and IT risks will continue to emerge. Continuous measurement of the IT performance is needed to support the business vision, and information risk management plays an essential part in the alignment of strategies and the constant drive for continual improvement.

Risk assessment process

The general principles of managing IT risks are similar to those of managing any other risks. The core steps involve context establishment (including scope, boundary and participants), identifying unwanted security events or incidents, analysing risks, evaluating risks, deciding how to manage the risks, considering options and implementing the most appropriate controls to manage the risks.

The main difficulty in assessing IT risks is determining the rate of occurrence, as historical information is usually not available on all kinds of past incidents. However, event and fault tree analysis can be used to understand these risks better.

The assessment process enables risks to be identified and prioritized so that they can be managed. This is a precursor to developing mitigating controls to drive cost and efficiency benefits. A simplified overview of this process is shown in Figure 7.1.4.

An IT risk matrix will be required to consider the likelihood and consequences of IT risks (see the example in Figure 7.1.5).

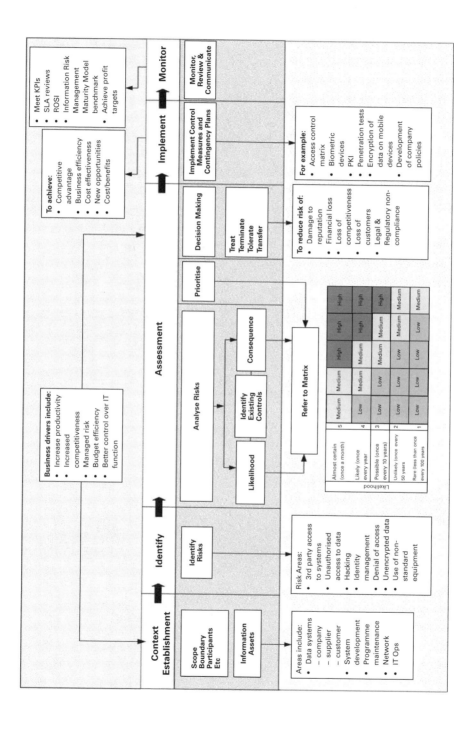

Figure 7.1.4 Simplified process overview

Likelihood			A	B	C	D	E
Almost certain (once a month)	5		Medium	Medium	High	High	High
Likely (once every year)	4		Low	Medium	Medium	High	High
Possible (once every 10 years)	3		Low	Low	Medium	Medium	High
Unlikely (once every 50 years)	2		Low	Low	Low	Medium	Medium
Rare (less than once every 100 years)	1		Low	Low	Low	Low	Medium
			A	B	C	D	E
Consequence			Negligible	Minor	Moderate	Major	Catastrophic
Financial loss			Loss up to £10,000.	Loss between £10,000 and £100,000.	Loss between £100,000 and £1,000,000.	Loss between £1,000,000 and £5,000,000.	Loss of more than £5,000,000.
Loss of competitiveness			Some business requirements not achieved.	System objectives not met (eg unable to determine identity of customer/supplier).	System not operating as required resulting in complaints from customers/suppliers.	Loss of confidence in systems and significant loss of orders, sales generated and revenue.	Unable to determine stock levels and productivity affected. Failure to meet contractual obligations, with potential loss of market share.
Non-delivery of IT project			System does not function as expected.	Some system objectives not met.	Key system objective is not met.	Key system objective is not met and project is late and/or over budget.	Failure to meet multiple key system objectives and system is very late/substantially over budget.
Non-compliance with legal and regulatory requirements			Some examples of non-compliance noted.	Attention from regulators.	Potential investigation by regulators.	Investigation and possible prosecution by Regulators.	Serious legal implications with likely prosecution, heavy fines and potential custodial sentences.
Reputation damage			Local press coverage.	Local and some national press coverage.	TV news and headline national press coverage.	Ongoing national press coverage and possible investigation by regulators.	International press coverage, serious legal implications and possible major fines.

Figure 7.1.5   Example: IT Risk Matrix

Summary

Information risk management, incorporating IT risk management, is not just a technical issue, although it has to deal with rapidly changing new technology and developments. It is increasingly seen by senior management not as a cost and necessary evil, but as an opportunity to provide their business with a competitive advantage.

Information and IT risk is inextricably linked to business risk; IT is an integral part of a business, so it is not surprising that IT risk should be an integral part of business risk. Some IT risks are well known, such as potential loss of data, corruption of data and loss of equipment. However, new threats emerge continuously, such as denial of service and loss of sensitive data if mobile devices are lost or stolen. These could all have an impact on business risk, leading to loss of customers, non-compliance with regulatory requirements and potentially damage to reputation.

Effective information risk management is a fundamental element in corporate governance and enables organizations to develop a reliable and trustworthy environment for conducting their business. Effective information risk management also enables organizations to streamline their key processes, capitalize on new technology opportunities to benefit their business, develop new routes to market and improve customer confidence, all with the knowledge and conviction that core systems and processes are in place to support and enable these activities.

Replicating data for business continuity

Leigh Griffiths, Hewlett-Packard

Most businesses are dependent on information technology for the day-to-day running of the business, and any downtime can have serious consequences. Unreliable systems and services will increase an organization's costs and negatively impact on revenue, customer retention, brand image and stock price. Moreover, in the event of a disaster, maintaining data availability and integrity is integral to a company's survival. Implemented properly, disaster-tolerant technology can provide your business with the highest level of business continuity and rapid recovery times, even following a major failure. But implemented poorly, it can lead to catastrophic data loss and unnecessary, extended application downtime.

One of the biggest mistakes that businesses make is to think it won't happen to them. Catastrophic events such as fire and flood seem like a remote prospect, but it only takes a single piece of bad luck to bring down a company. For example, during the Manchester terrorist attack of 1996 many companies in the city that hadn't been affected by the bombings nevertheless found themselves within an exclusion zone. With staff unable to reach their offices, those that hadn't made plans to replicate data remotely and relocate staff would have suffered serious damage to the business. Even small events such as power cuts lasting only an hour or so can have big consequences:

- E-mail and messaging failures will render the business unable to communicate with its customers, suppliers and partners and put vital information out of reach.
- Failures in real-time finance and payment systems will stop the business trading altogether.
- Supply chain failures directly affect suppliers' and customers' ability to operate.
- Customer relationship management (CRM) failures will render the business non-existent to customers.

The power of replication

When failures occur, no one either inside or outside the business is concerned whose fault it is. The test of a company's efficiency is how quickly its systems can be up and running again. Back-up is the first step. The business cannot be restored unless a record has been kept of all its transactions. The most common method until recently was tape back-up, a solution that is still popular with some companies. Tape is relatively inexpensive, but carries the problem that it is asynchronous, which means that back-up isn't performed as transactions are being created but at a later stage – usually overnight. This means that data are not immediately available in the event of an outage.

Modern disk technology is becoming more cost-effective, and therefore more attractive to small and medium businesses. With disk technology, it is possible to have synchronous back-up, which means that recovery is immediate after any downtime. The drawback of this is that real-time back-up, especially to a remote site, takes up valuable bandwidth and is therefore more costly than asynchronous back-up.

Table 7.2.1   Categories of threat

Unplanned	*Planned or predictable*
Power failure	Maintenance/upgrades
Hardware failure	Regular back-up and restore
Natural disaster	Human error
Human-caused disaster	Increased IT demand due to growth/new business
Partner/supplier failure	Mergers/acquisitions
Malicious sabotage	Government legislation
Security breach/data theft	

As part of the design of any good business continuity plan, businesses need to decide what data are essential and what are not, and offset that against the cost of storage and recovery. Some systems, such as commerce systems, will need to be available immediately. Others will need to be restored within the same day while other kinds of data can be stored for days or weeks. The most important systems should be replicated in their entirety off-site. This is the most costly solution but absolutely necessary for some operations and part of regulatory requirement for services such as hospitals.

Smart storage systems

For less serious outages such as human error or hardware failure, on-site storage to disk has become smarter and cheaper in recent years with the advent of storage area networks (SANs). Previously, storage was attached to individual servers, which meant that many devices were doing the same back-up job. With SANs, IT managers can consolidate this storage using disk arrays attached to a network, which significantly reduces the total cost of ownership and frees up the servers for day-to-day business applications.

More importantly, because SANs consolidate the data, they give IT managers the chance to replicate large amounts of information via mirroring, or replicating, to another disk, making it immediately available in case of an outage, or ready for migration to alternative locations for safekeeping.

However, probably the biggest advance in business continuity for small to medium-sized business is the electronic vaulting service (EVS), which has the dual purpose of backing up huge amounts of data off-site and making it immediately available if on-site systems fail. This managed back-up solution has become possible as the cost of bandwidth and storage has decreased, making it easy and efficient to quickly back up, store and retrieve large amounts of data.

The reason EVS works so well is that it makes techniques considered to be the preserve of enterprises available to ordinary businesses. EVS is based on mirroring, a synchronous process that replicates information as it is created. The data are then transmitted via a fibre optic network to a remote site, storing the information at the two locations at the same time. Once the information has been stored, it becomes immediately available in case of interruption at the original site.

The truly innovative aspect of EVS is that high bandwidth to the off-site data centre cuts down recovery times dramatically, while large amounts of data can be securely held away from the business in case of major disaster. As a managed solution, EVS is a huge step forward for companies that do not have substantial IT departments. Providers often offer the chance to restore only the data that have been lost, eg just one e-mail as opposed to the entire mailbox, and additional capacity can be added as required. Companies can therefore migrate their storage requirements in increments – starting with the mission-critical applications – and add the rest later.

Advanced EVS systems combined with total business continuity solutions offer more – the chance to resume operations using the stored data in the case of total failure. Because the data are being stored at one location across different platforms and applications, a full snapshot of the business is being taken at any one time, enabling full recovery.

The disaster-tolerant solution

For more complicated environments, one simple solution such as EVS may not be sufficient. A third-party business continuity provider can help design a system that will ensure absolutely essential applications such as e-commerce systems experience no outage whatsoever, while less essential systems are up and running within an acceptable time frame. The provider can also help a company rehearse and redefine its business continuity plan on a regular basis, so the solution is always suited to the business and IT staff are trained to administer the solution.

These systems for enterprises typically involve the use of at least two geographically distributed data centres that mirror each other. Recovery is facilitated by fail-over and fail-back, where clustered servers fail over to others in the event of an outage and then fail back to the original source when normal service has been resumed. Redundant arrays of independent disks (RAID) provide automatic back-up, controlled by replication software. These solutions allow for information to be tiered, so that mission-critical applications are the first to be restored.

But business continuity is about more than data – it's about people. Some kinds of disaster, such as fire, flood or a terrorist incident, won't take out just a network; they'll take out the entire office, possibly for weeks. In such a case it's important to know that there's somewhere for staff to go or that there's a way to provide staff with essential equipment.

Many providers will supply access to an entirely replicated office within a recovery centre. This will involve the company hiring space and equipment within a third-party data centre, which will act as a surrogate office if the original office is out of bounds. If this is the case, the recovery centre needs to be able to copy the working conditions of the company accurately, including phones securely redirected to the same number and access to the (replicated) network. Advanced recovery centres will even offer facilities such as meeting rooms and catering.

Whether a company has hired a recovery centre or not, in the event of major disaster staff organization is a key part of any business continuity plan. Staff need to know what your business continuity plans are and be involved in rehearsals. They should know, for example, whom to contact if the office has to be evacuated and where they need to go. Essential staff should be given the right equipment to maintain contact with the network if necessary. And, most importantly, these plans should continue to be revised. Outdated business continuity plans can be as bad as none at all.

Case study: Elsevier

The business continuity solution designed by publishing house Elsevier is the result of a 14-year association with provider HP. The key to success has been constant scrutiny, rehearsal and refinement by HP and Elsevier.

Workplace recovery is located at HP's Reading Recovery Centre where the company has 100 work-area positions available to rehouse staff from the Camden, Holborn, Oxford and Kidlington centres.

Working to a master crisis management plan, senior managers determine the nature of each incident and the recovery time. In an invocation, some key staff may go to other Elsevier offices and some staff may be sent home, but the majority will move to the Reading Recovery Centre.

'The beauty of the HP site is that it is just like any other Elsevier site', says Mike Hartshorne, EMEA facilities director with Elsevier. 'All the networking capability is in there and we just switch that on to become another Elsevier site. Within four hours of a major disaster, people will be up and running at the recovery centre with our standard desktop image on the PCs, just as though they were at their own desks.'

Well resourced

At the latest workplace recovery test 30 people from different business units at four different sites were sent to Reading in a real-life situation. HP specialists had everyone up and working within five minutes of arriving, complete with redirected phones, voicemail and network connectivity.

HP provides dedicated racks at the Reading Recovery Centre, and Elsevier has installed dedicated communications into the building. It also subscribes to syndicated or shared hardware. This cost-effective service can be made available in the recovery centre or through a ship-to-site service.

In charge of working with HP specialists to create the appropriate environment is Elsevier's operations manager Rob Innes. He says:

> In effect, we replicate the whole of our infrastructure services down to Reading so, if we lost Oxford, Reading would take over very quickly and we would not need to do a great deal of work to get it going. We run a tiered system rating business services according to various criteria such as whether they are revenue generating or customer facing. Business units getting a 'cold' service are restored in three to five days and those on the 'warm' service are up and running much quicker.

In a recent invocation, parent company Reed Elsevier accidentally deleted all Elsevier's public folders. This caused restore problems because exchange servers could not be running on-site at the same time. HP came to the rescue with the loan of some 30 servers, and staff worked round the clock to get data back on the live network.

Data vaulting with HP's new electronic vaulting service is part of future plans, with data back-ups to a SAN installed on the customer site and data replicated directly across to a back-up SAN at the recovery centre. Rather than recovery from tape, data would be restored from disk, which enables greatly reduced recovery time. It may also greatly reduce the amount of data that could be lost from an outage if contrasted with the data lost when using a daily tape back-up.

Case study: Shoosmiths

Widely regarded as one of the country's most progressive, innovative and technologically advanced law firms, Shoosmiths has grown rapidly in recent years and now has a network of seven regional offices employing a total of 1,400 people.

Increasing reliance on IT for the company has brought an awareness of how much the business would suffer if information systems were unavailable. Says Carol Light, firm-wide facilities manager at Shoosmiths: 'We are totally dependent on our computer systems. Granted, we have manual procedures that would enable us to continue to respond for a period of time, but we couldn't go on indefinitely.'

HP provided Shoosmiths with business continuity consultancy services over a period of eight months. The work involved a business impact analysis and risk assessment followed by the development of a continuity strategy. Business processes were examined as well as technology issues. For example, a need was identified to capture and document knowledge more effectively.

The consultancy work led to a requirement for a business continuity recovery solution. Shoosmiths awarded HP a three-year contract to provide seven customer sites across the UK with continuity services for IT and business work-area. This involves hundreds of servers and applications used by a total of 1,400 lawyers and support staff. The services make use of HP business recovery centres in Newbury, Wellingborough, Birmingham and Reading.

Under the terms of the contract, HP will provide Shoosmiths with access to the facilities of its business recovery centres within four hours of notification. For each end user, this includes the use of a desk, PC, telephone and peripherals, together with network access. In the event of complete IT failure, there is a 24-hour timetable for business recovery.

Customer satisfaction

According to Light, Shoosmiths has an obligation to show existing and potential customers that it has a structured business continuity capability. Thanks to HP, it can now do so. The emphasis on business continuity rather than just IT is seen as very important. Light points out that many companies think only of securing the information infrastructure, but Shoosmiths prefers to take a broader view. She says:

> To keep our clients satisfied we need to maintain a certain level of response, whatever happens. If one of our offices was out of action, for example, some of the business could be managed from other locations, but we also have to consider where our people would physically go in order to work. This is why we have asked HP to provide workplaces at several of its business recovery centres.

Information security governance and *The Wealth of Nations*

Paul Williams, Protiviti

What possible link could there be between the writings of an 18th-century economist and the management of information security in the 21st century? Would Adam Smith have something to say about today's world of Wi-Fi, public key infrastructure, VOIP and SOA? Could his famous quote 'when ownership and control of corporations are not fully coincident, there is potential for conflicts of interest between owners and controllers' still have relevance today in an information security context? Well, yes, because within that famous quote Smith was sowing the seeds of the need for governance, as much an imperative for effective and transparent information security in today's world as it has become for corporate behaviours in a post-Enron and Maxwell world.

Adam Smith's basic contention, as published in his seminal work *The Wealth of Nations* published in 1776, was that as hitherto owner-managed businesses expanded as a result of the industrial revolution there became a need for external sources of finance. This kick-started the trend towards reliance upon external shareholders and investors for the provision of business capital. In order to ensure that those responsible for the day-to-day running of the business properly protected the interests of the outside investors, who were not always themselves in a position to oversee the decisions made by the management, the need grew for systems of checks and balances to ensure that the interests of all those involved were properly protected. This led to the evolution of governance structures, processes and practices, which today include the statutory requirement for external audit, the need to comply with ever more complex financial reporting rules and standards, and the additional overhead necessitated by legislation such as Sarbanes–Oxley or the latest EC directives.

Amongst this complexity and regulation it is easy to lose sight of the basic premise behind Smith's original writings. All that he was saying was that, where there is a potential for interests that should be working towards a common goal (principally the creation of wealth) to diverge, there should be mechanisms in place to ensure equilibrium.

Relate this principle to information security

Recent UK regulation and guidance on governance has emanated largely from the Cadbury and Turnbull recommendations formulated following the corporate scandals of the 1980s and 1990s. The Cadbury Committee, for example, stressed the need for companies to strengthen their internal control and for boards to set strategic aims, provide leadership, supervise management and report to shareholders on their stewardship. Similarly the subsequent Turnbull Committee stated that it is the responsibility of the board to ensure the existence of appropriate and effective processes to monitor risk and the effectiveness of the system of internal control. Mitigating the risk of security breaches through a cohesive system of internal control, which should include information security policies and processes, falls firmly within this requirement.

There is little debate, in today's complex world of almost total business reliance on technology in all its forms, that information security has become a business imperative. Supplier–customer relationships and supply chain integrity are built upon trust, with each participant in the chain being able to rely upon the completeness, accuracy and validity of information passed up and down the chain. When, for example, an online customer pays for his or her purchase by using a credit card, that customer has the right to expect that the credit card details will be properly protected and that, as appropriate, the details of the transaction will remain confidential. The user of an internet banking service similarly has the right to expect that security measures established by the bank are sufficient to minimize the risk of unauthorized access to his or her account details. That user in turn has an obligation to the bank to protect his or her PIN numbers and other access codes from unauthorized disclosure and use. Thus responsibility for maintaining their own part of the security 'chain' pertains at all levels, from the most senior management of the business entity down to the individual users, whether internal or external to the entity.

However, as with all aspects of business it is with the board of directors that the buck stops. It is they who must bear ultimate responsibility for the success or failure of the security policies and processes that are put in place in their name to protect corporate and stakeholder assets. This is where the Adam Smith principles of governance come in because, although unambiguously it is the responsibility of the CEO and the board to protect the business assets, the actual processes put in place to provide that protection often are selected, implemented and managed by others, to whom those tasks are delegated. Although tasks may be delegated, the responsibility for ensuring that they are carried out effectively and that the results deliver the expected protection cannot be delegated. So how can the board satisfy themselves that those to whom the tasks have been delegated have properly and completely fulfilled the information security mandate?

Should board members become experts in technologies as various as wireless communications, PKI and biometrics? The answer of course is no. To gain such detailed knowledge would be impractical and unnecessary but, in order to carry out their governance mandate, board members must seek properly informed assurance that the security measures in place are appropriate to the risk and are effective and efficient in operation.

How this may best be done

The first step is always to recognize and understand the risk. There must also be a recognition that risk cannot be totally avoided. It is often said that the only completely secure computer is one that is turned off and buried 10 metres deep, fully encased in reinforced concrete. Such a secure environment may reduce risk to zero but the business benefit also would be zero. Therefore it is necessary to talk in terms of mitigating risk to the lowest practical level rather than of raising the security bar so high that normal business cannot take place.

But how real is the risk? Obviously the risk will vary depending upon the type of business, with financial services, for example, likely to carry a higher level of risk than a ball bearing manufacturer. However, whatever the type of business there is still a responsibility to identify key information security risks and implement effective and appropriate countermeasures. A key principle here is that we are talking about information security and not information technology security. This means that all aspects of securing information need to be considered and covered. This will include security not only of information held within IT systems but also of verbal communications, particularly relevant today with the advent of VOIP (Voice over Internet Protocol) technologies, and the written word. I am sure that many of us can recount examples of sitting next to fellow passengers on trains or planes who leave sensitive information on seats or tables whilst they visit the toilets or the bar, or who discuss their latest corporate deal on their mobile phones seemingly oblivious to who might be listening in.

Such examples stress the need for a high-level information security policy, endorsed and owned by the board, which will define key matters such as the types of information that require protection and the responsibilities of management and staff for security compliance.

The development of such a policy should be regarded as more than a theoretical exercise as it will be the foundation for the detailed structures and processes that will follow. Therefore the construction of a comprehensive yet manageable policy may require some training of board members and others in what such a policy should contain, how it should be managed and why it is important. For a policy to be effective it will be essential for board members to 'walk the talk' and set the tone from the top in endorsing its implementation. Such training is usually best done in facilitated workshop sessions providing ample opportunity for questions, open discussion and the reaching of consensus.

The principles of governance extend also to defining responsibilities for information security. What is being secured is business information and, whilst many of the techniques used to ensure and manage security may be technical solutions that require technical expertise to select, implement and manage, it is the business that has to bear the prime responsibility for its security and confidentiality. Only the business can decide on the levels of security that may be appropriate to diverse ranges of corporate information. For example, customer credit card information is likely to require a higher level of security than a fixed asset register. To treat all information in the same way would almost certainly lead to some being over-secured and some under-secured. Security measures must be appropriate to the risk if they are to be cost-effective.

Another key governance responsibility is to ensure that sufficient funds and resources are available to acquire, develop, implement and manage the appropriate security measures. It would be a major failure in governance if risks and responsibilities were properly identified but resources were not made available to mitigate the risks effectively. This is one of the reasons why boards are beginning to ask questions such as 'What proportion of our IT spend should be dedicated to security?' Although it might give a warm feeling if the answer came back that 'Our spend is above the industry average', this could be unhelpful, as no two organizations are the same and the level of spending appropriate to one might be totally inappropriate to another. However, some industry benchmarking can be useful from a governance angle, at least allowing board members to ask the right follow-on questions if, for instance, your percentage of security spending is less than your industry average. This might imply that your risk is not being adequately addressed. Conversely if you are spending more than the average, although this might imply that you are better addressing the need, it might imply equally that, from a value-for-money point of view, you are spending more than is necessary. External benchmarking will never give you the answer but it can help boards to frame the right questions.

Some organizations have taken the segregation of information security and information technology security a step further, creating two separate departments with their own budgets. This not only enables the board to track security spending more granularly, but can also act as an enabler for more robust policies and procedures (information security) with support from the right technologies (information technology security) as each department can focus on its core function. This segregation also has the positive side effect that the IT department is free to deal with actual IT issues.

A further key principle of governance is never to assume that all is well. Purely allocating responsibility for security tasks is insufficient to ensure that the right things are actually being done and that the right results are being achieved. Those responsible for governance, at all levels, need to obtain regular, informed assurance that this is happening. This requires the development of reporting mechanisms with appropriate metrics to prove to the board and others that information security is operating effectively and efficiently within the organization and that the risks have been properly and completely identified and mitigated.

Internal audit, whether in-house, outsourced or co-sourced, has a part to play in this as information security and its effectiveness should be part of the audit plan and a regular item on the audit committee agenda. Indeed within many organizations it is becoming standard practice for the chief security officer, or equivalent, also to have a reporting line to the audit committee.

The board may (and probably should) require direct reporting to them of specific security-related metrics such as:

■ numbers of security incidents in the past year (hopefully a downward trend year on year);
■ average loss per incident;
■ brief descriptions of the five most significant security breaches;
■ average cost of dealing with a security incident;
■ proportion of staff having received training in information security;
■ numbers of professionally qualified security staff (eg CISM or CISSP);
■ proportion of IT spend dedicated to security;
■ number of new implementations delayed by security concerns;
■ number of outstanding security-related audit issues.

There are many metrics that may be used. Selected metrics may be included in a management dashboard or a balanced scorecard. The common problem of paralysis by analysis needs to be avoided through the selective and focused use of metrics. However, the absence of any security-related metrics or any security-related reporting at board level is likely to imply shortcomings in security governance and a consequent failure of senior management to address properly what increasingly is becoming a significant business issue.

Of course, obtaining accreditation under security and related standards such as ISO 27000 will provide visible evidence, both within the company and to its trading partners and customers, that this is an organization that takes its information security responsibilities seriously.

The 2006 DTI Information Security Breaches Survey[1] identified that 87 per cent of larger businesses had suffered security incidents during 2005 and that this number was likely to increase rather than decrease. The direct losses arising from such incidents were also increasing as was the cost of repairing the damage. Any board, whether public or private sector, that ignores, or gives less than full attention to, information security governance will be failing in its stewardship responsibilities. There is much guidance available to help from organizations such as the DTI, ICAEW,

ITGI, etc.[2] Therefore there is now little excuse for business directors and managers not to be sufficiently knowledgeable on the topic to be seen to take it seriously.

Notes

1. www.dti.gov.uk/industries/informationsecurity
2. *Board Briefing on Information Security Governance* (www.itgi.org); *Information Security: An essential today* (www.itfac.co.uk).

Risk management and wireless security

Tim Pickard, RSA, The Security Division of EMC

Introduction: assessing wireless risk

Wireless networks are a boon to business. Workers with mobile phones are more productive, because they can communicate wherever they are. When voice communications are coupled with data, the benefits are even greater.

As a result, corporate use of wireless technology is booming. However, wireless is not without its potential risks, and if the benefits are to be fully realized they must be addressed.

It is difficult to apply risk management to any emerging technology: the risks are changing as the technology evolves. The benefits are also sometimes intangible. They change as new applications emerge, and are often oversold.

Yet the benefits of wireless technology outweigh the costs when deployments are assessed, planned and managed using thoroughly prepared risk management strategies.

The context: why wireless?

Wireless has become a basic necessity in business life. It allows staff to communicate more flexibly and respond more quickly. They become more productive and effective. For example, an executive who can access information in an airport lounge via a wireless hotspot can evaluate proposals and deliver decisions far more quickly than the same executive who has to return to the office to use the same resources.

Replacing wired networks with wireless in the office can cut cabling and costs related to administrative work when an employee moves within the office. Wireless can also support concepts such as location-aware badges for office staff and converged phones, which can reduce phone bills.

The umbrella term 'wireless networking' can include familiar and less familiar technologies:

■ mobile phones (cellular voice);
■ cellular data (text messaging, mobile e-mail, eg BlackBerry, and access to business applications such as CRM through mobile devices);
■ Wi-Fi access at public hotspots;
■ corporate in-building wireless networks, either as an add-on for conference rooms or guest use or as a replacement for traditional data cables;
■ short-range connections such as Bluetooth (and the forthcoming ultra-wideband), used among and between hand-held devices.

These all carry the same generic risks, which at the simplest level are as follows:

■ Data is carried over a radio link that can in principle be 'tapped', leaking potentially sensitive and confidential information to others.
■ Connections are made and remade, so identity can be difficult to ascertain, allowing opportunities for fraud and spoofing.

The advent of wireless

Two major approaches to wireless networking have developed in parallel. Firstly, the cellular network operators look on wireless data as a way to increase traffic (and profits) on their networks and are promoting sending business data over their networks (using GPRS and, eventually, 3G). Technologies include PDAs, e-mail and laptop data cards. Secondly, Wi-Fi technology provides short-range wireless networks using shared 'licence-exempt' radio spectra. This technology can be delivered as a paid-for service at hotspots, or used in a building to extend or replace wired networks.

There is a big overlap between these approaches, but also a difference in security models. Cellular networks are secured by the service provider (though the user has to secure the data and the device). Security on Wi-Fi networks, which operate on shared spectra and usually on equipment owned by the user, is entirely down to the user.

Wi-Fi standards are specified by the 802.11 working group of the IEEE. These include a set of increasingly fast basic transmission standards, 802.11b, 802.11g, 802.11a and (in 2007) 802.11n, which promises to allow wireless networks that operate as fast as today's wired office networks, at 100Mbit/s or more.

Alongside these are other standards, including the 802.11i standard for securing the network. This replaced an earlier effort, known as WEP (or Wired Equivalent Privacy), which used cryptography that turned out to be easy to crack.

The Wi-Fi Alliance has taken the IEEE's security specifications and created a branding programme: equipment bearing the WPA2 brand performs to current security specifications.

Serious problems

Although the problems with Wi-Fi security are well known in IT circles, they have apparently not been dealt with in practice. While the use of wireless networking continues to rise, network owners' use of security technology is not always keeping pace.

In 2006 the number of wireless access points found in London jumped by 57 per cent over the previous year, according to a survey carried out by RSA, the Security Division of EMC, which also checked levels of wireless adoption and security use in Paris and New York.

Shockingly, although higher security is available, only 1 per cent of all sites in these three cities were using anything more advanced than the inadequate WEP. It's some consolation to find that WEP is in use at three-quarters of sites – apart from public hotspots – as it does deter casual hackers.

Public hotspots rarely encrypt traffic at all, as this would make it hard for paying customers to log on. Instead, they rely on password protection to provide a gateway to the service. If users want security, it is generally up to them to encrypt their own data.

Managing wireless risks

Risk management entails the following steps:

- assessing the context;
- identifying the potential risks;
- assessing the actual risk level;
- managing those risks, by transfer, avoidance or mitigation;
- reassessing the risks regularly.

Identifying the risks

The two main risks that wireless networking brings are of insecure data and uncertain identity. More specifically:

- An unsecured wireless network can allow other people within or near an office building to access the corporate network, including critical data and resources.
- Information passing over a wireless network can in principle be detected and exploited by a third party, including perpetrations of identity theft.
- Information gathered from a wireless leak can be used in attacks on other parts of the company.
- Wireless networks are open to denial-of-service attacks. Wireless systems in the area can be overloaded or disabled if they are not properly secured.

- Seduced by the convenience of wireless connections, staff can potentially install their own access points outside the IT department's control and open the corporate network.
- 'Evil twin' or 'rogue' access points can mimic real access points and be used to commit identity theft, gathering passwords and other crucial information from users connecting to them.
- Wireless networks can break regulatory requirements, such as the need to ensure the security of customers' personal data. Increasingly, compliance with regulations such as Sarbanes–Oxley will require wireless security measures.
- A wireless security breach can seriously damage a company's brand and reputation.
- More indirectly the organization may be liable for harm done to third parties, by unauthorized users accessing the internet through a corporate wireless network.

Assessing the costs

The risks must be assessed according to their likelihood (how often they will occur) and their severity (the amount of damage they would inflict).

This part of the process depends on the organization in question. Banks, for instance, would suffer severe consequences if a transaction was interfered with or if customer information leaked. They are also likely to get more attacks, given the value of their data.

It can be useful to undertake a wireless penetration test run by experts, as a way of discovering any flaws in the organization's wireless network, and the ease with which they can be exploited.

The actual risk should then be presented in financial terms, in order to take the next steps – planning and cost-justifying any investment in mitigating the risk.

Planning to manage the risks

Once risks are identified, the organization's response to them will again be specific to the organization, but could involve:

- transferring risks to third parties – by insurance or outsourcing contracts;
- avoiding risks by not adopting wireless; and
- risk mitigation – applying wireless security.

Transferring risks is not a very easy option, but avoidance was a safe option in the early stages of the wireless industry. When the technology was primitive, the benefits were smaller because mobility seemed desirable in theory but in practice it was a lot of hassle. The security risks were greater too before WPA.

Avoiding wireless may still be a suitable strategy for some, but it is now harder to enforce, since wireless equipment has become a cheap consumer item, and wireless attack techniques are widely circulated. Preventing wireless attacks now requires wireless equipment to be installed, and monitoring the airwaves for any unauthorized equipment. What's more, the business benefits of wireless networks have become increasingly compelling, as equipment and applications have matured.

Most organizations will use wireless networking in one form or another. For them it is vital to mitigate the risks, using the following basic ground rules:

■ Start with the human level, setting up policies and education – and make sure users are prepared to abide by the policies.
■ The computer security department should approve all wireless equipment.
■ Implement products well. Change the factory-default security settings, which will be well known to attackers.
■ Encrypt data. The WPA scheme is considered adequate, and is now included in all business wireless networking equipment.
■ Any users outside corporate networks, connecting across the internet from home or public hotspots, should use virtual private networks (VPNs) to encrypt data.
■ All users should authenticate, through WPA, to the corporate security systems.
■ Authenticate devices too – where possible limit the network to devices whose unique network address (MAC) is already known.
■ Don't give away information needlessly – wireless LANs broadcast a network name (or SSID). Give that a name that doesn't reveal whose network it is, or stop broadcasting it.
■ Apply wireless intrusion detection and prevention. Wireless networks can monitor for attacks from unauthorized devices, and the presence of rogue access points. This function is often included within wireless networks, or can be added as an overlay using extra access points as sensors.
■ Limit the applications used on the wireless network.
■ Apply policies to mobile devices when they connect, ensuring they are patched, up to date and free from viruses before allowing them to join the network.
■ Remember that data is mobile while in devices, so secure hand-held devices such as phones and PDAs, and laptops, with passwords and remote management.

Completing and reviewing the plan

The aim is not to achieve the impossible and reduce risk to zero, but to limit it to a manageable level that allows the organization's work to continue.

Every security measure has an impact on usability, whether it be a requirement to create and change passwords, a requirement to use specific hardware, or a requirement to submit every laptop to quarantine until it has been updated with the latest patches and only then allowed to connect. Include the cost of any usability impact in your plan – and remember that users frustrated by over-draconian measures will find ways to bypass security measures.

Keep refining the plan as new wireless opportunities emerge and new wireless threats appear.

Prepare for the wireless future

Wireless networks have become an integral part of business life and therefore need to fit into the enterprise's risk management framework. However, this is an opportunity.

Early wireless networks extended the boundaries of the enterprise but did not take full account of the increased risk levels that would result. A more rigorous approach has evolved, which has not only secured wireless networks but can improve the security of the business as a whole.

Future wireless applications will bring plenty of benefits, so 'wireless avoidance' will carry the risk of losing competitive edge.

Among these benefits is voice over Wi-Fi (VoWi-Fi), a technique that allows companies to reduce mobile phone calls, many of which are made by users in the office or else at hotspots, where free or cheap Wi-Fi is available. Moving voice from the cellular to the Wi-Fi network could also bring benefits of integration between voice and data applications.

This will bring new potential risks. More complex mobile devices will be more susceptible to malware, and voice over IP (VoIP) brings with it other security issues, since such devices are accessible by other IP devices.

In the future, business communications will be 'wireless by default'. Users will expect to communicate wherever they are, regardless of wires. Security models designed with this in mind will bring benefits across the board.

The strength to cover business risks worldwide.

XL INSURANCE companies are chosen by the world's leading firms not only for the strength of our capital and the depth of our experience, but also for the quality and variety of our solution-focused products created to precisely meet your insurance requirements:

PROPERTY
Global All Risk Property Damage & Business Interruption | Energy & Construction All Risk | Fine Art | Jeweller's Block | Cash In Transit

CASUALTY
Primary Liability | Product Recall & Tamper | Workers' Compensation | Global Public & Products Liability | Excess Liability

PROFESSIONAL
Directors & Officers | Employment Practices | Professional Indemnity

SPECIALTY
Aviation & Space | Environmental Liability | Equine & Livestock | Marine & Offshore Energy

Experience our strength:
www.xlinsurance.com

The XL Insurance companies have one or more of the following ratings:
A+ by A.M. Best
A+ by Standard & Poor's
Aa3 by Moody's

XL INSURANC
FUNDAMENTAL STRENGTH – CAPITAL AND PEOP

The evolution of biometrics: why increased security could present the greatest risk of all

Thomas Stamm, XL Insurance

Biometrics as a means of monitoring individuals' movements has achieved a level of acceptability that could not have been contemplated even a decade ago. The growth of terrorism has undoubtedly played a role in this phenomenal growth – but it is not the only factor. Biometrics – defined as the science of measuring physical properties of living beings – has in fact been with us since the middle of the last century.

Automated fingerprint analysis has been consistently used since the 1960s to identify individuals, and today retina scans at airports are increasingly common. In California, Mineta San Jose International Airport uses hand geometry to speed up processing through customs. Many construction companies monitor employees' arrivals and departures on-site through face recognition. Even Disney now uses finger scanning to control entry to its parks. Growing concerns around international terrorism and transaction fraud are starting to outweigh fears about personal liberty and data protection, resulting in faster adoption of identification technologies. Yet arguably the use of biometrics and the logical extension of their use *should* be a matter for concern. Biometrics can help to protect lives, frustrate criminal activity and facilitate everyday activities, but as we will explore in this chapter the inherent risks are significant.

Biometric technology works by identifying individuals through measurement of their physical features, comparing the information with stored biometric reference data. The term 'biometrics' is often used to mean biometric authentication, which is the automated recognition of a living being using one or more body characteristics (these may vary according to the type of authentication system).

The attractions of biometric authentication methods are many and varied, including:

■ enhanced security and reduced fraud;
■ greater accuracy of timekeeping systems;
■ lower system support costs as they remove the need to maintain and reset passwords;
■ greater accuracy than PINs and passwords;
■ convenience;
■ cost-effectiveness;
■ increasing social acceptance;
■ creation of an audit trail.

However, these benefits come at a potential cost that is far higher than the physical implementation and maintenance of the authentication system. The technology that increases personal security could be used to manipulate human behaviour, curtail personal freedom and, taken to the extreme, change society as we know it.

Defining 'biometrics'

Biometrics refers to an automated process of recognizing, identifying or verifying individuals by their physical or behavioural characteristics. Examples are shown in Table 7.5.1.

Similar technologies to biometrics are also used in the same way and carry similar advantages and risks. For example:

■ *Forensics.* Forensics is a form of biometrics, but the required level of recognition is significantly higher than would be necessary in biometrics.
■ *DNA.* Opinion is split as to whether DNA is a biometric. Currently DNA recognition is not performed by an automated process, and therefore is generally not considered a biometric.

Table 7.5.1 Biometric types

Type	Example
Physical	Fingerprint: the pattern of the ridges and furrows. Facial recognition: distance of facial features such as eyes, nose and mouth in relation to each other. Iris pattern. Vascular scan: the pattern of the vein structure, ie on the retina or back of the hand. Hand geometry: measurement and analysis of the subject's hand. Finger geometry: the measurement of the subject's finger. Ear form: dimensions of the visible ear. Odour: chemical composition of one's odour. Speaker recognition: tone or timbre of the voice.
Behavioural	Gait: manner of walking. Signature: measurement of pressure and speed. Keyboard strokes: rhythm of keyboard strokes. Voice can also be considered a behavioural characteristic.

■ *Radio frequency identification (RFID).* RFID tagging is not technically a biometric, but it is closely linked, as will be seen later in this chapter. The identifying tags are not a physical part of the individual, but they can be inserted under the skin of a person or animal, enabling the subject to be uniquely identified. RFID tags are frequently used in conjunction with biometrics for recognition and verification.

The biometric recognition process

Personal data are typically collected using a 'sensor'. Having captured the sample data from the subject, the sensor converts them into digital format. The quality of the sensor has a direct impact on the recognition results. Sensors could be digital cameras, telephones or security scanners, for example at shop doorways. Once in digital format, the information is called a 'biometric template' and it is this template that is compared with the sample when the subject next attempts recognition.

There are subtle differences between recognition, identification and verification:

■ *Recognition.* This is a generic term used in biometrics. All biometric systems perform recognition when they compare a sample with a sample already in the database.
■ *Verification.* The individual states his or her identity and the system matches the biometric sample to the one stored in the database to verify the identity. Verification is sometimes called authentication.

■ *Identification.* The system attempts to determine the identity of an individual. The biometric sample is collected and compared to the samples held in the database. Identification is 'closed-set' if the subject is known to be in the database, and 'open-set' if the computer must also determine whether the individual is in the database.

While a living thing can be identified by personal characteristics, there are two practical drawbacks to using biometrics. First, it is impractical to collect a biometric sample from an animal, since it would have to be manually placed in front of a sensor. Second, a mass-produced product has no unique characteristic, except a barcode, which would also have to be manually placed in front of the sensor. RFID tags are therefore more effective in the tracking of goods and animals. They can be incorporated into credit cards, membership cards, passports, etc, which also makes them ideal for identifying people.

RFID works by means of a wireless device known as a transponder or RFID tag, which operates as a data storage system. The microchip and antenna contained in the tag transmit their unique ID code to a transceiver, which is capable of both activating the chip and providing its power source (see Figure 7.5.1).

RFID tags – also called 'smart tags' – have a broad range of possible uses, since they can be integrated into the smallest of objects, such as key rings for vehicle immobilizers, product packaging, credit cards, price tags and passports. They also have significant implications for risk management. Ensuring the control of products at any time, the tags can help to improve risk management across almost every industry sector. The use of RFIDs is not yet widespread, but the challenge will be to embrace this powerful technology while guarding against its misuse.

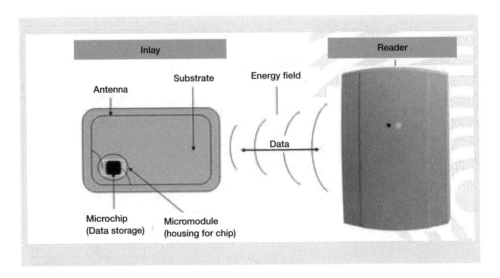

Figure 7.5.1   Smartrac NV

How identification technology can improve risk management

Identification technology, whether biometric or RFID, seems to have almost unlimited potential. Today it is commonly used for access control to buildings, alarm systems, public transport, at ski resorts, and in the area of logistics, such as tracking products for distribution. The following examples demonstrate the breadth of possibilities:

- *Livestock farming.* For a number of years RFID tags have been used in farm management, through implantation of microchips into the animals' ears. This technology has enabled smooth management of livestock databases, recording details such as milk production, origin and age. In the wake of the BSE outbreak, the tags became vital to controlling the production and distribution of meat products.
- *Public safety.* Recently, following public outcry over 'fighting dog' attacks on people in several European countries, demands are being made to tag certain breeds of dog to keep track of them and their ownership.
- *Product manufacturing.* Increasingly, businesses are investigating the use of RFID tags to keep track of the manufacture and distribution of their products. The technology saves time and money, especially when products prove deficient and need to be recalled. If they were used in conjunction with biometric data, people at a higher risk could be identified and prioritized.
- *Healthcare.* Impending healthcare reforms include the reorganization of procedures in hospitals and clinics both to cut costs and to improve services. In this scenario, RFID technology is gaining in importance. For example, when patients are admitted to hospital, they can be given bracelets with an RFID chip containing their medical history and current details. Precise identification could mean the difference between life and death, especially where the patient has a negative reaction to certain medications.
- *Government.* Many governments have introduced or are beginning to introduce biometric passports. These traditional-looking passports combine identity documents with biometric data to authenticate the citizenship of the passport holder. The passport's critical information is stored on an RFID tag. An embedded contactless chip that holds a digital signature ensures the integrity of the passport and the biometric data. Tags for the European version of the passport are expected to incorporate both digital imaging and fingerprint scans. This combination of biometrics is designed to create an unrivalled level of security and protection against counterfeiting and fraud.
- *Catering.* A school in England is using another aspect of identification technology in its canteen. Students no longer pay cash for their lunches and, instead, they are identified biometrically by an iris scan, enabling a computerized catering system to charge their account. The computer's database can also be used to store personal information about the student. For example, if a child's parents do not permit the child to eat hamburger and chips, but the child tries to order them anyway, the iris scan will notify the canteen personnel not to serve him or her the forbidden foods.

Risks of biometrics

There are two aspects to the risks of using biometrics. One concerns the operational risks of implementing and maintaining an authentication system, and the other relates to how we as a society use the technology.

Implementation and maintenance

Biometric technology is not used in isolation. It is part of a larger system architecture and, as such, involves multiple risks.

Operational risks

From an operational perspective, the biometric system must be appropriate for the task (eg where throughput is an issue, a finger scan taking approximately a second is much more practical than a fingerprint background check, which could take 24 hours). Cost versus benefit numbers must be analysed and validated; frequently the benefits can be overstated in an attempt to see the system adopted. Operators need to be appropriately trained, particularly where the means of collecting the data may be obtrusive. For example, some people might be reluctant to touch a finger scan sensor for reasons of hygiene, but if the scan is not completed correctly the results may be flawed. Here the operator can assist in reassuring the individual and ensuring the scan takes place correctly. Finally, the environment must be conducive to the biometric collection (eg face recognition may be difficult in an outdoor location where individuals could commonly be wearing hats or scarves that conceal their faces).

Security risks

From a security standpoint, biometrics enhances the accuracy of a system, but it cannot single-handedly solve a security problem. The system may be accessed by hackers, and the very existence of a database of biometric data could attract criminal behaviour. The greater the amount of personal data stored, the greater the temptation for misuse. There is also a serious concern that biometric data are permanent and cannot be reset like a password. This means that once compromised the data are compromised for ever, since one's physical characteristics cannot be changed, for example after a case of identity theft. Research is taking place currently to adapt biometric technology to address this concern, so that if security is later compromised a new biometric sample can be created.

Another widely publicized concern around the security of biometric authentication is the ease of forgery, cloning and fraudulent use, particularly with biometric passports. Researchers have found that RFID technology is vulnerable to 'skimming' or eavesdropping (ie being read by a concealed reader and/or interception of the transaction between passport and 'official' reader). Various mechanisms can be used to prevent this: first, a mesh of metal in the passport cover blocks access to the chip when the passport is closed and, second, the layout of passport control areas makes it difficult to get close enough to read the tag. However, shops and hotels that require passports to verify identification can be a risk, as their layout would tend to be more accessible. Additionally, other devices using RFID, such as identity cards, do not have covers, so cannot make use of the metal mesh protection.

Health risks

One development with a potential impact on health is the RFID 'chipping of humanity'. For example, a Spanish beach club offers its VIP members the option of having an RFID chip implanted, usually in the arm or fingertip. This chip, roughly the size of a grain of rice, permits guests to gain access to members-only rooms, and eliminates the need for them to carry cash, because they can be charged automatically. While the individuals obviously have to give their permission for the chips to be implanted, it is open to question whether they are totally aware of the consequences. It is not possible to determine precisely what the side effects might be, such as radiation or the body simply rejecting the chip. At the moment, such risks can only be guessed at.

Privacy risks

One of the greatest debates around biometrics is its impact on data protection and personal liberty. Biometric identification is extremely accurate and physical characteristics difficult to forge, so the greater risk comes from the system in which they are integrated. As discussed under 'Security risks' above, efforts are being made continually to safeguard information and protect against fraud. However, there is a more insidious risk concerning the use of biometric data. How can the usage be monitored and controlled? One only has to consider the volume of RFID tags in existence already – in passports, store loyalty cards, credit cards, membership cards, access passes, ID cards and public transport passes – to realize the scale of the risk we already face.

In some countries, personal data may only be gathered and used when specific permission has been given by the individual. This only ceases to apply when the processing of that information is considered necessary in the public interest, or to facilitate the work of such authorities as the state, the revenue services or the police. However, when individuals give their consent for an organization to collect their personal data, are they truly aware of how that information will be used today or how it might be used in the future?

Let us consider a supermarket scenario: Jane Smith does her weekly grocery shopping on a Friday. On each visit she is recognized by a sensor at the store entrance, which tracks her route past other sensors to the checkout. Analysis of Ms Smith's and her fellow shoppers' data reveals that many of them miss out a certain area of the store. The supermarket management can then rearrange the shop layout or position special offers to ensure that Ms Smith changes her route and visits more counters, potentially spending more time and money. Unbeknown to her, her shopping behaviour has been manipulated by the organization that holds her personal data.

Use of biometric technology

Despite the many benefits of this evolving technology, it is clear that the downside is potentially significant. Consumer associations and data privacy organizations are concerned that identification technology will in future allow for everything to be identified, all the time, everywhere – people, animals and products. If we apply this biometric technology to consumer goods and services – at the cinema, in department stores, at football grounds – then George Orwell's *1984* society, where Big Brother was constantly watching, changes from fiction to reality. Every now and then, human nature finds a way to circumvent the controls imposed by biometrics. Take the catering example above, and link it with the school in Rotherham that tried to impose healthy eating on its students: a group of activist parents began passing junk food to the children over the school gates, invalidating the school's good intentions and exposing the limits of too much control by the authorities. But the possibility of total surveillance is clear. The more widespread the use of identification technology, and the more familiar it becomes, the more widely it will be accepted and the less likely its use will be questioned.

The workplace exemplifies how simple access control could be manipulated. Where doors are controlled by systems using iris or finger scans, an employee could be monitored every time he or she left or entered the building, ostensibly for security or health and safety purposes but also revealing the amount of time spent at the office. The same employee wearing a badge containing an RFID chip could be tracked via sensors in different parts of the building, indicating time spent in the tea room or the toilets. Surveillance would be total. Yet many companies already require their employees to carry badges with integrated RFID tags, and very few employees object. The routine acceptance of RFID chips is most dangerous, because the negative aspects are rarely pointed out when we are given a name badge, apply for a credit card or pick up the key fob for our car.

A further issue of concern is the processing of sensitive personal data, which in a number of countries is subject to extremely strict legislation. 'Sensitive personal data' include information regarding racial or ethnic origins, political opinions, religious or philosophical convictions, membership of a trade union, sexual orientation or state of health. Such data may not, in general, be used by third parties. Yet through biometric technology political and religious information could be collected and analysed by the security services to avert terrorist acts. Can we be absolutely sure that innocent individuals would not be seen as potential terrorists by virtue of where they go, whom they meet or even where they live?

Conclusion

Undoubtedly our world can be made safer though greater use of biometrics and RFID technology. The constant pressure for greater security, the availability of improved production and distribution methods, and the constant quest for greater profits all combine to create a potential need for expanded usage and, maybe, greater acceptance.

Yet given the tremendous advances in identification technology, the question is: how can we meet the challenge of ensuring that personal data can be both monitored and kept secure? This is one of today's most complex ethical questions. The repercussions of getting the answers wrong would be felt far into the future.

8

Aspects of Environmental Risk

Managing environmental risks: a survey of international developments

Karl Russek, ACE European Group

The management of environmental risk has emerged as a significant issue for European businesses. The concept of long-term sustainability has been added to the traditional *raison d'être* of profitability. Many would argue that for enlightened managers these two concepts are closely intertwined. At the same time, more and more companies are driven by competition to expand their businesses elsewhere around the globe. In doing so, of course, companies open themselves up to new markets and opportunities, but also a variety of emerging risks, including environmental risk.

This chapter provides a brief overview of the environmentally based business risks that companies can expect to encounter as they venture beyond the UK. It is critically important to note that environmental risk and regulation are an extremely local phenomenon, and that no company should enter a new market without the benefit of experienced local technical and legal counsel.

In general terms, environmental risk can be defined in a number of ways and can range from compliance with local health and safety regulations all the way to issues associated with global climate change. The focus in this chapter will remain more on regional issues and the response of government in managing these issues.

Regulatory environment

The primary means by which most companies manage environmental risk is by working to comply with the applicable environmental regulations in force where they operate. As with many other business risks, this is by no means a static situation; regulations, and the zeal with which they are enforced, can change quite quickly in some parts of the world. In fact, in many parts of the world, one might consider regulatory risk as a form of political risk, so variable and capricious is its enforcement.

There are significant prerequisites for a well-developed system of environmental regulation and, by extension, of environmental liability. Among them is the development of a politically powerful middle class for whom placing a high priority on quality-of-life issues such as clean air and water translates into the political will to accept the economic consequences of regulation. A country whose citizens are more concerned with increasing their humble standard of living in an emerging industrial power (eg China) is likely to be somewhat more forgiving of the unintended consequences of that industrialization.

Legal system

Another important factor is the predictability and even-handedness of the legal system. Many countries are compelled to adopt fairly well-developed environmental laws and regulations as a consequence of their participation in various international treaties and trade agreements. However, many do not necessarily have the means or the will to enforce them. When enforcement does come, it is likely to be used as a political tool to further other agendas.

What follows is a region-by-region overview of trends in environmental awareness and regulation as they pertain to business, with country-specific examples where appropriate. It is by no means an exhaustive list.

Europe/EU

In so far as western Europe is made up of stable, industrial democracies with a strong middle class, it should be no surprise that it also enjoys a relatively stable, consistent approach to environmental law and regulation. Nevertheless, there can be significant country-by-country and even local nuances that significantly affect the burden of regulation.

Among the most significant developments in the environmental liability arena in the EU states in the past few years was the formalization of the EU Environmental Liability Directive (ELD) in April 2004. The directive itself will take practical effect when it is promulgated into national law in each of the member states. The deadline is April 2007, but certain key EU members (including the United Kingdom) will probably take longer to incorporate its requirements into their national regulatory schemes. Although the overall thrust of the ELD is the harmonization of the environmental liability regime among EU members (enshrining the 'polluter pays' principle and largely seeking to bring others up to the standard of Germany and the Scandinavian countries), there are several key concepts that warrant attention.

Significantly, the ELD holds polluters vulnerable to claims for direct, complementary and compensatory damages for impacts to biodiversity (protected habitats and natural resources). Further, it introduces the concept of strict liability for certain classes of polluters, particularly heavy industry. However, it is important to note that the EU does not seek to impose these requirements retroactively (as was the case with similar legislation in the United States). Thus in most member states the business impact of the ELD should be manageable. Obviously, however, companies operating in such places as Poland should be on the lookout for greater change that those currently operating in countries like Sweden.

The ELD is by no means the sole emerging factor in the EU. The REACH Directive seeks to require detailed human health impact information from chemical manufacturers and suppliers before their products can be sold in the EU. Whilst the aims of this directive are laudable, there are real questions as to its practicality, given the large numbers of compounds already in distribution or planned for distribution. The RoHS Directive bans certain substances outright. In the future we can expect additional directives governing soil and water/groundwater clean-up.

While we don't know the precise practical impact of these directives until they are transposed into national law, there is always the potential that certain member states will seek to 'gold-plate' certain aspects in order to enhance the government's green credentials – particularly near election time.

In addition to the EU activity, in response to some well-publicized incidents some countries are starting to show increased regulatory activism. For example, the government of Spain recently took up the matter of compulsory pollution insurance for certain businesses perceived to pose a higher risk. This was an idea mooted by the EU as part of the ELD, but ultimately thought to be premature based on the limited ability of the insurance markets to respond. Nonetheless, it remains a fairly popular political idea and one could expect the concept to bubble up from time to time.

Aspiring EU members in south-eastern Europe have some way to go before they provide a predictable legal and regulatory context for managing environmental risk. Nonetheless, there is an increasingly influential activist movement in many countries that can influence government decision making on key industries and large projects, but typically on a case-by-case basis.

Further east, Russia has demonstrated that environmental regulation and permitting can be distilled into a purely political tool, as the recent case of the permitting of the Shell-led Sakhalin island project bears out.

North America

Notwithstanding its reputation as the bastion of free enterprise, the United States has among the most onerous and rigid environmental regulatory schemes in the world. This is matched by a very active litigation climate. Because of this, many international companies have had negative experiences in the United States with environmental issues, particularly pollution legacy issues. The United States differs from most of Europe – where the retroactive nature of pollution liability is limited by a number of factors including former state ownership of industry – in that such liability is not only retroactive but also 'joint and several'. This means that in theory even a minor involvement with a former industrial site can result in full liability for the cost of clean-up and any attendant third-party claims. Caution is the key word when operating in the United States, and experienced local counsel is a necessity. Though much of the body of environmental regulation in the United States is well established and has been the subject of much case law, the overall trend over the past 10 to 15 years in the United States has been one of decentralization and the adoption of more user-friendly approaches, although much of this work has been done at the state level as opposed to the federal level. Thus the practical effect of environmental law in the United States is very much a state-by-state phenomenon.

Canada enjoys a very stable environmental regulatory system, modelled in some part on the US system – down to the province-by-province differences in interpretation and enforcement zeal. To its benefit, Canada tends to enjoy a more European enforcement and litigation environment, thus making it a somewhat less onerous jurisdiction in which to operate.

Latin America

Similarly, much of Central and South America has a well-documented, stringent scheme of environmental regulation – at least on paper. A problematic uncertainty in this part of the world lies with inconsistent enforcement of the existing regulations. While much of the region has signed up to a host of regulatory schemes as part of free trade agreements with the United States, compliance with many of these regulations is often ignored and enforcement is often used as a political tool.

In addition, tort systems can vary greatly from those experienced in the UK, particularly with respect to the intersection of civil and criminal law, so again caution and local guidance are the best advice here.

Asia

Notwithstanding its long industrial history and tradition of consensus-based government and industry relations, Japan has also developed a more stringent environmental regulatory scheme and, given the scarcity of land and the density of development in much of the country, contaminated property questions are front-burner issues for most industrial companies there. In addition, the increasing openness of the Japanese market to restructuring and foreign ownership means that legacy liability issues can no longer be kept under wraps by the major industrial companies.

However, the tort environment in Japan is quite different from that in the United States, and anyone seeking to undertake an assessment of potential liabilities there would be well served in seeking local guidance.

Elsewhere in Asia, the picture is quite mixed. Taiwan recently announced a scheme for mandatory insurance for certain polluters, whilst Singapore is likely to be not far behind. Both countries feature very strong regulatory schemes, but also a significant political component to enforcement and legal proceedings.

For much of the rest of the region, environmental issues appear to be taking a back seat in the rush to economic development. China is of course a perfect example. While certain high-profile incidents garner international attention and thus prompt government action, the story on the ground in most parts of the country is one of rampant development with little in the way of checks and balances and little faith in the sanctity of contracts or the rule of law. Signs of increased awareness of environmental issues among the growing middle class are starting to emerge, but a truly objective, comprehensive and sound liability scheme for environmental issues is probably a decade or more away. One can imagine that foreign firms will be the first to bear the brunt of any forays by the government in this direction.

Australia and New Zealand

Australia and New Zealand share an environmental regulatory climate very similar to that of the United States. Also, by virtue of their history of British common law, both countries have tort systems that would seem quite familiar to a UK risk manager, although there is much more of a US-style litigation environment. As such, environmental exposures are very much part of the liability landscape for business.

Africa

In the vast majority of African states, the focus is necessarily on economic development. NGOs and pressure groups can bring some pressure to bear with respect to particularly unpopular projects.

What should a risk manager do to avoid being taken unawares by these developing issues?

Consider the following:

■ Gain a thorough understanding not only of where your company currently operates outside the UK, but of where it has historically done so. In addition, look into whether any acquired subsidiaries or operations have or had significant operations overseas that could have resulted in an environmental legacy. Develop an understanding of the nature and extent of such past operations.
■ Consult with your real estate and legal departments to determine whether non-UK real estate or asset acquisitions are subject to the same level of environmental due diligence as such transactions in the UK.

■ Consult with your legal department to see if your company is protected from past or current environmental liabilities in leases, purchase agreements, service contracts and the like. Seek to have language protective of your company's interests inserted in all such agreements.

■ If your product is shipped or distributed overseas, ensure that your company is protected through appropriate contract language and insurances. Depending on the jurisdiction, even though the materials may be beyond your care, custody or control, you may be seen as a deep pocket by virtue of your company name.

■ Consult with your environmental, health and safety department to determine the standards to which non-UK facilities are managed. Many more sophisticated global companies manage their facilities to global environmental, health and safety standards, which often far exceed those in the applicable host jurisdiction. This represents a significant investment, but one well worth it when NGOs and pressure groups come knocking.

■ Review your foreign casualty programme with your broker to understand better the limitations on pollution cover in your existing programme. Look into coverage enhancements or stand-alone cover to fill those gaps. Consider the following areas, which are often significant and costly gaps in casualty programmes:

  – Does your programme offer cover of gradual pollution releases?
  – Does your programme offer cover for the clean-up of pollution, both on your property and off?
  – Does your programme offer cover for past releases, which may not yet have been discovered?

As the liability picture for environmental issues is still developing in many parts of the world, tools currently exist to identify and manage these emerging risks, and all risk managers would be well served in staying aware of them.

Managing occupational health and safety

Tony Boyle and Mike Thomas, HASTAM

Introduction

OHSAS 18001[1] is an occupational health and safety management system (OH&SMS) published by the British Standards Institution (BSI) and it is an alternative to the other two main OH&SMSs used in the UK, that is, the Health and Safety Executive's (HSE's) Successful Health and Safety Management[2] and the British Standard, BS 8800.[3]

This chapter describes how using OHSAS 18001 to manage OH&S produces very different results from using these other OH&SMSs. The chapter is based on the results of work in a number of organizations, in a wide variety of sectors, both public and private, in 2004–06.

The chapter begins with a description of the authors' findings with regard to the way OH&S was being managed in the organizations concerned and continues with a description of some key issues identified and addressed.

Existing OH&S management

In the organizations concerned, OH&S was being managed using a combination of OH&S legislation and Successful Health and Safety Management (HSG65). This created the following problems:

- Complying with OH&S legislation does not produce good OH&S management because, except in special situations such as safety case regimes, there is no legal requirement for key management activities such as planning, monitoring, measuring, audit and review.[4] Indeed, there is no legal requirement to investigate the majority of accidents, and the legal requirement to record accidents is social security legislation, not OH&S legislation.
- HSG65 is guidance; it is not a specification. This means that organizations can claim to be complying with HSG65 even when they are not carrying out many of the activities described in HSG65. For example, none of the organizations on which this chapter is based had a planning procedure, a measuring procedure, an audit procedure or a review procedure despite the fact that all of these activities appear in the HSG65 diagram. Incidentally, all of the organizations claimed to be on the second edition of HSG65, which is based on the concepts of workplace precautions and risk control systems, but none of the OH&S professionals concerned knew what these terms meant.

In addition, the organizations' documentation had the following main flaws:

- It was described as the OH&S policy, but was between 80 and 300 pages long. In environmental and quality management systems the policy is one or two pages long, and the excessive length of the OH&S policies arises because of a misreading of the Health and Safety at Work etc. Act 1974.[5] What the OH&S professionals referred to as their OH&S policies were akin to an OH&S manual, and this is how they are described from now on.
- The OH&S manuals consistsed mainly of paraphrased HSE guidance (with a random selection of transcription and interpretation errors) on a range of OH&S legislation, for example the risk assessment requirements from the Management of Health and Safety at Work Regulations 1999, or control of specific risks such as substances hazardous to health, display screen equipment and manual handling. The vast majority of the documentation described how to do things and there were few, if any, descriptions of who should do things, when and with what result.
- There was no particular structure to the documentation and no consistency from one section to another. Usually, different sections had been written by different people at different times (typically soon after new legislation had been enacted), and none of the organizations had document control procedures that specified document formats.
- In general, the content of the documentation suggested that it had been written by looking at OH&S legislation rather than looking at what an organization did, what management systems it already had in place and what it wanted to achieve by its health and safety management.

Once the existing situation had been identified, the next step was to carry out a gap analysis, comparing the existing situation with what is required by OHSAS 18001. In some of the organizations this was carried out by one of the authors, but in other organizations it was carried out by an author in conjunction with the organization's

OH&S professional. This co-working included mentoring, which enabled the OH&S professionals concerned to claim continuing professional development (CPD) points.[6]

Key issues

This section of the chapter describes a selection of the key issues identified and addressed during the work. The section is subdivided as follows:

- description of the OH&SMS;
- behavioural-based documentation;
- top management involvement;
- legal requirements;
- measuring OH&S performance;
- audit.

Description of the OH&SMS

OHSAS 18001 requires the following: 'The organization shall establish and maintain information, in a suitable medium such as paper or electronic form, that: a) describes the core elements of the management system and their interaction; and b) provides direction to related documentation.' In practice this means that OH&S professionals have to decide what they want their organization to do with regard to all of the procedures identified in OHSAS 18001. They then have to write this down, either in the description or as separate procedures. Once they are clear about what they would like to see happen, they have to obtain the relevant authorization, usually from top management, and this is dealt with in a later section.

The typical findings from this part of the work are that OH&S professionals have not thought about OH&S management in this way before. They have thought about compliance with the requirements of legislation, but not about compliance with the requirements of an OH&SMS. However, they all saw the benefits of managing OH&S more systematically and either prepared or procured appropriate descriptions of their intended OH&SMS.

Behavioural-based documentation

'Behavioural-based documentation' is used as a shorthand for documentation that contains descriptions of what people will do, when and with what result. This type of documentation is also referred to as standards-based documentation.

Preparing this type of documentation requires OH&S professionals to be clear about what they want other people to do and record it in the form, eg 'Job Title or Name will carry out risk assessment reviews annually and make any changes identified as necessary.' This is in contrast to more commonly used forms such as: 'Risk assessment reviews will be carried out annually' or 'The organization will carry out risk assessment reviews.'

The critical aim of behavioural-based documentation is to ensure that every required OH&S task is clearly allocated to a specified job title or a named individual since this is an essential prerequisite of the effective allocation of responsibility and accountability.

The behavioural-based documentation developed for and by the organizations, in addition to specifying, usually for the first time, who should do what, enabled two other major improvements: 1) It was structured according to the requirements of ISO/TR 10013[7] so that consistency between documents could be ensured. 2) It was linked to the description of the OH&SMS so that a structure was imposed on the complete documentation and particular information was easier to find.

Top management involvement

Two of the requirements of OHSAS 18001 are dealt with in this section: 1) the requirement for a management appointee; 2) the requirement for top management reviews.

Management appointee

OHSAS 18001 requires that a member of top management is appointed 'with particular responsibility for ensuring that the OH&S management system is properly implemented and performing to requirements in all locations and spheres of operation within the organization', and this management appointee has to have a defined role, responsibility and authority for a range of tasks.

In conformance with the use of behavioural-based documentation, the tasks the management appointee has to carry out have to be identified and recorded and it is also a good idea to estimate how long they will take since this is likely to be one of the first questions any proposed management appointee will ask.

It is essential that there is a management appointee, not only to satisfy the requirements of OHSAS 18001 but also because the management appointee is the person who will be able to authorize the other OH&S responsibilities and accountabilities identified in the behavioural-based documentation. The management appointee also has an important role in the management review, which is the subject of the next section.

Management review

OHSAS 18001 requires that: 'the organization's top management shall, at intervals that it determines, review the OH&S management system, to ensure its continuing suitability, adequacy and effectiveness'.

Management reviews are critical for two reasons:

1. They close the feedback loop. In any system like an OH&SMS, control is only possible if there is a feedback loop. In essence, the output of the system is measured and the level of the output used to determine what the system does next. In an OH&SMS, the feedback loop is created by the actions of people during the review

process and if these actions are not carried out the OH&SMS is out of control. Because the OH&SMS is complex, it is difficult to predict the consequences of this lack of control, but experience from major disasters has shown that they can be very severe.

2. They drive continual improvement. If an organization is to maintain an effective and efficient OH&SMS and meet the requirements of OHSAS 18001 it must have a procedure for continual improvement. As a minimum, this procedure should ensure that the OH&SMS adapts to meet internal and external changes and so stays up to date. However, OHSAS 18001 requires that organizations go beyond this and create absolute improvements.

However, none of the organizations involved had a formal management review procedure. When the idea of a management review procedure was described to the top management of the organizations it was accepted in all the organizations. Top managers seemed pleased that they were receiving practical guidance on what they had to do to manage OH&S, rather than threats of jail if they did not meet their responsibilities.

As with the other OHSAS 18001 procedures, the management review procedure should be documented, and there is good guidance on what the procedure should contain in OHSAS 18002.[8]

Legal requirements

OHSAS 18001 requires that: 'the organization shall establish and maintain a procedure for identifying and accessing the legal and other OH&S requirements that are applicable to it' and 'the organization shall keep this information up-to-date'.

All of the organizations had a policy commitment to complying with relevant OH&S legislation, but none of them had a list of the legislation with which they had to comply and none of them had a formal procedure for identifying and accessing new or changed legislation. Setting up and maintaining a list of relevant OH&S legislation (often referred to as a legal register) is an onerous task, and the majority of the OH&S professionals opted for HASTAM's legal register service, which maintains an up-to-date legal register on their behalf.

Measuring OH&S performance

All of the organizations measured loss data to some degree but there was no measurement of, for example, compliance with legislation or conformance with the organizations' OH&SMSs.

Measurement of loss data was easily improved by, for example, using number of days lost instead of just number of incidents, and by making estimates of accident costs. In one organization, a quick estimate of accident costs using a specially developed spreadsheet showed that the costs in the previous year were equivalent to the organization's deficit for that year.

Measurement of compliance with OH&S legislation was also easy to deal with by using HASTAM's monitoring, auditing and measuring software packages.

Measuring compliance with the organizations' OH&SMSs was more difficult, for two reasons:

1. As has been described, the organizations' existing documentation was not based on standards and was not, therefore, suitable for measuring conformance. It will be some time before all of the new documentation is implemented fully and amenable to compliance measurement.
2. The requirements of the new documentation have to be translated into question sets so that they are in a form that will enable measurement. This is an ongoing process but, as continual improvement is central to OHSAS 18001, it provides ways in which improvement can be achieved – more and better measurement of the performance of the OH&SMS.

Audit

In all the organizations, inspections were referred to as audits and in none of the organizations was there OH&SMS auditing. All but one of the organizations had as an objective achieving external accreditation to OHSAS 18001 and this means that they will be subject to external management system audits. These external audits will be conducted according to the requirements of ISO 19011[9] and for this reason it was necessary that the OH&S professionals learned these requirements. This was done either with an in-house course, for those organizations with a number of OH&S professionals, or by attendance at an appropriate public course.

Conclusion

Managing OH&S by complying with OHSAS 18001 takes OH&S professionals into areas not normally dealt with in OH&S training. This makes it challenging, but also a rich source of CPD activities. However, the benefits to the OH&S professionals are far outweighed by the benefits to the OH&S professionals' organizations, which, if OHSAS 18001 is implemented effectively, will have an OH&SMS that is the equal of the equivalent management systems for quality and environment. This will enable OH&S management to join quality and environmental management in being driven by the requirements of the organization, rather than by legislation.

Notes

1. BSI (1999) *Occupational Health and Safety Management Systems: Specification*, BSI, London.
2. HSE (1997) *Successful Health and Safety Management*, HSG65, HSE, London.
3. BSI (2004) *Occupational Health and Safety Management Systems: Guide*, BS 8800, BSI, London.

4. Regulation 5 of the Management of Health and Safety at Work Regulations 1999 requires activities of this type but only in so far as they relate to 'preventive and protective measures'.

5. The relevant section of the Health and Safety at Work etc Act is: 'it shall be the duty of every employer to prepare and as often as may be appropriate revise a written statement of his general policy with respect to the health and safety at work of his employees and the organisation and arrangements for the time being in force for carrying out that policy'. For some reason this has been misinterpreted by the OH&S community in general, and even the current (September 2006) edition of the National Examination Board in Occupational Safety and Health's Diploma syllabus includes the following:

   'Description of the general components of a health and safety policy document:
   – statement of intent – overview, safety goals and objectives
   – organisation – duties, responsibilities and organisational structure in relation to health and safety
   – arrangements – systems, procedures, standards, cross-reference to key documents.'

   It is not clear how this misinterpretation came about, but, so long as examination boards continue to say that this is what should be taught, the misinterpretation is likely to continue.

6. In the UK, OH&S professionals can become chartered members or chartered fellows of the Institution of Occupational Safety and Health. Maintaining this chartered status requires individuals to undertake a range of CPD activities, for which points are claimed.

7. BSI (2001) *Guidelines for Quality Management System Documentation*, ISO/TR 10013, BSI, London. Although the title of this document refers only to quality documentation, the text includes the following: 'This Technical Report may be used to document management systems other than the ISO 9000 family, for example environmental management systems and safety management systems.'

8. BSI (2000) *Occupational Health and Safety Management Systems: Guidelines for the implementation of OHSAS 18001*, OHSAS 18002, BSI, London.

9. BSI (2002) *BS EN ISO 19011: Guidelines for quality and/or environmental management systems auditing*, BSI, London. Although the title of this document refers only to quality and environmental management systems, the text includes the following: 'The application of this International Standard to other types of audit is possible in principle, provided that special consideration is paid to identifying the competence needed by the audit team members in such cases.'

The environmental and related business impacts of climate change

Deborah Evans and Anne-Marie Warris, LRQA and Anne Goodenough, University of Gloucestershire

Introduction

In an uncertain world, and dealing with an uncertain topic, there are two things of which risk managers can be sure: first that the need for climate change to be considered a serious and imminent risk to business cannot be overstated; and second that the motto 'Be prepared' has never been more apt.

Given the exponential increase in the scientific, media and sociological attention afforded to climate change over the past couple of decades, some 80 per cent of the FTSE 100 companies now identify the impacts of climate change as a potential business risk. However, there is still comparatively little understanding of what these risks entail, when and how they might impact upon business, or how they can be mitigated.

Accordingly, and even given the undeniable element of uncertainty as regards the impacts of climate change, a lack of understanding, forethought and planning means businesses may increase the risks they face unnecessarily.

The potential effects on business caused by the environmental impacts of climatic change are massive. The possible cost implications are high: the cost of insurance claims to cover damages resulting from sea-level rise, floods, droughts, storm surges and hurricanes has already risen sixfold in a decade and ultimately climate change could cost in excess of $300 billion per year. More importantly, many types of business are at risk, with one-eighth of the US economy, about $120 billion per year, estimated to be invested in sectors that are sensitive to climate change.

Businesses across the globe are using management systems such as ISO 9001 (quality) and 14001 (environment) to identify and manage their various risks. External drivers such as corporate governance codes, Sarbanes–Oxley in the United States, Turnbull and Cadbury's in the UK and most international securities/stock exchange commissions require businesses to protect shareholder rights, enhance disclosure and transparency, facilitate the effective functioning of the board and provide an efficient legal and regulatory enforcement framework. In order to do this, businesses compile risk registers covering all their activities, not just those seen as being operationally risky, and establish management system processes that include input and review from senior or board level.

It is only recently that businesses are considering perceived non-financial issues, ie those of environmental or societal concern when determining risk, or their 'material' issues. Today's materiality processes tend only to capture information relevant to short-term performance and risks. This is changing. Now businesses are seriously starting to consider long-term consequences of something going wrong.

Consequences of climate change

Some of the more common consequences are shown graphically in Figure 8.3.1, so that linkages can be appreciated.

In this chapter we cannot hope to cover in detail all the consequences of climate change. Instead we have selected a few of the more increasingly occurring environmental impacts of climate change to describe their impacts and exemplify their implications to business.

Flooding, storms and drought

Some of the most serious effects of climate change are likely to be on the hydrological cycle. Flooding is predicted to become an issue of ever greater importance, particularly in temperate and humid regions, where altered weather systems are likely to increase both the number of businesses at risk from flooding and the severity of the risk that they face. Precipitation in Britain and northern Europe has increased by 10–40 per cent in the last century and is predicted to carry on rising. More worryingly, rain is likely to come in shorter, more intense episodes, which would tax drainage systems beyond their capacity. Areas may be flooded more often, or to a greater extent, and flooding may occur in areas not previously associated with flooding risks, thereby increasing potential damage through a lack of flood defence precautions. Flooding can cause serious damage to the infrastructure and equipment of any industry, but

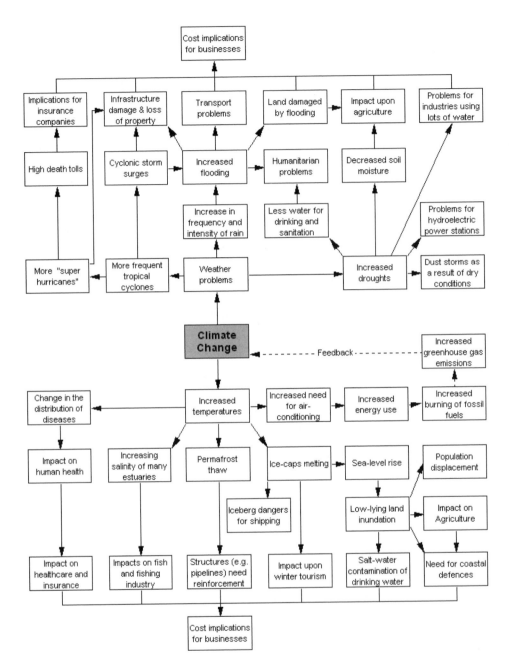

Figure 8.3.1 Consequences of climate change

some businesses are at additional risk, such as those using chemicals that could pose a pollution threat. Claims for flood damage in the UK are expected to increase from the current annual level of £1 billion to £25 billion by 2080. Worryingly, however, some 90 per cent of SMEs in the UK are under-insured for flood damage, given climate change, and 70 per cent of businesses in areas already at risk of flooding do not consider flooding a serious risk.

In addition to general changes in the hydrological cycle there is the specific threat of more frequent, more intense tropical cyclones and a rise in the number of super-hurricanes due to sea temperature rise. According to computer simulations, a rise in sea temperature of 2.2 °C in the north-west Pacific would result in hurricanes 10 per cent more intense than are currently experienced, while the number of people at risk of storm surges worldwide is predicted to double to 92 million. Salt-water inundation can contaminate freshwater resources – potentially a problem in south-east England – and cause salinity damage to land that can last for months or even years after the flood waters recede, which is already a problem for paddy fields in Bangladesh. Rescue and rebuilding operations following natural weather-related disasters could increase the global spend on climate change problems by $3 billion per annum, while insurance companies may experience record claims. Even single storms could incur international insurance costs of $67 billion, the estimated pay-out for damage caused by hurricanes Katrina and Rita in 2005 – over double the insurance cost of the World Trade Center attacks.

At the opposite extreme, changes in climate could exacerbate periodic and chronic water shortfalls leading to droughts in arid and semi-arid areas: the number of countries classified as water-scarce or water-stressed is expected to double to 38 by 2025. Drought causes problems for hydroelectric power stations and for water-intensive industries such as metal smelting, while agricultural industries have predicted losses of $42 billion as a result of drought, flood damage and yield reductions if carbon dioxide levels reach twice their pre-industrial level. In the United States, barley yields could decrease by up to 75 per cent by 2090, while total world cereal production may be reduced by 5 per cent. Dust storms and fires caused by drought and higher temperatures are also a problem: fire destroyed 20 per cent of the Greek island Samos in 2000, while the first-ever forest fire in the Mexican rainforest in 1998 caused the loss of over 500,000 hectares of forest and produced smoke that caused a health alert as far away as Texas. Globally, water industries are expected to face cost increases of $47 billion by 2050 in dealing with flood and drought-related issues.

Sea-level rise

Sea-level rise is another issue that could pose serious risks to business, especially in low-lying cities such as London, Tokyo and Bangkok. In the last century global sea levels have risen by 10–25 centimetres, a rise primarily caused by the thermal expansion of oceans, resulting in the current rate of sea-level rise at Chesapeake Bay in North America being an estimated three times higher than the natural historical rate. Future thermal expansion and the injection of melt water from ice caps are likely to cause continued sea-level rise, though the extent and immediacy of this is still uncertain. Such sea-level rise would cause significant land inundation, resulting in the displacement of millions of people and industries, particularly in low-lying countries such as Bangladesh, which has already lost 7,500 hectares of land in this way in the last 30 years. A 50-centimetre rise in sea level (well below the maximum suggested by the Intergovernmental Panel on Climate Change) could inundate 8,500–19,000 square kilometres of dry land and expand the current flood plains by more than 23,000 square kilometres in North America alone, while, for some island nations such as the Maldives, mitigating against sea-level rise is essentially impracticable.

Higher temperatures

Higher temperatures are also likely to cause problems *per se*. Thawing of permafrost may lead to lowered water tables in some areas but cause the permanent flooding of thaw lakes in other areas. Structures, particularly gas pipelines, that have been built on permafrost may need structural modification owing to subsidence, a concern in many areas, including Alaska where thawing since the 1960s has already caused subsidence of up to 10 metres. In just 35 days, one Antarctic ice sheet known as the Larsen B ice shelf, which measured 3,263 square kilometres (the size of the English county of Wiltshire) and was the same thickness as a 60-storey building, disintegrated into icebergs that caused problems for the shipping industry. Up to 95 per cent of alpine ice and snow fields could disappear by 2100, potentially damaging the winter tourism industry. More generally, buildings and entire cities throughout the world will have to be adapted to warmer climates, particularly heatwaves, in order to maintain functionality. The increased use of energy for summer cooling is likely to far outweigh any savings from reduced energy use for winter heating, and will also shift the energy demand pattern. Warmer temperatures might also reduce air circulation and lead to higher levels of near-surface ozone and other pollutants, reducing air quality and potentially causing health problems. There may also be a substantial increase in heat-related mortality, with the number of people in the United States expected to die each year from heat exposure in cities such as Minneapolis predicted to double by 2020 compared with the baseline figure for 1964–91. In addition, more people are likely to be at risk from tropical diseases, as such diseases, or the insects that carry them, expand their ranges. For example, model predictions suggest that the proportion of the global population exposed to malaria could grow from 45 per cent to 60 per cent by the latter half of this century. Such issues would have direct effects for the healthcare and insurance industries, as well as knock-on effects for government spending and aid agencies.

Implications

Businesses need to understand how these predictions will impact on their operations and then mitigate the risks. After all, human-produced climate change and the need to cut global greenhouse gas emissions are universally acknowledged as a significant challenge. In a carbon-constrained imminent future, greenhouse gas emissions will become financial liabilities on many companies' balance sheets.

Management systems will allow businesses to identify and manage risk, monitor their greenhouse gas emissions and set improvement targets. Some typical examples of management approaches that have been and can be adopted by businesses in order to mitigate their consequences of climate change are outlined below.

Exploring market opportunities

Develop new products that are sustainable. This is of particular interest both to business and to developing countries, which receive commercial benefits and environmental improvements respectively. For example, producing a lighting unit for sale in countries whose population has limited access to grid electricity and is reliant on fuel burning for both light and heat. Removing the need to burn fuel for light alone reduces carbon dioxide emissions but also improves the quality of life.

Introducing preventative measures

Improve drainage systems on-site to match extreme weather events (flooding) as predicted by local meteorological departments or to capture rainfall by diverting the water into storage tanks for use in auxiliary processes when potable water supplies are threatened (drought).

Changing operational controls

■ Draw up emergency plans and infrastructure such as:
  – sluice gates that prevent the ingress of water, whether it be from flooding or from sea-level rise, into the site's premises thus preventing loss of revenue from goods being damaged and subsequent insurance claims having to be made – these can also be used to protect watercourses from catastrophic rainfall washing off material from the site;
  – protective bund walls whose capacity is designed not only to stop catastrophic failure but to protect against flood or rain waters washing out any chemical residues into the local watercourse and polluting it.
■ Change the manufacturing process's reliance on high-quality water, especially in drought-affected areas. Ask whether the water for the first wash or cleaning of equipment needs to be of potable standard. Not only does this conserve drinking water for the local community but cost savings for the business can also be generated.
■ Invest in and install new alternative technologies that do not generate large quantities of greenhouse gas emissions. This demonstrates that you are going beyond compliance with environmental legislation in many cases and also that your business is committed to being socially responsible.

Conclusion

The movement of climate change on a business's risk register from the category of 'important *but* immaterial' to 'important *and* material' is a measure of progress. Not only does it allow businesses to demonstrate and deliver sustainability outcomes but it sets apart real business leaders, ie those who have 'got it' as against those who are still primarily avoiding their environment-related business risk problems.

Credible, independent endorsement of your business managing these environment-related business risks will help ensure that your business can deliver on the promises it makes.

Appendix: Contributors' contact list

ACE European Group Limited
The Ace Building
100 Leadenhall Street
London EC3A 3BP
Tel: +44 (0) 20 7173 7000
Fax: +44 (0) 20 7173 7852
Contact: Karl Russek
e-mail: karl.russek@ace-ina.com
Contact: Emma Watkins
e-mail: emma.watkins@ace-ina.com
Contact: Richard Coello
e-mail: richard.coello@ace-ina.com
Contact: Steve Capon
e-mail: steve.capon@ace-ina.com
www.aceeuropeangroup.com

BMW Group
Risikomanagement
80788 Munich
Germany
Tel: +49 (89) 382 20245
Fax: +49 (89) 382 25564
Contact: Dr Elmar Steurer
e-mail: Elmar.Steurer@bmw.de
www.bmwgroup.com

Centre for Effective Dispute Resolution (CEDR)
70 Fleet Street
London EC4Y 1EU
Tel: +44 (0) 20 7536 6000
Fax: +44 (0) 20 7536 6001
Contact: Andy Rogers
e-mail: arogers@cedr.co.uk
www.cedr.co.uk

Centre for Technology Management
Institute for Manufacturing, Cambridge University
Engineering Department
Mill Lane
Cambridge CB2 1RX
Tel: +44 (0) 1223 766401
Contact: Clare Farrukh
e-mail: Cjp2@eng.cam.ac.uk
www.ifm.eng.cam.ac.uk/ctm/

Chartered Institute of Management Accountants (CIMA)
26 Chapter Street
London SW1P 4NP
Tel: +44 (0) 20 7663 5441
Contact: Lottie Muir
e-mail: Lottie.Muir@cimaglobal.com
www.cimaglobal.com

Chartered Institute of Purchasing and Supply (CIPS)
Easton House
Easton on the Hill
Stamford PE9 3NZ
Tel: +44 (0) 1780 756777
Fax: +44 (0) 1780 751610
Contact: Liz Cullen
e-mail: liz.cullen@cips.org
www.cips.org

Chiltern plc
3 Sheldon Square
London W2 6PS
Tel: +44 (0) 20 7153 2290
Fax: +44 (0) 7899 062125
Contact: Louis Cooper
e-mail: cooperl@chilternplc.com
www.chilternplc.com

Commercial Security International Limited (CSI)
125 Aldersgate Street
London EC1A 4JQ
Tel: +44 (0) 20 7553 7960
Contact: Neil Miller
e-mail: neil.miller@comsec-international.com

Companycare Communications
154 Castle Hill
Reading
Berkshire RG1 7RP
Tel: +44 (0) 118 939 5900
Fax: +44 (0) 118 959 9595
Contact: Kevin Taylor
e-mail: kevin@companycare.com
www.companycare.com

DNV
Cromarty House
67–72 Regent Quay
Aberdeen AB11 5AR
Tel: +44 (0) 1224 335000
Fax: +44 (0) 1224 593311
Contact: Joyce Dalgarno
e-mail: joyce.dalgarno@dnv.com

Federation of European Risk Management Associations (FERMA)
4 rue de la Presse
1000 Brussels
Belgium
Tel: +32 (0) 2 227 1144
Fax: +32 (0) 2 227 1148
Contact: Marie-Gemma Dequae
e-mail: info@ferma-asso.org
www.ferma-asso.org

HASTAM
The Old Bakehouse
Fullbridge
Maldon
Essex CM9 4LE
Tel: +44 (0) 1621 854111
Fax: +44 (0) 1621 851756
Contact: Tony Boyle
e-mail: tony@hastam.co.uk
www.hastam.co.uk

Heineken International
PO Box 28
1000 AA Amsterdam
The Netherlands
Tel: +44 (0) 31 20 5239338
Fax: +44 (0) 31 20 5239537
Contact: Eric Bloem
e-mail: Eric.Bloem@heineken.com
www.heineken.com

Hewlett-Packard
29 Valepits Road
Garrets Green
Birmingham B33 0TD
Tel: +44 (0) 121 784 7445
Fax: +44 (0) 121 783 4015
hpbc.uk@hp.com

HSBC Insurance Brokers
Bishops Court
27–33 Artillery Lane
London E1 7LP
Tel: +44 (0) 20 7661 2511
Contact: Anna Moreno
e-mail: Anna.Moreno@hsbc.com
www.hsbc.com

ICM Computer Group
ICM House
Oakwell Park
Oakwell Way
Birstall
West Yorkshire WF17 9LU
Contact: Frances Longley
e-mail: frances.longley@icm-computer.co.uk
www.icm-computer.co.uk

The Institute of Risk Management
6 Lloyd's Avenue
London EC3N 3AX
Tel: +44 (0) 20 7709 9808
Fax: +44 (0) 20 7709 0716
Contact: Rebecca Brueton
e-mail: rebecca.brueton@theirm.org
www.theirm.org

KPMG LLP
Risk Advisory Services
8 Salisbury Square
London EC4Y 8BB
Tel: +44 (0) 20 7694 3282
Fax: +44 (0) 20 7311 8864
Contact: Andrew Fields
e-mail: andrew.fields@kpmg.co.uk
www.kpmg.co.uk

KSB Law LLP
Elan House
5–11 Fetter Lane
London EC4A 1QD
Tel:+44 (0) 20 7822 7567
Fax: +44 (0) 20 7822 7600
Contact: Jennifer Paynter
e-mail: jpaynter@ksblaw.co.uk
www.ksblaw.co.uk

Liquid Public Relations Ltd
Number 1, Greenbox
Westonhall Road
Stoke Prior
Bromsgrove
Worcestershire B60 4AL
Tel: +44 (0) 870 232 0300
Fax: +44 (0) 870 232 0301
Contact: Elisabeth Lewis Jones
e-mail: lis@liquidpr.co.uk
www.liquidpr.co.uk

Lloyd's Register Quality Assurance Ltd (LRQA)
LRQA Centre
Hiramford
Middlemarch Office Village
Siskin Drive
Coventry CV3 4FJ
Tel: +44 (0) 24 7688 2386
Contact: Anne-Marie Warris
e-mail: anne-marie.warris@lrqa.com
www.lrqa.com

Middlesex University
Centre for Decision Analysis and Risk Management
Queensway
Enfield
Middlesex EN3 4SA
Tel: +44 (0) 20 8411 6822
Fax: +44 (0) 20 8411 6580
Contact: John Watt
e-mail: j.watt@mdx.ac.uk
www.mdx.ac.uk/risk

Norland Managed Services Limited
454–460 Old Kent Road
London SE1 5AH
Tel: +44 (0) 20 7231 8888
Contact: Paula Ansell
e-mail: Paula.Ansell@norlandmanagedservices.co.uk
www.norlandmanagedservices.co.uk

Protiviti
Protiviti UK
6th Floor, Rex House
10 Regent Street
London SW1Y 4PE
Tel: +44 (0) 20 7024 7549
Fax: +44 (0) 20 7930 8807
Contact: Sean Holohan
Tel: +44 7917 761030
www.protiviti.com

RSA Security UK Ltd
RSA House
Western Road
Bracknell
Berkshire RG12 1RT
Tel: +44 (0) 1344 781000
Fax: +44 (0) 1344 781001
Contact: Natasha Staley
e-mail: nstaley@rsa.com
www.rsa.com

Siemens Insight Consulting
5 The Quintet
Churchfield Road
Walton on Thames
Surrey KT12 2TZ
Tel: +44 (0) 1932 241000
Fax: +44 (0) 1932 236868
Contact: Robert Chapman
e-mail: robert.chapman@siemens.co.uk
www.siemens.co.uk

XL Group
XL House
70 Gracechurch Street
London EC3V 0XL
Contact: Paula Wilson
e-mail: Paula.Wilson@xlgroup.com
www.xlgroup.com

Index

Index of advertisers